Crime and Society

Dr. Poonam Rani

Crime and Society

ISBN 978-93-5111-626-4

Published in 2015 in India by

RANDOM PUBLICATIONS

4376-A/4B, Gali Murari Lal, Ansari Road
New Delhi-110 002
Phone : +9111-43580356, 011-23289044, 011-43142548
e-mail: sales@randompublications.com,
info@randompublications.com, randomexports@gmail.com

Reprint, 2022

Type Setting by : Friends Media, Delhi-110089
Digitally Printed at Replika Press Pvt. Ltd.

Preface

Crime and society are closely linked – for better and for worse. Society is strongly affected by crime, both due to the cost of crime, as well as the decline in the quality of life that citizens suffer as a result of crime.However, society can also play a role in reducing and deterring crime. Many agencies and programs in the crime prevention field are based on societal and community efforts.

The label of "crime" and the accompanying social stigma normally confine their scope to those activities seen as injurious to the general population or to the State, including some that cause serious loss or damage to individuals. Those who apply the labels of "crime" or "criminal" intend to assert the hegemony of a dominant population, or to reflect a consensus of condemnation for the identified behaviour and to justify any punishments prescribed by the State. Usually a natural person perpetrates a crime, but legal persons may also commit crimes.

Society refers to a group of people who share a defined territory and a culture. Society is often understood as the basic structure and interactions of a group of people or the network of relationships between entities. A distinction is made between society and culture in sociology. Culture refers to the meanings given to symbols or the process of meaning-making that takes place in a society. Culture is distinct from society in that it adds meanings to relationships. All human societies have a culture and culture can only exist where there is a society. Distinguishing between these two components of human social life is primarily for analytical purposes—for example, so sociologists can study the transmission of cultural elements or artifacts within a society. This chapter will present a brief overview of some of the types of human societies that have existed and continue to exist. It will then present some classic approaches to understanding society and what changing social structure can mean for individuals.

The book will also be of immense use to criminologists, social workers, research students and academicians involved in the study of violent expressions of social conflicts.

I would like to thank my team for standing beside me throughout my career and writing this book. My special thanks go to "Random Publications" who have published the book.

– Dr. Poonam Rani

Contents

1

Introduction to Crime

CRIME

Crime is the breach of rules or laws for which some governing authority can ultimately prescribe a conviction. Individual human societies may each define crime and crimes differently. While every crime violates the law, not every violation of the law counts as a crime; for example: breaches of contract and of other civil law may rank as "offences" or as "infractions". Modern societies generally regard crimes as offences against the public or the state, distinguished from torts. When informal relationships and sanctions prove insufficient to establish and maintain a desired social order, a government or a state may impose more formalized or stricter systems of social control.

With institutional and legal machinery at their disposal, agents of the State can compel populations to conform to codes, and can opt to punish or attempt to reform those who do not conform. Authorities employ various mechanisms to regulate certain behaviours in general. Governing or administering agencies may for example codify rules into laws, police citizens and visitors to ensure that they comply with those laws, and implement other policies and practices which legislators or administrators have prescribed with the aim of discouraging or preventing crime. In addition, authorities provide remedies and sanctions, and collectively these constitute a criminal justice system. Legal sanctions vary widely in their severity, they may include incarceration of temporary character aimed at reforming the convict. Some jurisdictions have penal codes written to inflict permanent harsh punishments: legal mutilation, capital punishment or life without parole. The sociologist Richard Quinney has written about the relationship between society and crime. When Quinney states "crime is a social phenomenon" he envisages both how individuals conceive crime and how populations perceive it, based on societal norms.

The label of "crime" and the accompanying social stigma normally confine their scope to those activities seen as injurious to the general population or to the State, including some that cause serious loss or damage to individuals. Those who apply the labels of "crime" or "criminal" intend to assert the hegemony of a dominant population, or to reflect a consensus of condemnation for the identified behaviour and to justify any punishments prescribed by the State. Usually a natural person perpetrates a crime, but legal persons may also commit crimes.

DEFINITIONS OF CRIME

The following section examines the three major approaches to defining crime. This is not to say that these are the only approaches, or even the best approaches; rather that they are the most widespread. New ways of viewing crime are continually being developed, such as the critiques presented from a feminist perspective. However, for the present purpose the three main approaches will suffice. *The consensus view* The consensus approach to defining crime stems from the functionalist school within sociology. The basic tenet of this school of thought is that society functions as an integrated structure, its stability depending upon agreement, or consensus, among its members about the norms, rules, and values which are to be uniformly respected. Thus, a society's legal system is a reflection of the consensus of what, within that particular society, will and will not be tolerated as acceptable conduct. A crime is therefore a violation of the criminal law, an act which meets with the disapproval of the majority.

A definition of crime following this tradition would be of the style exemplified by Williams: 'A crime is an act that is capable of being followed by criminal proceedings, having one of the types of outcome known to follow these proceedings'. This definition clearly has a number of important consequences. First and foremost an act has to be committed before a crime can be said to have occurred; thought without some action is not a crime. Further, the act must be legally forbidden; 'antisocial' behaviour in itself is not a crime unless specifically and explicitly prohibited by law. In keeping with this, in the majority of instances the individual must also have had criminal intent in committing the act, the exception being crimes of *strictliability* such as health and safety regulations. An interesting discrepancy arises here between what might seem *morally* wrong, as opposed to 'wrong' in the legal sense. Racism and sexism, for example, may raise great moral issues, but are not well established in criminal law.

This is not to preclude the possibility that they might: criminal law has to have the flexibility to accommodate shifting societal values. Sutherland and Cressey illustrate this latter point, noting that at various times in the past activities such as printing a book, having gold in one's house, or driving with reins have all been criminal acts. More recently abortion, suicide, and consenting homosexual behaviour in adults over the age of 21 years have all been removed from the criminal law domain. The reverse can also happen: acts once not punishable by law are turned into crimes. In the USA it was perfectly legal to own and sell marijuana until the federal law was amended in 1937. In this country changes have been made regarding the sale of solvents to certain age groups, criminalizing a once legal activity— within, of course, the specific boundaries of the law itself. In other instances, technological advances are at present proving challenges to the law-makers: video piracy and computer fraud are contemporary acts which criminal law is having to address. While there are those acts which may pass in and out of criminal law, and can be thought of as 'statutory' crimes, there are other acts which are almost universally deemed 'wrong' or 'bad in themselves'.

Such acts would include those which inflict harm on another's person, for example murder, assault, and rape; or would inflict harm on the other person's property, for example burglary, malicious damage, and trespass. Thus the function of criminal law is to ensure the maintenance of these agreed aims of society, that is to protect the individual's person and property. However, as N.Walker points out, criminal law adopts a wider brief in seeking to achieve this aim. Laws also exist for the defence of the Realm, and to prevent public acts which might shock, corrupt, or deprave. It can be seen that such laws can be comfortably accommodated within a consensus framework: they act to preserve the stable society within which the individual lives and his or her possessions exist. An important part of criminal law is the delivery of retribution to those who transgress the commonly agreed boundaries of acceptable conduct.

The concept of punishment is not a simple one, raising many practical, legal, and ethical issues. For example, most people would agree that not all crimes merit the same punishment. Some system is needed which can differ between crimes of varying severity and magnitude. The tradition in this country is to distinguish between serious offences, sometimes referred to as *indictable* or *notifiable* offences, such as theft, fraud, and violence against the person; and less serious, or *Non-indictable* or *summary,* offences such as minor traffic offences and petty damage to property. This dichotomy of serious and Non--serious offences can be broken down still further: for example Siegal summarizes findings from the American National Survey of Crime Severity of public perceptions of crime seriousness. In this survey the five most serious crimes, as nominated by a sample from the American public, were all crimes of violence against the person. The most serious of all was: 'Planting a bomb in a public building. The bomb explodes and twenty people are killed.' The crimes judged least serious were being drunk in public, trespass, and least serious of all the 204 crimes in the survey was a 'youngster under sixteen years plays hooky from school'. If criminal law reflects the consensual views of society, then the punishments it delivers must also reflect the consensual view of the seriousness of different types of crime.

The Conflict View

The conflict view of crime stands directly opposed to the consensus view. It argues that rather than functioning as an integrated unit, society is best seen as a collection of competing diverse groups—professional bodies, unions, students, industrialists, and so on. These groups are in conflict with each other on a range of fronts as, given the unequal distribution of wealth and power within society, some are poor and dissatisfied while others are wealthy and powerful. This inequality in the distribution of power creates a social atmosphere based on conflict, which in turn, it is argued, promotes crime. The conflict view of crime grew in both popularity and sophistication in the late 1960s and early 1970s. It is most closely associated with the writings of criminologists such as Turk, Quinney, and Chambliss and Seidman; although the contribution of earlier writers such as Vold and Dahrendorf should not be neglected.

The conflict view of crime developed into a distinct branch of criminology with the introduction of Marxist theory, a merger generally credited to the book *The New Criminology* by I.Taylor, Walton, and Young. Specifically Marxist or new criminology views crime as a function of a capitalist system which produces those who have wealth and power and those who do not. While each group, or class, within society commits crimes, the type of crime is dictated by the system: the poor commit crimes within their scope, such as theft, murder, and burglary; the middle class commit typical 'white-collar' crimes such as tax evasion and theft from employers; while the wealthy and powerful upper class indulge in activities such as exploitation, profiteering, and environmental pollution and damage—acts which are not accorded the status of crime. As theories based on conflict are clearly political and economic in orientation, the function of the criminal justice system is viewed in very much the same terms.

Criminal laws exist for the express purpose of protecting the rich and powerful from the remainder of the population. In Marxist terms, the 'justice' system exists to preserve capitalist interests —that is the interests of the capitalist bourgeoisie—ensuring power remains with the wealthy and not the proletariat. Thus inequalities in sentencing can be used to support the position of conflict theories. Laws which exact harsher penalties for offences against property rather than against people, and cases in which the poor are imprisoned for minor offences while the rich receive lesser sentences for more serious crimes, appear to offer evidence for a conflict view of crime. Conflict theories have attracted a great deal of criticism. Klockars has pointed specifically to a number of gaps and flaws in Marxist theories: for example the neglect of individual differences—why do not all people within a capitalist system commit crimes? It should be noted that Marxists have responded to these criticisms and are seeking to refine their theories of criminology.

The Interactionist View

While the consensus and conflict view of crime stand directly opposed, the interactionist view falls between these two camps. With its beginnings in a school of thought within sociology known as *symbolic interactionism*, this view of crime rests on a number of critical assumptions. The first of these assumptions is that each individual's behaviour is guided by their interpretation of reality and the meaning which events hold for them. The second assumption has its focus on the learning of meaning, a process seen as resulting from the way in which other people react, either positively or negatively, Towards any given individual or situation. Finally, the third assumption holds that the evaluation of one's own behaviour is made just as to the meanings learned and acquired from other people. In focusing so sharply on meaning, the interactionist view of crime moves away from the moral stance of 'right' and 'wrong' central to the consensus view. Thus, while taking the life of another person is a criminal act, this does not *always* have to be the case: self-defence, in battle during war, and state execution are examples of 'legitimate' killing.

The decision as to when an act becomes a crime is not a matter of consensus, rather a statement of the preferences of those who hold social power and are able to impose their preferred definition on society. However, unlike the conflict views of crime, the interactionist view does not suggest that economic and political considerations are the driving motivations for those in power. Becker used the term 'moral entrepreneurs' to describe those individuals who advance to positions in society which allow them to influence the rule making process.

Thus the interactionist view is concerned with the way in which changing moral standards—not therefore seen as fixed or absolute—relate to changes in legal standards. Interactionist views were at their most influential in the 1960s but have rather declined in popularity since then within the criminological community. Some of those who held interactionist views have moved to a conflict position while others shifted to a consensus view: it is probably true to say that in the 1980s the conservative consensus view is once again gaining the ascendancy.

THEORIES OF CRIME

The three views have clearly placed very different constructions around the phenomenon of crime. The view taken by the individual criminologist, together with his or her own background in sociology, psychology, and so on, will influence the way in which research evidence is gathered, data interpreted, and theories constructed. The following section briefly examines how the three views have been translated into theories of crime.

CLASSICAL AND POSITIVIST THEORIES

The consensus view of crime is linked to two schools of thought within criminology. The *classical* theorists hold central the concept of free will in explaining why a person commits a crime. When the opportunity for crime arises, the individual has a free choice between criminal and non-criminal behaviour. If the payoffs for the criminal act are greater than the retribution it will bring, so the probability of a crime increases. At its most basic this suggests that severe retribution will deter people from any criminal act. Indeed, this simple philosophy was one which guided the process of justice through to the mid-1700s and even into the early 1800s, when acts such as stealing or vagrancy were punishable by severe physical punishment such as flogging or even death. The eighteenth-century Italian economist Cesare Beccaria was in accord with the general view of the time that humans are rational beings, able to choose and control their behaviour. Beccaria was also concerned that the punishment should fit the crime and so argued, with eventual success, that extreme measures are unnecessary and, indeed, may be counter-productive.

There is more than a grain of truth in the saying that 'it is as well to be hung for a sheep as a lamb'. Around the turn of the eighteenth century, the British philosopher Jeremy Bentham similarly argued that a balance between profit and pain guided the free choice of a criminal act. Bentham formulated a number of rules by which to regulate the administration of punishment; with the justification for punishment always presented in terms of its preventing a greater evil than it creates.

Classical theory, as presented by Beccaria and Bentham, was the dominant force in Europe and America in the late eighteenth and nineteenth centuries, guiding both judicial philosophers and criminal justice system of the time. With the advent of positivist theories the classical school waned in popularity and influence throughout the twentieth centry. However, the 1970s and 1980s have seen a renewed interest in classical criminology.

The *Neo-classical* or *conservative* criminologists have emerged as a strong voice in contemporary theorizing. Fuelled by a general failure of positivist theories to discover the causes of crime and to develop effective strategies for controlling crime, some of the basic ideas associated with classical theories are beginning to return. The call for greater deterrence in the form of longer prison sentences, the return of the death penalty, and the notion of 'just deserts' for lawbreakers, has been heard increasingly over the past decade.

The *positivist* theorists, while sympathizing with the consensus view of crime, differ from classical theorists with respect to the role of free will in determining behaviour, including criminal behaviour. Positivist theories grew from the arguments, advanced from the mid-nineteenth century onwards, that influences outside the realm of free will are the most important in determining behaviour. As theories have advanced and fallen so these influences have ranged from biological factors such as genetic transmission, to psychological constructs such as personality, learning, and moral development.

While from a more sociological perspective, there are *social structure* theories which emphasize concepts such as 'anomie', and 'strain' which result from class structure and poverty; and *social process* theories which focus on the effects of, for example, education, peer relationships, and the family. Positivist theories are generally seen as more liberal in orientation, with their suggestions that some form of helpful intervention—be it welfare at a social level or treatment at an individual level—is the optimum strategy for reducing crime.

Radical Criminology

While conflict views of crime encompass a range of opinions, it was those theorists who emphasized the Marxist position who advanced the framework for a new model within criminology. The new criminology promised by I.Taylor *et al.* quickly became more popularly known as radical criminology. It is incorrect to say that radical criminology represents a unified theory; rather since 1973 it has put forward a series of associated coherent statements which combine to form a body of knowledge and opinion. While radical criminology has its roots in the writings of Marx and Engels, it was theorists such as Willem Bonger who began to formulate a full Marxist critique of crime. In contrast to classical theories it is proposed that no act in itself is naturally immoral or criminal; definitions of crime are socially determined, reflecting current social values. This emphasis on social determination also runs counter to those positivist theories which incorporate genetic or other biologically based explanations of crime.

Within a radical framework, criminal law is designed to suit the purposes of the dominant ruling class, those within society who hold wealth and power. In a capitalist system, the unequal distribution of wealth means that those without finance have to resort to crime to enjoy the luxuries and advantages seen to be enjoyed by others. Crime therefore is in some instances a function of poverty.

The rich also commit crimes for the purpose of gaining further wealth and power. However, as the rich control the means of regulating crime, their legal sysem will discriminate against the poor. So while the poor, the proletariat, may commit the same number of crimes as the wealthy, the bourgeoisie, they are arrested and punished with much greater frequency. A number of modern writers have clarified, elaborated, and extended the position defined by Bonger and articulated by I.Taylor *et al.*

In terms of a solution for crime, radical criminology suggests that changes must occur at economic, political, and social levels. Specifically if progress from the present capitalist system to monopoly capitalism can be made, then redistribution of wealth can take place. It is argued that crime will then no longer be necessary; any crimes which do occur will be the result of individual psychopathology. T.Platt presents a blueprint for the formulation of alternatives to the present system of 'law and 'order' which follow a radical criminological approach. Radical criminology has been subjected to fierce criticism, with some carefully constructed commentaries and others with more than a touch of naivety.

Labelling Theory

The interactionist view of crime gave rise to a theory of criminology which relies on a mixture of social and semantic processes to explain deviance. In common with conflict theories, labelling theory suggests that the law is applied to the benefit of those who hold social and economic power. Thus disadvantaged groups within society, such as the lower socioeconomic classes and minority groups, are more likely to be prosecuted and to receive harsher penalties. An individual becomes a criminal when the people who hold power—judges, parents, police, teachers, etc. —decide to confer the label 'criminal'. As Becker notes: 'Deviant behaviour is behaviour that people so label'.

Here there is a clear contrast with a moral view: behaviour is not seen as 'right' or 'wrong', rather 'deviant behaviour' is a judgement by certain sections of society towards certain classes of behaviour. This argument does not, of course, apply only to criminal behaviour: the same reasoning has been used to explain the creation of groups variously labelled 'alcoholic', 'mentally ill', 'sexually deviant', and so on. While writers such as Gove have offered explanations within a labelling theory framework to account for the involvement of people in criminal acts, the main force of labelling theory has been to examine the consequences of labelling. Two consequences are emphasized—the creation of stigma and modification of self-image. The term *stigma* refers to the public attitude of condemnation of the deviant and the associated exclusion of the labelled individual from some parts of society.

The label 'criminal' is associated with undesirable traits and so, in the public eye, the criminal is a person to be avoided and treated with suspicion. Thus the criminal will find that he or she is barred from certain types of employment; the young offender may find that their school or their family is unwilling to offer a welcome; those with criminal records may attract an undue amount of attention from the police. The force of these social pressures can lead to the second major consequence of the label: the individual comes to believe society's judgement and so modifies his or her self-image to match the label. The prophecy becomes self-fulfiling: the individual becomes the person described by the label. As the label becomes a role for the labelled individual, so the role is reinforced so that the person's life changes to suit the role. More crimes are committed, the peer group changes to others playing the same role, the person's identity becomes that of a 'criminal' with all its associated values, attitudes, and beliefs. Lemart calls this process *deviance amplification*.

The irony of any attempt at intervention, either by punishment or treatment, is that it serves only to reinforce the individual's self-perception of him- or herself as a criminal. Like all other theories of crime, labelling theory has its critics. There are a range of objections from a failure to specify why some individuals set off on a path of crime, to a failure to acknowledge that some crimes such as murder and rape are universally judged as 'wrong'.

As Siegal points out, several criminologists who were at one time strong advocates of labelling theory have in the 1970s and 1980s shifted ground to favour more radical theories, principally the conflict theories. In summary, it can be seen that the three influential theories explain crime in very different ways. It is true that there is a degree of overlap between certain aspects of some theories, which has been examined by experimental methods but in the main the theories remain independent of each other. While these theories offer explanations for crime, they do not inform us as to the numbers of crimes committed.

Knowledge of the numbers of crimes committed is important both theoretically and practically: if crime is a low frequency behaviour then criminals may differ in some important way from those who do not perform such acts; if on the other hand it is a high frequency behaviour this may mean quite the reverse. The practical reasons are concerned with the allocation of finance to those establishments concerned with controlling crime: if there is a great deal of crime, and it is society's wish to control it, then the forces of law and order will demand a proportion of the public purse—the higher the frequency of crime, the greater the demand on the purse.

WHITE COLLAR CRIME

White collar crime tends to refer to crimes committed at a business by a businessman or woman. Such crimes might include embezzlement or fraud. Criminology expert and sociologist, Edwin Sutherland, in a 1939 speech, coined the term. Sutherland posited that people are more likely to commit crimes when they are surrounded by criminal behaviour of others. This philosophy relates to punishment of white collar crime by the US justice system. A white collar criminal is considered less likely to commit another crime, and punishment may be softer than for crimes involving violence. Today the definition of white collar crime may also refer to the socio-economic status of the person committing the crime. A person from the middle or upper classes commits a white collar crime simply because of his origin.

However, if the crime is violent in nature, it still is likely not considered a white collar crime. Most believe that white collar crime is a less punishable offense, than for example a mugging where violence is threatened. However, white collar crimes like embezzlement, the stealing of company funds, may ultimately harm more people. If funds are irrecoverable, a white collar criminal might technically steal all the savings of people who depend upon those savings in order to live. When the money cannot be recovered, the white collar criminal has caused more damage by his actions than the mugger. However, the mugger is likely to receive a stiffer sentence.

Since white collar crime tends to occur among those of higher socio-economic standing, an advantage is gained. Most people can afford a better lawyer to argue in their defence. Those of lower socio-economic standing are not likely to be able to afford a private lawyer and must rely on the overworked state defence attorneys. It has been statistically shown that most clients fare better with a private lawyer. Generally, a white collar criminal also has the advantage of being housed in a minimum-security prison. Such an environment offers greater freedom and is generally considered a safer environment than maximum-security prisons. Thus a white collar crime is not considered with the same gravity as other offenses, even when a person has damaged beyond repair the lives of others.

ORGANISED CRIME

Organised crime is the name for illegal acts committed by a criminal organisation or group, working together to achieve a common goal—usually to make money. For many people, organised crime stirs TV and movie images of gangsters from the Italian and Sicilian mafia in the five major crime families identified in New York City by the Federal Bureau of Investigation. Real-life organised crime, however, also includes mobsters from Russia and Eastern Europe. Organised crime rings from African and Asian countries are involved in everything from prostitution and trafficking people and drugs to pornography, financial scams, computer crimes, genocide, and terrorism. The FBI estimates these groups of organised criminals around the world annually earn $1 trillion US Dollars in profits. In some places, organised crime has infiltrated legitimate businesses and industries, such as construction and garbage disposal. The legitimate businesses are often used to launder money and help cover up illegal activities. Organised criminals in Italy have been known as the mafia since the 1800s. These criminal organisations have been in the United States since the early 1900s. One of the most famous of the Italian mobsters in the US was Charles "Lucky" Luciano, who came from Sicily in 1907, when he was still a boy. He is credited with helping establish the modern mafia, or La Cosa Nostra, which is the organisation of Italian and Sicilian crime families that operate mainly in US cities on the East Coast.

Since the early 1990s, organised criminals have been coming to the United States from countries that comprised the former Soviet Union. Their activities include human smuggling and prostitution, fraud, money laundering, drug trafficking, auto theft, and extortion. In Russia, they have been regarded as the leading threat to national security because of the threat they pose to political institutions and the economy. Asian groups of organised criminals have been active in the United States since the early 1900s. In addition to China and Japan, most of these gangsters have ties to Korea, Thailand, the Philippines, Cambodia, Laos, and Vietnam.

They have begun to participate in white-collar crime and use legitimate businesses to cover their criminal activity. They are involved in crimes ranging from gambling and prostitution, to smuggling aliens, and trafficking heroin and methamphetamine. They are also known to commit financial fraud and produce counterfeit computers and clothing. Of the organised groups of criminals from African countries, those in Nigeria are considered the most significant threat. They operate in more than 80 countries, including the United States. Much of their criminal activity is centred around drug trafficking and financial fraud.

COLLECTIVE VIOLENCE

Collective violence receives a high degree of public attention. Violent conflicts between nations and groups, state and group terrorism, rape as a weapon of war, the movement of large numbers of people displaced from their homes, and gang warfare—all these occur on a daily basis in many parts of the world. The effects of these different types of event on health in terms of deaths, physical illness, disabilities and mental anguish are vast. Collective violence may be defined as: the instrumental use of violence by people who identify themselves as members of a group—whether this group is transitory or has a more permanent identity—against another group or set of individuals, in order to achieve political, economic or social objectives.`

The Extent of The Problem:

- Besides the many thousands killed each year in violent conflicts, there are huge numbers who are physically injured as a result—including some who are permanently disabled or mutilated.
- In 2000, over 300, 000 people died as a direct result of violent conflicts. Rates varied from less than 1 per 100, 000 population in high-income countries to 6.2 per 100, 000 in low and middleincome countries.
- The 20th century was one of the most violent periods in human history. An estimated 191 million people lost their lives directly or indirectly as a result of conflict, and well over half of them were civilians.
- Torture and rape are also used to terrorize and undermine communities, although exact numbers of people subjected to these abuses are difficult to determine. Many people hide the trauma they have suffered and parties to a conflict often try to manipulate or conceal evidence of torture and rape.
- Worldwide, the highest rates of conflict-related deaths are found in Africa.

The Consequences of Collective Violence: The impact of violent conflicts on health can be very great in terms of mortality, morbidity and disability. Increased mortality rates of civilians during violent conflicts are usually due to:

- Decreased access to food, leading to poor nutrition
- Diminished access to health services
- Increased risk of communicable diseases
- Injuries
- Poor environmental conditions
- Psychosocial distress
- Reduced public health programmes

Infants and refugees are among the groups most vulnerable to disease and death in times of conflict. Increases in morbidity and mortality rates among these two groups can be dramatic. The violence and cruelty of conflicts are associated with a range of psychological and behavioural problems, including depression and anxiety, suicidal behaviour, alcohol abuse and post-traumatic stress disorder. Conflicts disrupt trade and other business activities, and divert resources to defence from other vital services and sectors. They also have an impact on food production or distribution and displace thousands of people from their homes. Famine related to war, other armed conflicts or genocide is estimated to have killed 40 million people in the 20th century.

RISK FACTORS FOR COLLECTIVE VIOLENCE

The roots of violent conflict are generally deep and may be the result of long-standing tensions between groups. There are a number of factors that put states at risk of violent conflict.

They include:

- A lack of democratic processes and unequal access to power. The risk is especially high when power stems from ethnic or religious identity, and when leadership is repressive and disposed to the abuse of human rights.
- Control by a single group of valuable natural resources, such as diamonds, oil, timber and drugs.
- Rapid demographic change that outstrips the capacity of the state to provide essential services and job opportunities
- Social inequality marked by grossly unequal distribution of, and access to, resources. Conflict is most likely in situations where the economy is in decline, thus exacerbating social inequalities and intensifying competition for resources.

WHAT CAN BE DONE TO PREVENT COLLECTIVE VIOLENCE

There are a number of measures that can be taken to prevent collective violence and—where it occurs—to lessen its impact.

Some of the general policies needed to reduce the potential for violent conflicts include:

- Ensuring the promotion and application of internationally agreed treaties, including those relating to human rights.
- Reducing access to biological, chemical, nuclear and other weapons.
- Reducing inequality between groups in society.
- Reducing poverty, both in absolute and relative terms, and ensuring that development assistance is targeted so as to make the greatest possible impact on poverty.

National governments can help prevent conflicts by upholding the spirit of the United Nations stage, which calls for the prevention of aggression and the promotion of peace and security. At a more detailed level, this involves adhering to international legal instruments, including the 1949 Geneva Conventions and their 1977 Protocols. Investing in health development can contribute to the prevention of violent conflict. A strong emphasis on social services can help maintain social cohesion and stability. Early manifestations of situations that can lead to conflicts can often be detected in the health sector. Health care workers have a significant role to play in drawing attention to these signs and in calling for appropriate social and health interventions.

TERRORISM

GENERAL INFORMATION ABOUT TERRORISM

Terrorism is the use of force or violence against persons or property in violation of the criminal laws of the United States for purposes of intimidation, coercion, or ransom.

Terrorists often use threats to:

- Create fear among the public.
- Get immediate publicity for their causes.
- Try to convince citizens that their government is powerless to prevent terrorism.

Acts of terrorism include threats of terrorism; assassinations; kidnappings; hijackings; bomb scares and bombings; cyber attacks; and the use of chemical, biological, nuclear and radiological weapons. High-risk targets for acts of terrorism include military and civilian government facilities, international airports, large cities, and high-profile landmarks. Terrorists might also target large public gatherings, water and food supplies, utilities, and corporate centres. Further, terrorists are capable of spreading fear by sending explosives or chemical and biological agents through the mail. Within the immediate area of a terrorist event, you would need to rely on police, fi re, and other officials for instructions. However, you can prepare in much the same way you would prepare for other crisis events.

The following are general guidelines:

- Be aware of your surroundings.
- Be prepared to do without services you normally depend on—electricity, telephone, natural gas, gasoline pumps, cash registers, ATMs, and Internet transactions.
- Learn where emergency exits are located in buildings you frequent. Plan how to get out in the event of an emergency.
- Move or leave if you feel uncomfortable or if something does not seem right.
- Take precautions when traveling. Be aware of conspicuous or unusual behaviour. Do not accept packages from strangers. Do not leave luggage unattended. You should promptly report unusual behaviour, suspicious or unattended packages, and strange devices to the police or security personnel.

- Work with building owners to ensure the following items are located on each fl oor of the building:
  - First aid kit and manual.
  - Fluorescent tape to rope off dangerous areas.
  - Hard hats and dust masks.
  - Portable, battery-operated radio and extra batteries.
  - Several flashlights and extra batteries.

EXPLOSIONS

Terrorists have frequently used explosive devices as one of their most common weapons. Terrorists do not have to look far to find out how to make explosive devices. The materials needed for an explosive device can be found in many places including variety, hardware, and auto supply stores. Explosive devices are highly portable using vehicles and humans as a means of transport.

They are easily detonated from remote locations or by suicide bombers. Conventional bombs have been used to damage and destroy financial, political, social, and religious institutions. Attacks have occurred in public places and on city streets with thousands of people around the world injured and killed.

BIOLOGICAL THREATS

Biological agents are organisms or toxins that can kill or incapacitate people, livestock, and crops. The three basic groups of biological agents that would likely be used as weapons are bacteria, viruses, and toxins. Most biological agents are difficult to grow and maintain. Many break down quickly when exposed to sunlight and other environmental factors, while others, such as anthrax spores, are very long lived. Biological agents can be dispersed by spraying them into the air, by infecting animals that carry the disease to humans, and by contaminating food and water.

Delivery methods include:

- Aerosols—biological agents are dispersed into the air, forming a fi ne mist that may drift for miles. Inhaling the agent may cause disease in people or animals.
- Animals—some diseases are spread by insects and animals, such as fleas, mice, flies, mosquitoes, and livestock.
- Food and water contamination—some pathogenic organisms and toxins may persist in food and water supplies. Most microbes can be killed, and toxins deactivated, by cooking food and boiling water. Most microbes are killed by boiling water for one minute, but some require longer. Follow official instructions.
- Person-to-person—spread of a few infectious agents is also possible. Humans have been the source of infection for smallpox, plague, and the Lassa viruses.

CHEMICAL THREATS

Chemical agents are poisonous vapours, aerosols, liquids, and solids that have toxic effects on people, animals, or plants. They can be released by bombs or sprayed from aircraft, boats, and vehicles. They can be used as a liquid to create a hazard to people and the environment. Some chemical agents may be odourless and tasteless. They can have an immediate effect or a delayed effect. While potentially lethal, chemical agents are difficult to deliver in lethal concentrations. Outdoors, the agents often dissipate rapidly. Chemical agents also are difficult to produce. A chemical attack could come without warning. Signs of a chemical release include people having difficulty breathing; experiencing eye irritation; losing coordination; becoming nauseated; or having a burning sensation in the nose, throat, and lungs. Also, the presence of many dead insects or birds may indicate a chemical agent release.

NUCLEAR BLAST

A nuclear blast is an explosion with intense light and heat, a damaging pressure wave, and widespread radioactive material that can contaminate the air, water, and ground surfaces for miles around. A nuclear device can range from a weapon carried by an intercontinental missile launched by a hostile nation or terrorist organisation, to a small portable nuclear devise transported by an individual. All nuclear devices cause deadly effects when exploded, including blinding light, intense heat, initial nuclear radiation, blast, fi res started by the heat pulse, and secondary fires caused by the destruction.

Hazards of Nuclear Devices

The extent, nature, and arrival time of these hazards are difficult to predict. *The geographical dispersion of hazard effects will be defined by the following*:

- *Existing meteorological conditions*: Wind speed and direction will affect arrival time of fallout; precipitation may wash fallout from the atmosphere.
- *Height above the ground the device was detonated*: This will determine the extent of blast effects.
- *Nature of the surface beneath the explosion*: Some materials are more likely to become radioactive and airborne than others. Flat areas are more susceptible to blast effects.
- *Size of the device*: A more powerful bomb will produce more distant effects.

Radioactive Fallout

Even if individuals are not close enough to the nuclear blast to be affected by the direct impacts, they may be affected by radioactive fallout. Any nuclear blast results in some fallout. Blasts that occur near the earth's surface create much greater amounts of fallout than blasts that occur at higher altitudes. This is because the tremendous heat produced from a nuclear blast causes an updraft of air that forms the familiar mushroom cloud. When a blast occurs near the earth's surface, millions of vapourized dirt particles also are drawn into the cloud. As the heat diminishes, radioactive materials that have vapourized condense on the particles and fall back to Earth. The phenomenon is called radioactive fallout.

This fallout material decays over a long period of time, and is the main source of residual nuclear radiation. Fallout from a nuclear explosion may be carried by wind currents for hundreds of miles if the right conditions exist. Effects from even a small portable device exploded at ground level can be potentially deadly. Nuclear radiation cannot be seen, smelled, or otherwise detected by normal senses. Radiation can only be detected by radiation monitoring devices. This makes radiological emergencies different from other types of emergencies, such as floods or hurricanes. Monitoring can project the fallout arrival times, which will be announced through official warning channels. However, any increase in surface build-up of gritty dust and dirt should be a warning for taking protective measures.

Electromagnetic Pulse

In addition to other effects, a nuclear weapon detonated in or above the earth's atmosphere can create an electromagnetic pulse, a high-density electrical field. An EMP acts like a stroke of lightning but is stronger, faster, and shorter. An EMP can seriously damage electronic devices connected to power sources or antennas. This includes communication systems, computers, electrical appliances, and automobile or aircraft ignition systems. The damage could range from a minor interruption to actual burnout of components. Most electronic equipment within 1,000 miles of a high-altitude nuclear detonation could be affected. Battery-powered radios with short antennas generally would not be affected. Although an EMP is unlikely to harm most people, it could harm those with pacemakers or other implanted electronic devices.

Protection from a Nuclear Blast

The danger of a massive strategic nuclear attack on the United States is predicted by experts to be less likely today. However, terrorism, by nature, is unpredictable. If there were threat of an attack, people living near potential targets could be advised to evacuate or they could decide on their own to evacuate to an area not considered a likely target. Protection from radioactive fallout would require taking shelter in an underground area or in the middle of a large building In general, potential targets include:

- Centres of government such as Washington, DC, and state capitals.
- Important transportation and communication centres.
- Major ports and airfields.
- Manufacturing, industrial, technology, and financial centres.

- Petroleum refineries, electrical power plants, and chemical plants.
- Strategic missile sites and military bases.

The three factors for protecting oneself from radiation and fallout are distance, shielding, and time:

1. *Distance*—the more distance between you and the fallout particles, the better. An underground area such as a home or office building basement offers more protection than the first floor of a building. A floor near the middle of a high-rise may be better, depending on what is nearby at that level on which significant fallout particles would collect. Flat roofs collect fallout particles so the top floor is not a good choice, nor is a floor adjacent to a neighbouring flat roof.
2. *Shielding*—the heavier and denser the materials—thick walls, concrete, bricks, books and earth—between you and the fallout particles, the better.
3. *Time*—fallout radiation loses its intensity fairly rapidly. In time, you will be able to leave the fallout shelter. Radioactive fallout poses the greatest threat to people during the first two weeks, by which time it has declined to about 1 per cent of its initial radiation level.

RADIOLOGICAL DISPERSION DEVICE (RDD)

Terrorist use of an RDD—often called "dirty nuke" or "dirty bomb"—is considered far more likely than use of a nuclear explosive device. An RDD combines a conventional explosive device—such as a bomb—with radioactive material. It is designed to scatter dangerous and sub-lethal amounts of radioactive material over a general area. Such RDDs appeal to terrorists because they require limited technical knowledge to build and deploy compared to a nuclear device. Also, the radioactive materials in RDDs are widely used in medicine, agriculture, industry, and research, and are easier to obtain than weapons grade uranium or plutonium. The primary purpose of terrorist use of an RDD is to cause psychological fear and economic disruption. Some devices could cause fatalities from exposure to radioactive materials. Depending on the speed at which the area of the RDD detonation was evacuated or how successful people were at sheltering-in-place, the number of deaths and injuries from an RDD might not be substantially greater than from a conventional bomb explosion. The size of the affected area and the level of destruction caused by an RDD would depend on the sophistication and size of the conventional bomb, the type of radioactive material used, the quality and quantity of the radioactive material, and the local meteorological conditions—primarily wind and precipitation. The area affected could be placed off-limits to the public for several months during cleanup efforts.

PROSTITUTION

Human Rights Watch, there are approximately 15 million prostitutes in

India. There are more than 100,000 women prostitution in Bombay, Asia's largest sex industry centre. Girl prostitutes in India, Pakistan and the Middle East are tortured, held in virtual imprisonment, sexually abused, and raped. Girl prostitutes are primarily located in low-middle income areas and business districts and are known by officials. Brothel keepers regularly recruit young girls. Girl prostitutes are grouped as common prostitutes, singers and dancers, call girls, religious prostitutes or devadasi, and caged brothel prostitutes. Districts bordering Maharashtra and Karnataka, known as the 'devadasi belt', have trafficking structures operating at various levels.

The women here are in prostitution either because their husbands deserted them, or they are trafficked through coercion and deception. Many are *devadasi,* dedicated into prostitution for the Goddess Yellamma. An oft-repeated cause of prostitution is poverty. But poverty is not the only reason. The helplessness of women forces them to sell their bodies. Many girls from villages are trapped for the trade in the pretext of love and elope from home, only to find themselves sold in the city to pimps, who take money from the women as commission. The other causes of prostitution include ill treatment by parents, bad company, family prostitutes, social customs, inability to arrange marriage, lack of sex education, media, prior incest and rape, early marriage and desertion, lack of recreational facilities, ignorance, and acceptance of prostitution.

Economic causes include poverty and economic distress. Psychological causes include desire for physical pleasure, greed, and dejection. Most enter involuntarily. India, along with Thailand and the Philippines, has 1.3 million childrens in its sex-trade centres.

The childrens come from relatively poorer areas and are trafficked to relatively richer ones. India and Pakistan are the main destinations for children under 16, who are trafficked to South Asia. What is causing alarm both in governmental and Non- Governmental Organisations circles is the escalation in trafficking of young girls, in the last decade. NGOs like STOP and MAITI in Nepal, report that most trafficking in India is for prostitution. And 60 per cent of those trafficked into prostitution are adolescent girls in the age group of 12 to 16 years. These are corroborated by a study done by the Department of Women and Children in 13 sensitive districts of Uttar Pradesh. It revealed that all sex workers who formed a part of this survey had entered the profession as young girls. Many transsexuals, called *hijiras*, are sex workers. The families of *hijiras* reject them. They face opposition from the public, and with the denial of employment, they take to begging and then enter the sex market.

Globalisation, professionalisation of trafficking syndicates, feminisation of poverty and rise in sex tourism—all have contributed to an increase in trafficking. This problem is further compounded because of two factors: linkages of trafficking with the spread of HIV/AIDS and the clandestine nature of the activity. Studies now show that while women of all ages are more vulnerable to the infection than men, young girls are even more at risk because their genital tracts are immature. In addition, they have absolutely no control over sexual relations and sexual health. So a physical vulnerability is compounded by gender vulnerability. The study done in 13 districts of Uttar Pradesh showed that in a sample of 1,341 sex workers, brothel-based prostitution was 793 and family-based prostitution came close at 548. Since prostitution is not legal, the police can arrest sex workers at any time. The police, whose main function is to protect and serve, turn out to be robbers, stealing the little money that these workers "earn". Interventions are increasingly based on issues like combating stigma related to HIV/AIDS, developing empowering strategies for victims and involving communities in the rehabilitation of rescued women and girls.

But there is a lot that still needs to be done. Involvement of communities is of the greatest significance here since, it has been seen that their families and communities do not accept rescued women and girls. The situation becomes worse, if someone is tested positive for HIV, then she is immediately labeled a prostitute—a perception that creates a complex situation in the rehabilitation programmes. Even if trafficked returnees can avoid such treatment, they have few options for survival. What is needed is a multi-pronged strategy, which can help in curbing trafficking and empowering communities and which also has scope for rescue and rehabilitation processes. The task is not just daunting; given the political priorities of most governments, it has not been given the importance it deserves.

CAUSES OF PROSTITUTION

- Bad company.
- Early marriage and desertion.
- Economic causes include poverty and economic distress.
- Family prostitutes.
- Ill treatment by parents.
- Inability to arrange marriage
- Lack of recreational facilities, ignorance, and acceptance of prostitution.
- Lack of sex education, media.
- Prior incest and rape.
- Psychological causes include desire for physical pleasure, greed, and dejection.
- Social customs.

Notorious red light districts of India include GB Road in Delhi, Sonagachi in Kolkata, Kamathipura in Mumbai, Budhwar Peth in Pune and Reshampura in Gwalior. There are around 2.8 million prostitutes in the country and their number is increasing, as informed by Lok Sabha. Most of the girls are brought from Nepal and Bangladesh. Young girls are trafficked from Nepal to brothels in Mumbai and Kolkata at an average age of twelve. They are trapped into the vicious cycle of prostitution, debt and slavery. By the time they are in their mid-twenties, they are at the dead end.

In modern India different kinds of prostitution is prevailing apart from prostitutes in brothel there are:

- Bar dancers
- Beat prostitutes
- Call girls
- Child prostitutes
- Escort girls
- Fricatrice prostitutes
- Gimmick prostitutes
- Religious prostitutes
- Road side brothel
- Street prostitutes

Prostitution is a problem in itself and child prostitution is making it more complex. Quoting a study on 'Girls/Women in prostitution in India', Minister for Women and Child Development Renuka Chowdhury said that out of the total number of prostitutes in the country, 35.47 per cent entered the trade before the age of 18 years.

Though in cases like Gaurav jain vs. Union of India direction where given for the upliftment of prostitutes and establishment of the juvenile home for the children's of prostitutes.

THE PROSTITUTION LEADS TO MANY HEALTH PROBLEMS

In a country like India where most of the people indulge themselves in unprotected sex with prostitutes it is very difficult to eradicate the problem of AIDS. Historically, the AIDS epidemic in India was first identified amongst sex workers and their clients, before other parts of society became affected. The sex workers are themselves taking steps to combat with aids in some brothels in India for example,

Sonagachi a brothel in Kolkata; where the sex workers are insisting their clients for use of condoms in order to avoid AIDS. But in all the other brothels in India social workers and NGO,s are trying to acquaint the sex workers about the ill effects of AIDS and are insisting them for using condoms

- Cervical cancer
- HIV
- Psychological disorders
- Sexually transmitted diseases
- Traumatic brain injury

STEPS THAT SHOULD BE TAKEN IN ORDER TO FIGHT WITH PROSTITUTION

- Adequate publicity, through print and electronic media including child lines and women help lines about the problem of those who have been forced into prostitution.

- Awareness generation and legal literacy on economic rights, particularly for women and adolescent girls should be taken up.
- Culturally sanctioned practices like the system of *devadasis, jogins, bhavins,* etc. which provides a pretext for prostitution should be addressed suitably.
- Formal education should be made available to those victims who are still within the school going age, while non-formal education should be made accessible to adults
- Rehabilitation and reintegration of rescued victims being a long-term.
- Recruitment of adequate number of trained counsellors and social workers in institutions/homes run by the government independently or in collaboration with non-governmental organisations.
- The Central and State Governments in partnership with non-governmental organisations should provide gender sensitive market driven vocational training to all those rescued victims who are not interested in education.

SHALL INDIA LEGALIZE PROSTITUTION

Some people opine that prostitution shall be made legal in India and accept them as a part of society because the problem of prostitution is inevitable. The benefit of legalizing prostitution in India will be that atleast as suggested, have a track record of Sexworkers as for example when dance bar in Bombay were closed most of the bar dancers migrated to Gujarat and Karnataka and other neighbouring state and started their business undercover. Legalising prostitution will see these women, who live life on the edge everywhere, gaining access to medical facilities, which can control the spread of AIDS. There is a very strong need to treat the sex industry as any other industry and empower it with legal safeguards.The practical implications of the profession being legal would bring nothing but benefits for sex workers and society as a whole. Keeping prostitution illegal also contributes to crime because many criminals view prostitutes and their customers as attractive targets for robbery, fraud, rape, or other criminal acts. The criminals realise that such people are unlikely to report the crimes to police, because the victims would have to admit they were involved in the illegal activity of prostitution when the attacks took place, now if it is legal then they will easily go and report this to police.

Benifits of legalizing prostitution are:

- Legalization of prostitution and the sex industry will stop sex trafficking.
- Legalization of prostitution will control the sex industry.
- Legalization of prostitution will decrease clandestine, hidden, illegal and street prostitution.
- Legalization of prostitution will promote women's health as they can have easy access to medical facilities which they don't have when it is illegal.

- Legalization of prostitution will protect the women in prostitution as they will have rights.
- Recognizing prostitution as an economic activity, thus enabling women in India to obtain working permits as "sex workers".
- Women in systems of Prostitution want the sex industry legalized as they are the one who suffers the most as they don't have any rights.

SEX-RELATED CRIMES

Being involved in a sex-related crime can be a complicated process because of all the details that help to define where the lines fall for the crime. There are many different types of sex crimes depending on what kind of situation was involved with the crime. The technical definitions for sex crimes can become very complicated because it's somewhat hard to define what is classified as a sex crime and what is classified as consensual sex. The area to define each type of sex-related crime can become a very grey area because of the age of consent and other details. The first thing that you should understand is that every sex crime is a crime that involves forcing someone to commit some type of sexual act without their direct consent. This means that any type of sexual act that is forced by another person could be consider a sex crime depending on the circumstances.

No matter what the person may say later, if the person said no at any time and the event still occurred, it would technically be considered a sex crime. Understanding this fact will help in any sex crime case that you may be involved with. The next factor that you should consider is that every sex-related crime will have some sort of punishment no matter what the circumstances of the event may have been. The next thing you should realise is that there many different types of sex-related crimes. Rape is considered to be a sex crime because of all the things that it entails. Rape is technically defined as forcing someone to have sexual intercourse without their consent to the actions. This means that someone is forced to have sex with another person without their consent to the actions that happened. The convictions for a rape charge as well as the consequences to go along with it can be quite severe with a lifetime of changes that will always affect your life. Some of the consequences could be jail time or even prison time as well as a rather large fine. The court can also assign you a long probation period as well as up to 1000 hours of community service time that you must complete in a certain amount of time. These are just some of the many consequences that go along with some of the other sex-related crimes as well.

COGNITION AND CRIME

The term 'cognition' is an imprecise one, used in a variety of ways by different authors: in general terms it refers to concepts such as memory, imagery, intelligence, and reasoning; although perhaps its most widely used meaning is as a synonym for thinking. In explanations of offending, cognition is implicit in the theories of a number of writers who suggest that various styles of thinking, such as 'impulsive' or 'concrete', are characteristic of criminal populations. The link between cognition and crime is perhaps at its most explicit in the controversial writings of Samuel Yochelson and Stanton Samenow.

In the first volume of *The Criminal Personality,* Yochelson and Samenow describe their conclusions drawn from interviews with male offenders referred to their hospital for 'determination of competency'. From these interviews, they claim to have discovered the 'criminal thinking patterns' which characterize all criminals. While cautious social scientists might exercise some restraint in accepting the conclusions of investigators who assert that 'The criminal has revealed the working of his mind to us' and 'We fractionate the criminal's mind and then synthesize it', it cannot be denied that Yochelson and Samenow present some fascinating and idiosyncratic views.

They describe a number of styles and errors of thinking—Ross and Fabiano have counted fifty-two—which define the criminal mind. These thinking patterns include concrete thinking, fragmentation, failure to empathize with others, a lack of any perspective of time, irresponsible decision-making, and perceiving themselves as victims. While there is much of interest in this work, there are a number of criticisms and shortcomings, some methodological, others theoretical. The sample used by Yochelson and Samenow is an unusual one in that it consisted of 240 persistent offenders, many of whom had been judged 'Not Guilty by Reason of Insanity'. It is questionable just how far it is possible to generalize from this sample to the remainder of the offender population. Their conclusion that all criminals share the same thinking pattern, must therefore be treated with caution. Further, as they failed to include a non-offender control group, it is not established that the thinking patterns they describe are peculiar to criminal populations. The interview method of data-gathering, while a rich source of material, does require a check for reliability and validity which is not given. Similarly, there is no indication of any attempt at standardization across interviews. At a theoretical level two principal issues arise: the first is with the concept of 'mind' and the associated assumption that thinking caused behaviour.

There are a number of theoretical variations on both mind and the primacy of cognition over behaviour, none of which is fully explored. The second issue lies in their assertion that, by processes which are not well explained, criminals are like a different breed of person. Indeed, comments of this latter type have led to charges of 'neo-Lombrosian' being levelled against this work. In summarizing the cognitive approach of Yochelson and Samenow, Ross and Fabiano express regret at the shortcomings of this work, which has led to a great deal of controversy rather than establishing a valuable contribution to clinical criminology. However, the approach of Yochelson and Samenow is not that of other cognitive models of criminal behaviour. More recent studies have looked for more explicit cognitive variations between offenders and non-offenders. Although the distinction may not be exact, Ross and Fabiano distinguish between *im*personal cognition and *inter*personal cognition. The former is that aspect of cognition which 'deals with the physical world'; the latter is concerned with 'understanding people and their actions', sometimes called social cognition. While impersonal cognition may be a factor in the development of criminal behaviour—for example the research which points to intellectual imbalances in offender samples— Ross and Fabiano argue that interpersonal cognition may well be more important in understanding crime. In reviewing studies of social cognition with criminal populations, Ross and Fabiano described a variety of types or styles of cognition which characterize offenders.

A failure in *self-control,* leading to *impulsivity,* figures repeatedly in explanations of crime. Ross and Fabiano suggest that impulsivity may be seen 'as a failure to insert between impulse and action a stage of reflection, a cognitive analysis of the situation'. This failure, they further suggest, may be due to one of a number of factors: a failure to learn to stop and think; a failure to learn 'effective thinking'; a failure to generate alternative responses; or a reflection of hopelessness. The empirical evidence is mixed. Some studies suggest that offenders are more impulsive than non-offenders others that offenders are unable to delay reward. However, other studies have not found such differences.

The difference between studies may be due to differing definitions and measures of impulsivity, and the heterogeneity of the offender population. The concept of *locus of control* refers to the degree to which individuals perceive their behaviour to be under their own *internal* control, as opposed to being controlled by *external* agents such as luck or authority figures.

A number of studies have shown that offenders tend to external control, that is they explain their behaviour as being controlled by influences beyond their personal control. However, other studies have failed to show any difference in locus of control between offender and non-offender samples; while Lefcourt and Ladwig found offenders to be more *internally* controlled than Non-offenders. The varied findings are probably due to two unfounded assumptions: that locus of control is a unitary concept, and that offenders form a homogeneous population.

With regard to the former point, a number of studies have shown that there are several dimensions to locus of control, such as belief in control over one's immediate environment as opposed to belief in control over political events. In terms of the latter point, locus of control within an offender population may be a function of race; type of offence, for example, violent offenders tend to external control or time spent in prison. If locus of control does have some relationship with offending, it will require rather more sophisticated research than is presently available to discover its exact role. As social perception develops so the ability to 'see things from the other person's point of view' matures and influences our own behaviour.

A long-standing finding with offenders is that they see situations only from their own perspective, not appreciating the view of the other person. This is reflected in low scores on measures of empathy and role-taking ability: although variations have been reported just as to length of criminal career and type of offence. If social perception is the ability to discriminate social cues and understand their significance, then the next step requires using these perceptions to decide upon suitable social behaviour.

This requires a range of cognitive skills such as the ability to generate a range of solutions to a social problem, considering the various consequences of the different solutions, and planning the steps to achieve the different outcomes.

These cognitive skills have become more widely known as 'cognitive problem-solving' over the past few years. Several studies have found that offenders show poorer social problem solving than Non-offenders. Although some doubt has been expressed about the validity of one of the measures used in some of these studies, and also about the functional relationship of these cognitive skills with offending. In total the evidence does indicate some differences in social cognition between offenders and non-offenders. However, two points require clarification: the relationship between impersonal and interpersonal cognitive abilities, particularly with regard to offender populations; secondly, and perhaps more importantly, the process by which the cognition results in offending.

It seems likely that the answer to this latter point will come from studies, not yet attempted, of social *decisionmaking* in offenders. While social decision-making in offenders has not been researched, decision-making regarding the commission of crime has received a growing amount of attention.

This line of enquiry portrays the offender as a rational decision-maker, a 'reasoning criminal'. The beginnings of this cognitive view of crime are, somewhat ironically, to be found in studies which focused on environmental rather than individual factors in explaining the crime. Simply, this view suggests that for a crime to be committed, the opportunity must be afforded for the offence to occur; the criminal is one who decides to take advantage of this opportunity. L.E.Cohen and Felson elaborated on this view of 'crime as opportunity', suggesting that for example the increase in burglaries over the past decade can be explained in terms of increased opportunity as more family members go out to work, so leaving houses empty for longer periods.

Studies have similarly investigated the effects of opportunity on car theft violence robbery and theft and vandalism. The cognitive component involves the decision-making process when the opportunity to offend arises. A crime is seen therefore as the result of the offender's consideration of the risks and costs of offending; indeed previous studies have addressed the relationship between risk perception and likelihood of offending. Cornish and Clarke summarize this view of crime:

- Its starting point was the assumption that offenders seek to benefit themselves by their criminal behaviour; that this involves the making of decisions and choices, however rudimentary on occasion these processes might be; and that these processes exhibit a measure of rationality, albeit constrained by limits of time and ability and the availability of relevant information.

Cornish and Clarke also make the distinction between criminal *involvement* and criminal *events*. The former is the process by which individuals choose to become involved in crime, while the latter refers to the short-term, immediate decisions in a given set of circumstances. Thus the approach is an interactional one, in which the offender reacts in a reasoned manner to environmental opportunities. While this represents a move away from 'dispositional' theories which focus exclusively on the offender, it does not dismiss the importance of personal variables, but rather attempts to place such variables in a wider context. As an example Cornish and Clarke work through the process of an individual's initial involvement in the crime of burglary, followed by the event decision for a specific burglary, and finally the process underlying the individual committing more and more such offences.

The initial involvement includes factors such as type of upbringing and other social variables; the event decision considers the influence of factors such as the presence of a dog or a burglar alarm on the decision to enter a particular house; while the increase in frequency is related to a growing sense of 'professionalism' in committing the crime, and accompanying changes in self-evaluation, life-style, and peer group. As well as burglary the rational choice model has been applied to shoplifting, robbery and drug use.

The rational choice model can also be applied to the decision to give up crime. In total, the traditional learning theories have concentrated upon the acquisition of criminal behaviour through reinforcement and modelling. The cognitive theories have followed this trend, but have recently considered the alternative of explaining why offending does *not* occur even when the opportunity arises. This notion of not offending is central to another group of theories which see crime as a failure to learn control behaviour.

THE CRIMINAL JUSTICE SYSTEM IN STOPPING VIOLENCE AGAINST WOMEN

Comprehensive, effective, and Non-discriminatory implementation of criminal justice system powers is essential to ending violence against women, both for freeing individual women and for ending the world wide epidemic of violence against women. No doubt, all segments of society must make profound changes before violence against women will be eliminated. But once there is violence or threat of violence, the criminal justice system is the only sector of society that has the power and authority to step in and stop the violence. The criminal justice system alone is invested with the power and authority to enforce the laws against violence, to carry out a criminal investigation, to arrest and detain a perpetrator, and to provide justice for criminal offences. If the criminal justice system doesn't fully do its part to put the perpetrator under control, you can social work these cases endlessly. In all likelihood the perpetrator will just turn around and easily undo any peace and equilibrium you and the victim have been able to establish in her life.

The pivotal importance of the criminal justice system in stopping violence against women can be illustrated in both the positive and the negative. On the positive side, a handful of diverse jurisdictions around the country that have implemented a consistent, aggressive, and modern criminal justice response to domestic violence have been able to reduce their domestic violence homicide rates by over 60% in just a matter of years. If domestic violence were a disease, this kind of dramatic reduction in deaths would be heralded a miracle cure.

You may recall a series of studies from the late 1980's which found that arresting perpetrators resulted in only minimal reduction of future violence in the relationship. These studies are still used to argue against the necessity of a strong criminal justice system response, so it's important to be aware of a core flaw, not in the studies themselves, but in the conditions at the time. The system in place at the time consisted principally of arrests by themselves, without the crucial follow-up investigations and prosecutions in place. It was like trying to make the airplane fly with only one wing. It's easy to see that if perpetrators are merely arrested and detained for a couple days and then let go without follow-through, they are likely to be even more dangerous to victims.

It wasn't until the early 1990's when a few jurisdictions, most notably San Diego, CA and Quincy, Massachusetts, began to pioneer the more modern, comprehensive law enforcement approach to domestic violence. In addition to pro-arrest policies, the new approach included a complete police investigation with an eye to prosecution, prosecutorial follow-up, no diversion/no-drop policies, victim support, and intensified probation monitoring and/or correctional follow through. It was only when this full spectrum criminal justice response was applied to domestic violence that the immediate and dramatic reductions in domestic violence homicides took place in those pioneering cities. These positive and striking results have now been successfully reproduced in a number of other jurisdictions throughout the country.

No other approach to domestic violence-not educational, therapy based, and not diversion programmes-has shown anywhere near the effectiveness and impact obtained by the implementation of a comprehensive criminal justice response. If anything, studies of non-criminal justice remedies to domestic violence repeatedly demonstrate their ineffectiveness in bringing about any significant reduction in the levels of violence. Given the proven and unequivocal benefits of a full criminal justice response, it's sad that still today, the pivotal importance of good criminal justice system response is still more often manifested in the negative. On the negative side, the consequences of law enforcement failures to implement their powers on behalf of women are all too evident by tracing law enforcement histories leading up to domestic violence homicides. What's found in case after case where women have been murdered by their partners is a history of gross failures of law enforcement to respond properly to the victims' previous requests for help.

Half-baked investigations, officer bias against women, contempt of victims, inadequate prosecution, slap-on-the-wrist sentencing, careless follow-up, and overall system disregard paves the road to one domestic violence homicide after another. Sloppy law enforcement response emboldens the perpetrators, throws the women into despair, and leads to an incalculable number of severe injuries and deaths to women.

A year 2002, Domestic Violence Fatality Review from Washington State aptly names this all too common inadequate law enforcement response to domestic violence "the meaningless processing of cases". All too often, instead of implementing their powers on the victim's behalf, criminal justice officials were found to be carelessly handing the cases off from one to the next. Perpetrators were never really held accountable despite multiple rounds through the system, and ultimately the women were murdered.

When the criminal justice system withholds its powers from victims of rape and domestic violence, it bolsters the perpetrators, and, in fact, increases the danger to the victim. The perpetrators are emboldened by the immense authority behind the system's could-care-less attitude. The perpetrators feel they've been given the ultimate green light to carry on with the violence or to escalate. In fact, once law enforcement responds carelessly, it's not uncommon for perpetrators to invoke law enforcement authority in taunting the victim. "Go ahead, call the Sheriff," Avelino Macias would taunt his estranged wife Teresa, "The Sheriff protects me more than they protect you."

The victim, on the other hand, is dangerously weakened and driven into despair by the system's denial of help. Right at the moment she takes the great risk of exposing her intent to confront the perpetrator by bringing in law enforcement, she is betrayed by inadequate law enforcement response in front of the perpetrator. "Instead of helping me," Teresa had told her mother regarding authorities' responses to her calls for help, "they sunk me even more." Like many victims of domestic violence homicide, Teresa had been driven into such deep despair by the Sheriff's repeated disregard of her more than 25 calls for help, she had given up on calling the Sheriff for help in the weeks before Avelino lay in wait and executed her. Nor do you have to limit your observations to domestic violence homicides to see the harm of law enforcement disregard for violence against women. The same can be seen in the law enforcement histories of so many cases where there are serious injuries. Or in cases of serial rapists or serial child molesters. If you dig out the law enforcement histories in these felony cases, here again you'll most always find a trail of law enforcement disregard of the perpetrator's prior lower level violence against women and children.

Given the increased danger to women created by official's denial of protection and justice, it should be clear that any police officer or prosecutor who routinely mishandles violence against women, over the course of his or her career, or even over the course of a year, is more dangerous to women than a hundred batterers and rapists. What's more, if you look at the law enforcement history in cases of serial killers and mass murderers, you'll also frequently find a trail of inadequate law enforcement response to the perpetrator's earlier violence against women. A current case in the news is that of John Muhammad whose sniper killing spree in the fall of 2002 held the entire populace of Washington DC under siege for weeks and resulted in the killing of 13 people and the wounding of 5.

In the two years prior to that killing spree at least three police agencies, the Tacoma PD, the Bellingham PD, and the area Sheriff's Department had failed to respond properly to Muhammad's domestic violence related crimes against his wife and children and against the mother of Jahn Malvo, Muhammad's juvenile accomplice in the killing spree. These law enforcement agencies never once arrested Muhammad, nor obtained an arrest warrant for these crimes, despite the fact that Muhammad had abducted and concealed his children from his wife for over a year, despite the fact that he had made threats to kill that were heard by credible witnesses, and despite the fact that law enforcement was in touch with Muhammad and had ample evidence to prove those crimes.

As a point of insight into Tacoma Police mentality it's worth noting that in that same time period Tacoma PD had obtained an arrest warrant for Muhammad-But that arrest warrant had nothing to do with domestic violence. Tacoma PD obtained the arrest warrant because Muhammad had shoplifted $27 worth of meat from a Tacoma store. The Tacoma PD took stronger action on behalf of the store owner's loss of $27 worth of meat than on behalf of Muhammad's wife, including when Muhammad abducted and concealed their three children for over a year.

It's also worth noting that in April, 2003, Tacoma Police Chief Brame shot and killed his own wife in front of their two children. The Fallacy of Avoiding the Criminal Justice System. If you are a victim advocate reading this, it may seem silly to belabor the point that effective criminal justice system response is essential to stopping violence against women. But there are many women in the violence against women movement who are so disgusted by the sexism, the racism, and all the other abuses of power in the criminal justice system, that they are desperately looking for ways to circumvent the system altogether. They point not only to the system's mishandling of violence against women, but also to the system's persistent discriminatory violations of defendant's rights as well, especially abuses against defendants of Colour. And the point is undeniably true. The criminal justice system, probably more than any other public entity, abuses its powers in a highly discriminatory manner, and, in fact, frequently actively uses its immense powers to enforce existing inequalities and injustices in the social order. But it would be as foolhardy to divert women's energies away from the criminal justice system as it would be to advise a minority community not to call the fire department because their current fire department responds in such racist ways. What alternate solution could we possibly create that could respond at one in the morning when a woman has a knife to her neck? Who's going to investigate when the perpetrator says she started it and he was acting in self defence? Who's going to invest in the necessary equipment, training, and salaries to respond to millions of these cases? And when the perpetrator promises to stay away from the house, by what authority are we going to stop him when he breaks the promise?

And if, for the sake of argument, we were to create such a system, is there any question that the current law enforcement system would not sit idly by? They would, of course, immediately begin to arrest the members of our alternative system the moment we moved to restrict a perpetrator's freedom. So doesn't that bring us inevitably right back to the confrontation with the current justice system that we wanted to avoid in the first place? What then? Are we going to make the millions of women who now call the police to secure their safety give up their housing and go into shelters? The kids too? And for how long? And let the violent perpetrators run free? To find more victims? And what about justice? Do we say, oh well, she may have been beaten to a pulp, but as long as she's safe, she doesn't need justice? Do we say that first we must stop all justice system abuses of male defendant's before we demand justice for women? Or do we create an alternate justice system as well as an alternate system of first response?

Or are we going to prevent this violence from happening in the first place? With education? And how many women are we willing to let die before the prevention education sinks in? And since most young boys turn to violence after growing up in violent homes, isn't stopping the current violence against women the first priority of any successful prevention programme? And doesn't that bring us right back to the original dilemma? Who's going to step in and stop the current violence that's ravaging millions of women's lives today? What good does it do to tell kids not to play with matches if there's a wildfire raging all around them and the firemen won't budge?It doesn't take but a few minutes thought to see that when it comes to intervening in the rampant existing violence against women, the criminal justice system as exclusively authorized and empowered by the state is as pivotal and irreplaceable as the fire department is to fighting fires.

But it's worth doing the mental exercise if only to beat down once and for all the temptation to give up on dealing with the criminal justice system. It's true the criminal justice system is permeated with abuses. And it's true these abuses can easily endanger and re-victimize victims, as well as victimize defendants. But this is all the more reason we need to confront this system head on, and to remake the current justice system into a system that responds adequately, equitably, and even handedly.

2

Psychology and Crime

INTRODUCTION

One of the challenges of crime is that any attempt at its understanding demands knowledge across a wide range of disciplines. Writers and researchers from anthropology, economics, jurisprudence, medicine, philosophy, psychology, and sociology have all contributed to the study of crime. As the study of crime became more refined so it evolved into the specialism of criminology: An integrated approach to the study of crime, in which the elements of other disciplines are used to develop theories and explanations for the phenomenon of crime. There is some debate as to whether criminology has achieved the status of an independent discipline.

Critics suggest that as criminology relies so heavily on other disciplines its independence is doubtful and so it would be better considered as a specialization within another established field such as, say, sociology. This argument may have had some force in the past but seems altogether less tenable in the 1980s. I am persuaded by the arguments of writers such as Wolfgang and Ferracuti who claim that criminology has achieved the status of an independent discipline with its own data base, methodologies, and theories. With this in mind, I am able to set this book into perspective. I make no imperialist claims on behalf of psychology; crime cannot be explained solely by psychological theory.

However, what I believe psychology can do is to contribute to criminology both in terms of its methodology, and by the application of some of its own data base and theory. Further, crime and criminals raise a number of practical issues, principally in two fields. First, how can it be determined whether or not an individual has committed an offence when so accused? Second, when an individual has committed an offence how, if at all, are we to respond to that person? Psychology on its own cannot provide all the answers but, once again, I believe it has a contribution to make. In this light, therefore, the emphasis of this book will be the *contribution* psychology can make to the study of crime.

Of necessity the bulk of each stage is concerned with psychological research and theories as applied to some aspect of crime. Each stage ends with a short section labelled 'Perspective'. The function of these sections is precisely as the name suggests: to provide a sense of perspective by addressing some point raised in the preceding material. At the outset, however, there are three fundamental points which must be addressed: What is psychology? What is crime? What is the relationship between psychology and crime?

POLICE RECORDING OF CRIME

If an offence is reported to the police is it guaranteed to appear in the official statistics? An American study cited by Hood and Sparks suggests not: only about two-thirds of serious crimes which victims claimed to have reported to the police were actually recorded in police files. A British survey similarly found that there were discrepancies between reported crime and police-recorded crime: the percentage shortfall— crimes reported but not recorded—ranged from 75 per cent for robbery to 27 per cent for bicycle theft. However, three offence categories—sexual offences, thefts of motor vehicles, and theft in a dwelling—showed no shortfall between reporting and police recording.

While human error may play a part in misrecording or 'losing' crimes, and the exact figures involved may be open to question, it is also true that the police have considerable discretion over the recording of reported crime. Bottomley and Pease present a full discussion of police work and criminal statistics; however, for present purposes the emphasis will be on the process of recording. As Hough and Mayhew note, the police may, with justification, feel that a reported 'crime' is a mistake, or there is a lack of evidence to support the report. In other instances an informal caution may be given in which case the offence will not appear in the official figures.

In a similar vein, the criminal incident may be satisfactorily resolved by the appearance of a police officer: family disputes and arguments in public houses are examples of this type of situation in which the crime is reported but goes unrecorded. Alternatively it could be that after reporting a crime the injured party asks for the crime to be dropped and so the incident is written off as 'no crime' —again failing to appear in the criminal statistics. In a survey of three London areas, Sparks *et al.* found that 'no crime' cases accounted for between 18 per cent and 28 per cent of all initially recorded crimes. The time lapse between the committing of the crime and its reporting to the police is also important; those judged as being too 'stale' to merit investigation may fail to be recorded. Thus for these and perhaps other reasons the discrepancy between the number of crimes actually committed and the number recorded by the police suggests that the official statistics are not telling the full story—at least for some types of crime. While crimes can be 'lost' and so distort official figures, variations in police activity can also cause fluctuations in the crime statistics. A crackdown on some criminal group, say drug offenders, can cause a 'bulge' in the figures. Of course this does not mean that there has been a dramatic increase in that type of crime—despite what some newspaper headlines might say—rather that, to use an experimental metaphor, improved sampling has given a better estimate of the true population. In other words, the official figure moves closer to reality.

Similarly a change in public attitude or improving the means of communication—it is more convenient to telephone the police at 2 am than to walk to the station—may shift both the quality and quantity of crimes reported to the police. So while, say, the real amount of violent crime in society is decreasing, higher levels of reporting can cause an *increase* to appear in the official figures. The first British Crime Survey showed that victims were selective in the crimes they reported to the police: there was, for example, a high rate of reporting for theft of a motor vehicle but a low rate for theft in a dwelling. M. Hough and Mayhew also examined the reasons offered by victims for not reporting a crime. The main reasons were the view that the crime was too trivial, or that the police could do nothing, or that it was appropriate to deal with the matter personally. In total these explanations show why victims may decide not to report a crime, although other factors can also be considered.

The victim, or perhaps witness, may not realise an act is criminal: physical violence, for example, may be perceived as bullying rather than assault. In cases of fraud or theft from an employer the victim might be unaware of the crime. Alternatively the individual may be a 'willing victim': for example, some homosexual behaviour, drug dealing, and prostitution all involve willing victims. Finally there are 'victimless crimes': if a telephone box is vandalized, or a false income tax return submitted, who is the victim to report the crime? In summary, crimes are committed, some serious, which fail to appear in the criminal statistics. The amount of this 'unknown' crime is traditionally referred to as the *Dark Figure*. In attempting to shed light on the magnitude of the Dark Figure researchers have turned away from official bodies towards the other two parties involved in crime—the offenders and the victims.

OFFENDER SURVEYS

In the 1960s a number of offender surveys were carried out for which reviews are available. The most commonly employed methodology was to select a sample either on the basis of age or geographical location, then to ask the members of the sample whether they had committed any crimes, either detected or undetected. This information was gathered either by questionnaire or interview, conducted with the target person themselves or with someone who knew them well. A British study of theft conducted by Belson illustrates a typical survey. A sample of 1,445 boys, aged from 13 to 16 years, was randomly selected from a large sample of London households. Interviews with the boys revealed that approximately 70 per cent of the sample had stolen from a shop, and about 17 per cent had stolen from private premises.

Thus the majority of boys had committed an offence for which, had they been caught, they would have been liable to prosecution. The general picture which emerges from the self-report studies is that the official figures underestimate the true extent of crime, especially amongst the young. Indeed, Hood and Sparks suggest that the official figures represent on average only one-quarter of those who actually commit offences; in other words, they estimate that the Dark Figure is actually about four times greater than the official figure. The initial impact of the self-report studies was to give pause for thought about whether crime, especially in the young, can legitimately be considered a deviant activity.

If so many people are committing offences perhaps that is the norm rather than remaining within the limits of the law. Critics of self-report studies pointed to several shortcomings, the principal one being confidence in the veracity of the data. Does the respondent always tell the truth? Are some crimes withheld, others invented or exaggerated? Further research showed that a number of interviewer and interviewee characteristics—age, sex, socioeconomic status, and race—could influence the quality of information. Additionally there may be sampling problems: if a survey is carried out at a school, for example, it will lose those absent or playing truant—who may be engaged in committing the more serious crimes. Advocates of self-report studies pointed to the advantages of the methodology in that it not only gives a picture of crime involving victims, but also includes 'victimless' crimes such as drug abuse and vandalism. Such doubts led a number of investigators to refine the self-report methodology to include reliability checks on the data.

The most frequently used verification technique is to compare selfreport with police records. Studies using this check have found high degrees of agreement between the two measures of offending. Other verification methods include using peer informants to ensure reports match; testing respondents twice to determine if their answers remain constant; and including lie questions in the schedule as a general check on honesty. Hindelang *et al.*, following a comprehensive review of self-report methodology, conclude that the match is a good one between self-report data and official recording. However, despite the assurances of researchers such as Hindelang *et al.*, the trend in recent times has moved away from offender surveys to victim surveys. One reason for this is that not only can victim surveys reveal information about crime, but also they can be used to gather data on other issues such as public attitudes towards crime and public fear of crime.

VICTIM SURVEYS

The first contemporary victim surveys were carried out in the USA in the late 1960s, followed by the first American national survey in 1972. Similar surveys were carried out in other parts of the world including Australia and the Scandinavian countries. Smaller-scale victim surveys have been conducted in specific parts of a country, for example in England surveys have been conducted in the Midlands, in Islington in London and on Merseyside or in areas of the same city, such as the survey in different parts of London. Victim research has a range of available methodologies but *household surveys* offer perhaps the most important means of data collection. This methodology is typified by the first British Crime Survey. This survey selected 16,000 households from the Electoral Register, with the aim of interviewing one person aged 16 years or older from each household.

The survey achieved an 80 per cent success rate in striving to achieve that particular sample. In the context of an interview respondents answered questions about any crimes in which they had been the victim, gave details of the crime and answered questions on their attitudes towards crime. Surveys such as the British Crime Survey have thrown up a vast amount of data, but across studies a consistent pattern of findings emerges. The most notable is the extent of crime, as Sparks notes: 'Criminal victimization is an extremely rare event...crimes of violence are extremely uncommon'. The first British Crime Survey was in agreement with Sparks's observations.

Trivial crimes such as theft from a motor vehicle are the most common, while serious offences such as assault and robbery have a very low frequency of occurrence. Indeed, M.Hough and Mayhew estimate that the 'statistically average' person over the age of 16 years can expect to be burgled once every 40 years, and to be robbed once every 500 years. Crime is not, however, a random event and crime surveys illustrate this point.

The majority of respondents, Sparks estimates about 90 per cent, report no experience of crime. On the other hand, some people report being involved in a series of incidents, having been the victims of two, three, four, or even more crimes. This leads to the important distinction between the *incidence* of victimization and the *prevalence* of victimization.

The incidence is the average crime rate over the whole population; the prevalence is that percentage of the population who actually experience crime. Thus surveys reveal that burglaries are most prevalent in inner city areas; cars parked on the street at night are more likely to be stolen; and that it is not the elderly but young males, who typically have assaulted others themselves, who are the most likely victims of assault. If surveys are repeated over regular periods trends in crime rates may be described.

Sparks discusses some figures from the American National Crime Survey over the period 1973–79: rates for burglary and robbery dropped over that period, while rates for household and personal larceny fluctuated over that time. In Britain such trends cannot be calculated as only two national crime surveys have been completed.

The second of these showed rises in almost all categories of offence. It can also be seen that the rises detected by the survey closely parallel changes in the amount of crime recorded by the police.

Table. Percentage change in British Crime Survey Estimates and Offences Recorded by the Police in the same Period

Offences	Survey estimates	Recorded offences (per cent Change)
Vandalism	+ 9	+ 15
Theft from a motor vehicle	+ 7	+ 12
Burglary in a dwelling	+ 21	+ 24
Theft of motor vehicle	0	– 2
Bicycle theft	+ 34	+ 13
Theft in a dwelling	+ 2	+ 13
Theft from a person/robbery	+ 9	– 1
Total	+ 10	+ 12

MORAL DEVELOPMENT AND CRIME

The process of socialization is linked with moral development in the theories of both Piaget and Kohlberg. There are various accounts of Piaget's theories on moral development and Aronfreed compares the views of Piaget and Kohlberg. However, Kohlberg has used his theory to develop an explanation for offending and therefore this particular theory is of interest here. Kohlberg, like Piaget, argues that moral reasoning develops in a sequential manner as the individual attains maturity. Kohlberg describes three levels of moral development, with two stages at each level.

At the lower stages moral reasoning is concrete in orientation, becoming more abstract at the higher stages and involving concepts such as 'justice', 'rights', and 'principles'. Offending, Kohlberg argues, is associated with a delay in the development of moral reasoning so that given the opportunity for offending the individual does not have the internal mechanisms to control and resist the temptation. A number of recent reviews have both elaborated this basic premise and discussed the empirical evidence. The main body of experimental evidence compares the moral judgements of delinquents and non-delinquents. The results are mixed with some studies finding that young offenders use less mature reasoning than non-offenders; others failing to show any distinction between the two groups.

There are two procedural explanations for these varied results: the first is the failure to control for behavioural and personality correlates of moral development; the second is the possibility of variations just as to the type of offence within the offender population. Indeed, Thornton and Reid reported that convicted criminals who had offended for no financial gain showed more mature moral judgement than those who offended for money. Thus, as Jurkovic notes: 'Not only do they vary from one another in stage of moral judgement, but they also fluctuate in their own reasoning level on different moral problems'. As both Ross and Fabiano and Arbuthnot and Gordon point out, the concept of moral development is not a simple one and a number of important distinctions require clarification within the overall framework. While research has focused on the *content* of the offender's moral code, that is the offender's beliefs and attitudes, this contextual aspect can be contrasted with the *process* of moral reasoning. It is an assumption that process is related to content: while delayed development may be the cause of an antisocial moral code, it is also possible that as Ross and Fabiano suggest: 'One can argue eloquently and convincingly about social/moral issues yet have a personal set of values which are entirely self-serving, hedonistic or anti-social'.

Further, the assumption of a relationship between moral reasoning, moral values, and behaviour must also be queried: several well-known experiments have shown that people will behave in ways which they believe or know to be wrong. In summary, there are a number of doubts about the general applicability of moral development theory to crime. A direct causal link between moral functioning and criminal behavour remains to be established.

Further, tests of moral development which assess answers to hypothetical moral and social issues have also been criticized as having little relevance to the type of thinking an offender engages in when deciding whether to commit a crime. Indeed, studies of thinking prior to offending show that the criminal is not concerned with moral issues, but rather with the likelihood of being successful. Cognitive, social, and moral development are the subjects of much recent research and it may be that these advances will be applied to delinquent populations in the future to respond to some of the doubts expressed.

Eysenck's Theory of Crime

Eysenck's theory, which is also a control theory, incorporates biological, social, and individual factors. The basis of the theory is that through genetic endowment some individuals are born with cortical and autonomic nervous systems which affect their ability to learn from, or more properly to *condition* to, environmental stimuli. An individual's behaviour, influenced by both biological and social factors, defines that person's *personality*. H.J.Eysenck defined two dimensions of personality, *extroversion* (E) and *neuroticism* (N); later work described a third dimension, *psychoticism* (P). Each of these dimensions is conceived as a continuum with most people falling in the middle range and, it follows, with comparatively few people at the extremes of each scale. Extraversion runs from high to low; similarly neuroticism runs from high to low; as also does psychoticism. The extravert is considered as cortically *under*aroused and therefore is continually seeking stimulation to maintain cortical arousal at an optimal level: thus the extravert is impulsive and seeks excitement.

The introvert is cortically *over*aroused and therefore tries to avoid stimulation to keep arousal levels down to a comfortable, optimal level: introverts are therefore characterized by a quiet, reserved demeanour. In terms of conditioning, that is learning by Pavlovian conditioning or association rather than operant conditioning the theory maintains that extraverts condition less efficiently than introverts. Neuroticism, sometimes called emotionality, is argued to be related to the functioning of the autonomic nervous system. Individuals at the high extreme of this continuum are characterized by a very labile ANS, which causes strong reactions to any unpleasant or painful stimuli: High N individuals display moody, anxious behaviour. Low N individuals have a very stable ANS and so display calm, eventempered behaviour even when under stress.

As with E, N is also linked with conditionability: High N leads to poor conditioning because of the vitiating effects of anxiety; Low N leads to efficient conditioning. As assessed by standard psychometric tests, each individual scores on both E and N; therefore their position on these two dimensions of personality can be plotted as shown in Figure. As conditionability is related to levels of E and N it is further suggested that stable introverts will condition best; stable extraverts and neurotic introverts will be at some mid-point; while neurotic extraverts will condition least well.

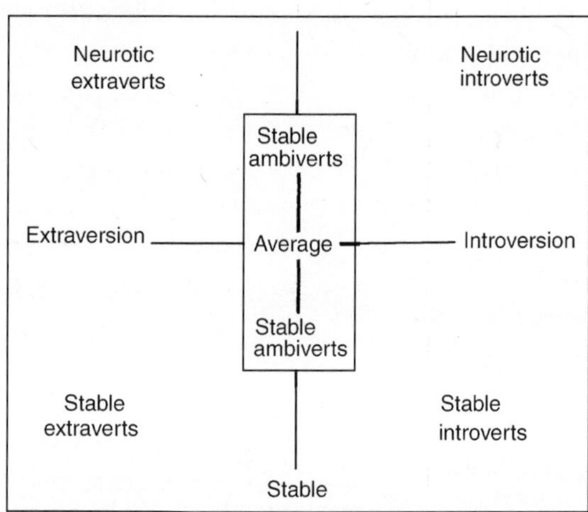

Fig. Eysenck's Personality Dimensions of Extraversion and Neuroticism

The third personality dimension, psychoticism is not so well formulated as E and N: while maintaining a genetic basis for P, its biological basis has not been described in detail. Indeed, various descriptions of P have been offered: initially intended to distinguish the personality underlying psychosis, as opposed to neurosis, the suggestion was later made that P might better denote psychopathy than psychoticism. The P scale assesses attributes such as a preference for solitude, a lack of feeling for others, sensation-seeking, toughmindedness, and aggression. Although recently revised, there is still some doubt about what exactly the P scale is measuring.

The relationship between personality and crime has been described and refined by H.J.Eysenck, and recent summaries are available. The principal assumption is that children learn to control antisocial behaviour through the development of a 'conscience': this conscience, Eysenck maintains, is a set of conditioned emotional responses to environmental events associated with the antisocial behaviour. For example the child who misbehaves incurs parental wrath; the fear and pain this brings is associated with the antisocial act, and through this conditioning process the child becomes socialized. The speed and efficiency of social conditioning will mainly depend upon the individual's personality in terms of E and N. As the High E-High N combination leads to poor conditionablity then such individuals will be least likely to learn social control and therefore, it is predicted, will be over-represented in offender populations. Conversely Low E-Low N would lead to effective socialization, so that these individuals would be predicted to be under-represented in offender groups.

The remaining two combinations, High E-Low N and Low EHigh N, fall at some intermediate level and so would be expected in both offender and non-offender groups. The third personality dimension, P, is also argued to be strongly related to offending, particularly with crimes which involve hostility towards other people. H.J.Eysenck suggests that 'In general terms, we would expect persons with strong antisocial inclinations to have high P, high E, and high N scores'. It is important to note the use of the term *antisocial*: as H.J.Eysenck is at pains to point out, not all crimes are antisocial in the general sense of that term. There are politically motivated crimes, impulsive crimes, crimes committed by the intellectually disadvantaged, and so on. In other words, some allowance has to be made for the heterogeneity of the offender population. Eysenck's theory of crime has generated a great deal of empirical research and there are several reviews of the findings up to 1980.

The broad position is that there is unanimous support for the contention that offenders will score highly on P, and the majority of studies show that offender samples score highly on N. The evidence is mixed for E: some studies reported high E scores as predicted in offender samples, others found no difference between offender and non-offender samples, and a small number of studies reported *lower* scores in offender groups. The general pattern for P, E, and N is similar with both young and adult offender groups. In seeking to account for the discrepant findings for E, S.B.G.Eysenck and H.J.Eysenck suggested that E might be split into two subscales, Sociability and Impulsiveness, with only the latter related to offending. A study by S.B.G.Eysenck and McGurk confirmed that an offender sample scored higher than a non-offender sample on Impulsiveness, with no difference between the two samples on a measure of Sociability.

There are two important points to note with regard to these early investigations: the majority of studies have examined the personality traits singly rather than in combination; and few studies have attempted to control for the type of crime. It will be recalled that Eysenck's theory is specifically concerned with the combined effects of different personality traits and with antisocial crimes. A small number of studies have attended to these specific aspects of the theory. Two studies by Allsopp and Feldman suggested that P, E, and N in combination provided support for Eysenck's theory.

The most compelling evidence is presented in a more recent study by McGurk and McDougall. McGurk and McDougall report the results of a cluster analysis of the P, E, and N scores of 100 delinquents and 100 non-delinquent college pupils. The analysis showed four personality clusters in each group: both groups contained Low E-High N and High E-Low N clusters, but the clusters predicted to be related to criminal behaviour—High E-High N and High P-High EHigh N—were, indeed, found only in the delinquent sample. The Low E-Low N group, which the theory would predict to be highly socialized, was found only in the non-delinquent group.

McEwan attempted a similar analysis with a delinquent population and also found four personality clusters. With a more rigorous definition for 'high' and 'low', McEwan's analysis gave rather different clusters to McGurk and McDougall. While the High E-High N combination figures prominently, the other groups show varying degrees of dissimilarity with those reported in the previous study. Another study by McEwan and Knowles also produced four clusters, once again with similarities and differences to the other studies. With regard to type of offence, Hindelang and Weis found mixed support for the predicted relationship between personality type and nature of offence.

Their findings indicated that the High E-High N cluster was significantly associated with general deviancy but not with major theft and aggression. S.B.G.Eysenck *et al.* compared the P, E, and N scores of groups of offenders: 'conmen' showed lower P scores than the other groups, while property and violent offender groups had lower N scores. The groups did not differ on the E scale. McEwan and Knowles failed to show any significant variation in the types of offences committed by the personality clusters in their study. In terms of numbers of offences, McEwan compared the criminal records of the subgroups defined in the first part of his study.

The subgroup with the high P score proved to have significantly more previous convictions than the other subgroups. The weight of empirical evidence lends support to Eysenck's thesis that there is a relationship between personality and crime. Indeed, a self-report study of a range of predictors of delinquency showed that P was by far the strongest predictor. Exposition of the theory Feldman concludes that the 'Eysenckian personality dimensions are likely to make a useful contribution to the explanation of criminal behaviour'. While this may prove to be the case, a number of reservations, as Eysenck acknowledges, need to be made. The theory does not explain all crime and, with its concentration on extremes of the scale, is not applicable to all offenders.

Further, one of the theoretical bases of the theory, the link between classical conditioning and socialization, remains to be established satisfactorily.

On a broader front the Eysenckian personality traits are not the only personality traits to have been described; studies have pointed to other personality dimensions which may be associated with criminal behaviour. Still further, the theory demands acceptance of a trait theory of personality which is only one of a number of ways of conceptualizing 'personality' and one which has come under fierce attack. In summary, Eysenck's theory is important, emphasizing the interaction between biological, environmental, and psychological factors. Integration of the theory into mainstream criminology, bearing in mind the various shortcomings, would be one way of bringing individual factors into more sociologically oriented views of crime.

PSYCHOLOGICAL THEORIES OF AGGRESSION AND VIOLENCE

It should be noted that there is a variability in terminology in the literature: three terms are in common, sometimes interchangeable, use, *aggression, violence,* and *criminal violence*. Megargee and Siann discuss the issue of definition and have informed the meaning of the terms as used here: aggression refers to the intention to hurt or gain advantage over other people, without necessarily involving physical injury; violence involves the use of strong physical force against another person, sometimes impelled by aggressive motivation; criminal violence involves directly injurious behaviour which is forbidden by law. While concern here is with psychological theories, there are theories from other disciplines, such as anthropology and biology. A number of texts cover the full range of theories, while Mednick *et al*. review biological factors, Merikangas discusses neurological theories, and Riches details the anthropology of violence. In turning to psychological theories it is plain that there is considerable overlap with other theories. This is true of the first class of theories to be discussed, those theories which postulate some instinctual drive towards aggressive and violent behaviour.

INSTINCT THEORIES

A number of theorists have used the notion of an instinct, an innate impulse, to account for aggression and violence. Within Freud's writings, for example, there is the view that human behaviour is driven by two basic instincts, the life instinct and the death force. In the conflict between the instincts of life and death the destructive energy is displaced to the external world. Aggression can be likened to a safety valve as it reduces the energy levels within the system to acceptable levels. If the aggressive behaviour can take the form of non-destructive and socially acceptable acts, then the probability of violence is correspondingly reduced. Such cathartic release might take the form of anger or participating in acceptable aggression such as sport.

This 'neutralizing' of the aggressive instinct can go astray so that the aggression becomes 'internalized', potentially culminating in violence, murder, or suicide. Lorenz approached the study of aggression from an ethological perspective. Following observation and study of animals, Lorenz proposed that aggression stems directly from an innate 'fighting instinct'. This instinct, it is suggested, has evolved over generations owing to its benefits for the survival of the species—*homo sapiens* included. As with Freud's explanation, aggressive energy is seen as continually mounting within the individual and so has, at some point, to be vented. This venting can occur in two ways: a specific environmental aggression-releasing stimulus triggers an aggressive act; or, if the build-up of energy is not released in 'safe' amounts, a violent eruption relieves the tension. Storr sought to fuse the psychoanalytic and ethological theories of aggression. Storr agreed that aggressive behaviour stems from an instinctive impulse, biologically determined, which seeks discharge before reaching critical levels.

Storr extended the argument by suggesting that the way in which an individual manifests aggression in later life results from unconscious motivations derived from childhood emotional experiences. Further, should negative events occur in the period when the individual seeks to deal with the aggressive drive, then the psychopathological aspects of aggression—typified by depression, schizoid behaviour, and paranoia—may result from the unresolved drive. Fromm, while primarily working within a psychoanalytic tradition, argued that it is necessary to go beyond individual factors and consider the role of social, economic, and political influences in precipitating aggression and violence. The criticisms of instinct theories centre on conceptual ambiguities and a lack of empirical verification. There is little hard evidence to demonstrate an instinctual biological drive, nor do there appear to be environmental releasers of aggression in humans. Critics suggest that in the balance between innate and learned behaviour, instinct theories inadvisedly prefer biological to social forces—although Storr, for example, has attempted to meet this point.

Drive Theory

An alternative to explanations based on an innate aggressive instinct followed the development of the concept of a reac-tive drive. A 'drive' which motivates a particular behaviour, including violence, was seen as being acquired through experience rather than being innate. As the level of the drive increased so the individual is motivated to find conditions in which behaviours can take place which reduce the drive. This amalgam of ideas from psychoanalytic and early behavioural psychology as a means of explaining aggression was advanced by Dollard *et al.*. The theory proposed that if a goal was blocked and expected rewards were not forthcoming, this produces a state of frustration; the frustration instigates aggression leading to aggressive or violent behaviour.

The aggressive or violent behaviour may be directed at either the source of the frustration, or displaced to other targets which have some relationship with the primary source of the frustration. Later work pointed to the distinction between 'hostile aggression' and 'instrumental aggression': the former being where the aggression is intended to injure the victim, the latter where the aggression is simply a means to an end as in, for example, armed robbery. Dollard *et al.*'s thesis generated a body of research work which led to a number of reformulations of aspects of the initial theory. Berkowitz proposed one such modification which has gained prominence. In contrast to the original drive theory, Berkowitz suggested that frustration produces a state of emotional arousal, or 'anger', which creates a potential for aggression.

In order for this potential to be realised, an 'anger-eliciting cue' must be present: this cue, or stimulus, takes the form of something the individual associates with aggression, such as another person's behaviour or the presence of a weapon. This view was taken a stage further with the suggestion that a strong environmental stimuli could produce aggression or violence in the absence of the prior angry state. One of the strengths of drive theory was that it offered hypotheses which could be tested experimentally. As a body of research duly amassed, it became apparent that the theory lacked full explanatory power and so attention turned to a search for new theories. As Bornstein *et al.* note: 'As a result of the deteriorating empirical status of instinct and drive theories of aggression, the social learning perspective...has grown rapidly in popularity and support in the past decade'.

Social Learning theory

Bandura suggested that there are three crucial aspects to an understanding of aggression: the *acquisition* of the aggressive behaviour; the process of *instigation* of the aggression; and the conditions which *maintain* the aggression. Social learning theory argues that acquisition of behaviour occurs through the process of learning, either through direct experience or by observation. There is empirical evidence to suggest that aggressive behaviour can be acquired through direct reinforcement, and via observation. With regard to instigation, Bandura noted that the anticipated outcome, in turn the product of previous learning, was vitally important. The anticipation, signalled by environmental cues previously associated with aggression, not only made aggression more likely, but also pointed to the potential victims of the aggression.

Alongside anticipated outcome, Bandura also suggested that aversive environmental conditions such as high temperatures, air pollution, and crowding can act to raise emotional arousal and so facilitate the instigation of aggression. A suggestion supported by recent research findings; while it has also been shown that verbal and physical provocation can have a similar effect. The effects of provocation have been explained both in terms of the anticipated consequences, such as loss of self-esteem, of failing to respond; and also in terms of the cognitive appraisal of the provocation. An act *perceived* as provocative and antagonistic is liable to increase 'angry' arousal and aggression.

Although as Novaco notes, there may be a reciprocal relationship between cognition and anger such that particular cognitions induce anger, while experiencing anger can lead the individual to think in an aggressive manner.

Similar reciprocal relationships, as shown in Figure, may function between cognition and behaviour, and between anger and behaviour. Finally, from a social learning theory perspective, the maintenance of aggression is through the three types of reinforcement: external reinforcement, vicarious reinforcement, and self-reinforcement.

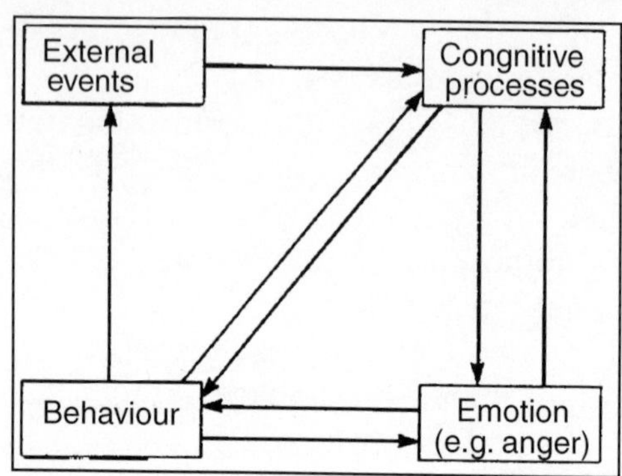

Fig. Schematic representation of the relationship between cognition, emotion and behaviour

Siann makes a number of criticisms of psychological theories of aggression as detailed thus far: as a result of laboratory-based research they show a too narrow approach to aggression; they are limited by positivist methodology; and they show a poor conception of human motivation. Siann suggests that aggression might best be considered as a *social* phenomenon; a phenomenon best studied 'in the real world of perceived and actual inequalities, environmental stress and political conflict'.

Social Accounts

Toch presents the details of a series of interviews with violent men in an attempt to place violence within a social context and so move towards a 'phenomenology of violence'. Toch's work views violence from the offender's perspective, being concerned with the meaning or sense of the act for that person within the social context in which the act occurred. Toch describes different uses of violence such as alleviating tension in awkward social situations or for defending personal reputations.

Typically violence occurs when another person is seen as a threat and some action is taken to respond to the threat; the other person reacts, the instigator responds again, and the *interaction* escalates towards violence.

A tradition of social research has followed this style of investigation, with recent work examining the 'rules of disorder'. This research has shown that some violence, such as between football fans, is rule-bound to the extent that it is agreed that fights should take place between equal numbers and that certain forms of fighting are not allowed. Other accounts, mainly from sociologists rather than psychologists, have concentrated even further on the social setting.

Wolfgang and Ferracuti argued that there are subcultures, usually involving young men, in which violence is the legitimate norm: the function of the violence is to provide excitement and a means of achieving status. This argument is supported by the various studies which have shown that violence is prevalent in parts of large cities, and involves a disproportionate number of young males. In accounting for these violent subcultures it has been suggested that they are the result of the anger and frustration caused by social and economic inequalities A radical criminology approach, arguing that 'violence' is defined by the powerful social classes for the purposes of social control.

Thus deaths resulting from the failure to test a drug properly, or inadequate health and safety precautions in a workplace, are not seen as 'murder', but are described as 'accidents' or 'regrettable incidents'. This strategy serves two basic functions: it deflects culpability from the privileged classes; and it locates 'real' crimes in the lower classes. As with most social accounts two problems arise: the difficulty of including the full range of social factors; and the tendency to exclude individual factors.

It is difficult to resist the conclusion that an interactive theory is required, one which seeks to place individual behaviour within a social and political context. Psychological research has contributed to both strands: in the following parts research is discussed which has examined both the situations in which violent crime occurs, and the characteristics of the violent person.

MENTAL ILLNESS AND CRIME

In truth, the term 'mental illness' causes more problems than it solves: Ashworth and Gostin note that mental illness is not defined in the Mental Health Act and therefore 'much will depend upon medical opinion'. In practice the term is used for a wide range of diagnostic categories including psychoses, affective disorders, anxiety states, hysteria, and so on. Inspection of admissions to Special Hospitals shows that by far the greatest number of mentally ill serious offenders are diagnosed as schizophrenic, with depression the next most frequent diagnosis. Does any special relationship exist between these two particular disorders and crime?

SCHIZOPHRENIA

The most important indicators of schizophrenia, which would *not* all be found in one person, include disturbances of thought, perception, affect, and motor behaviour. Thought disorder refers to a disturbance of the process of making associations between thoughts. Perceptual disturbances are evinced by hallucinations, which may be visual or tactile but are most commonly auditory, typically as voices commenting or giving instructions. Affect can be flat and expressionless or alternatively it can be inappropriate such as anger without provocation, or laughter at misfortune. Finally, motor disturbances can take the form of bizarre facial grimaces, repeated gesturing, or excited agitation of the body; alternatively unusual postures can be adopted and held, in a state of immobility, for long periods. As noted, not all these behaviours would be found in the same person, although some pattern does emerge: disorganized or hebephrenic schizophrenia is characterized by hallucinations, delusions, and inappropriate affect; catatonic schizophrenia by motor disturbances; and paranoid schizophrenia by delusions of persecu-tion, incorporating 'ideas of reference' in which personal significance is continually perceived in the actions of other people. Given this range, it may well be expedient to think of schizophrenia as a group of disorders rather than a single disorder which always manifests itself in the same fashion.

While of uncertain aetiology, contemporary theories favour a complex interaction between genetic, neurochemical, and social factors as an explanation for schizophrenia. It is generally accepted that the incidence of schizophrenia is close to 1 per cent in the general population: this sets a baseline against which to compare the rates of schizophrenia in offender populations. Spry reviews the evidence on the incidence of schizophrenia and crime and notes a division in research findings: with studies of Non-disordered offender groups the incidence of schizophrenia is around the 1 per cent mark with selected samples of offenders referred for psychiatric treatment, typically having committed serious offences, the incidence is much higher.

For example, Green reports that 74 per cent of a sample of fifty-eight men admitted to a Special Hospital having committed matricide were schizophrenic. Does this suggest that schizophrenia is related to serious offences? As Spry notes, many people associate schizophrenia with crime, particularly violent crime. Indeed, there are indications that a relationship may exist between paranoid ideas and violence, and that the victims of violent attacks are often those who figured in the schizophrenic's delusions.

Crimes of this type catch the public imagination: Prins notes the case of Ian Ball, in which delusional thought processes were manifest in a plot to kidnap a member of the royal family: Prins discusses the crimes of Peter Sutcliffe, the 'Yorkshire Ripper', in which there was some controversy as to the role of his paranoid schizophrenia in the murders he committed. It should be stressed, however, that the publicity generated by these cases is in inverse proportion to their frequency; the deluded and paranoid people who commit such crimes are rare. While these extreme cases are infrequent, the finding remains that schizophrenics are slightly more likely to commit violent offences than other disordered groups or the general population.

While schizophrenia may be directly related to violence, with delusional and paranoid beliefs of apparent importance, a simple relationship between the disorder and the crime is unlikely to exist. P.J.Taylor suggests that: 'It is not unusual to find that the violent act of a schizophrenic cannot be directly explained by the current psychopathology. This does not, however, negate the relevance of the illness...social and illness variables must be considered together'. The point Taylor makes is an important one: as well as considering a causal relationship between schizophrenia and violence, attention should also be paid to the similarities in social, environmental, and organic antecedents common to both violence and schizophrenia. More recent findings by the same researcher reinforce this point. From a survey of 121 psychotic offenders, Taylor concluded that '20% of the actively psychotic were directly driven to offend by their psychotic symptoms, and a further 26% probably so'. When social factors such as homelessness were considered along with the nature of the crime, so that 'the direct and indirect consequences of psychosis are considered together, then over 80% of the offences of the psychotic were probably attributable to their illness'.

Depression

Clinically two types of depression are distinguished: *major depression* and *bipolar disorder*. Major depression is characterized by profoundly sad mood, overwhelming feelings of selfblame, guilt, and worthlessness, appetite disturbances, fatigue and long periods of sleep, lethargy, and recurrent thoughts of death and suicide. Bipolar disorder is typified by bouts of mania as well as periods of depression: during the manic phase the individual shows elated or irritable mood, high levels of furious physical activity, goes long periods without sleep, and displays a general air of self-importance and inflated self-esteem.

Of the two, major depression is by far the most common, with estimates suggesting that 8 per cent to 11 per cent of men and 18 per cent to 23 per cent of women will be clinically depressed at least once in their life; bipolar disorder is less frequent, appearing in about 1 per cent of the population. Theories of depression incorporate a wide range of biological, cognitive, behavioural, and social factors. As with schizophrenia—or, indeed, any mental illness—there are difficulties in establishing the relationship between depression and crime.

A range of possibilities exists: the crime may have been committed because the offender was depressed; the offender may become depressed after the crime, either because of guilt or imprisonment; the offender may have been depressed when committing the crime, but the depression was not instrumental in causing the crime. In terms of a direct causal link, one of the more familiar and tragic associations between depression and crime occurs when an individual becomes convinced that life is hopeless and before committing suicide kills his or her children and other members of the family. West studied seventy-eight cases of murder followed by suicide and estimated that twenty-eight of the offenders were depressed at the time of the offence. Lawson suggests that a general pattern in certain murders by depressives lies in the 'social circumstances and pathological features of the domestic killing'.

The social circumstances involve a negative life event such as an upset in a long-term relationship, while the act itself shows no sign of planning or even malice. As well as murder, depression has been associated with other crimes including shoplifting and violence. With regard to violence, Häfner and Böker found that the violence was principally directed at relatives, suggesting similarities with the 'extended suicides'. As Howells notes, depressed in-patients are not a violent population, suggesting that the relationship between depression and crime is closely tied to social, particularly interpersonal, factors. Although most studies do not indicate which type of depression is present, it is reasonable to assume that major depression is involved.

However, McCulloch and Prins do describe a case involving a manic episode, a car salesman, and violence towards property. While Blumberg suggested that, after schizophrenia, manic depressive episodes were the disorder most commonly found in arsonists; Gunderson similarly suggested that firesetting during a manic state may be more common than is generally acknowledged. The broad picture which emerges for mental illness and crime does not really take us much further than the general evidence for 'mental disorder' and crime. Mental illness, particularly schizophrenia and depression, are found in criminal populations but the exact nature of the relationship between the two remains unclear. P.J.Taylor's work is however beginning to show how psychosis and crime may be seen as complex psychosocial phenomena, rather than in a simple relationship in which one factor has a linear causal effect on the other.

MENTAL HANDICAP AND CRIME

The Mental Health Act seeks to define a group of offenders characterized by 'arrested or incomplete development of mind which includes... impairment of intelligence and social functioning'. The Act distinguishes between 'severe' and 'significant' mental impairment although the difference between the two is not clarified. The group the Act refers to are those generally referred to as mentally handicapped, although other terms such as mentally retarded and mentally subnormal are sometimes used. It should of course be emphasized that mental *handicap* is not the same as mental *illness*. The former refers to the person's enduring level of intellectual and social ability; the latter is an episodic disturbance which does not necessarily affect intellectual functioning.

The assessment of mental handicap relies on a combination of results from tests of intellectual and social ability. While there is no legal level of IQ score by which to define impairment, in clinical assessment it is generally taken that an IQ in the region of 70 points is taken as 'borderline'. Thus a score of 70 or below, in conjunction with a low level of social functioning, may be indicative of some degree of handicap. IQ scores below 50 usually indicate a substantial degree of impairment. The 'two group theory' suggests a division between two types of mental impairment. The first is a 'normal impairment', as defined by those individuals who are at the lower end of the IQ distribution.

This may be because of family factors, including genetic endowment, or because of poor schooling or other environmental factors. While low in terms of IQ points, such individuals are usually well adapted socially. The second group are those who score very low on IQ tests and show poor social adaptation. Unlike the first group, there is usually an identifiable cause for the impairment: this may be a genetic or chromosomal abnormality such as Down's syndrome; a biological disturbance such as phenylketonuria; damage or infection *in utero,* as with rubella; birth complications such as anoxia; childhood disease like meningitis; head injury resulting in brain damage; or poisoning such as by lead, radiation, or toxic chemicals. In examining the relationship between mental handicap and crime two approaches have been used: the study of the intellectual functioning of offenders generally, and investigation of the specific offences of mentally handicapped offenders.

Before looking at the evidence it is as well to make a number of points about measuring intelligence. Most research comparing offender and non-offender groups has used IQ tests to measure intellectual ability. However, the possibility must be considered that this means of measurement introduces unwanted variance into the results: in other words, are the tests biased against offender groups? The important point is whether the standardization of the test included offenders. Standardization can be thought of as the estimation of test norms, that is, the levels or standards present in the general population. A properly standardized IQ test should in theory always yield the same average score in a random sample from the general population.

It should not, for example, be possible to score higher on an IQ test simply because, say, of age: the average score on a properly standardized test should be the same for any age level; if not, then the test is biased against some age groups. Thus if the population sample on which the test was standardized did not include offenders, then the possibility cannot be discounted that any difference in IQ between offender and non-offender groups may be due to test bias. Of course it is also the case that any differences may be due to social class, cultural, and educational differences between offender and non-offender samples. This is not test bias, rather a reflection that intellectual performance is affected by environmental factors. To be sure that real differences in IQ exist between offender and non-offender samples it is necessary to be confident that the particular IQ test employed is not biased against offenders, and that effects due to differences in class, educational background, and so on have been controlled or allowed for in the research.

In practice the environmental variables are likely to exert a greater influence on IQ test scores than variations in standardization. Nevertheless, both points should be held in mind when considering the evidence on intelligence and offending.

Intelligence in Offender Populations

Opinion on the nature of the relationship between intelligence and crime has gone through a number of historical phases. Charles Goring, a contemporary of Lombroso, studied 3,000 English convicts and found them to be of generally low intelligence. Goring suggested that crime was therefore the result of a lack of intelligence, in turn determined by genetic factors. As criminology grew in sophistication such simplistic, unitary causes of crime were replaced by complex multidimensional theories, often with a strong sociological content. The inclusion of individual characteristics such as intelligence into such theories gradually passed out of fashion. Indeed, the occasional study suggested that there was little to be gained from such a line of investigation: Woodward calculated that on average offenders were not more than eight IQ points below the population mean—a small difference, say 92 as compared to 100.

However, in the 1960s and 1970s research once again began to suggest an association between IQ and crime. An American study by Hirschi found a significant association between IQ and self-reported delinquency, an association which remained even after allowing for the influence of race and social status. A longitudinal study of boys living in London reported by West and Farrington found a strong correlation between IQ and recidivism, with boys of lower IQ more likely to become recidivists. The correlation remained when the analysis controlled for family size and income. These and other studies led Hirschi and Hindelang to reintroduce intelligence as an important factor in understanding the development of criminal behaviour.

More recent studies have added confirmatory evidence to this line of thought. If the correlation appears reasonably strong, its meaning is less clear. West and Farrington extended their analysis and discovered that lower IQ was also associated with problem behaviour in early life, suggesting that the link between IQ and delinquency was via this earlier association. Richman *et al.* similarly showed that the IQ link with behavioural disorders could be found by 3 years of age.

It seems likely therefore that IQ and crime are associated via one or more other pathways. Rutter and Giller suggest two possible routes. The first is that low IQ leads to educational failure, which leads to low self-esteem and emotional disturbance, in turn leading to conduct disorder and criminal behaviour. While there is support for a relationship between learning disability and crime, this does not account for the findings which suggest that the associations are present at pre-school ages.

The second hypothesis is that IQ and conduct disorder share a common aetiology, the exact nature of which is open to speculation: this could be a biological, social, or familial influence; or even another individual factor such as temperament. Other research has examined the IQs of convicted offender populations.

As with all studies of offender populations, it should be remembered that these are a highly selected sample and may be unrepresentative of the general offender population, especially with regard to intelligence. Craft collated information from fifteen studies of IQ in convicted prisoners carried out between 1931 and 1952. The earlier studies show low mean IQs, ranging from a mean of 71 to a mean of 88: the most recent studies show a marked difference, all finding mean IQs of 92.

This may reflect changes in IQ tests, as well as policy changes over the decades regarding the disposal of offenders with low IQs. Although significant fluctuations in prison population IQ levels over a short period of time have been recorded. It should be pointed out that most of the studies discussed this far are not concerned with very low IQ scores, but rather more with IQs which tend towards the 'below average' classification. While low IQ is as common among men first convicted in adulthood as among boys first convicted as juveniles, this does *not* imply that criminals are, by definition, mentally handicapped.

Offenders may display a lower IQ on average—but this means that some offenders will have normal or above normal IQs. Further, mental handicap is as much concerned with social functioning as with IQ, but the research has mainly been concerned with intelligence. A number of studies have been concerned with very low IQ scores in offender populations. Craft reports that in convicted prisoners the percentage with IQ scores less than 70 varied from a high of 31 per cent in a 1931 study, to about 10 per cent in 1940s studies, to a low of 4.2 per cent in a 1950 study. Prins presents a similar survey, noting a high of 28 per cent of convicted offenders deemed 'subnormal' in a 1918 study, falling to 2.4 per cent in a 1964 study.

This probably reflects changes over time in the disposal of mentally handicapped offenders. More recent studies have controlled for variables such as type of test and time of testing and have found about 2.5 per cent of the prison population have IQ scores below 70. The importance of social functioning is seen in a survey by Denkowski and Denkowski of the prevalence of mentally handicapped inmates in the prisons of twenty states in the USA. From their figures on individually tested prisoners, it can be calculated that 2.25 per cent of prisoners are classified as retarded in those states which rely on IQ testing and do not use a formal means of assessing adaptive behaviour.

In the five states where IQ and adaptive behaviour was assessed the percentage of mentally handicapped prisoners is 1.28 per cent. These lower figures—in the region of 2–2.5 per cent—are similar to the incidence of mental handicap in the non-offender population. Therefore mental handicap is unlikely, in itself, to be a strong factor in the aetiology of crime: nevertheless mentally handicapped people do commit crimes —is there anything remarkable about this group?

Offending and Mental Handicap

N.Walker compared the indictable offences of 305 males ordered over a one-year period to be committed to hospital as mentally handicapped, with the offences of all other male offenders dealt with by the courts in the same year. While there were no differences in the frequency of violent and property offences, the percentage of handicapped offenders sentenced for sexual offences was six times as great as that for the other offenders. Similarly A.Shapiro found that in a sample of compulsorily detained mentally handicapped offenders, 35 per cent had committed a sexual offence.

Tutt, with a sample from a 'subnormality hospital', found that almost 16 per cent had been convicted of a sexual offence prior to admission. These rates are much higher than the expected figure for sex offences in the general offender population, which would be of the order of 3 per cent. Robertson carried out a follow-up study of the offences of a group of over 300 mentally handicapped offenders who appeared before the courts for a criminal offence and had received a hospital order and had subsequently been released into the community. Most of the offences are not unusual, although the rate of sex offences in males is relatively high.

Table. Principal Offences of Mentally Handicapped Offenders

	Male	Females
Larceny	54	60
Breaking and entering	33	9
Sexual Indecency	12	–
Soliciting	–	9
Arson	3	1
GBH/wounding	2	3
Rape	1	–
Manslaughter	1	0
Robbery	1	0

Robertson also compared the male mentally handicapped offenders with a sample of male mentally ill offenders. In personal terms, the handicapped offenders were much younger and less likely to have been married. The handicapped group had fewer hospital admissions, with about half having been in-patients prior to the Section 60 order, compared to about 80 per cent of the mentally ill group. With regard to criminal history, the handicapped group were younger when receiving their first conviction and had committed many more offences as juveniles. Despite this, the mentally ill group had more court appearances and had spent longer in prison. While the incidence of theft was similar in the two groups, the mentally ill offenders had been convicted of more violent offences such as assault and criminal damage, with more sexual offences in the handicapped group. As Robertson comments, apart from the sexual offences, the pattern shown by the handicapped offender of petty juvenile crime developing in later life to various acquisitive offences is similar to that found in the general offender population.

This contrasts sharply with the atypical pattern seen in the mentally ill population in which, as Robertson notes, 'juvenile offending is rare and where criminality may be one consequence of a general social deterioration following chronic illness'. It is, however, important to note several ways in which the mentally handicapped offender is disadvantaged compared to his or her more able contemporaries. The mentally handicapped offender may not have learned the difference between acceptable and unacceptable behaviour, therefore a 'crime' cannot be elevated to the status of a 'right' or 'wrong' act in the sense that the person knowingly transgressed the law.

The handicap may mean that the crime itself is carried out less efficiently, leading to easier detection, or the mentally handicapped person may be exploited by more able offenders. In some cases mental handicap is associated with emotional outbursts, particularly following some stressful event, which may in turn precipitate aggressive acts. A lack of social skills may mean that acts intended to be friendly are seen by others as aggressive or hostile, resulting in unfortunate consequences. A similar point may hold for sexual skills: as Craft and Craft note, the sexual experimentation of mentally handicapped people may be more visible and hence more upsetting than convention allows. Thus the high sexual offending of this group may reflect a paucity of skills in making acceptable sexual approaches; such social naivety may be seen by the 'victim' as assault and criminal proceedings are likely to follow. In the discussion of theories of mental handicap, the distinction was made between 'normal' mental handicap and those cases where the handicap results from some known, usually organic, cause. Research into mental handicap and offending has not considered this distinction: a point which may be something for future research to address as the aetiology of mental handicap in the offender may be informative theoretically, and have practical implications in terms of management and the services offered to this type of offender.

PSYCHOPATHIC DISORDER

The 1983 Act defines psychopathic disorder as 'a persistent disorder or disability of mind which results in abnormally aggressive or seriously irresponsible conduct'. As various commentators have noted, this is a less than perfect definition in that it does not specify what is meant by 'persistent', 'abnormally aggressive', or 'seriously irresponsible'. To complicate matters further, the American system varies the terminology: as Davison and Neale note, 'In current usage the terms *sociopath* and *psychopath* appear interchangeably with antisocial personality'. Given this, what characteristics identify such an ill-defined category of offenders?

Identifying the Psychopath

Cleckley identified the psychopath by listing the characteristics observed in clinical practice: these identifying characteristics place emphasis on the emotional and social emptiness of the psychopath.

Cleckley's Characteristics of the Psychopath:

- Superficial charm and good intelligence

- Absence of delusions and other signs of irrational thinking
- Absence of 'nervousness' or other psychoneurotic manifestations
- Unreliability
- Untruthfulness and insincerity
- Lack of remorse or shame
- Inadequately motivated antisocial behaviour
- Poor judgement and failure to learn by experience
- Pathologic egocentricity and incapacity for love
- General poverty in major affective reactions
- Specific loss of insight
- Unresponsiveness in general interpersonal relations
- Fantastic and uninviting behaviour with drink and sometime without
- Suicide rarely carried out
- Sex life impersonal, trivial, and poorly integrated
- Failure to follow any life plan

Hare conducted a factor analysis of data derived from the Cleckley criteria and found five factors, which offer a succinct description of the psychopath: they show an inability to develop warm, empathic relationships; an inability to accept responsibility for their antisocial behaviour; an absence of intellectual and psychiatric problems; weak behavioural control. Blackburn and Maybury performed a similar analysis on the Cleckley checklist which 'yielded results which are broadly in agreement with those of Hare in indicating that a unitary dimension describable as lack of empathy or affection pervades most of the criteria'. However, as numerous commentators have noted, many of the terms used by Cleckley are vague and imprecise, causing difficulties for clinicians and researchers alike. Hare constructed a more precise scale for the assessment of psychopathy in criminal populations: this scale is shown in full in below.

Psychopathy Checklist:

- Glinbness/superficial charm
- Previour diagnosis as psychopath (or similar)
- Egocentricity/grandiose sense of self-worth
- Proneness to boredom/low frustration tolerance
- Pathological lying and deception
- Conning/lack of sincerity
- Lack of remorse or guilt
- Lack of affect and emotional depth
- Callous/lack of empathy
- Parasutuc life-style
- Short-tempered/poor behavioural controls
- Promiscuous sexual relations
- Early behaviour problems
- Lack of realistic, long-term plans

- Impulsivity
- Irresponsible behaviour as a parent
- Frequent marital relationships
- Juvenile delinquencey
- Poor probation or parole risk
- Failure to accept responsibility for own actions
- Many types of offence
- Drug of alcohol abuse not direct cause of antisocial behaviour

Factor analysis showed that the new scale also contained five factors, similar to those found in the factor analysis of the original Cleckley checklist. Analysis also showed high agreement between the new scale and Cleckley's original criteria. Hare has subsequently shortened the list to give a *Psychopathy Checklist* for use by clinicians and researchers. The approach adopted by Cleckley and Hare to identifying the psychopath rests on clinical observation of the defining characteristics; statistical techniques are then used to produce a reliable psychometric instrument based on the observations. A different approach to the same task is to use existing psychometric measures to define a particular 'psychopathic' personality.

The work of the British psychologist Ronald Blackburn is of particular significance here. Blackburn's original psychometric research described four types of violent offender, within which the distinction was made between *primary psychopaths* and *secondary psychopaths*. The primary group is characterized by high levels of hostility, low anxiety levels, and has few psychiatric problems. The secondary psychopaths also show high levels of hostility but with attendant anxiety, guilt, and psychiatric disturbance. Blackburn has shown that the original four groups can be described in terms of two factors, psychopathy and sociability. Primary psychopaths are high on psychopathy and sociability; secondary psychopaths also score highly on psychopathy but are low on sociability.

Blackburn presents data which suggest that primary psychopaths are more likely to commit violent acts, while secondary psychopaths are more likely to commit sex offences. Hare compared a variety of assessment procedures including the checklist shown and various self-report inventories including the MMPI. Hare concludes that 'Self-report inventories simply do not sort subjects in the same way that clinical-behavioral procedures do': Hare recommends the twenty-two-item Psychopathy Checklist as a valid measure of psychopathy as it relates strongly to 'criminal activities, violence, institutional behaviour, and outcome on con-ditional release, including parole', although, as Hare points out, agreement is not perfect among such clinical assessments. Further, despite its clinical utility, this checklist approach does little towards contributing to the understanding of the aetiology of psychopathy and the development of a theoretical model of the disorder. A third level of identification is a more informal one, but none the less important for that, the criteria used by practitioners to diagnose psychopathy.

W.Davies and Feldman asked a sample of over thirty 'forensic specialists' to rate the importance of twenty-two signs of psychopathy. In summary, what has been identified about the psychopath? It is not a well-defined condition, nor is it universally popular, yet it is one which is used and cannot be ignored. A publication by the Department of Health and Social Security and the Home Office offers a pragmatic, operational definition:

- The consensus view is that psychopathic disorder is not a description of a single clinical disorder but a convenient label to describe a severe personality disorder which may show itself in a variety of attitudinal, emotional and inter-personal behaviour problems. The core problem is impairment in the capacity to relate to others—to take account of their feelings and to act in ways consistent with their safety and convenience.

While there is debate about the means of identification of the psychopath,indeed about the utility of the term psychopath, a body of research evidence has accumulated which seeks to examine a range of correlates of psychopathy. The force of this approach is that it may provide an empirical means of differentiating the psychopath from the Non-psychopath and, should the distinction be established, so move towards a theory of psychopathy. The research falls into the three areas of background variables, physiological functioning, and cognitivebehavioural factors.

Background Variables in Psychopathy

The most cited aetiological variables in psychopathy are the familiar ones of family functioning, childhood behaviour, and genetic influences. W.McCord and J.McCord suggested that lack of affection and severe parental rejection were primary aetiological factors, while a longitudinal study by Robins pointed to a variety of early behavioural problems which were strongly associated with psychopathic behaviour as an adult. These problems included early referral to a child guidance clinic for theft or aggression, a history of truancy, lying, non-compliance, no signs of guilt or remorse, and general irreponsibility regarding school and family routines. As with the McCord and McCord study, family characteristics of little or no discipline were also associated with later psychopathic behaviour, as was antisocial behaviour shown by the father.

However, it should be added that this pattern of a wayward childhood is a predictor of many disorders in later life, including criminal behaviour not labelled psychopathic, as well as a range of clinical disorders from neuroses to psychoses. Therefore these findings do not point exactly to the particular antecedents of psychopathy. Some investigators have suggested that the basis of psychopathy, viewed as an extreme of antisocial behaviour, lies in genetic transmission. The evidence in support of a genetic component to antisocial behaviour, noting findings from adoption and twin studies which support the proposition. Cadoret extends this argument to psychopathy. While family, longitudinal, and genetic studies suggest various correlates of psychopathy, they do not provide all the answers: how does the genetic transmission work and what factors mediate poor parenting to produce psychopathic behaviour? An answer may lie in a suggestion made by Cantwell that adult psychopathy is associated with childhood hyperactivity, the common thread being a similar neurological abnormality of possible genetic origin. Is the key to unlocking psychopathy physiological in nature?

Physiology and Psychopathy

There is a considerable body of research evidence on physiological and psychophysiological functioning and psychopathy: For the most part investigators have concentrated on the central nervous system and the autonomic nervous system. Studies of CNS functioning have relied on the electroencephalogram, a recording of the electrical activity of the brain. A review by Syndulko pointed to the methodological difficulties of EEG studies, but nevertheless suggested high frequencies of EEG abnormality in psychopaths; the problem is, however, that not all psychopaths show EEG abnormalities, and in those that do the pattern of abnormality is not consistent.

Further, the pattern varies across situations: Hare and Jutai found abnormal EEGs when the psychopaths were resting, but normal EEGs when the psychopaths were in an active state. Blackburn found little evidence to support the notion of a general association between EEG arousal and aggression; but suggested that differences may exist between primary and secondary psychopaths. The primary psychopaths showed the lowest levels of EEG arousal, while the secondary psychopaths appeared more alert even when resting. Studies of ANS functioning in psychopaths have concentrated upon reactivity and arousal levels as indices of ANS activity. One of the most cited results from this line of research is that when resting, psychopaths have unduly *low* levels of electrodermal reactivity, but in stressful situations there are very *high* levels of cardiac reactivity. This can be viewed as a fast heart-rate indicating the 'gating out' of sensory input and so lowering cortical arousal, meaning that the psychopath is effectively 'tuning out' unpleasant environmental cues. Skin conductance is therefore low because to all intents and purposes environmental stimuli, especially aversive stimuli, are being ignored. While of interest, these physiological findings assume greater significance when considered in the context of cognitive-behavioural evidence.

Cognitive-behavioural Performance in Psychopaths

Cleckley suggested that one of the main characteristics of the psychopath was a failure to learn from experience. This poor learning is evident in the psychopath's failure to avoid the negative consequences of antisocial behaviour. A number of studies have experimentally tested this suggestion employing the technique of *passive avoidance learning* in which the subject learns to respond to anticipatory cues in order to avoid some unpleasant outcome. The findings indicate that psychopaths perform poorly on passive avoidance learning tasks: a result taken to indicate that psychopaths are in a low state of ANS arousal and are relatively anxiety-free.

The physiological evidence on ANS functioning suggests how this might occur: high cardiac arousal gates out the cues indicating the forthcoming unpleasant event, leading in turn to lower arousal and impaired avoidance learning. However, this picture becomes a little more complicated by evidence which showed an effect of the type of aversive event. When the aversive consequence of poor learning was physical pain or social disapproval the psychopaths performed poorly as compared to Non-psychopathic controls; however, if the outcome was financial penalty, the psychopaths learned more efficiently than the controls. The introduction of a cognitive component might account for this difference in responding: for example some 'punishments' may have little or no meaning for psychopaths. Thus a prior cognition 'signals' a stressful event which, in turn, is gated out as indicated by the levels of physiological functioning. If the experimental learning task is made more complex by including the competing goals of monetary reward for good performance and avoiding monetary loss for poor performance, then psychopaths perform at a lower level than controls. As psychopaths are equal to controls with financial loss only, it may be that psychopaths have difficulty attending to competing contingencies once they are trying to gain a reward. Newman *et al.* employed an experimental task in which money could be gained and lost: they found that while controls were able to adjust their performance to allow for increases in the probability of losing, psychopaths failed to make such adjustments and so lost accordingly.

This pattern of behaviour is termed 'response perseveration': the continuation of the same action regardless of the consequences it produces. In other words, a failure to learn from experience. Newman *et al.* found that if a 5-second delay was forced between one response and the next, so as to interrupt response set and allow increased time to attend to feedback from the last response, then the deficit between psychopaths and controls was reduced. The reason for this effect of delay is uncertain. These learning difficulties, as demonstrated in experimental tasks, may—perhaps in conjunction with physiological variables—be related to the under-socialization and poor social performance of psychopaths.

While psychopaths may commit crimes of aggression and brutality, this type of behaviour does not seem to be specific to particular types of situations: Blackburn found that even in a hospital ward psychopaths were rated by nurses as more aggressive, more likely to use threatening behaviour to both staff and other patients, and less likely to follow institutional rules than other patients. The pattern of Non- conformity to social rules and subsequent lack of remorse can be seen as a failure to learn to avoid social censure; alongside response perseveration in that the same behaviour is continually repeated regardless of the situational demands. Blackburn and Lee-Evans examined the anticipated reactions of primary and secondary psychopaths to anger-evoking situations. They found that psychopaths reported stronger anticipated reactions than controls, particularly for situations involving personal attack. The primary psychopaths anticipated less strong reactions than the secondary psychopaths: this is in accord with Blackburn's earlier suggestion that the aggression of primary psychopaths is more likely to be 'incentive-motivated', while that of secondary psychopaths is 'annoyance-motivated'.

Blackburn and Lee-Evans suggest that the cognitive processes associated with the angry reaction may be of particular importance, particularly with regard to the attentional bias in perceiving hostility in social cues. This suggestion is at odds with a view of psychopathy which suggests a lack of sensitivity to social cues in proposing that the psychopath's aggressive behaviour is in fact a maladaptive strategy in interpersonal problem-solving. In total the psychology of the psychopath is not clearly understood despite contributions such as those discussed and others from areas as diverse as ego psychology, analogies with child development, and conceptualizations in terms of an interpersonal circumplex. Indeed the psychopath remains something of a puzzle: the most reliable fact is that there are relatively small numbers as reflected in official records.

In England and Wales in 1984 there were 410 restricted patients classified as psychopathic detained in hospital. Of this number, 200 had been convicted of homicide or other offences against the person, 90 of arson, and 70 of sexual offences. The number of unclassified psychopaths is, of course, unknown. When compared to mentally ill and mentally handicapped offenders, psychopaths are much more 'criminal': they have committed more offences, particularly theft and assault; received more prison sentences; and spent more time in prison: which all suggests that the prison population may contain substantial numbers of psychopathic offenders. Thus the difficulties posed by the psychopath are numerous: the term itself is ill defined both legally and empirically; the diagnosis of psychopathy is correspondingly unreliable, but once delivered is a powerful label; and there is disagreement about the concept of psychopathy. Two strategies present themselves for resolving this state of affairs.

PREDICTORS OF CRIME AND VIOLENT OFFENDING IN FAMILY STUDIES

In the Cambridge Study in Delinquent Development, 383 boys from a low-income London suburb were followed up to age 32, and the conviction records of children and their parents were compared. At the age of 24–25 years, 51% of the convicted fathers vs. 24% of the non-convicted fathers, had a delinquent son. Of the criminal fathers, 38% had a recidivistic son compared with 12% of the Non-criminal fathers. Only 6% of the sons accounted for 52% of the recorded convictions.

There was a close link between paternal convictions from a long time previously, before the son was born, and the delinquency of the sons. Among the sons whose mother, but not father, had convictions, 45% had been convicted. Among those sons whose father, but not mother, had convictions, 45% had been convicted. Among the sons with both parents convicted, 65% were delinquents, compared with only 22% of the sons with no parents convicted. In the whole cohort, up to age 32, 37% of the sons had been convicted of criminal offences. The peak age for the number of offences was 17 years.

Those who were convicted at the earliest ages tended to become the most persistent offenders, committing a large number of offences at high rates and over long time periods. The convicted men differed significantly from the Non-convicted men in most aspects of their lives. The most important childhood predictors of crime were socio-economic deprivation, poor parenting, family deviance, school problems, hyperactivity-impulsivity-attention deficit, and antisocial behaviour as a child. The familial precursors of violent offending and chronic offending were parental criminality, poor parental supervision and separation from parents. In the Copenhagen birth cohort with follow-up time up to age 34, violent offences were predicted by the combination of birth complications and maternal rejection, but not by either of these alone. This combination also differentiated violent and non-violent offenders, and predicted the most serious forms of violent crimes, such as robbery, rape or murder, in comparison with all other subjects, being associated with violent offending before age 18. Poor social circumstances were independently predictive. Early separation from parents was associated with increased risk for violent offending and violent recidivism among males separated at birth from their parents for an average of seven months because of tuberculosis in Finland. The risk of criminal behaviour was slightly increased among both males, and females. It is common for mothers of children with conduct problems to have histories of neglect or abuse themselves.

These mothers also often have adult relationships characterized by violence. In a family study of 816 Australian children born between 1981–1984 in Brisbane, paternal, but not maternal, alcohol use disorders predicted violent and non-violent delinquency of children. Executive functioning mediated the relationship between paternal AUD and the violent delinquency of a child, whereas family stress mediated the relationship between paternal AUD and both violent and Non-violent delinquency. The authors suggested that paternal AUD may be associated with child executive functioning and family stress, which may in turn lead to child delinquency.

Aggressive behaviour is a stable trait that predisposes a child to later antisocial behaviour, criminality and physical aggression In a family study by Huesman et al, the stability of aggression across generations within a family, when measured at comparable ages, was even higher than the stability across ages. The authors assessed psychological tests, self rated aggressive incidents and some criminal records of the followed-up index children and their children. However, the aggressiveness of the parents of the index children was evaluated only from the parents' reports of the severity of punishments they would use in response to specific misdeeds by the index children.

Since this study and several other studies have demonstrated intergenerational continuity in parenting, it has remained unclear whether it was the method of parenting or the aggressive behaviour that was shared by all three generations. Among followed-up twins in the UK, violent crime was independently predicted by adult APD and reading problems, and also by any previous crime. The absence of childhood aggression did not, however, indicate a good prognosis when multiple other CD and hyperactivity symptoms were present.

A study of the risk factors for crime and violent offending in SCH compared the health care registers and criminal records of persons born in Helsinki between 1951 and 1960. Poor educational attainment, poor grades for attention at school, higher birth weight and larger head circumference were significantly associated with the risk for criminal offending in adulthood among persons with SCH. The association between delivery complications and later violent offending among males was of borderline significance.

ADOPTION STUDIES

Most adoption studies of children separated at birth from their biological parents have demonstrated an association between parental and offspring criminal offending, but only non-significant association between parental and offspring violent offending. Bohman found no association between parental and adoptee criminality in the Swedish adoption data. However, when he compared the later criminality of both adopted children of biological parents with serious crimes and adopted children of severe alcohol abusers with the criminality of matched control adoptees, whose parents were neither criminal offenders nor alcohol abusers, only the children of the alcohol abusers differed significantly from the controls. Late adoption placement was associated with a higher prevalence of alcohol abusers.

Bohman concluded that if a genetic composition existed for criminality, it was related to alcoholism. Criminality was prevented by adoption, whereas adoption was not so influential when the biological parent had alcoholism.

The genetic and environmental factors affecting antisocial behaviour have been described since the 1970s. Cadoret et al. reported that parental APD predicted increased risk of CD, adolescent aggressiveness, adult APD and drug abuse among offspring. Substance abuse and PDs in biological parents were associated with later criminal behaviour of adopted sons. It was suggested that adverse adoptive home environment interacted with a genetic background of APD to result in significantly increased aggressiveness and CD in adopted persons in the presence, but not in the absence, of parental APD. Male gender, foetal alcohol exposure and adverse environment were risk factors for adult antisocial syndrome. The individual differences in aggression seem to result from both heritable and environmental factors.

TWIN STUDIES

Estimates of the heritability of antisocial behaviour are between 41% and 80% depending on the definition of the genotype. Heritability estimates for psychopathy are even higher. Heritability of individual symptoms of CD may differ. In a twin study of 1,100 twin pairs, heritability estimates were 49% for aggressive domain, 55% for non-aggressive domain, and 53% for full-scale CD. Gelhorn et al. have suggested that DSM-IV CD domains are influenced by unique genetic and environmental factors, but also share some common genetic and environmental influences. Genetic influences on antisocial behaviour were more important in socioeconomically advantaged environments, while environmental factors were more influential in less advantaged environments, in a longitudinal twin study including 1,480 twin pairs carried out in Sweden.

Heritability of antisocial behaviour was higher for girls than for boys. A common genetic factor loaded substantially on both psychopathic personality traits and antisocial behaviour. However, a common shared environmental factor loaded exclusively on antisocial behaviour. Larsson et al. suggested that the genetic overlap between psychopathic personality traits and antisocial behaviour may reflect a genetic vulnerability to externalizing psychopathology. The finding of shared environmental influences in antisocial behaviour only suggests an etiological distinction between psychopathic personality dimensions and antisocial behaviour. The Environmental Risk Longitudinal Twin Study, a nationally representative birth cohort of 1,116 twin pairs and their families, investigated how genetic and environment factors shape children's development. The results indicated that physical maltreatment plays a causal role in the development of children's antisocial behaviour. The association between childhood educational difficulties and antisocial behaviour resulted primarily from environmental factors common to both. This association was stronger for boys.

The candidate environmental factors only weakly mediated the association. For boys, poor reading ability led to antisocial behaviour, and antisocial behaviour led to poor reading ability. By contrast, the correlation between reading achievement and ADHD was best explained by common genetic influences. Positive adjustment in children exposed to socio-economic deprivation was promoted by maternal warmth, stimulating activities, and the child's outgoing temperament. Resilience was partly heritable. The protective processes operated through both genetic and environmental effects. Maternal depression following, but not preceding, the birth of the twins was associated with child antisocial behaviour at 7 years of age. The combination of depression and APD symptoms in mothers posed the greatest risk for the children's later antisocial behaviour. A twin experiencing maternal negativity and less warmth had more antisocial behaviour problems. Maternal emotional attitude towards the child may play a causal role in the development of antisocial behaviour.

BEHAVIOURAL GENETIC STUDIES

Gene-environment interaction occurs when the effect of exposure to an environmental pathogen is conditional on a person's genotype, or when the environmental experience moderates the effect of genes on health. Behavioural genetic studies have empirically measured some geneenvironment interaction processes resulting in antisocial and criminal behaviour. The gene provides a blueprint for the chain of amino acids that forms the proteins and enzymes that do the actual work. For many genes, the environment can influence whether or not the genes are transcribed to build the proteins. For example, environmental stress influences the expression of many genes by initiating the transcription of some genes, inhibiting the transcription of others, and changing the level of transcription of still other genes. Early adverse experiences during sensitive phases of development alter a constellation of physiological and behavioural processes.

For example, prenatal stress reduces brain neuron proliferation and may affect the number of neurons throughout life in rats. Elevated rates of glucocorticoid hormones facilitate cell death particularly in the hippocampus, the brain area important for learning and memory. The atrophy of dendrites after a brief exposure is reversible, but may become permanent with prolonged exposure to high glucocorticoid levels. However, these effects could be counteracted by Neo-natal handling, suggesting that infantile maternal stimulation may also reverse the appearance of behavioural disorders induced by early life stress. Appropriate parental input is critically important for normative development of the hypothalamic-pituitary-adrenal axis and neurotransmitter system function. Primates removed from their mothers and deprived of early participation in social groups later exhibit aberrations in neurochemical function, neuroendocrine stress axis activity, and many aspects of social behaviour.

In humans, Caspi et al. reported that one particular gene predicted antisocial behaviour in conjunction with childhood adversity. Genotypes associated with high levels of monoamine oxidase A activity protected against the effect of childhood maltreatment and adversity on the development of antisocial behaviour and CD. Maltreatment was defined by Caspi et al. as a composite index including prospective information about maternal rejection, repeated loss of a primary caregiver, harsh discipline, and retrospective self-reports of physical and sexual abuse. Foley et al. replicated the finding for CD. They defined "maltreatment" as parental neglect as reported by the parent, together with interparental violence and inconsistent discipline reported by the child. Maltreated males whose genotype conferred low levels of MAO-A developed

CD, personality disposition towards violence, and APD significantly more frequently than those with high-activity MAO-A. They were also significantly more often convicted of violent crimes in adulthood than the children with highactivity MAO-A. On the other hand, the males with high MAOA activity had no elevated antisocial outcomes, even when they had experienced childhood maltreatment. As many as 85% of the severely maltreated men having a lowactive MAO-A genotype in the Dunedin birth cohort developed some form of antisocial behaviour.

Caspi et al. suggested that deficient MAO-A activity may dispose the organism towards neural hyperactivity to threat, and that a functional polymorphism in neurotransmitter-metabolizing enzyme MAOA moderates the influence of childhood maltreatment on neural systems implicated in antisocial behaviour. Later the buffering effect of high activity MAO-A genotype against increased risk of violent and/or antisocial behaviour was replicated in the E-risk study among white children, but not among non-white. More recently, several other associations have been documented. For example, interaction between increased paternal alcohol abuse and dopamine receptor 4 gene polymorphism was associated with temperamental novelty-seeking in a preliminary Finnish study. Variations in human serotonin transporter gene promoter region moderate psychopathological reactions to stressful experiences from early developmental periods onwards.

The shorter allele having lower transcriptional activity has been associated with lower levels of serotonin uptake, type 2 alcoholism, and violent behaviour. A prospective study in children with ADHD from England and Taiwan indicated that a common haplotype of dopamine transporter gene was associated with ADHD and mediated the effect of maternal alcohol use during pregnancy on the development of ADHD.

TRANSMISSION OF PSYCHIATRIC DISORDERS ASSOCIATED WITH VIOLENT CRIME

Hicks et al. used structured equation modelling of the Minnesota Twin Family Study to estimate simultaneously the general and specific transmission mechanisms of CD, adult APD, alcohol dependence and drug dependence. Transmission of general vulnerability to all these externalizing disorders accounted for most familial resemblance. This general vulnerability was highly heritable. Disorder-specific vulnerabilities were also detected for CD, alcohol dependence and drug dependence.

The authors concluded that the mechanism underlying the familial transmission of externalizing disorders is primarily a highly heritable general vulnerability. The latent correlation between mother and father externalizing disorders revealed substantial assortative mating. Assortative mating is very common among substance abusing parents and those with APD. The familial aggregation of SUD and antisocial behaviour disorders tends to be the same among men and women, although women may require greater familial loading before expressing the disorder. The estimates of the heritability of SUD on the basis of family, twin, and adoption studies of persons with alcohol dependence range from 50% to 60%.

This effect may be partially explained by the concurrent familial distribution of APD, which may predispose to the development of SUD. Cadoret suggested, on the basis of adoption data, that there are two genetic pathways to drug abuse/ dependency. One proceeded directly from the biological parent's SUD to SUD among the offspring.

The other commenced with APD of the biological parent and proceeded through intervening variables of adoptee aggressiveness, CD and APD to drug use/dependency. A Norwegian twin study of 1,386 twin pairs suggested that the twin resemblance of illicit drug abuse was largely due to genetic factors. The heritability of drug abuse or dependence ranged from 58% to 81%. Among the twins from the Vietnam Era Twin Registry, genetic factors, shared environment and non-shared environment had significant influences of similar magnitude on the individual's risk of developing a drug use disorder.

Parental behaviour during child-rearing years is associated with elevated risk of offspring PD in adulthood. In the Children in the Community study, significant effects were found to be low parental nurturing and aversive harsh punishment.

The risk of PD was not attributable to offspring behavioural and emotional problems or parental psychiatric disorder, and did not diminish over time. Low parental affection or nurturing was associated with increased risk for offspring APD, BPD, paranoid, avoidant, and schizoid PD. Harsh punishment was associated with increased risk for offspring BPD, paranoid PD, passiveaggressive PD, and schizotypal PD. The authors concluded that parenting behaviour may mediate the association of childhood behavioural and emotional problems and parental psychiatric disorder with risk for the development of offspring PD. BPD is five times more common among first-degree relatives of persons with BPD than in the general population.

PSYCHIATRIC DISORDERS AND VIOLENT CRIME IN THE GENERAL POPULATION

Several studies have reported the association between psychiatric disorders and violent crime. The optimal study design might be a prospective study, comparing the occurrence of violent behaviour between persons with and without clinically assessed psychiatric disorders in large, unbiased birth cohorts with validated psychiatric diagnoses and unbiased method to clarify the criminal behaviour. Birth cohort studies are very laborious and expensive, and few have been carried out. The Copenhagen and Stockholm and Oulu studies were carried out using registered data of both crime and mental disorders, and the Dunedin study using both crime registers and selfreported crime and psychiatric disorders.

The risk of violent crime in the Dunedin Study was 1.9 among persons with alcohol dependence, 3.8 among persons with marijuana dependence and 2.5 among persons with schizophrenia-spectrum disorder. Persons with at least one of these disorders constituted one fifth of the sample, but accounted for half of the violent crimes. In birth cohort studies from Finland, Sweden, and Denmark, and studies using psychiatric case registers in Australia and the UK the risk of becoming a violent offender was two to six-fold for males and two to eight-fold for females among persons with MMDs, compared to the same-aged general population.

In the 26-year Prospective Study of the 1966 Northern Finland Birth Cohort data, 14% of persons with SCH and 17% of persons having mood disorders with psychotic features had committed violent crimes. The OR of violent offending was 7.0 for all cohort members with SCH, and 8.0 for those having mood disorders with psychotic features. When the lowest and the highest socioeconomic classes were compared with the reference group, no marked correlation between criminality and socioeconomic status was found. The association of specific psychiatric disorders with violent crime was clear in the Epidemiologic Catchment Area (ECA) Study on a cross-sectional population sample of 18,571 adults in years 1980 and 1984 at five sites in the US. DSM-III psychiatric disorders at any time of life were obtained from personal interviews, and comprehensively linked with self-reported crime at three sites. The sample was weighted to represent the structure of the nation, including institutional residents.

A greater proportion (55%) of people with a psychiatric disorder, compared to those without one (20%), reported violent behaviour in the past year. The most prevalent disorders among violent persons were SUDs. Since the ECA study was based on selfreporting of arrests and convictions, and lacked independent verification of criminality or psychiatric history, the results were likely to be underestimates. Recently, a cross-sectional interview survey of national household population in England, Wales and Scotland reported associations between DSM-IV psychiatric disorders and the severity, chronicity and victims of violence. Hazardous drinking was associated with over half of the incidents involving injury.

Persons who reported violent behaviour when intoxicated were more likely to report injuring a victim and being injured. Violence when intoxicated was increased 5-fold by alcohol dependence and nearly 3-fold by drug dependence. Occurrence of a PD doubled the risk of violence when intoxicated. APD independently increased the risk of violence when intoxicated by 3.3-fold. Nearly one in three persons with APD reported being violent when intoxicated. Persons with PDs and substance dependence were more likely to report violent incidences, injuries to their victims, injuries to themselves, multiple violent incidences and multiple victim types. APD brought the greatest risk, over 4-fold, of injury to the victim. The population attributable risk for victim injuries of the disorders was 24% for APD, 30% for alcohol dependence, 21% for drug dependence, 37% for any PD, 51% for hazardous drinking, 14% for neurotic disorders and only 1% for psychosis. Thus, prevention of APD would have reduced the proportion of persons reporting injuries to others by almost a quarter. Psychosis was independently associated only with an increase in recidivistic violence.

The study measured self reported victim injuries in self-reported psychosis, and lacked objective data, like many community studies. Self-reported crime rates may supply more information about total criminal behaviour than crime registers because of the high rate of unregistered less severe violent crimes. However, the studies may exclude the most severely violent, psychotic and antisocial individuals, who live in institutions or antisocial subgroups or are homeless, and therefore underestimate the association between the most severe psychiatric disorders and criminal behaviour.

VIOLENT OFFENDING AMONG PERSONS WITH MMD

Fazel and Grann compared the hospital discharge registers and crime registers in Sweden to study the population attributable risk of persons with MMDs. Among persons with MMDs, 6.6% had been convicted of violent crime, with a mean of 3.2 times per psychotic person. About 0.3% of patients vs. 0.1% of the general population were convicted at least 10 times. The overall crude OR for violent crime was 3.8. The OR was higher among women. Psychotic male patients committed approximately nine times more violent crimes than female patients.

The OR of males was the highest among those aged 25–39 years, while the OR of females was highest in the age group over 40 years. For SCH, the OR was 6.3, and for other psychoses 3.2. The population attributable risk fraction was, however, higher for other psychoses than for SCH.

The highest risk fractions among persons with MMD were reported for homicide and attempted homicide, 18.2%, and arson, 15.7%. The PAFs for other crimes were 7.5% for threats and harassment, 6.3% for assaulting an officer, 4.9% for sexual offences, 3.6% for robbery, and 3.1% for common assault. In several studies, the effect of MMDs has been higher for women than for men. Nearly a fifth of community-dwelling women with chronic psychosis in UK committed assault during a two-year follow-up study.

Assaultive behaviour was associated with previous violence, non-violent convictions, victimization, and cluster B personality. The risk of violence among persons with MMD is associated with many factors such as medication non-compliance, and active psychotic symptoms.

The National Clinical Antipsychotic Trials of Intervention Effectiveness project investigated the correlates and prevalence of minor and serious violence during the previous six months. The family and self-reports of 1,410 inpatients and outpatients with SCH living in the community at 56 sites in the US were studied. Inclusion criteria included SCH, decision-making capacity, and *e.g.* suboptimal antipsychotic treatment. Treatment resistant and mentally retarded patients were excluded.

The results indicated that positive psychotic symptoms, such as persecutory ideation, increased the risk of minor and serious violence, but only when the scores for negative symptoms were low. Five out of seven positive symptoms on the Positive and Negative Symptom Scale were significantly associated with serious violence: hostility, suspiciousness/persecution, hallucinatory behaviour, grandiosity, and excitement. In particular, the combination of delusional thinking with suspiciousness/ persecutory ideation was strongly associated with serious violence. Five out of seven specific PANSS negative symptoms decreased the risk of serious violence: lack of spontaneity and flow of conversation, passive/apathetic social withdrawal, blunted affect, poor rapport and difficulty in abstract thinking.

Childhood conduct problems were significantly associated with any violence. Serious violence was associated with psychotic and depressive symptoms, CD, and victimization. The authors concluded that specific clusters of symptoms may increase or decrease violence risk in SCH patients.

THE PREVALENCE OF MMD AMONG HOMICIDE OFFENDERS

SCH is over-represented among homicide offenders. In UK prisons, 10.9% of males convicted of homicides had SCH. However, the prison samples exclude those in hospitals. Among 1,423 arrested homicide offenders in Finland over a 12 year period, 93 individuals, amounting to 7% of male and 7% of female homicide offenders had SCH diagnosis in forensic psychiatric evaluations for court proceedings. The types were paranoid SCH in 50%, undifferentiated SCH in 23%, disorganized SCH in 11%, residual SCH in 3% and catatonic SCH in 1% of offenders.

Paranoid, schizoaffective and residual types were over-represented in comparison with the rates occurring in the general population. Schizoaffective disorder was diagnosed in 12% of offenders. Among 36 homicide recidivists convicted in Finland over 13 years, 67% had alcoholism, 64% PD, 11% SCH, and 6% major depression. In Austria, DSM-IV diagnoses of homicide offenders with MMDs investigated between the years 1975–1999 were made on the basis of hospital files. 77% of males and 70% of females with MMD had SCH. The paranoid subtype was the commonest among males among females. Major depressive or manic episodes were not associated with increased likelihood of committing homicide.

PSYCHOLOGY AND CRIME: THE SOCIAL CONTEXT

Rates of crime, its seriousness, and the frequency of different types of it, all vary considerably from one country to another. That could of course be a reflection of varying definitions and recording methods rather than underlying differences. But large-scale studies suggest that in England and Wales in recent years, there have been in the region of 12–17 million crimes per annum. Those figures come from successive sweeps of the British Crime Survey. The subjectively experienced fear of crime also shows sizeable variations, but they are only circuitously related to the patterns of crime recorded in official statistics. Whatever the exact details, the upshot is that directly or indirectly, crime touches the lives of nearly everyone. Given that context, it is rarely out of the media spotlight.

Research shows that crime events take the largest single share of stories in every news medium. Furthermore, the proportion of news devoted to crime has been rising over the last 50 years. The level of saturation is such that almost everyone has an opinion, and a theory, and some evidence to back them up. Yet discussion of law-and-order inexorably reveals what could be described as an attitudinal minefield. Individuals' perspectives are more likely to be shaped by their prior attitudes and beliefs on a range of social issues than by systematic evidence concerning crime itself. Can an approach that claims to be scientific really be applicable to what most people think of as moral or political questions? In the prevalent imagery, science aims towards detachment and objectivity. Surely that prohibits an appreciation of subjective experiences, meanings, ideals, values and other elemental qualities of the human condition. On the contrary: psychology is very much concerned with those spheres. Moreover, a scientific outlook can be perfectly compatible with exploring them, and with a system of values. If psychology is to inform social action or public policy, it needs to take account of ethical and political dimensions. Nevertheless, there is a view that its methodological aspirations and close connection with biological sciences render it unsuitable for addressing social problems. If it does have a stance, its focus on individual differences leads some writers to perceive it as affiliated, intrinsically, to the conservative end of the political spectrum.

INDIVIDUAL AND COMMUNITY

Let us examine these issues first at the individual level. Working with persons who have broken the law raises a number of complex ethical questions. There is an inherent tension between providing services to meet individual needs while also attempting to serve collective or community interests. Recalling the terminology used by Garland many of the activities described earlier might make it sound as if psychology has switched its historic allegiances. While traditionally it looked like part of the Lombrosian project in criminology, perhaps it has now been assimilated into the governmental project. Psychologists help the police with their inquiries, assist courts of law in evaluating evidence, assess risk levels of offenders, and develop methods of managing them inside the penal system.

Their basic agenda is to help explain crime and find means of controlling it. In Garland's view, such a 'science of causes' is a 'deeply flawed' undertaking.

And all of it is done in the service of the state! But before the idea takes off that this is one-sidedly part of a totalitarian agenda, note that much of it can also help individual citizens. It may safeguard them from being wrongfully convicted; reduce severity of punishments if they are; and protect potential victims from genuine risks of exploitation or assault. Outside criminal justice, psychology has many further uses in health, education and the workplace. Furthermore, it is possible simultaneously to meet the needs of both society *and* of the individual who has broken the law. The behaviour of those who frequently offend is evidently troublesome for the community. But much research suggests that often, members of that group are themselves very troubled people. Helping such individuals re-orient their lives can be of immense value both to them as well as to others if it effectively reduces offending.

For the 1,527 young people followed in the Denver Youth Survey, there was a strong association between numbers of self-reported problems and seriousness of offending. 'Amongst those facing only one problem, 7% are serious offenders, but among those facing four problems, 85% are serious offenders'. This pattern emerged for both males and females. The experience of personal difficulties across several areas of life is unfortunately sometimes accompanied by a lack of skills for addressing those problems and solving them in an effective way. For example, Wesner found poorer problem-solving skills among offenders than in a non-offending comparison sample. Whitton and McGuire gave a series of questionnaires designed to assess aspects of problems and styles of coping to young people under the supervision of youth offender teams in the Manchester conurbation, and to a matched sample of non-offenders in a secondary school.

Young offenders reported a significantly higher frequency of serious problems in their lives, and this was correlated with their numbers of previous convictions. However, in depicting the ways they coped, they showed higher rates of using fairly futile, unproductive methods, and lower rates of more active, problem-focused coping. In a study we have encountered before, Zamble and Quinsey interviewed highly repetitive adult offenders, with an average of 25 previous convictions, concerning factors that appeared to contribute to new offences. The crimes for which they were re-arrested were often preceded by difficulties in coping and by poor self-management, characterized by an absence of a positive problem-oriented approach. For example, individuals ignored problems they were experiencing, so allowing them to accumulate to intolerable levels, then adopted drastic solutions. In other research on how adult prisoners cope with problems, Zamble and Porporino found that more poorly adjusted prison inmates had more limited problem-solving skills. Morrison-Dyke found that having limited skills for solving problems was associated with homelessness among offenders with mental disorder.

Exploring the factors that were associated with giving up offending in an adult community sample, Farrall observed that 'as the total number of "problem" social circumstances facing the probationer increased, so desistance became less likely'. Many structured interventions are expressly designed to impart skills in solving personal problems but focus in addition on difficulties posed by the situations in which participants live. Programme materials often emphasize the importance of finding solutions that are most likely to work given certain constraints; depending on circumstances that may generate courses of action that involve changing external situations. Participants in this form of exercise are not extracted or dislodged from their environments. Training enables them to locate the sources of their difficulties, which does not automatically imply that problems reside solely within themselves.

ETHICAL DILEMMAS: RISK ASSESSMENT, PREDICTION AND CHANGE

The ethical tension alluded to above becomes particularly sharp in relation to assessment and prediction of risk, and different writers have taken conflicting stances on whether such a task can be performed ethically. Whether that is feasible depends on the predictive accuracy of the methods used. Some authors have designated a level of accuracy that should be reached before predictions can be ethically acceptable. Whatever that standard might be, it is important only to use the outputs from such assessments in conjunction with various other sources of information, and to inform decisions rather than dictate them. Writing reports and making recommendations are not value-free processes. The principal objective of a psychological report is to change the beliefs and influence the actions of the person who will be reading it. It is incumbent upon psychologists to pay attention to ethical dimensions arising in such work. Other dilemmas arise when contemplating the process of change. This has several interconnected aspects. The paramount question is whether participation in 'change-related activities' should be entirely voluntary, or can somehow be required by criminal justice staff. Even if we believe that someone would change if compelled to do so, is it ethical to enforce compliance?

From one perspective, the right to decide whether to participate resides solely with individuals themselves. From another, society can overrule the offender and is entitled to impose change. Having disregarded the rights of others, it is argued, he or she has forfeited the right to be left alone. We would expect that for people to make meaningful changes, for example of the immensity required when learning to control substance use, it is a prerequisite that they should participate in services on a purely voluntary basis. That is certainly the optimal arrangement. But some findings show that there are also circumstances in which a compulsory framework can be conducive to change.

Farabee *et al.* reported a review of 11 evaluation studies of treatment programmes for drug-abusing offenders. The programmes varied in the extent of legal pressure applied, but in all of them participation was coerced to some extent. Of the 11 studies, 'five found a positive relationship between criminal justice referral and treatment outcomes, four reported no difference, and two studies reported a negative relationship'. The authors challenged the orthodox view that the existence of external pressure implies that individuals lack any internal motivation to change. On the contrary, change often results from a complex interplay of internal and external factors. The authors concluded that the findings supported 'the use of the criminal justice system as an effective source of treatment referral, as well as a means for enhancing retention and compliance'. The importance of the latter was underpinned in further work by Fiorentino *et al.*. But change might not need to be coerced; it can be induced. With reference to high-frequency behaviours such as occur in substance abuse, it is possible to influence people towards change by a refined form of counselling known as *motivational interviewing*. This involves the use of a number of interactive strategies on the part of counsellors. They include, for example, encouraging clients to make statements that attribute to themselves the capacity to change, and drawing to their attention discrepancies between the things they say and the things they do.

While this is not blatantly coercive, it nevertheless raises ethical difficulties. Subtly influencing someone in this way is done without their full, informed consent and is open to the charge of being manipulative. Blackburn has discussed whether there are circumstances in which coercion could be ethically justifiable. This is based on a recognition that psychologists and other professionals working with offenders in criminal justice services are in a dual role, 'simultaneously helper and agent of social control', a conflict that can cause considerable strain. Evidence that coercion achieves desirable ends does not in itself excuse its use. But given certain types of offence or risks of harm, 'total rejection of compulsion does not seem a viable option'.

PROFESSIONAL CODES OF ETHICS

The need to address complexities such as these has led the national psychological associations of most countries to develop and publish professional codes of ethics. Such codes are usually based on the *deontological* approach to moral reasoning: the doctrine that actions have immanent properties of rightness or wrongness independently of their consequences, and that fundamental moral values can be deduced from first principles. It is contrasted with a *utilitarian* approach in which the morality of actions is decided by their consequences or net outcomes. Although the precise contents of ethics codes vary, most enunciate several basic precepts:

- *Beneficence*: the acceptance of a responsibility or obligation to do good.
- *Non-maleficence*: the acceptance of a responsibility to avoid doing harm.
- *Autonomy*: observing individuals' freedom of thought and action, and their right to self-determination.
- *Justice*: basing actions on justice and fairness between individuals.

- *Integrity*: trustworthiness and faithfulness to commitments; acting within one's competence.

The American Psychological Association first published its code of ethics in 1953. It has since undergone several revisions. In 1995, the constituent members of the European Federation of Psychologists' Associations formulated a joint *meta-code* of ethics. Codes are binding upon members of the respective regulatory bodies, and violations of them may lead to disciplinary action. However, they cannot possibly cover all the concrete situations in which an ethical problem might surface. Some psychologists have developed problem-solving and decision-making sequences to apply in circumstances like these, an approach known as *practical ethics*.

AUGMENTING MODELS: RISK FACTORS AND GOOD LIVES

Many current developments in criminal justice programmes are derivatives of the *risk–needs* model propounded by Andrews and Bonta. Some critics contend that dissecting persons in this way represents them solely as a package of risks, a 'dissolution of the subject into a cluster of factors', so denigrating their individuality and completeness. While that misconstrues the approach in important ways, recently a few researchers have proposed major revisions to risk–needs analysis.

Some revive a long-standing assumption that in helping people to change, it may be necessary to alter the 'whole person'. Based on such a critique, Ward and Stewart have forwarded an alternative to the risk factors model, which they contend provides a sounder basis for integrating what have been called criminogenic needs within a wider analysis of motivation and change. They argue that what Andrews and Bonta term *needs* are not ones that offenders themselves would recognize. Rather, they reflect factors that other members of society would wish to change if doing so will lead to lowered rates of recidivism. Ward and Stewart propose instead that we can enrich and strengthen our understanding of need by locating it within a general model of human motivation. Within this they outline certain basic motives and 'primary human goods'. These include, for example, health, selfdirectedness, freedom from turmoil, and relatedness to or intimacy with others.

This leads to a framework for providing offender services that Ward and Stewart call the *good lives* model, in which the objective is promotion of general psychological well-being. Bonta and Andrews have retorted that risk–needs assessment encompasses a very broad range of areas, and offenders should have access to high-quality services to meet all their needs. The question is whether it is the appointed role of criminal justice services to address ones not demonstrably linked to offending. Arguably, criminal justice personnel have no clear mandate to probe factors in an individual's life other than his or her criminal acts, and to attempt more than that is invasive. Davison and Stuart distinguish *minimal goals*, the reduction of problematic behaviour, from *optimal goals*, the enhancement of other aspects of individual functioning. The relative weight given to each may have to be negotiated afresh in every case.

DESISTANCE THE WHOLE PERSON

One of the most consistent findings in criminology, the *age–crime curve*, shows lucidly that as age increases from approximately 20 onwards, there is a substantial decline in the portion of the population committing crimes. Until recently, comparatively little was known about this process. However, several researchers have explored the reasons individuals give when they have successfully reduced their involvement in crime. One important discovery is that this is far more like a journey than a sudden event. As with the pathway into offending, it involves changes of speed and reversals of direction, as individuals' priorities and lifestyles unevenly evolve. Jamieson found that many of the young people they interviewed talked straightforwardly about growing up, maturing, and making other transitions in terms of jobs, education, partners, breaking away from offending peers, taking on responsibilities and 'settling down'. Maruna reported a series of in-depth interviews explicitly focused on desistance processes, and found that offenders need to make sense of their lives, and in doing so they construct life stories or *personal narratives* developed around specific themes. These *generative scripts* helped them to forge evolving identities within which, metaphorically speaking, they gradually become different people, or new versions of themselves, capable of acting in different ways.

In a study of the impact of probation supervision, Farrall found that the process of desistance bore relatively little relation to the efforts of supervising officers, and was much more a function of life events and circumstances. Externally, progress in desistance was associated with getting jobs, meeting partners and other key events. Others who were stuck in a pattern of offending attributed this to a 'lack of change' in their lives, meaning unsatisfactory circumstances with regard to jobs and relationships. These studies have in common an emphasis on what might be called the 'whole person' approach. While to some extent it challenges the more analytical risk factors model, the two can be complementary, as Maruna's work amply illustrates.

3

Women and Crime

INTRODUCTION

It appears, then, that women, like men, drift into criminal actions whenever the structure of opportunities is such that it seems a reasonable response to their situation. The particular situations in which they find themselves are determined by the ways in which sex–gender identities are institutionalized in their society, and so their patterns of criminality are gendered.

Cultural stereotypes about men and women, as suggested, show, are also a major influence on the nature of the social reaction to female criminality. The absence of strong punitive responses to most forms of female crime means that the progression from primary to secondary deviation is less likely to occur. Women may drift into crime, but they only rarely pursue criminal careers.

A form of female crime that seems to be the principal exception to this rule is prostitution. In law, a prostitute is someone who sells sex, and this is almost invariably seen as a female offence. Men involved in prostitution, other than as clients, tend to be seen as engaged in acts of 'indecency' rather than of 'soliciting' for prostitution. Under British law, a woman who has been arrested and convicted for soliciting is officially termed a 'common prostitute' and is liable to re-arrest simply for loitering in a public place. As most prostitution is arranged in public, on the streets, it is difficult for women so labelled to avoid the occasional spell in custody.

They may also find it difficult to live a normal life off the streets:

- It is virtually impossible for them to live with a man or even another woman as it is immediately assumed that such people are living off immoral earnings, thereby making themselves vulnerable to a criminal charge. Also, the legal definition of a brothel, as a dwelling containing two or more prostitutes, has made it difficult for two women to live together even where only one is a prostitute.

In 2006 the government in Britain announced its intention to change the law to allow up to three prostitutes to work together without their place of work being defined as a brothel. The reaction of the police is critical in determining whether a woman who breaks the law is defined as a criminal. Police work is structured around the cop culture, a culture that strongly emphasizes masculinity and that underpins the harassment and abuse of female police officers and the derogation of many female offenders.

Prostitutes, for example, are seen as flouting the domesticity of the conventional female role and have been subject to harassment and entrapment. Nevertheless, prostitutes are often able to establish a mutual accommodation with the police, an arrangement in which each can get on with their job with the minimum of interference from the other. When there is pressure on the police to take action, however, such arrangements break down. In these circumstances, prostitutes are highly vulnerable and can be quite susceptible to police persuasion and suggestion. On the other hand, women who conform to conventional role expectations are seen as in need of protection, and cautioning is more widely used for female offenders than it is for males. There is some evidence that this differential treatment of male and female offenders also occurs in the courts.

Sexist assumptions in court practices have led some to suggest that women experience greater leniency than men. Others, however, have suggested that greater harshness is more likely. Heidensohn correctly points out that this may simply reflect the well-known lack of consistency in sentencing, though she reports evidence that supports the view that women are treated more harshly.

Indeed, Edwards has suggested that women are subjected to much closer scrutiny in courts precisely because the female offender is seen as unusual or unnatural. Women are on trial not only for their offence but for their deviation from conventional femininity. Their punishment or treatment is intended to ensure that they adjust themselves back to what is seen as a natural feminine role. Very few convicted women are given custodial sentences.

Men are two or three times more likely to be imprisoned for an offence than are women, and their sentences tend to be longer. The women who are imprisoned are mainly those who have been convicted of such things as theft, fraud, forgery, or violence. Prisons do make some attempt to recognize that women's domestic commitments are different from those of men, and a number of motherand- baby units have been set up. Some well-publicized cases have been reported, however, of pregnant prison inmates who have been forced to give birth while manacled to a prison officer. Studies of female prisons in the United States have shown how these prisons are important sources of emotional and practical support for their inmates, often involving the establishment of lesbian family relationships. This appears to be less marked in Britain.

GLOBALIZATION'S EFFECTS ON WOMEN

Women have become more vulnerable, and violence against them has become more prevalent, under economic systems in which governments' strategic approach to poverty is to open up the land and labour to multinational corporations at the expense of national sovereignty and people's rights to food, land, and resources. Promoting privatization and the growth of multinational corporations under the guise of creating jobs and boosting economies, governments and corporations have increased the wealth of only a small sector of their economies, the wealthiest, while destroying access to independent means of economic survival, safety, and security for large numbers of people.

The liberalization of trade among nations based on agreements such as the North American Free Trade Agreement—and the efforts of international economic organizations such as the World Trade Organization to increase growth of large industries in debt-ridden countries—has had complex effects on many working people worldwide. Established in 1994, NAFTA lifted most tariffs on goods traded among the United States, Mexico, and Canada, aiming to facilitate cross-border movement of goods and services and substantially increase investment.

Its core provisions grant foreign investors a remarkable set of new rights and privileges that have promoted relocation abroad of factories and jobs, and the privatization and deregulation of essential services, such as water, energy, and Health care. The WTO, established in 1995, is an international organization that deals with the rules of trade between nations. It is a multilateral trading system for administering trade agreements, facilitating trade negotiations, and resolving trade disputes.

It provides training and technical assistance for developing countries. The WTO is one of the main mechanisms of corporate globalization. Critics worldwide see it as primarily functioning to open markets for the benefit of transnational corporations at the expense of national and local economies; workers, farmers, indigenous peoples, women, and other social groups; health and safety; the environment; and animal welfare.

Anuradha Mittal, codirector of Food First/The Institute for Food Development Policy, one example of how the organization functions is the WTO Agreement on Agriculture, which requires that countries open their economies and import agricultural products from other countries. American markets are saturated, so the United States is aggressively—and successfully—pressuring foreign markets to import U.S. products. One out of three U.S. acres produces food or fibre for export.

The United States subsidizes agriculture, which benefits agribusiness, but these subsidies are denied to poor farmers, and they lower world prices. For example, the United States exports wheat at 46 per cent and corn at 20 per cent below cost of production; family farmers in the United States, and in countries with which the United States trades, can't afford to sell their produce below cost. So, as Mittal explains, the WTO agreement puts control of the food system in the hands of large businesses, export producers, and the wealthy few. Before NAFTA, Mexico used restrictive licensing and high tariffs to control its grain imports.

Now, though, the United States and Canada pay no tariffs for grain exports to Mexico. Economist Debbie Seidband reported in 2004 that Mexico, once self-sufficient in producing basic food needs, now imports 95 per cent of its soy, 58 per cent of its rice, 49 per cent of its wheat, and 40 per cent of its meat. Mexico's demand for U.S. corn reached record highs in 2004.

As a result, Mexican corn farmers are being put out of business. Two million of Mexico's extreme poor are corn farmers; they can't compete with subsidized American agribusiness. Mittal estimates that six hundred peasant farmers are forced off their land every day. This is happening in many other countries as well. Although some see the movement of labour from small farms to wage-earning factory jobs as improving a nation's standard of living, these efforts have led to the economic and cultural dislocation of rural and indigenous people in regions of South and Central America and the Asia Pacific countries.

The growth of large-scale industries, such as mining, logging, power generation, and agriculture, operated by multinational corporations, has caused poverty, loss of land and traditional sources of livelihood, and inconsistent access to food. Multinational companies forming agribusiness ventures have turned subsistence farmers from landowners to cheap labourers who have no control over pricing, land use, or distribution of produce.

To survive poverty and to support their families, hundreds of thousands of men and women have joined the pool of cheap labour; many have migrated to cities where they can earn wages. Women and children are the worst affected. Migration of men to cities often leaves women to fend for themselves as well as for their households and their communities. Migration of women and girls to cities leaves them poor and far from their communities and families, where they are more vulnerable than ever to sexual harassment, sexual assault, trafficking, and sexual slavery.

Since NAFTA was signed in 1994, more than twenty-seven hundred sweatshops producing goods for export have begun operations in Mexico; they employ more than 1.3 million workers, mostly young women. Women's pay averages 50 cents an hour, without job security or benefits, and they are often subject to unsafe working conditions and sexual harassment. These women live in a harsh environment that often denies them access to effective protection from the criminal justice system. Radhika Coomaraswamy, the UN Special Rapporteur on Violence Against Women, in Hong Kong alone there were 237,110 foreign domestic helpers in 2002, the majority coming from the Philippines, Indonesia, and Thailand, all women.

In Southeast Asia, women and girls are being trafficked for the sex industry as well as for sweatshop labour, forced marriage, and street begging. Coomaraswamy has said that the problem of trafficking in women and girls has increased in recent years as part of the "feminine side" of globalization. Private market interests are reducing the role of governments, and subcontracting of manufacturing by large corporations has led to deregulation, an absence of laws to protect workers, and the increase of "sweatshop" labour in jobs that offer no fixed incomes or benefits. While globalization has created economic opportunities for women in some areas, increased poverty and loss of sources of income have led thousands of women to migrate to factory towns in search of work, which often makes them vulnerable to abuse, exploitation, and violence.

criminal justice system still skewed against women

We keep being told that feminism has had its day. Women have pulled down all the barriers to their aspirations, have renegotiated their relationships with men and are now scaling the heights that were formerly beyond their reach. The f-word cannot be mentioned without a boo from the sidelines. Girls are doing better than boys in education; they are filling the universities; they are becoming priests. Childcare is being shared, new men are staying at home while their women bring home the bacon. If we are to believe certain newspapers our preoccupations now are simply to ensure our pay is high and our weight is low. A few more legislative changes and all will be well with the world. In many respects it is true that the battle for formal equality has been won. For the most part, old-fashioned rank prejudice has gone since the laws which underpin formal equality were introduced in 1976. Examples of crude, in-your-face prejudice are much more rare. The case which now has to be made is for substantive equality-treatment as equals, taking account of the real experiences of women and the context of their lives. There has to be greater understanding of the differential effects of policies which, on the face of it, are neutral. It is also important to acknowledge that women are not just one homogenous group. Discrimination now is much more subtle and nuanced and often operates most fiercely at that junction where different forms of prejudice intersect.

When race and class overlap with the social vector of gender, we see in sharp focus the disadvantages still suffered by so many women. Being poor and female makes for a very different experience from that of the middle-class professional. Add the brickbats of racism, and the burden of multiple discrimination can be unbearable. The backlash against feminism takes many forms. Men are the ones we are now to be concerned about. They are being battered; they are having false claims made against them of child abuse because of false memory syndrome; they are being refused access to their children; they are falling prey to shameless hussies who try to get money out of tabloids for their stories. All of it does happen. Men can be used and abused too. Their pain at false accusation is no less. Their loss of their children is just as raw a wound. But the smoke and mirrors used to enlarge these claims are the products of fear that the old arrangements between the sexes might be reconfigured in ways that may be less to the satisfaction of some men. After September 11, American evangelical preachers even claimed that the events were a punishment for the behaviour of feminists and other deviants. The creation of pilot programmes, where special domestic violence courts will operate a speedy, multi-agency response to abuse is a major development. The many projects within the police, prosecution and penal service to address women's concerns are to be welcomed. There is a desperate need for special units to deal with rape cases and the Crown Prosecution Service is putting them in place. A lot has improved within the courts and legal system. We have more women on the bench and practising in the courts. There is no doubt that the government has taken on many women's issues and taken women's experience of victimisation to the heart of criminal law policy.

However, there has been a rolling of women's concerns into a generalised rhetoric about victims. All victims are bundled up together, when policy-makers should be brave enough to say that cases involving abuse of intimacy and the historic discrimination against women deserve special treatment. However, many ministers live in fear of being ridiculed as being in the thrall of "feminists"; they recoil from the reality that the most ill-treated victims within our system are women and children, and that this is still a reflection of some very disconcerting facts about male violence. What is the gender of most children abused over a long period and eventually killed by parents? From Jasmine Beckford to Victoria Climbie, go through the files of the NSPCC and you will find that they are almost invariably girls. Of course, boy children are also killed in outbursts of rage or to wreak revenge but the slow torture of children is most often directed at girls. What is the gender of the partner most often beaten in a relationship? What is the gender of those most often sexually violated? When we hear a body has been found, someone killed in a park by a stranger, what sex is the victim? When we hear of honour killings who is found dead? The gendered nature of certain crimes and their victims and the gendered nature of so much law, because it is largely created and administered by men, is still insufficiently recognised or discussed.

Instead of debating all these questions boldly, politicians hide behind the much more acceptable cloak of a generalised heading, marked "victims". Often with victims as their alibi, huge inroads are made into civil liberties. The most troubling and pressing questions are never asked. What is it about men that they are so much more disposed to criminality as a sex? Is masculine violence a feature of a patriarchal culture and why is so much of it directed at women? If so what are we doing about it within the education system? What are we doing to divert men from abuse? Discussions about violence never get to the heart of these issues because they are so disconcerting for us, reaching into dark places where primordial power-play simmers.

If we consider just how our law has historically criminalised aggression-how certain types of antisocial behaviour have been targeted, while others have been either formally or practically left unregulated-then it seems that such law is about male patterns of behaviour and about male standards of acceptable conduct. The law on rape and the minimising of domestic violence are the paradigm examples of this perspective; the law is gendered, especially in relation to violence, and the new gender-neutral language of legislation does not fully disguise this fact. It is why we had to go through such contortions to get the defence of provocation to work for women in domestic killings. Women rarely killed in a sudden blind rage; as the law required, more usually their loss of control arose from despair, like the final surrender of frayed elastic. Only now are the courts shifting to accommodate this different reality. Despite the fact that we know that men and women behave differently and seem to act for different reasons, we still watch governments provide universal theories of crime and formulate general criminal laws that are meant to work in a gender neutral manner. We are just not prepared to face the facts of crime. Sex is the most salient variable when it comes to offending.

Until women and children get justice in the system, certain special processes are justified, including anonymity for complainants in sexual offence cases and anonymity for children at all times. However, at regular intervals, we have to rehearse the arguments about why accused men should not be given the cover of anonymity in some spurious call for equality. Open justice means anonymity should be used sparingly. The coverage of a rape case at times leads to the discovery that the male accused is a multiple offender, because other women are given the confidence to come forward.

Redressing the profound historic failures in relation to women means having to take special steps and the government should be upfront about this. "Gender bias" does include bias against men, and there are cases, particularly those involving child custody, where this certainly applies. The difference is that the majority of men in court are stereotypically viewed as powerful, credible and independent. The men who do invoke negative stereotypical assumptions-homosexual, black, Irish, Arab, vagrant, Gypsy, unemployed-can suffer just as women do.

The law is also disfigured by pernicious stereotypes of women. The punitive pursuit of Maxine Carr, Ian Huntley's former girlfriend, who was acquitted of any involvement in the Soham murders, reveals a continuing belief that women have a special, nurturing responsibility towards children. Women who don't fulfil our expectiations of good womanhood are judged by double standards.

Increasingly, the arena of political change has moved to the courts, where individual cases become a way of raising wider political issues. As Rahila Gupta of Southall Black Sisters says, "It is as though individual pain is the only point of entry into an understanding of a systemic disorder." Law has become a political space for women that is capable of being used as an engine of change. Some of the most high-profile and important cases heard in the courts in recent years have involved women asserting their rights and testing the boundaries of the law: the case of Diane Pretty, who suffered from motor neurone disease, over the right to die; Diane Blood over the right to conceive using the sperm of her dead husband; the women in the military who were dismissed once they became pregnant. And then we have had the terrible appeals involving sudden infant deaths, such as those of Angela Cannings and Sally Clark, where women have been victims of miscarriages of justice, their mothering called into question. The law is changing but the process is slow and sometimes cosmetic. The old myths and stereotypes of women are still alive, well and being enriched with new cliches; we now have women painted as "ladettes" and binge drinkers to show they were asking for it. What has changed during my professional life is women's expectations. Women are very clear that they will not settle for a system that does not listen to them or take account of their lives; the legal system is becoming wise to that fact. Women have gone through the stage where they did the adjusting; now they expect the institutions to change. The symbol of justice may be a woman but none of us will settle for symbols.

DEFINITIONS OF GENDER JUSTICE

The literature on gender justice as understood in law reflects several different understandings of the concept in the South Asian context. There are at least three distinct perspectives that are discernible in the literature, which in turn affect understandings of law and development, citizenship and entitlement. (Kapur and Cossman 1996) These three approaches are: protectionism, equality and patriarchy. Each is described in the following section, and I offer examples highlighting how the literature on gender justice fits into each category. These categories are flexible, and clearly not all writings on gender justice in the arena of law fit neatly and unequivocally into a single category.

PROTECTIONISM

Perhaps the most problematic articulation of gender justice in law is the one that posits the relationship between women and law as one of protection. Scholars who endorse this approach have reinforced an essentialist understanding of gender difference, assuming that women are naturally weaker than men. This position of helplessness is so much visible among women in general that it has ceased to be any longer of much significance even to themselves.

The protectionist approach accepts the traditional and patriarchal discourses that construct women as weak, biologically inferior, modest and incapable of decision-making. Such so-called feminine characteristics are perceived as natural, immutable and thus, as the appropriate starting place for legal regulation. Writers within this approach often extol the role of women within the family—roles which are assumed to be natural, selfless and sacred. Atray writes: A woman's position as a wife has been given the highest place over all other roles which she is required to play because it is here that she is required to perform the most arduous of duties and the most difficult of responsibilities... As a wife, she is beyond everything else and sits on a pedestal as high and as glorious as the imagination can reach. Women's roles as mothers are similarly celebrated, and naturalized as an inevitable consequence of the biological differences between women and men. In this literature, the role of law is unproblematically asserted as protecting women.

Laws that continue to treat women differently than men are accepted as a necessary part of this protection. This protectionist approach is often reflected in judicial approaches to the question of the relevance of gender difference. Since women are seen as weak and subordinate—and thereby in need of protection—they must be treated differently in law. Any differential treatment of women is deemed to be intended for women's protection and, therefore, for their benefit.

Some recent examples of law enacted ostensibly for women's benefit include the imposition of minimum age limits on female workers going abroad for employment by Bangladesh, India and Nepal. In 1998, Bangladesh banned women from going abroad as domestic workers. In 2002, the government of Bangladesh announced it was considering removing the ban. However, the ban appears to have remained in effect. In the same vein, although not entirely prohibiting migration by women, the Nepal Foreign Employment Act, 2042 (1985) prohibits issuance to women of employment licences to work overseas without the consent of the woman's husband or male guardian.

Women's ostensibly natural differences are deployed to justify any differential treatment in law, and in effect, operate to preclude any entitlement to equality. This approach is firmly located within patriarchal discourses. It does not problematize the way in which law treats women, nor does it consider women's subordinate status. Gender justice is located exclusively within a protectionist framework, whereby laws are enacted in order to protect women as they are unable to decide and act for themselves. The effect is to infantilize women and pursue an agenda that merely reinforces this infantilization as it is contingent on male or state protection. While it is concerned with women as subjects of law, and even as subjects of rights, this literature is not within a feminist theoretical tradition. It is an approach that tends to essentialize the difference—that is—to take the existence of gender difference as natural and inevitable. It is an approach that affirms the legal relevance of gender difference and thus risks reinscribing this difference along with the underlying social relations that produced it. The legal recognition of this difference—within a protectionist approach—tends to both reflect and reinforce the common-sense understanding of this discrepancy as natural and inevitable.

This conception of gender justice is reproduced in the discourse of progressive groups, such as women's groups as well as the discourse of the religious and conservative groups as I will illustrate later. It is a conception that is highlighted as it continues to be relevant in the contemporary moment and because it has had a significant effect on how gender justice has come to be understood in law.

Equality

A second and perhaps more familiar approach to gender justice in the literature is one that is based on promoting equality. The literature has primarily focused on providing empirical reviews of laws that affect women. Writers within this approach have tended to provide comprehensive reviews of a range of legal provisions affecting women, from personal laws to criminal and labour laws.

This literature highlights both laws that continue to discriminate against women and successful challenges to such discriminatory laws. Writers within this approach have also tended to emphasize problems in relation to the under-enforcement of existing legal provisions governing women's equality rights (Sarkar *et al.* 1990). Implicit in much of this work is the assumption that law can play an important role in advancing women's equality by removing the legal obstacles that have limited women's full and equal participation. While this work recognizes there is still some distance to go before women's rights are adequately protected in law and gender justice fully achieved, there is a general optimism regarding the extent to which much of this road has already been travelled. Again, the positive role of law has more often been assumed than questioned.

An important feature of this approach is the conception of law upon which it is based. The depiction of law that emerges within this literature is its role in social engineering. For example, the 1975 *Report of the Committee on the Status of Women in India* placed considerable importance on the role of law: 'One of the main characteristics of modern society is a heavy reliance on law to bring about social change.' (Committee on the Status of Women in India 1975:102). This role is highlighted in postcolonial states: The tasks of social reconstruction, development and nation building all call for major changes in the social order, to achieve which legislation is one of the main instruments. It can act directly, as a norm setter, or indirectly, providing institutions which accelerate social change by making it more acceptable.

While the Report includes recommendations for sweeping legal reforms, this emphasis on the role of law in social engineering is not unqualified. For example, the Report also notes some of the limitations of law in this process. 'But legislation cannot by itself change society. To translate these rights into reality is the task of other agencies. Public opinion has to be moulded to accept these rights.' The Report, while noting the role of the judiciary and the executive levels of government in this process, further observes that neither level of government has fulfilled this role.

With regard to the Courts, the Committee notes that legislation has often been narrowly interpreted, and that the courts have often 'failed to give effect to the principles underlying the legislation.' The subsequent focus of the Report is on revealing the areas in which the implementation of the law falls short of the principles it articulates. Other government reports have also echoed this view of the limits of law. The *National Perspective Plan for Women* on India has observed: It is...necessary to realize that there are limits to the extent to which changes can be effected by law. Attempts at bringing about changes in women's status through either legislation or judicial activism can achieve little success without a simultaneous movement to change the social and economic structures and the culture of society. (Government of India 1988:135)

The view that emerges from both the *Report of the Committee on the Status of Women and the National Perspective Plan* is that law is a necessary but insufficient part of a more general strategy of bringing about social change. These reports, along with other literature in which the role of law is qualified, go some distance in recognizing the limitations of law in bringing about social change. However, they remain firmly located within the law as a social engineering thesis. As such, this literature does not question law's commitment to social change, nor does it consider the role of law in the subordination of women, beyond the discriminatory character of some laws (Singh 1989). This understanding is important as it has been influential in shaping programmes for pursuing gender justice in different parts of South Asia.

There is an assumption that equality can be achieved through mere reform of the law and enforcement, which is a vision of equality for women found in the context of liberal feminism. Such feminism begins from the basic premises of liberal theory: individualism and equality. Accordingly, the focus of liberal feminism has been on women as individuals—in particular, the extent to which women have been denied the status of individuals, and denied the liberal goal of equality. Liberal feminism has placed considerable attention on law in pursuing gender justice. According to this approach, law has contributed to women's oppression by exclusion. Women's oppression is understood largely as a result of discriminatory treatment. Thus, law can contribute to overcoming oppression by the creation of a legal order that includes women on an equal footing. Liberal feminist perspectives focus on eliminating statutory provisions and language that explicitly discriminate on the basis of sex, and which reinforces sexual stereotypes. According to this perspective, in order to achieve gender justice, women should be treated the same as men, and gender difference should be irrelevant in law.

Liberal feminist perspectives on law have also developed a concern with ensuring equality for women through equal opportunity. In order to create conditions of equality for women, liberal feminists may argue in favour of affirmative action, that is, for rules that treat women preferentially in order to create substantive equality. Liberal feminism provides some important insights into the legal regulation of women. It has focused on and identified the various forms of discrimination against women in law, and has provided a major impetus for waves of law reform establishing formal legal equality for women that have taken place throughout South Asia. However, it is also limited in some very significant respects. There is, for example, no analysis within liberal feminism of the underlying structures of oppression. The focus on the individual, and in particular, on the equal treatment of the individual in law leaves the economic, social, cultural and political institutions that produce and reinforce women's oppression uninterrogated. There is, accordingly, no consideration of the role of law in transcending this oppression—the role of law is simply assumed rather than problematized.

The liberal feminist approach is based on a very specific conception of equality—that is, it is based on the prevailing conception of equality as sameness. In this vision of equality, women are understood as the same as men—so, for the purposes of law they are the same, and must be treated the same. According to this version, any legislation or practice that treats women differently than men is seen to violate guarantees of equality. This sameness approach has been used to strike down provisions that treat women and men differently. It has, however, also been used to preclude any analysis of the potentially disparate affect of gender-neutral legislation. In some ways, this approach to equality is a reaction to the protectionist approach, which reinforced gender difference, instead of realizing gender justice. Thus it simply reproduced the processes of subordination under which women lived. Some feminist approaches have endorsed this conception of equality.

According to them, gender difference ought to be irrelevant, and women ought to be treated exactly the same as men. Advocates of this approach argue that so-called 'special treatment' has historically been a double-edged sword, because under the guise of protection, it has been used to discriminate against women. They point to the use of gender difference in the past in prohibiting women to vote, to be elected to government, to be admitted to the legal profession, and other such participation in the economic, political and cultural dimensions of society.

Similarly, in South Asia, an emphasis on equality as sameness is characterized by the same insights and limitations as liberal feminism. There is a focus on laws that treat women differently, and the need to reform such discriminatory laws. The starting assumption is one of equality, not difference.

Like liberal-feminist perspectives to law, more generally this approach has been important in challenging prevailing assumptions about women, in revealing the extent to which women continue to be discriminated against in law, and in demanding that laws be reformed to better reflect and promote women's right to full and equal participation in the world around them. The role of law is assumed, while the underlying structures of oppression are given little attention.

It is also not enough to draw attention to the under-enforcement of law, as this approach does, and recommend ways to ensure more efficient enforcement. The emphasis of this approach is on increasing women's access and enforcement through such means as sensitizing the judiciary to women's issues, legal aid, family courts and increased legal awareness for women. Similarly, it assumes that if law is effectively enforced, it can remedy the social problems for which it is designed. This emphasis on enforcement obscures the role that law plays in women's subordination: that it cannot simply be deployed at will with the belief that it will produce progressive outcomes for women and gender justice.

Eliminating discrimination and improving enforcement are not insignificant reforms. However, without a deeper understanding of the role of law in women's subordination, these reforms may only lead to further disillusionment with the legal system.

Patriarchy

A third approach in the literature on gender justice is one in which law is seen as an instrument of patriarchal oppression. In this approach, the focus of gender justice is to challenge the patriarchal assumptions on which law is based. Laws throughout South Asia continue to reflect patriarchal oppression and discriminate against women. These laws, and the judicial interpretations of these laws, are connected to the patriarchal social relations in which women have been oppressed.

Fareeda Shaheed's work is an example of the law as patriarchy approach. She argues that patriarchy in Pakistan results in inequalities to women. (Shaheed *et al.* 1986) Law is used to entrench social and behavioural codes that are labelled as Islamic and used to counter Westernization, including feminism. She argues that law is used as a way of vindicating patriarchy. The three sources of such laws are customary law, religious law, and British civil and criminal law. She discusses how customary and religious laws currently endorse Muslim practices that promote the superiority of men and rejection of Islamic teachings promoting women's rights. Customs such as the practice of *purdah* are designed to restrict women's participation in economic and political life. They simultaneously reinforce the control of men in the public domain.

Lina Gonsalves' analysis in her study *Women and the Law* is also an example of scholarship within the law as patriarchy framework. Gonsalves focuses on the enforcement (and lack thereof) of laws that were intended to benefit women, and argues that 'law enforcers...discriminate between women and men and unconsciously tend to reflect traditional and rigid attitudes towards women' (Gonsalves 1993:xiii). She attempts to highlight the extent to which 'the police, public prosecutors and the judges, who are products of patriarchal society, are by and large biased against women, and...help to perpetuate and preserve the oppression of women (Gonsalves 1993:xii). Gonsalves examines a broad range of laws affecting women—succession, maintenance, custody, divorce, rape and dowry—and attempts to illustrate the patriarchal biases in the courts' interpretation of these laws.

The study is important in its effort to reveal the biases and unstated assumptions about women that inform the case law and undermine women's rights. In her introduction and conclusion, Gonsalves is careful to state she does not believe the law is unimportant in women's struggles. Her focus is on the need to eliminate the patriarchal biases affecting the implementation of laws. However, at times her analysis of specific laws seems to undermine this position. For example, she concludes not only that laws intending to address violence against women such as India's *Dowry Prohibition Act*, 'have achieved little in transforming the social order and uprooting dowry as a social evil', but that: The outcome of trials and the unwillingness of the police to probe violence against women at home and in society has led to a situation in which the law as a whole can easily be taken to be an instrument of patriarchal oppression. This literature views law as an instrument of patriarchy. It can be seen to loosely correspond to a 'dominance feminist perspective' on law. Dominance feminism attempts to provide a more structural analysis of women's oppression, based on the concept of patriarchy. As Supriya Akerkar succinctly describes 'the context of dominance feminism is that gender inequalities are the outcome of an autonomous system of patriarchy and that gender inequalities are the primary form of social inequality.' (Akerkar 1995:2)

The law as a patriarchy (or dominance feminism) approach tends to examine the ways in which gender justice in law is informed by and serves to reinforce patriarchal social relationships. A primary concern includes the way in which law reinforces male control over women's sexuality, together with the way in which law continues to exclude or marginalize women's values and needs in the legal processes. Law is regarded as being based on male norms, male experience and male domination. The focus of analysis is often on the legal regulation of sexuality and of violence. Dominance feminism has made an important contribution in attempting to locate women's oppression within broader structures of gender oppression, as well as in exposing how even the most intimate space of the home and family is political. In the context of law, it has been crucial in revealing the importance of the legal regulation of sexuality and of violence in the oppression of women.

However, it is a perspective that is also limited in some important respects. It has been criticized for its understanding of patriarchy as ahistorical, decontextualized and universalistic; for its essentialist construction of women only as victims, rather than as agents of resistance and change; as well as for its focus on gender oppression to the exclusion of other forms of oppression. The exclusive focus on sexuality as the site of women's oppression leaves out other sites that contribute in significant ways to gender injustice, such as the family and the economy. The complex and specific nature of relations of oppression tends to be reduced to monolithic and highly general explanations.

Dominance feminist perspectives on law have been important in highlighting the negative and deeply problematic stereotypes of women that inform law and law enforcement. Further, such perspectives are also an important contribution in directing attention to the deeper structures of law and legal discourse, and suggesting a connection between these structures and women's oppression. However, this framework does not go far enough in explaining the role of law in women's oppression nor in women's struggles. It is not sufficient to simply assert that law is patriarchal, or that the lawmakers are sexist. The vision of law as an instrument of patriarchy tells us very little about the precise workings of the law, and even less about if and how women can use law. These three approaches to gender justice influence the ways in which this issue is addressed in law. Each has shortcomings as set out in this section. There is a need to further problematize the concept of gender justice from a postcolonial perspective and to contextualize the role of rights and legal discourse in promoting specific understandings of gender justice.

CRIMES OF THE AFFLUENT

The crimes of the affluent, the prosperous, and the powerful can be explained in terms of the same motives as any other criminal act. They differ from 'ordinary' theft and burglary only in terms of their social organization and the social reaction to them. The character and motivation of those involved are no more, and no less, pathological than those of any others who drift into crime. White-collar crimes, however, are much less likely to result in full-time criminal careers.

The nature of the social reaction makes the development into secondary deviation much less likely. Much corporate and occupational crime takes place in the financial services industry, where changing patterns of regulation have created greater opportunities for illicit activities. The British financial system was, for much of the nineteenth and twentieth centuries, regulated in a highly informal way. Recruitment to banks, insurance companies, and other financial enterprises took place through an old-boy network centred on the public schools and the Oxford and Cambridge colleges.

The Stock Exchange, as the central institution in the financial system, was at the heart of this system of informal regulation. The system rested on trust and loyalty: those who had been to school together and shared a similar social background felt that they could trust one another in their business dealings. The motto of the Stock Exchange was 'My word is my bond', and many deals were sealed on the shake of hands rather than with a written contract. During the 1970s the government introduced a number of changes to this system of regulation in response to the growing internationalization of the money markets.

This culminated in the so-called Big Bang of October 1986, when the Stock Exchange was finally opened up to foreign competition. New codes of practice were introduced to reflect the more diverse social backgrounds of those involved in the buying and selling of currency, shares, and commodities. The old system of trust could no longer be relied on, and more formal mechanisms were required. The Bank of England was given greater powers of control and supervision, and in 1997 the Labour government created a new Securities and Investment Board to regulate the whole system.

The offences with which the new system of regulation has had to deal are those that have been made possible by the changing structure of the financial system. The investment management firm of Barlow Clowes, for example, set up new offshore investment funds to provide high returns to its wealthy clients who wanted to minimize their tax bills. The head of the company was found to have financed an extravagant lifestyle at the expense of the investors in the funds.

The growth of domestic takeover business made possible massive fraud by some directors and managers associated with Guinness and its financial advisers in 1986. These directors and managers manipulated share dealings to keep up the price of Guinness shares on the stock market and to help its takeover of another company. Their actions were the subject of an official enquiry and, later, a criminal trial that resulted in some of them being imprisoned. Much white-collar crime is low in visibility.

It tends to occur in the context of normal business routines, and it is less likely to be noticed, even by its victims. Fiddling business expenses, for example, is almost undetectable, and many employers treat it as a source of tax-free perks for their employees. Large-scale fraud, when discovered, is more likely to result in an official reaction, though it will often be hushed up if it might suggest a failure of supervision or control by senior managers. Crimes of the affluent are far more likely to be regulated by specialized enforcement agencies than by the police, and this has important consequences for the nature of the social reaction.

These agencies—the Health and Safety Executive, the Factory Inspectorate, the Inland Revenue, and so on—generally have a remit to maintain and promote high standards of business and trading, and the enforcement of the criminal law is only one part of this remit. Their officials, therefore, develop 'compliance strategies' that stress persuasion and administrative sanctions aimed at crime prevention, rather than the detection and punishment of offences. The level of prosecutions is, therefore, very low. Few cases go to court, and very few result in imprisonment. In these ways, the transition to secondary deviation is avoided.

LEGAL CONTROL OF CRIME

Crime is that form of deviance that involves an infraction of the criminal law. Not all laws are 'criminal'. Lawyers recognize civil law, constitutional law, and various other categories of legal norm. Civil law, for example, concerns relations among private individuals, such as the contractual relations involved in such areas as employment relations and consumer purchasing.

A person who breaks a contract by, say, unfairly dismissing someone from her or his job or failing to supply goods that are 'fit for their purpose' has infringed the civil law, and action can be taken only by the particular individual affected. The police have no right to become involved, and a completely separate system of courts is involved in hearing any civil case. The outcome of a successful civil case is some kind of 'restitution', such as financial compensation or 'damages'.The criminal law, by contrast, consists of those legal norms that have been established by the state as a public responsibility, and which the police and the criminal courts have been designated to enforce. Someone who infringes the criminal law can be arrested, charged, and tried at public expense and, if found guilty, will be subject to repressive or punitive penalties such as a fine or imprisonment. The criminal law of a society can cover a wide range of actions.

In Britain, for example, it covers such acts as driving above the legal speed limit, stealing a car, breaking into a house, possessing certain drugs, forging a signature on a cheque, murdering someone, and arson. Penalties attached to these offences range from small fines for speeding to life imprisonment for murder, and, until 1998, execution for treason. The crimes that are most visible or that are perceived to be the most threatening are not necessarily those that have the greatest impact in real terms.

In practice, many minor crimes are normalized: few people report cases of speeding or dropping litter, and the police may often choose to disregard such offences. A different picture emerges, however, from the British Crime Survey, which draws its evidence from a sample survey of the general public.

This survey of victims and potential victims showed a fall in the amount of crime between 1995 and 2005. The peak in 1995, but crime had fallen by 44 per cent by 2005. Both vehicle crime and burglary fell by over a half, while violent crime fell by 43 per cent. The chances of being a victim of crime fell from 40 per cent in 1995 to 24 per cent in 2005. This is the lowest level since 1981. Young men, however, are far more likely to be a victim of crime, while relatively few of those aged over 65 have been victims.

People's attitudes, however, reflected the official statistics and their reporting in the media, with 61 per cent of people believing that crime had risen in the country as a whole. Government policy on minor crime and delinquency in Britain has recently centred around the issue of 'anti-social behaviour' and the 'respect' agenda that emerged during the 2005 general election campaign.

The 'respect' agenda is based on the idea that the low-level criminality and nuisance behaviour that upsets people on a day-to-day basis—petty vandalism, rudeness, drunkenness—should be dealt with through local communities themselves, by inculcating a climate of respect towards other people's property. Improving discipline in schools, for example, is seen as a way of establishing such control. This is seem as an extension of an earlier policy of controlling more serious petty criminality through the issuing of Anti-social Behaviour Orders.

These are orders issued by a civil court, rather than a criminal court, prohibiting a person from specific acts of concern to complainants. Although these are civil court orders, a breach of an ASBO is a criminal offence and can bring the offender under legal control. Public concern over crime relates mainly to theft and violence, which are regarded as being serious enough to warrant sustained attention from the police. This concern, reflected in periodic moral panics, tends to ensure that many of those who are involved in theft and criminal violence do so as a form of secondary deviation.

As a result, many of them develop a criminal identity. In this part as suggested, look at forms of professional and career crime and at those normalized forms of crime commonly called white-collar crime. As suggested, also look at the gendered nature of criminal activity, in relation both to the undertaking of criminal acts and to becoming the victim of crime.

PROFESSIONAL AND CAREER CRIME

Theft—stealing property belonging to another person—is one of the few forms of crime to have a highly organized character and to offer the chance of a career or profession to those engaged in it. Theft includes burglary, robbery, forgery, confidence tricks, pickpocketing, and numerous other fraudulent activities. Not all of these are organized as career crime, of course, and not all of those who drift into theft even make the transition from primary deviation to secondary deviation. School children who steal from shops, for example, rarely continue into a career of thieving.

Nevertheless, theft is, indeed, one of the most organized forms of crime. Career crime is nothing new. Mary McIntosh traces it back to the actions of pirates, bandits, brigands, and moral outlaws who often combined criminal with political aims. If the Robin Hood image of the rural outlaw is a rather idealized fiction, it nevertheless grasps an important element in pre-modern theft. With the growth of towns in the early modern period, opportunities for street and house crime became much greater, and there was a growth in the amount of what McIntosh calls craft crime.

This is the small-scale, skilled theft engaged in by pickpockets, cutpurses, and confidence tricksters. These forms of career crime proliferated through the eighteenth and nineteenth centuries and remain an important part of everyday crime. McIntosh traces the origins of what she calls project crime to a later period. This is large-scale robbery and fraud, and became fully established only in the early years of the twentieth century. It has become the predominant form of theft only since the 1950s.

CRIME AND THE UNDERWORLD

Where rural bandits and outlaws were enmeshed in the surrounding social life of the rural communities from which they were drawn, urban craft crime tended to be based in a distinct criminal underworld. The growth of such criminal areas was first reported in the sixteenth century, but it was in the eighteenth and nineteenth centuries that they achieved their fullest development. The criminal underworld of a city such as London comprised various 'rookeries' that formed the dwelling places and meeting places of craft criminals of all kinds. Segregated from the rest of society, the underworlds provided for the security, safety, shared interests, and concerns of the craft thieves. The underworlds were rooted in the surrounding slum districts of the poor working class. Poverty, unemployment, overcrowding in poor physical conditions, and a lack of leisure opportunities other than the pub, were the conditions under which many people drifted into crime and some became confirmed in a criminal career.

An urban underworld formed an occupational community with a subculture that established norms of criminal behaviour, a slang and argot, and an esprit de corps that sustained the shared identity of the thieves. Central to the underworld code was the injunction not to 'squeal', 'squawk', 'grass', or inform on others. Association with other thieves, and a lack of association with the targets of their theft, inhibited any concern for the feelings of the victims of crime. It also meant that thieves could learn from other thieves the techniques and skills that would help them in their own crimes.

In addition, their leisuretime associates formed a pool of partners in crime. They were able to find markets for their stolen goods, and they could attain a degree of protection and insulation from detection and law enforcement. Underworld life, however, has been fundamentally altered by the urban redevelopment of the inner-city areas and the dispersal of population to the suburbs. One of the principal roots of the London underworld had been in the Spitalfields and Cable Street districts of the East End, where there has been much redevelopment.

While certain central pubs and clubs remain important venues for career criminals, much activity is now more dispersed through the city, and the underworld forms an extended social network rather than being confined to a particular physical locale. Even in the 1960s, however, a tradition of craft crime still survived in Spitalfields, and the surrounding district had high levels of crime: there were especially high levels of burglary, violence against the person, gambling, and prostitution. Much crime, however, was 'petty, unsophisticated, unorganized and largely unprofitable—if often squalid and brutal'.

A subculture of crime continues to sustain career crime, which has, however, changed its character. Alongside older forms of craft crime, project crime has become more significant, and this has also helped to transform the structure of the underworld. Where craft theft involved the stealing of small amounts of money from large numbers of people, project crime involves a much smaller number of large thefts. Growing affluence and, in particular, the increasing scale of business activity have meant that the potential targets of theft have become much bigger.

As a result, criminals have had to organize themselves more effectively and on a larger scale if they are to be successful against these targets. Improved safes, alarm systems, and security vans can be handled only by organized teams of specialists: safe-breakers, drivers, gunmen, and so on. Such crimes, organized as one-off projects, require advanced planning and a much higher level of cooperation than is typical for craft crime. Teams for particular projects are recruited through the cliques and connections that comprise the underworld, and these may sometimes be organized on a semi-permanent basis. The criminal underworld that existed in the East End of London from the Second World War until the 1960s, for example, contained numerous competing gangs that were held together largely by the violent hegemony of the Kray twins and their associates. The east London gangs engaged in violent feuds with their counterparts from the south London underworld, and the leading members of the East End and south London gangs occasionally met on the neutral ground of the West End.

It is through the subculture of crime that people can be socialized into criminal identities, whether as a craft thief or a project thief. The professional thief, like the professional doctor, lawyer, or bricklayer, must develop many technical abilities and skills. He must know how to plan and execute crimes, how to dispose of stolen goods, how to 'fix' the police and the courts, and so on. These skills must be acquired through long education and training, and it is through his involvement in the underworld that the thief can acquire them most effectively. Based on his detailed study of a professional thief, Sutherland has shown how the person who successfully learns and applies these techniques earns high status within the underworld.

The beginning thief, if successful, is gradually admitted into closer and closer contact with other thieves. It is they who can offer him 'better' work and from whom he can learn more advanced skills. Once successful, the thief dresses and behaves in distinct ways and proudly adopts the label 'thief ' in order to distinguish himself from a mere 'amateur', small-time criminal.

As well as gaining respect within the underworld, he may also gain a degree of recognition and respect from police, lawyers, and newspaper crime writers. These people are aware of his activities and have often accommodated themselves to professional crime: apart from the corruption that sometimes occurs, there may also be shared interests in not reacting immediately and punitively towards all crime.

BURGLARY AS A WAY OF LIFE

One of the few contemporary investigations of career theft in Britain is an investigation of domestic burglaries. Burglary is illegal entry into a building with the intent to steal. Domestic burglary was, for a long time, subject to the death penalty, and from 1861 to 1968 it carried a maximum sentence of life imprisonment.

Following the Theft Act of 1968, the maximum penalty has been fourteen years' imprisonment. In practice, only just under a half of convicted burglars have been given custodial sentences. Recognizing the problems involved in assessing rates of crime, Maguire and Bennett concluded that about 60 per cent of all burglaries were committed by a relatively small number of persistent, career criminals. The remaining 40 per cent were committed by juveniles who had drifted into delinquency and would, for the most part, drift out of it again.

Maguire and Bennett interviewed a number of persistent burglars, most of whom were committed to their criminal careers. They had, typically, carried out between 100 and 500 break-ins during their careers. They combined this with involvement in car theft, burglary from commercial premises, and cheque forgery.

They were mainly young, single, and with no dependants. The men described themselves as 'thieves', or simply as 'villains', and they described their crimes as 'work' from which they could earn a living and from which they would eventually retire. Maguire and Bennett are, however, more critical of this self-image than Sutherland had been. In particular, they highlight a number of ways in which the thieves sought to neutralize the moral implications of their actions through self-serving rationalizations.

Thieves claimed, for example, that any distress suffered by the victims was no concern of theirs. They were simply doing a job, carrying on their trade, and this distress was an unavoidable consequence of their routine, professional activities. This claim was further bolstered by the claim that, in any case, they stole only from the well-to-do, who could easily afford it and who were well insured. In fact, many of their victims were relatively poor council house residents who could ill afford to be burgled.

Similarly, the thieves sought to boost their own status by disparaging the amateurism of the majority of 'losers', 'wankers', 'idiots', and 'cowboys' who carried out unsuccessful thefts. However, Maguire and Bennett argue, it is more accurate to see the persistent career thieves as divided into low-level, middle-level, and high-level categories on the basis of the scale of their crimes. Thieves move up and down this hierarchy a great deal over the course of their careers. High-level burglaries are undertaken by thieves who are members of small networks of committed criminals who keep themselves separate from other, small-time criminals. Sometimes they work alone, and sometimes in pairs, but always they keep their principal criminal contacts within their network. Middle-level burglaries are carried out by those who are involved in larger and less exclusive networks of thieves with varying abilities and degrees of commitment. There is less consistent adherence to the code of mutual support, and less effective contacts with receivers of stolen goods and with other specialist criminals.

Finally, low-level burglaries are undertaken by individual thieves with only loose connections to one another and who are indiscriminate in both their criminal connections and their choice of crimes. It is at the lower level that people first enter burglary, as the loose social networks are closely embedded in the surrounding structure of the local community. In most cases, this is a process of drift by some of those who have previously been involved in juvenile delinquencies.

When describing their careers, however, the thieves minimized the element of drift and presented a self-image of themselves as people who had chosen to enter careers of crime. Those who drift into lower-level burglary and become at all successful may graduate, in due course, to middle-level or high-level burglary through the contacts and connections that they make. Those in the networks carrying out the high-level burglaries were, in a sense, at the pinnacle of the career hierarchy, though Maguire and Bennett show that they are unlikely to be at all involved in large-scale project crimes undertaken by the London gangs.

Their activities are confined to housebreaking, shop-breaking, car theft, shoplifting, and cheque forgery. They have little or no involvement in such specialist crimes as hijacking lorries, bank raids, or embezzlement. Very few burglars—even those at the high level—make a major financial success of their chosen careers, and most spent at least one period in prison. Imprisonment is not, however, a purely negative experience, as it gives the burglar an opportunity to 'widen his circle of criminal acquaintances, learn new techniques and be encouraged to try his hand at more lucrative offences'.

Nevertheless, few burglars continued with burglary beyond their thirties or forties. Most drifted into what they hoped would be safer forms of work. Entry into legal employment is difficult for someone with a criminal record, and few make the transition successfully. Walsh has shown that some burglars are able to combine career crime with a continuing involvement in legitimate employment—typically short-term jobs in the building and construction industry or in other casual work such as catering and cleaning.

It seems likely that some who retire from burglary may be able to continue or to re-enter such casual and temporary work. Career crime has probably never been a completely self-contained, full-time activity. Even in the heyday of the Victorian underworld of the East End, criminal activities were combined with casual labour and street trading, one type of work supplementing the earnings from the other.

Hobbs has shown how the East End has long been organized around an entrepreneurial culture of wheeling and dealing, trading and fixing, that makes no sharp distinction between legal and illegal activities. Theft may, indeed, be career crime, a way of life, but it does not take up all of a thief 's time and cannot usually provide him with a regular or substantial income. Those involved in thieving, then, must combine it with other ways of gaining an income. Casual labour is combined with their own thieving and the performance of the occasional criminal task for other, more successful thieves. Those who are themselves more successful may be involved as much in trading and dealing as in thieving, and their entrepreneurial activities are likely to range from the legitimate, through various 'shady' deals, to the criminal. The fulltime criminal is not a full-time thief, even if he stresses this aspect of his life in constructing his own identity. Much thieving is undertaken by those who are in lowpaid or semi-legitimate work or who are unemployed. There is considerable evidence that the growth of the drugs market in the 1980s has sharpened a distinction between the full-time criminal and the mass of ordinary thieves. The establishment of a large and extensive market in drugs has connected together the criminal networks of London, Manchester, Birmingham, Glasgow, and other large cities. This has allowed a greater degree of organization to be achieved in the project crimes that sustain drugtrafficking. Those who are involved in this organized crime, however, have highly specialized skills—for example, in relation to VAT fraud—and are very different from those who steal hi-fis and videos from domestic premises.

The significance of the drug market for ordinary thieves is that it offers possibilities for casual and occasional trading in small quantities of drugs that supplement their more established sources of income.

GENDER, ETHNICITY, CLASS, AND CRIME

The public perception of crime concentrates on robbery, burglary, theft, mugging, rape, and other crimes of theft and violence. The popular view sees this crime as male, working-class activity. Professional crime is seen as the work of certain adult males and as expressing conventional notions of masculinity. This point of view does get some support from the criminal statistics, which seem to show the very small number of women who are convicted of criminal offences; 5.9 per cent of all men in 2000 were found guilty or were cautioned for a notifiable offence, compared with 1.2 per cent of women.

It also appears that the kinds of crimes committed by women are less 'serious' than those committed by men. All parts of Britain show that women have very little involvement as offenders in domestic or commercial theft, vehicle theft, or street violence, though they are often, of course, involved in these as victims. They are, however, more heavily involved in shoplifting than are men, prostitution is an almost exclusively female crime, and only women can be convicted of infanticide. There is some evidence, however, that the number and types of crime committed by women may have altered since the 1960s. In a similar way to the crimes of women, many middleclass crimes are not generally regarded as 'real' crimes. While there is a great public fear of street violence and domestic burglary, there is relatively little concern about fraudulent business practices, violations of safety legislation, or tax evasion.

While such offences, arguably, have much greater impact on people's lives than does the relatively small risk of theft or violence, they are either invisible to public opinion or are not seen as proper 'crimes'. In this part as suggested, assess the adequacy of these views of crime, exploring aspects of the crimes of women, ethnic minorities, and the affluent.

DISTRIBUTION BY GENDER, ETHNICITY, AND CLASS

The kinds of crimes that are committed by women, like those committed by men, reflect the gender-defined social roles that are available to them. Both men and women are involved in shoplifting, for example, but women are more likely to steal clothes, food, or low-value items. Men are more likely to steal books, electrical goods, or high-value items. This reflects the conventional domestic expectations that tie women to shopping for basic household goods in supermarkets, while men are able to shop for luxuries and extras. Put simply, both men and women tend to steal the same kinds of items that they buy. Similarly, men are heavily involved in vehicle crimes, including car theft, while women are heavily involved in prostitution. This involvement in prostitution can be seen as an extension of a normal feminine role that allows implicit or explicit bargaining over sex.

This connection between crime and conventional genderroles is particularly clear in the patterns of involvement that women have in offences related to children. Those who are most responsible for childcare are, other things being equal, more likely to be involved in cruelty to children, abandoning children, kidnapping, procuring illegal abortions, and social-security frauds. Theft by women generally involves theft from an employer by those involved in domestic work or shop work.

Even when involved in large-scale theft, women are likely to be acting in association with male family members and to be involved as receivers of stolen goods rather than as thieves. There are, of course, problems in estimating the actual number of offences from the official statistics but the overall pattern is clear. Because women are less likely to be arrested and convicted for certain offences—something that we look at below—the difference between male and female involvement in crime is exaggerated by the official figures.

The differing patterns of offence do, however, exist. Only in the case of sexual offences is the pattern for male and female involvement more equal, the apparent predominance of women resulting from the fact that their sexual behaviour is more likely to be treated in ways that result in conviction. The sexual double standard means that the authorities normalize much male sexual delinquency, but express moral outrage at female sexual delinquency.

As Smart argues:

- None of these types of offences requires particularly 'masculine' attributes. Strength and force are unnecessary and there is only a low level of skill or expertise required. The women involved have not required training in violence, weapons or tools, or in specialised tasks like safe breaking. On the contrary the skills required can be learnt in everyday experience, and socialization into a delinquent subculture or a sophisticated criminal organisation is entirely unnecessary.

There is growing evidence that members of ethnic minorities in Britain have become more heavily involved with the legal system since the 1960s. They are now especially likely to appear as offenders and, more particularly, as victims of crime and as police suspects. Housebreakings and other household offences show little variation among the various ethnic groups, about one-third of all households being victims of such crime. African Caribbeans, however, are almost twice as likely as whites to be the victims of personal attacks. This is, in part, a consequence of the fact that African Caribbeans live, disproportionately, in inner-city areas where such crimes are particularly likely to take place.

However, their experiences also have a racially motivated character. The growing victimization of black and Asian people reflects a real growth in racial violence and racist attacks by members of the white population. While criminal acts carried out during the urban riots of the 1980s often had a racial aspect to them, blacks and Asians are far more likely to be the targets of racial crimes than they are to commit them. There has, nevertheless, been a growing involvement of young African Caribbeans in many kinds of street crime. The police hold to a widely shared prejudice that African Caribbeans, in particular, are heavily involved in crime and that special efforts need to be taken to control them. Many studies have shown the racism inherent in police actions that stop black people in the street and subject them to closer scrutiny than other members of the population.

African Caribbeans are more likely than whites, and members of other ethnic minorities, to be approached by the police on suspicion, to be prosecuted, and to be sentenced. This is reflected in a growing hostility of ethnic minorities towards the police, who are often seen as racists rather than as neutral defenders of law and order. Offences carried out by men from the middle classes are generally described as white-collar crime. This term originally referred to crimes and civil-law infractions committed by those in non-manual employment as part of their work.

It is now used a little more broadly to refer to three categories of offence:

1. Occupational crimes of the affluent: offences committed by the relatively affluent and prosperous in the course of their legitimate business or profession. Examples are theft from an employer, financial frauds, and insider dealing in investment companies.
2. Organizational crimes: offences committed by organizations and businesses themselves—that is, by employees acting in their official capacities on behalf of the organization. Examples are non-payment or under-payment of VAT or Corporation Tax, and infringements of health and safety legislation leading to accidents or pollution.
3. Any other crimes committed by the relatively affluent that tend to be treated differently from those of the less affluent. An example is tax evasion, which is treated differently from social-security fraud.

The concept of white-collar crime, then, is far from clear-cut. It does, however, help to highlight the class basis of much crime. The number of people involved in whitecollar crimes is barely apparent from the official statistics, as many go unrecorded. Its status as hidden crime, however, is paradoxical in view of its financial significance.

It was estimated that the total cost of reported fraud alone in 1985 was £2,113 million, twice the amount accounted for by reported theft, burglary, and robbery. Official estimates suggest that the actual cost of all fraud in Britain in 2003 was £13,800 million. The relatively low representation of women in recorded crime is the main reason why female criminality has been so little researched. Lombroso and Ferrero set out a deterministic theory, based on the claimed peculiarities of female biology, which still has some influence in the late 1990s.

They held that women were less highly evolved than men and so were relatively 'primitive' in character. They were less involved in crime, however, because their biology predisposed them to a passive and more conservative way of life. They were, however, weak willed, and Lombroso and Ferrero saw the involvement of many women in crime as resulting from their having been led on by others.

The female drift into crime was a consequence of their weak and fickle character. The extreme position set out by Lombroso and Ferrero has long been abandoned, but many criminologists do still resort to biological assumptions when trying to explain female criminality.

Pollak, for example, held that women are naturally manipulative and deceitful, instigating crimes that men undertake. What such theories fail to consider is that, if women do indeed have lower rates of criminality, this may more usefully and accurately be explained in terms of the cultural influences that shape sex–gender roles and the differing opportunities available to men and to women. Like the crimes of women, the crimes of the affluent have been little researched.

Early discussions of white-collar crime were intended as criticisms of the orthodox assumption that criminality was caused by poverty or deprivation. Those who carried out thefts as part of a successful business career, Sutherland argued, could not be seen as acting out of economic necessity. Sutherland's own account stressed that white-collar crime was learned behaviour and that, in this respect, it was no different from other forms of criminality.

All crime, he held, resulted from the effects of 'differential association' on learning: those who interact more frequently with others whose attitudes are favourable to criminal actions are themselves more likely to engage in criminal acts. This implies that patterns of conformity among the affluent and the deprived, among men and among women, are to be understood in the context of their wider role commitments and the interactions in which they are involved with their role partners.

Those who are predisposed to see criminal actions as appropriate will, if the structure of opportunities allows it, drift into crime. There is no need to assume that women are fundamentally different from men, or that the working classes are fundamentally different from the middle classes.

THE FUNCTIONS OF CRIME CONTROL

According to control theorists, people do not engage in crime because of the controls or restraints placed on them. These controls may be viewed as barriers to crime—they refer to those factors that prevent them from engaging in crime. So while strain and social learning theory focus on those factors that push or lead the individual into crime, control theory focuses on the factors that restrain the individual from engaging in crime. Control theory goes on to argue that people differ in their level of control or in the restraints they face to crime. These differences explain differences in crime: some people are freer to engage in crime than others.

Control theories describe the major types of social control or the major restraints to crime. The control theory of Travis Hirschi dominates the literature, but Gerald Patterson and associates, Michael Gottfredson and Travis Hirschi, and Robert Sampson and John Laub have extended Hirschi's theory in important ways. Rather than describing the different versions of control theory, an integrated control theory that draws on all of their insights is presented.

This integrated theory lists three major types of control: direct control, stake in conformity, and internal control. Each type has two or more components.

Direct control. When most people think of control they think of direct control: someone watching over people and sanctioning them for crime. Such control may be exercised by family members, school officials, coworkers, neighbourhood residents, police, and others. Family members, however, are the major source of direct control given their intimate relationship with the person. Direct control has three components: setting rules, monitoring behaviour, and sanctioning crime.

Direct control is enhanced to the extent that family members and others provide the person with clearly defined rules that prohibit criminal behaviour and that limit the opportunities and temptations for crime. These rules may specify such things as who the person may associate with and the activities in which they can and cannot engage.

Direct control also involves monitoring the person's behaviour to ensure that they comply with these rules and do not engage in crime. Monitoring may be direct or indirect. In direct monitoring, the person is under the direct surveillance of a parent or other conventional "authority figure."

In indirect monitoring, the parent or authority figure does not directly observe the person but makes an effort to keep tabs on what they are doing. The parent, for example, may ask the juvenile where he or she is going, may periodically call the juvenile, and may ask others about the juvenile's behaviour. People obviously differ in the extent to which their behaviour is monitored. Finally, direct control involves effectively sanctioning crime when it occurs. Effective sanctions are consistent, fair, and not overly harsh. Level of direct control usually emerges as an important cause of crime in most studies. Stake in conformity. The efforts to directly control behaviour are a major restraint to crime. These efforts, however, are more effective with some people than with others. For example, all juveniles are subject to more or less the same direct controls at school: the same rules, the same monitoring, and the same sanctions if they deviate. Yet some juveniles are very responsive to these controls while others commit deviant acts on a regular basis. One reason for this is that some juveniles have more to lose by engaging in deviance. These juveniles have what has been called a high "stake in conformity," and they do not want to jeopardize that stake by engaging in deviance.

So one's stake in conformity—that which one has to lose by engaging in crime—functions as another major restraint to crime. Those with a lot to lose will be more fearful of being caught and sanctioned and so will be less likely to engage in crime. People's stake in conformity has two components: their emotional attachment to conventional others and their actual or anticipated investment in conventional society.If people have a strong emotional attachment to conventional others, like family members and teachers, they have more to lose by engaging in crime. Their crime may upset people they care about, cause them to think badly of them, and possibly disrupt their relationship with them. Studies generally confirm the importance of this bond. Individuals who report that they love and respect their parents and other conventional figures usually commit fewer crimes. Individuals who do not care about their parents or others, however, have less to lose by engaging in crime.

A second major component of people's stake in conformity is their investment in conventional society. Most people have put a lot of time and energy into conventional activities, like "getting an education, building up a business, [and] acquiring a reputation for virtue". And they have been rewarded for their efforts, in the form of such things as good grades, material possessions, and a good reputation. Individuals may also expect their efforts to reap certain rewards in the future; for example, one might anticipate getting into college or professional school, obtaining a good job, and living in a nice house. In short, people have a large investment—both actual and anticipated—in conventional society. People do not want to jeopardize that investment by engaging in delinquency.

Internal control. People sometimes find themselves in situations where they are tempted to engage in crime and the probability of external sanction (and the loss of those things they value) is low. Yet many people still refrain from crime. The reason is that they are high in internal control. They are able to restrain themselves from engaging in crime. Internal control is a function of their beliefs regarding crime and their level of self-control. Most people believe that crime is wrong and this belief acts as a major restraint to crime. The extent to which people believe that crime is wrong is at least partly a function of their level of direct control and their stake in conformity: were they closely attached to their parents and did their parents attempt to teach them that crime is wrong? If not, such individuals may form an *amoral orientation* to crime: they believe that crime is neither good nor bad. As a consequence, their beliefs do not restrain them from engaging in crime. Their beliefs do not propel or push them into crime; they do not believe that crime is good. Their amoral beliefs simply free them to pursue their needs and desires in the most expedient way. Rather then being taught that crime is good, control theorists argue that some people are simply not taught that crime is bad.

Finally, some people have personality traits that make them less responsive to the above controls and less able to restrain themselves from acting on their immediate desires. For example, if someone provokes them, they are more likely to get into a fight. Or if someone offers them drugs at a party, they are more likely to accept. They do not stop to consider the long-term consequences of their behaviour. Rather, they simply focus on the immediate, short-term benefits or pleasures of criminal acts. Such individuals are said to be low in "self-control."

Self-control is indexed by several personality traits. According to Gottfredson and Hirschi, "people who lack self control will tend to be impulsive, insensitive, physical (as opposed to mental), risk-taking, short-sighted, and nonverbal". It is claimed that the major cause of low self-control is "ineffective child-rearing." In particular, low self-control is more likely to result when parents do not establish a strong emotional bond with their children and do not properly monitor and sanction their children for delinquency. Certain theorists also claim that some of the traits characterizing low self-control have biological as well as social causes.

Gottfredson and Hirschi claim that one's level of self-control is determined early in life and is then quite resistant to change. Further, they claim that low self-control is the central cause of crime; other types of control and other causes of crime are said to be unimportant once level of self-control is established. Data do indicate that low self-control is an important cause of crime. Data, however, suggest that the self-control does vary over the life course and that other causes of crime are also important. For example, Sampson and Laub demonstrate that delinquent adolescents who enter satisfying marriages and obtain stable jobs (*i.e.*, develop a strong stake in conformity) are less likely to engage in crime as adults.

In sum, crime is less likely when others try to directly control the person's behaviour, when the person has a lot to lose by engaging in crime, and when the person tries to control his or her own behaviour. Crime control model refers to a theory of criminal justice which places emphasis on reducing the crime in society through increased police and prosecutorial powers and. In contrast, The "due process model" focuses on individual liberties and rights and is concerned with limiting the powers of government. Crime control prioritizes the power of the government to protect society, with less emphasis on individual liberties.

Those who take a stance favoring tough approaches to crime and criminals may be characterized as proponents of crime control, while those who seek to curb government intrusions and harassment of suspects favour a due process control model.

A THEORY OF CRIME PROBLEMS

The crime triangle (also known as the problem analysis triangle) comes striaght out of one of the main theories of environmental criminology-routine activity theory. "Routine Activity Theory" provides a simple and powerful insight into the causes of crime problems. At its heart is the idea that in the absence of effective controls, offenders will prey upon attractive targets. To have a crime, a motivated offender must come to the same place as an attractive target. For property crimes the target is a thing or an object. For personal crimes the target is a person. If an attractive target is never in the same place as a motivate offender, the target will not be taken, damaged, or assaulted. Also, there are controllers whose presence can prevent crime. If the controllers are absent, or present but powerlessness, crime is possible.

First, consider people who are influential in the lives of potential offenders. In the case of juveniles these might be parents, close relatives, siblings, peers, teachers, coaches, and other similarly placed individuals. In the case of adults these people may include intimate partners, close friends, relatives, and sometimes their children. These people are called "handlers" in routine activity theory. Crimes will take place where handlers are absent, weak, or corrupt. Next consider targets, or victims. Guardians try to protect targets from theft and damage and potential victims from attack and assault. Formal guardians include the police, security guards, and others whose job is to protect people and property from crime. Informal guardians include neighbours, friends, and others who happen to be in the same place as the attractive target. Parents, teachers, peers and others close to potential victims are also potential guardians. A target with an effective guardian is less likely to be attacked by a potential offender than a target without a guardian. If the guardian is absent, weak, or corrupt little protection is provided the target.

Finally, consider places. Someone owns every location and ownership confers certain rights to regulate access to the site and behaviours of people using the site. The owner and the agents of the owner (*e.g.*, employees) look after the place and the people using the place. Owners and their agents are called place managers. Place managers control the behaviour of offenders and potential victims. Examples of place manager include merchants, lifeguards, parking lot attendants, recreation and park workers, janitors, and motel clerks. In the presence of an effective place manager, crime is less likely than when the manager is absent, weak or corrupt.

All of the people in this theory use tools to help accomplish their criminal or crime control objectives. Tools that gang members use may include spray paint cans, guns, and cars. Offenders without access to tools are less likely to be able escape handlers, enter unauthorized places, and overcome victims, guardians, and managers. Guardians may use light to increase surveillance, engraving devices to mark property, and other devices to help reduce the chances of victimization. Place managers can use gates, fences, signs and other tools to regulate conduct. With effective tools handlers, victims, guardians, and managers will have a greater chance of keeping crimes from occurring. The tools used are often highly specific to the crime in question. The tools an offender needs for a burglary (*e.g.*, a screw driver) are likely to be different from those needed for a robbery (*e.g.*, a gun), for example.

The relationship of the actors, places and tools is depicted in the problem triangle. Problems occur when offenders are at the same places as targets, without any effective controller. If one or more of the controllers is present, however, the chances of crime are greatly reduced. The effectiveness of the people involved will depend, in part on the tools they have available. Adding or subtracting various elements in this model will alter the chances of crime.

The presence of attractive targets, weak handlers, ineffective guardianship, and indifferent management is not randomly distributed across places. Offenders do not wander aimlessly across the landscape. Like everyone else, offenders have routine behaviours that take them away from handlers and lead them to discover places with attractive targets. Potential victims also follow routines that separate them from effective guardians in places with weak management. The spatial ordering of crime opportunities and the routines of offenders and victims creates many of the crime problems we see.

This theory of crime also suggests ways of preventing these problems. The questions in the guide and the responses list are organized around each of the eleven elements. The guide asks problem solvers a series of questions about offenders, handlers, targets, guardians, places, managers, and the tools used by each. The answers to these questions, which will vary by problem, suggest possible responses. Thus, responses are problem specific (for example, a residential burglary problem in a neighbourhood of single family residences may require different responses than one in a large apartment complex, and a residential burglary problem in an apartment complex near a heavily travelled highway may require different responses than one in an apartment in a more isolated location).

Though responses are problem specific, there are often several possible responses to any specific problem. Few problems will have unique responses. Instead, the special insight of problem solvers is to choose among possible responses that can be implemented. Further, if one approach does not work, other backup responses are usually possible. Though it is possible to use the guide and responses list without understanding the basics of routine activity theory, knowing this theory helps use the guide and list with greater flexibility. For example, if someone proposes a potential solution to a problem, it is possible to determine if the solution is appropriate. To do this the problem solver identifies which of the 58 possible responses the proposed solution resembles most closely. The problem solver then works backwards from the solution list to the questions. The questions describe the types of answers needed for the solution to fit the problem. If the answers to the questions are consistent with the solution, the proposed solution may be appropriate. In short, the more familiar one is with routine activity theory, the more adaptable the guide and solution list will be. Additional information on routine activity theory can be found in the references cited below, particularly Clarke (1997) and Felson (1994).

4

Challenges of Cyber Crime

DEFINITIONS OF CYBER CRIME

Most reports, guides or publications on cyber crime begin by defining the term "cyber crime". One common definition describes cyber crime as any activity in which computers or networks are a tool, a target or a place of criminal activity. One example for an international approach is Art. 1.1 of the Draft International Convention to Enhance Protection from Cyber Crime and Terrorism (CISAC) that points out that cyber crime refers to acts in respect to cyber systems. Some definitions try to take the objectives or intentions into account and define cyber crime more precisely, defining cyber crime as "computer-mediated activities which are either *illegal or considered illicit* by certain parties and which can be conducted *through global electronic networks*". These more refined descriptions exclude cases where physical hardware is used to commit regular crimes, but they risk excluding crimes that are considered as cyber crime in international agreements such as the "Convention on Cyber crime".

For example, a person who produces USB -devices containing malicious software that destroy data on computers when the device is connected commits a crime as defined by Art. 4 Council of Europe Convention on Cyber crime. However, the act of deleting data using a physical device to copy malicious code has not been committed through global electronic networks and would not qualify as cyber crime under the narrow definition.

This act would only qualify as cyber crime under a definition based on a broader description, including acts such as illegal data interference. This demonstrates that there are considerable difficulties in defining the term "cyber crime". The term "cyber crime" is used to describe a range of offences including traditional computer crimes, as well as network crimes.

As these crimes differ in many ways, there is no single criterion that could include all acts mentioned in the Stanford Draft Convention and the Convention on Cyber crime, whilst excluding traditional crimes that are just committed using hardware. The fact that there is no single definition of "cyber crime" need not be important, as long as the term is not used as a legal term.

TYPOLOGY OF CYBER CRIME

The term "cyber crime" includes a wide variety of crime. Recognised crimes cover a broad range of offences, making it difficult to develop a typology or classification system for cyber crime. An interesting system can be found is found in the Council of Europe Convention on Cyber crime.

The Convention on Cyber crime distinguishes between four different types of offences:

1. Offences against the confidentiality, integrity and availability of computer data and systems;
2. Computer-related offences;
3. Content-related offences; and
4. Copyright-related offences.

This typology is not wholly consistent, as it is not based on a sole criterion to differentiate between categories. Three categories focus on the object of legal protection: "offences against the confidentiality, integrity and availability of computer data and systems"; content-related offences; and copyright-related offences. The fourth category of "computer-related offences" does not focus on the object of legal protection, but on the method. This inconsistency leads to some overlap between categories. In addition, some terms that are used to describe criminal acts (such as 'Cyber terrorism' or 'phishing') cover acts that fall within several categories. Nonetheless, the categories provided by the Convention on Cyber crime serve as a useful basis for discussing the phenomena of cyber crime.

GENERAL CHALLENGES OF CRIMES

RELIANCE ON ICTS

Many everyday communications depend on ICTs and Internet-based services, including VoIP calls or e-mail communications.

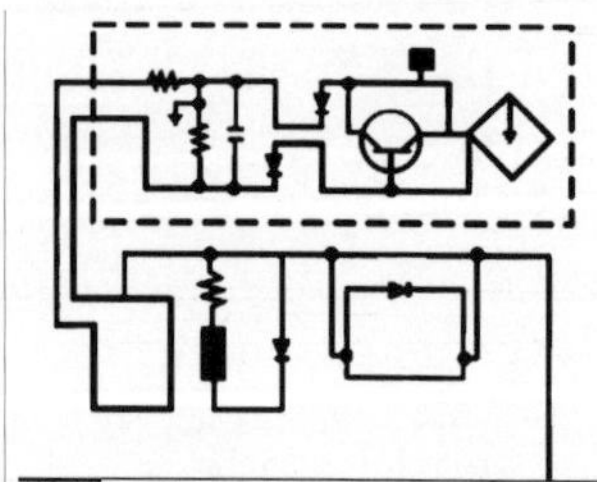

Fig. Information Technology and Electronic Devices are Increasingly Substituting Manual Functions.

ICTs are now responsible for the control and management functions in buildings, cars and aviation services. The supply of energy, water and communication services depend on ICTs. The further integration of ICTs into everyday life is likely to continue. Growing reliance on ICTs makes systems and services more vulnerable to attacks against critical infrastructures. Even short interruptions to services could cause huge financial damages to e-commerce businesses - not only civil communications could be interrupted by attacks; the dependence on ICTs is a major risk for military communications. Existing technical infrastructure has a number of weaknesses, such as the monoculture or homogeneity of operating systems.

Many private users and SMEs use Microsoft's operating system, so offenders can design effective attacks by concentrating on this single target. The dependence of society on ICTs is not limited to the western countries - developing countries also face challenges in preventing attacks against their infrastructure and users. The development of cheaper infrastructure technologies such as WiMAX has enabled developing countries to offer Internet services to more people.

Developing countries can avoid the mistakes of some western countries that concentrated mainly on maximising accessibility, without investing significantly in protection. US experts explained that successful attacks against the official Web site of governmental organisations in Estonia could only take place due to inadequate protection measures. Developing countries have a unique opportunity to integrate security measures early on. This may require greater upfront investments, but the integration of security measures at a later point may prove more expensive in the long run. Strategies must be developed to prevent such attacks and develop countermeasures, including the development and promotion of technical means of protection, as well as adequate and sufficient laws enabling the law enforcement to fight cyber crime effectively.

NUMBER OF USERS

The popularity of the Internet and its services is growing fast, with over 1 billion Internet users worldwide. Computer companies and ISPs are focusing on developing countries with the greatest potential for further growth. In 2005, the number of Internet users in developing countries surpassed the number in industrial nations, while the development of cheap hardware and wireless access will enable even more people to access the Internet.

With the growing number of people connected to the Internet, the number of targets and offenders increases. It is difficult to estimate how many people use the Internet for illegal activities. Even if only 0.1 per cent of users committed crimes, the total number of offenders would be more than one million.

Although Internet usage rates are lower in developing countries, promoting cyber security is not easier, as offenders can commit offences from around the world. The increasing number of Internet users causes difficulties for the law enforcement agencies because it is relatively difficult to automate investigation processes. While a keyword-based search for illegal content can rather easily be carried out, the identification of illegal pictures is more problematic. Hash-value based approaches are for example only successful if the pictures were rated previously, the hash value was stored in a data base, and the picture that was analysed was not modified.

AVAILABILITY OF DEVICES AND ACCESS

Only basic equipment is needed to commit computer crimes, which generally requires the following elements:

- Hardware;
- Software; and
- Internet Access.

With regards to hardware, the power of computers grows continuously. There are a number of initiatives to enable people in developing countries to use ICTs more widely. Criminals can commit serious computer crimes with only cheap or secondhand computer technology - knowledge counts for far more than equipment. The date of the computer technology available has little influences on the use of that equipment to commit cyber crimes. Committing cyber crime can be made easier through specialist software tools.

Offenders can download software tools designed to locate open ports or break password protection. Due to mirroring techniques and peer-topeer exchange, it is difficult to limit the widespread availability of such devices.

The last vital element is Internet access. Although the cost of Internet access is higher in most developing countries than in industrialised countries, the number of Internet users in developing countries is growing rapidly. Offenders will generally not subscribe to an Internet service to limit their chances of being identified, but prefer services they can use without (verified) registration. A typical way of getting access to networks is the so called "wardriving". The term describes the act of driving around searching for accessible wireless networks.

The most common way of access to network connections by offenders are:

- Public Internet terminals;
- Open (wireless) networks;
- Hacked networks; and
- Prepaid services without registration requirements.

Law enforcement agencies are taking action to restrict uncontrolled access to Internet services to avoid criminal abuse of these services. In Italy and China, for example, the use of public Internet terminals requires the identification of users. However, there are arguments against such identification requirements. Although the restriction of access could prevent crimes and facilitate the investigation of law enforcement agencies, such legislation could hinder the growth of the information society and development of e-commerce.

It has been suggested that this limitation on access to the Internet could violate human rights. For example, the European Court has ruled in a number of cases on broadcasting that the right to freedom of expression applies not only to the content of information, but also to the means of transmission or reception. In the case Autronic v. Switzerland, the court held that extensive interpretation is necessary since any restriction imposed on the means necessarily interferes with the right to receive and impart information. If these principles are applied to potential limitations on Internet access, it is possible that such legislative approaches could entail violation of human rights.

AVAILABILITY OF INFORMATION

The Internet has millions of webpages of up-to-date information. Anyone who publishes or maintains a webpage can participate. One example of the success of user-generated platforms is Wikipedia, an online encyclopaedia where anybody can publish. The success of the Internet also depends on powerful search engines that enable the users to search millions of webpages in seconds.

This technology can be used for both legitimate and criminal purposes. "Googlehacking" or "Googledorks" describes the use of complex search engine queries to filter many search results for information on computer security issues.

For example, offenders might aim to search for insecure password protection systems. Reports have highlighted the risk of the use of search engines for illegal purposes. An offender, who plans an attacks can find detailed information on the Internet that explain how to build a bomb by using only those chemicals that are available in regular supermarkets. Although information like this was available even before the Internet was developed, it was however, much more difficult to get access to that information. Today any Internet user can get access to those instructions.

Criminals can also use search engines to analyse targets. A training manual was found during investigations against members of a terrorist group highlighting how useful the Internet is for gathering information on possible targets.

Using search engines, offenders can collect publicly available information (*e.g.,* construction plans from public buildings) that help in their preparations.

It has been reported that insurgents attacking British troops in Afghanistan used satellite images from Google Earth.

MISSING MECHANISMS OF CONTROL

All mass communication networks - from phone networks used for voice phonecalls to the Internet - need central administration and technical standards to ensure operability. The ongoing discussions about Internet governance suggest that the Internet is no different compared with national and even transnational communication infrastructure. The Internet also needs to be governed by laws and law-makers and law enforcement agencies have started to develop legal standards necessitating a certain degree of central control.

The Internet was originally designed as a military network based on a decentralised network architecture that sought to preserve the main functionality intact and in power, even when components of the network were attacked.

As a result, the Internet's network infrastructure is resistant to external attempts at control. It was not originally designed to facilitate criminal investigations or to prevent attacks from inside the network.

Today, the Internet is increasingly used for civil services. With the shift from military to civil services, the nature of demand for control instruments has changed. Since the network is based on protocols designed from military purposes, these central control instruments do not exist and it is difficult to implement them retrospectively, without significant redesign of the network.

The absence of control instruments makes cyber crime investigations very difficult. One example of the problems posed by the absence of control instruments is the ability of users to circumvent filter technology using encrypted anonymous communication services. If access providers block certain Web sites with illegal content (such as child pornography), customers are generally unable to access those Web sites.

But the blocking of illegal content can be avoided, if customers use an anonymous communication server encrypting communications between them and the central server. In this case, providers may be unable to block requests because requests sent as encrypted messages cannot be opened by access providers.

INTERNATIONAL DIMENSIONS

Many data transfer processes affect more than one country. The protocols used for Internet data transfers are based on optimal routing if direct links are temporarily blocked. Even where domestic transfer processes within the source country are limited, data can leave the country, be transmitted over routers outside the territory and be redirected back into the country to its final destination.

Further, many Internet services are based on services from abroad *e.g.,* host providers may offer webspace for rent in one country based on hardware in another. If offenders and targets are located in different countries, cyber crime investigations need the cooperation of law enforcement agencies in all countries affected. National sovereignty does not permit investigations within the territory of different countries without the permission of local authorities. Cyber crime investigations need the support and involvement of authorities in all countries involved. It is difficult to base cooperation in cyber crime on principles of traditional mutual legal assistance. The formal requirements and time needed to collaborate with foreign law enforcement agencies often hinder investigations. Investigations often occur in very short timeframes. Data vital for tracing offences are often deleted after only a short time. This short investigation period is problematic, because traditional mutual legal assistance regime often takes time to organise. The principle of dual criminality also poses difficulties, if the offence is not criminalised in one of the countries involved in the investigation.

Offenders may be deliberately including third countries in their attacks to make investigation more difficult. Criminals may deliberately choose targets outside their own country and acting from countries with inadequate cyber crime legislation. The harmonisation of cyber crime-related laws and international cooperation would help. Two approaches to improve the speed of international cooperation in cyber crime investigations are the G8 24/7 Network and the provisions related to international cooperation in the Council of Europe Convention on Cyber crime.

INDEPENDENCE OF LOCATION AND PRESENCE AT THE CRIME SITE

Criminals need not be present at the same location as the target. As the location of the criminal can be completely different from the crime site, many cyber-offences are transnational. International cyber crime offences take considerable effort and time. Cybercriminals seek to avoid countries with strong cyber crime legislation.

Preventing "safe havens" is one of the key challenges in the fight against cyber crime. While "safe havens" exist, offenders will use them to hamper investigation. Developing countries that have not yet implemented cyber crime legislation may become vulnerable, as criminals may choose to base themselves in these countries to avoid prosecution. Serious offences affecting victims all over the world may be difficult to stop, due to insufficient legislation in the country where offenders are located.

This may lead to pressure on specific countries to pass legislation. One example of this is the "Love Bug" computer worm developed by a suspect in the Philippines in 2000, which infected millions of computers worldwide. Local investigations were hindered by the fact that the development and spreading of malicious software was not at that time adequately criminalised in the Philippines. Another example is Nigeria, which has come under pressure to take action over financial scams distributed by e-mail.

AUTOMATION

One of the greatest advantages of ICTs is the ability to automate certain processes.

Automation has several major consequences:

- It increases the speed of processes;
- It increases the scale and impact of processes;
- It limits the involvement of humans.

Automation reduces the need for cost-intensive manpower, allowing providers to offer services at lower prices. Offenders can use automation to scale up their activities - many millions of unsolicited bulk spam messages can be sent out by automation.

Hacking attacks are often also now automated, with as many as 80 million hacking attacks every day due to the use of software tools that can attack thousands of computer systems in hours.

By automating processes offenders can gain great profit by designing scams that are based on a high number of offences with a relatively low loss for each victim. The lower the single loss is the higher is the chance that the victim will not report the offence.

PETRO VOICE HOLDING
Hot Stock in Momentum play for week

OTC: PHVC
This company is nasdaq bound

Petro Voice in on a roll earning Contrac

This is not a Fly by Night
Real market Cap, Real Earnings

Fig. One Example for Automation Processes is the Dissemination of Spam. Millions of E-mails can be sent out within a Short Period of Time.

Automation of attacks affects developing countries in particular. Due to their limited resources, spam may pose a more serious issue for developing countries than for industrialised countries. The greater numbers of crimes that can be committed through automation pose challenges for law enforcement agencies worldwide, as they will have to be prepared for many more victims within their jurisdictions.

RESOURCES

Modern computer systems that are now coming onto the market are powerful and can be used to extend criminal activities. But it is not just increasing power of single-user computers that poses problems for investigations. Increasing network capacities is also a major issue.

One example is the recent attacks against government Web sites in Estonia. Analysis of the attacks suggests that they were committed by thousands of computers within a "botnet" or group of compromised computers running Programmes under external control. In most cases, computers are infected with malicious software that installs tools allowing perpetrators to take control. Botnets are used to gather information about targets or for high-level attacks.

Over recent years, botnets have become a serious risk for cyber security. The size of a botnet can vary, from a few computers to more than a million computers. Current analysis suggests that up to a quarter of all computers connected to the Internet could be infected with software making them part of a botnet.

Botnets can be used for various criminal activities, including:

- Denial of Service attacks;
- Sending out spam;
- Hacking attacks; and
- File-sharing networks.

Botnets offer a number of advantages for offenders. They increase both the computer and network capacity of criminals. Using thousands of computer systems, criminals can attack computer systems that would be out of reach with only a few computers to lead the attack.

Botnets also make it more difficult to trace the original offender, as the initial traces only lead to the member of the botnets.

As criminals control more powerful computer systems and networks, the gap between the capacities of investigating authorities and those under control of criminals is getting wider.

SPEED OF DATA EXCHANGE PROCESSES

The transfer of an e-mail between countries takes only a few seconds. This short period of time is one reason for the success of the Internet, as e-mails have eliminated the time for the physical transport of a message.

However, this rapid transfer leaves little time for law enforcement agencies to investigate or collect evidence. Traditional investigations take much longer. One example is the exchange of child pornography. In the past, pornographic videos were handed over or transported to buyers.

Both the handover and transport gave law enforcement agencies the opportunity to investigate. The main difference between the exchange of child pornography on and off the Internet is transportation. When offenders use the Internet, movies can be exchanged in seconds. E-mails also demonstrate the importance of immediate response tools that can be used immediately. For tracing and identifying suspects, investigators often need access to data that may be deleted shortly after transfer. A very short response time by the investigative authorities is often vital for a successful investigation.

Without adequate legislation and instruments allowing investigators to act immediately and prevent data from being deleted, an effective fight against cyber crime may not be possible.

"Quick freeze procedures" and 24/7 network points are examples for tools that can speed up investigations. Data retention legislation also aims to increase the time available for law enforcement agencies to carry out investigations. If the data necessary to trace offenders are preserved for a length of time, law enforcement agencies have a better chance of identifying suspects successfully.

SPEED OF DEVELOPMENT

The Internet is constantly undergoing development. The creation of a graphical user interface (WWW) marked the start of its dramatic expansion, as previous command-based services were less user-friendly. The creation of the WWW has enabled new applications, as well as new crimes - law enforcement agencies are struggling to keep up.

Further developments continue, notably with:

- Online games; and
- Voice over IP (VoIP) communications.

Online games are ever more popular, but it is unclear whether law enforcement agencies can successfully investigate and prosecute offences committed in this virtual world. The switch from traditional voice calls to Internet telephony also presents new challenges for law enforcement agencies. The techniques and routines developed by law enforcement agencies to intercept classic phone calls do not generally apply to VoIP communications. The interception of traditional voice calls is usually carried out through telecom providers. Applying the same principle to VoIP, law enforcement agencies would operate through ISPs and service providers supplying VoIP services. However, if the service is based on peer-to-peer technology, service providers may generally be unable to intercept communications, as the relevant data are transferred directly between the communicating partners.

Therefore, new techniques are needed. New hardware devices with network technology are also developing rapidly. The latest home entertainment systems turn TVs into Internet Access Points, while more recent mobile handsets store data and connect to the Internet via wireless networks.

USB (Universal Serial Bus) memory devices with more than 1 GB capacity have been integrated into watches, pens and pocket knives. Law enforcement agencies need to take these developments into account in their work - it is essential to educate officers involved in cyber crime investigations continuously, so they are uptodate with the latest technology and able to identify relevant hardware and any specific devices that need to be seized. Another challenge is the use of wireless access points. The expansion of wireless Internet access in developing countries is an opportunity, as well as a challenge for law enforcement agencies. If offenders use wireless access-points that do not require registration, it is more challenging for law enforcement agencies to trace offenders, as investigations lead only to access points.

CHALLENGES IN DRAFTING NATIONAL CRIMINAL LAWS

Proper legislation is the foundation for the investigation and prosecution of cyber crime. However, law-makers must continuously respond to Internet developments and monitor the effectiveness of existing provisions, especially given the speed of developments in network technology.

Historically, the introduction of computer-related services or Internet-related technologies gave rise to new forms of crime, soon after the technology was introduced. One example is the development of computer networks in the 1970s – the first unauthorised access to computer networks occurred shortly afterwards. Similarly, the first software offences appeared soon after the introduction of personal computers in the 1980s, when these systems were used to copy software products. It takes time to update national criminal law to prosecute new forms of online cyber crime – some countries have not yet finished with this adjustment process. Offences that have been criminalised under national criminal law need to be reviewed and updated – for example, digital information must have equivalent status as traditional signatures and printouts. Without the integration of cyber crime-related offences, violations cannot be prosecuted. The main challenge for national criminal legal systems is the delay between the recognition of potential abuses of new technologies and necessary amendments to the national criminal law. This challenge remains as relevant and topical as ever as the speed of network innovation accelerates. Many countries are working hard to catch up with legislative adjustments.

In general, the adjustment process has three steps: Adjustments to national law must start with the recognition of an abuse of new technology. Specific departments are needed within national law enforcement agencies, which are qualified to investigate potential cyber crimes. The development of computer emergency response teams (CERTs), computer incident response teams (CIRTs), computer security incident response teams (CSIRTs) and other research facilities have improved the situation.

The second step is the identification of gaps in the penal code. To ensure effective legislative foundations, it is necessary to compare the status of criminal legal provisions in the national law with requirements arising from the new kinds of criminal offences. In many cases, existing laws may be able to cover new varieties of existing crimes (*e.g.,* laws addressing forgery may just as easily be applies to electronic documents). The need for legislative amendments is limited to those offences that are omitted or insufficiently covered by the national law. The third step is the drafting of new legislation. Based on experience, it may be difficult for national authorities to execute the drafting process for cyber crime without international cooperation, due to the rapid development of network technologies and their complex structures. Drafting cyber crime legislation separately may result in significant duplication and waste of resources and it is also necessary to monitor the development of international standards and strategies. Without the international harmonisation of national criminal legal provisions, the fight against trans-national cyber crime will run into serious difficulties due to inconsistent or incompatible national legislations. Consequently, international attempts to harmonise different national penal laws are increasingly important. National law can greatly benefit from the experience of other countries and international expert legal advice.

NEW OFFENCES

In most cases, crimes committed using ICTs are not new crimes, but scams modified to be committed online. One example is fraud – there is not much difference between someone sending a letter with the intention to mislead another person and an e-mail with the same intention. If fraud is already a criminal offence, adjustment of national law may not be necessary to prosecute such acts. The situation is different, if the acts performed are no longer addressed by existing laws.

In the past, some countries had adequate provisions for regular fraud, but were unable to deal with offences where a computer system was influenced, rather than a human. For these countries, it has been necessary to adopt new laws criminalising computer-related fraud, in addition to the regular fraud. Various examples show how the extensive interpretation of existing provisions cannot substitute for the adoption of new laws.

Apart from adjustment for well-known scams, law-makers must continuously analyse new and developing types of cyber crime to ensure their effective criminalisation.

One example of a cyber crime that has not yet been criminalised in all countries is theft and fraud in computer and online games. For a long time, discussions about online games focused on youth protection issues (*e.g.,* the requirement for verification of age) and illegal content (*e.g.,* access to child pornography in the Online game "Second Life").

New criminal activities are constantly being discovered – virtual currencies in online games may be "stolen" and traded in auction platforms. Some virtual currencies have a value in terms of real currency (based on an exchange rate), giving the crime a 'real' dimension. Such offences may not be prosecutable in all countries. In order to prevent safe havens for offenders, it is vital to monitor developments worldwide.

INCREASING USE OF ICTS AND THE NEED FOR NEW INVESTIGATIVE INSTRUMENTS

Offenders use ICTs in various ways in the preparation and execution of their offences. Law enforcement agencies need adequate instruments to investigate potential criminal acts. Some instruments (such as data retention) could interfere with the rights of innocent Internet users. If the severity of the criminal offence is out of proportion with the intensity of interference, the use of investigative instruments could be unjustified or unlawful.

As a result, some instruments that could improve investigation have not yet been introduced in a number of countries. The introduction of investigative instruments is always the result of a trade-off between the advantages for law enforcement agencies and interference with the rights of innocent Internet users.

It is essential to monitor ongoing criminal activities to evaluate whether threat levels change. Often, the introduction of new instruments has been justified on the basis of the "fight against terrorism", but this is more of an far-reaching motivation, rather than a specific justification *per se*.

DEVELOPING PROCEDURES FOR DIGITAL EVIDENCE

Especially due the low costs compared to the storage of physical documents, the number of digital documents is increasing. The digitalisation and emerging use of ICT has a great impact of procedures related to the collection of evidence and its use in court. As a consequence of the development digital evidence was introduced as a new source of evidence. It is defined as any data stored or transmitted using computer technology that supports the theory of how an offence occurred. Handling digital evidence is accompanied with unique challenges and requires specific procedures. One of the most difficult aspects is to maintain the integrity of the digital evidence. Digital data is highly fragile and can easily be deleted or modified. This is especially relevant for information stored in the system memory RAM that is automatically deleted when the system is shut down and therefore requires special preservation techniques.

In addition, new developments can have great impact on dealing with digital evidence. An example is cloud-computing. In the past investigators were able to focus on the suspects premise while searching for computer data. Today they need to take into consideration that digital information might be stored abroad and can only be accessed remotely, if necessary. Digital evidence plays an important role in various phases of cyber crime investigations.

It is in general possible to separate between four phases:

1. Identification of the relevant evidence;
2. Collection and preservation of the evidence;
3. Analysis of computer technology and digital evidence; and,
4. Presentation of the evidence in court.

In addition to the procedures that relate to the presentation of digital evidence in court, the ways in which digital evidence is collected requires special attention. The collection of digital evidence is linked to computer forensics. The term 'computer forensics' describes the systematic analysis of IT equipment with the purpose of searching for digital evidence. With regard to the fact that the amount of data stored in digital format constantly increases, highlights the logistic challenges of such investigations. Approaches to automated forensic procedures by, for example, using hash-value based searches for known child pornography images or a keyword search therefore play an important role in addition to manual investigations.

Depending on the requirement of the specific investigation, computer forensics could for example include the following:

- Analysing the hardware and software used by a suspect;
- Supporting investigators in identifying relevant evidence;
- Recovering deleted files;
- Decrypting files; and,
- Identifying Internet users by analysing traffic data.

COMPUTER RELATED CRIMES

This category covers a number of offences that need a computer system to be committed.

Unlike previous categories, these broad offences are often not as stringent in the protection of legal principles, including:

- Computer-related fraud;
- Computer-related forgery, phishing and identity theft; and
- Misuse of devices.

FRAUD AND COMPUTER RELATED FRAUD

Computer-related fraud is one of the most popular crimes on the Internet, as it enables the offender to use automation and software tools to mask criminals' identities. Automation enables offenders to make large profits from a number of small acts. One strategy used by offenders is to ensure that each victim's financial loss is below a certain limit. With a 'small' loss, victims are less likely to invest time and energy in reporting and investigating such crimes. One example of such a scam is the Nigeria Advanced Fee Fraud.

Although these offences are carried out using computer technology, most criminal law systems categorise them not as computer-related offences, but as regular fraud. The main distinction between computer-related and traditional fraud is the target of the fraud. If offenders try to influence a person, the offence is generally recognised as fraud. Where offenders target computer or data-processing systems, offences are often categorised as computer-related fraud. Those criminal law systems that cover fraud, but do not yet include the manipulation of computer systems for fraudulent purposes.

Online Auction Fraud

Online auctions are now one of the most popular e-commerce services. In 2006, goods worth more than USD 20 billion were sold on eBay, the world's largest online auction marketplace. Buyers can access varied or specialist niche goods from around the world. Sellers enjoy a worldwide audience, stimulating demand and boosting prices. Offenders committing crimes over auction platforms can exploit the absence of face-to-face contact between sellers and buyers. The difficulty of distinguishing between genuine users and offenders has resulted in auction fraud being among the most popular of cyber crimes.

The two most common scams include:

1. Offering non-existent goods for sale and requesting buyers to pay prior to delivery; or
2. Buying goods and asking for delivery, without intention to pay.

In response, auction providers have developed protection systems such as the feedback/comments system. After each transaction, buyer and sellers leave feedback for use by other users as neutral information about the reliability of sellers/buyers. In this case, "reputation is everything" and without an adequate number of positive comments, it is harder for offenders to persuade targets to either pay for non-existent goods or, conversely, to send out goods without receiving payment first. However, criminals have responded and circumvented this protection through using accounts from third parties. In this scam called "account takeover", offenders try to get hold of user names and passwords of legitimate users to buy or sell goods fraudulently, making identification of offenders more difficult.

Advance Fee Fraud

In Advanced Fee Fraud, offenders send out e-mails asking for recipients' help in transferring large amounts of money to third parties and promise them a percentage, if they agree to process the transfer using their personal accounts. The offenders then ask them to transfer a small amount to validate their bank account data (based on a similar perception as lotteries – respondents may be willing to incur a small but certain loss, in exchange for a large but unlikely gain) or just send bank account data directly.

Once they transfer the money, they will never hear from the offenders again. If they send their bank account information, offenders may use this information for fraudulent activities. Evidence suggests that thousands of targets reply to e-mails. Current researches show, that despite various information campaigns and initiatives advance fee frauds are still growing – with regard to the number of victims as well as with regard to the total losses.

COMPUTER RELATED FORGERY

Computer related forgery describes the manipulation of digital documents - for example, by:

- Creating a document that appears to originate from a reliable institution;
- Manipulating electronic images (for example, pictures used as evidence in court); or
- Altering text documents.

The falsification of e-mails includes the scam of "phishing" which is a serious challenge for law enforcement agencies worldwide. "Phishing" seeks to make targets disclose personal/secret information. Often, offenders send out e-mails that look like communications from legitimate financial institutions used by the target. The e-mails are designed in a way that it is difficult for targets to identify them as fake e-mails. The e-mail asks recipient to disclose and/or verify certain sensitive information. Many victims follow the advice and disclose information enabling offenders to make online transfers, etc. In the past, prosecutions involving computer-related forgery were rare, because most legal documents were tangible documents. Digital documents play an ever more important role and are used more often. The substitution of classic documents by digital documents is supported by legal means for their use *e.g.*, by legislation recognising digital signatures.

with the hope, that the term will be ex-
them to transfer a rather small amount.

Fig. Compared to the Falsification of Classic Documents, Electronic Data can Rather Easily be Manipulated. Technical Solutions Such as Digital Signatures can Prevent Unrecognised Manipulations.

Criminals have always tried to manipulate documents. With digital forgeries, digital documents can now be copied without loss of quality and are easily manipulated. For forensic experts, it is difficult to prove digital manipulations, unless technical protection is used to protect a document from being falsified.

IDENTITY THEFT

The term identity theft–that is neither consistently defined nor consistently used–describes the criminal act of fraudulently obtaining and using another person's identity. These acts can be carried out without the help of technical means as well as online by using Internet technology.

In general the offence described as identity theft contains three different phases:

1. In the first phase the offender obtains identity-related information. This part of the offence can for example be carried out by using malicious software or phishing attacks.
2. The second phase is characterised by interaction with identity-related information prior to the use of those information within criminal offences. An example is the sale of identity-related information. Credit card records are for example sold for up to 60 US dollars.
3. The third phase is the use of the identity-related information in relation with a criminal offence. In most cases the access to identity-related data enables the perpetrator to commit further crimes. The perpetrators are therefore not focusing on the set of data itself but the ability to use them in criminal activities. Examples for such offence can be the falsification of identification documents or credit card fraud.

The methods used to obtain data in phase one cover a wide range of acts. The offender can use physical methods and for example steal computer storage devices with identity-related data, searching trash ("dumpster diving") or mail theft. In addition they can use search engines to find identity-related data. "Googlehacking" or "Googledorks" are terms that describe the use of complex search engine queries to filter through large amounts of search results for information related to computer security issues as well as person information that can be used in identity theft scams.

One aim of the perpetrator can for example be to search for insecure password protection systems in order to obtain data from this system. Reports highlight the risks that can go along with the legal use of search engines for illegal purposes. Similar problems are reported with regard to file-sharing systems. The United States Congress discussed recently the possibilities of file-sharing systems to obtain personal information that can be abused for identity theft. Apart from that the offenders can make use of insiders, who have access to stored identity-related information, to obtain that information.

The 2007 CSI Computer Crime and Security Survey shows that more than 35 per cent of the respondents attribute a percentage of their organization's losses greater than 20 per cent to insiders. Finally the perpetrators can use social engineering techniques to persuade the victim to disclose personal information. In recent years perpetrators developed effective scams to obtain secret information (e.g. bank account information and credit card data) by manipulating users through social engineering techniques.

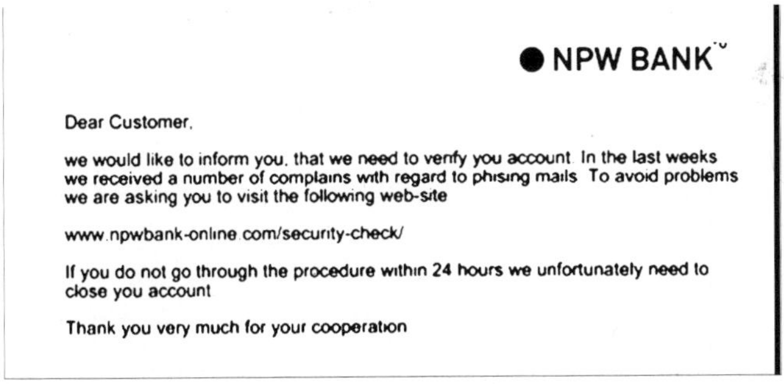

NPW BANK

Dear Customer,

we would like to inform you, that we need to verify you account In the last weeks we received a number of complains with regard to phising mails To avoid problems we are asking you to visit the following web-site

www.npwbank-online com/security-check/

If you do not go through the procedure within 24 hours we unfortunately need to close you account

Thank you very much for your cooperation

Fig. Phishing Mails are Used to Obtain Secret Information (Such as Account Information, Password and Transaction Numbers) from Targets. This Information can be used by Offenders to Commit Offences.

The type of data the perpetrators target varies. The most relevant data are:

- *Social security number (SSN) or passport number*: The SSN that is for example used in the United States is a classical example of a single identity-related data that perpetrators are aiming for. Although the SSN was created to keep an accurate record of earnings it is currently widely used for identification purposes. The perpetrators can use the SSN as well as obtained passport information to open financial accounts, to take over existing financial accounts, establish credit or run up debt.
- *Date of birth, address and phone numbers*: Such data can in general only be used to commit identity theft if they are combined with other pieces of information (*e.g.* the SSN). Having access to additional information like the date of birth and the address can help the perpetrator to circumvent verification processes. One of the greatest dangers related to that information is the fact that it is currently on a large scale available in the Internet – either published voluntarily in one of the various identity-related fora or based on legal requirements as imprint on Web sites.

- *Password for non-financial accounts*: Having access to passwords for accounts allows perpetrators to change the settings of the account and use it for their own purposes. They can for example take over an e-mail account and use it to send out mails with illegal content or take over the account of a user of an auction platform and use the account to sell stolen goods.
- *Password for financial accounts*: Like the SSN information regarding financial accounts is a popular target for identity theft. This includes checking and saving accounts, credit cards, debit cards, and financial planning information. Such information is an important source for an identity thief to commit financial cyber crimes.

Identity theft is a serious and growing problem. Recent figures show that, in the first half of 2004, 3 per cent of United States households fell victim to identity theft. In the United Kingdom, the cost of identity theft to the British economy was calculated at 1.3 billion British pounds every year.

Estimates of losses caused by identity theft in Australia vary from less than 1 billion USD to more than 3 billion USD per year. The 2006 Identity Fraud Survey estimates the losses in the United States at 56.6 billion USD in 2005. Losses may be not only financial, but may also include damage to reputations. In reality, many victims do not report such crimes, while financial institutions often do not wish to publicise customers' bad experiences.

The actual incidence of identity theft is likely to far exceed the number of reported losses. Identity theft is based on the fact that there are few instruments to verify the identity of users over the Internet. It is easier to identify individuals in the real world, but most forms of online identification are more complicated. Sophisticated identification tools (*e.g.,* using biometric information) are costly and not widely used. There are few limits on online activities, making identity theft easy and profitable.

MISUSE OF DEVICES

Cyber crime can be committed using only fairly basic equipment.

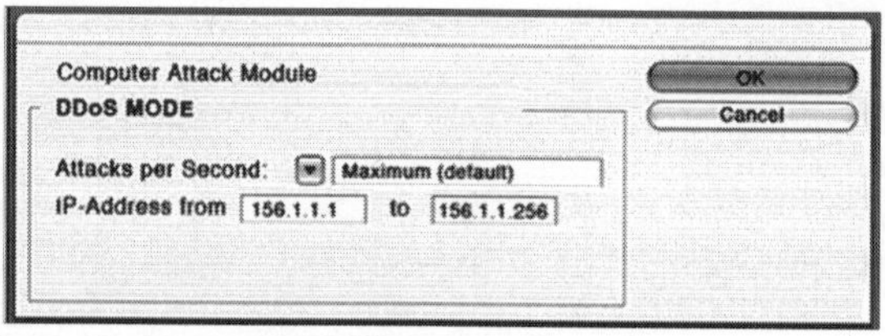

Fig. A Number of Tools are Available that Enable Offenders to Automate attacks against all Computer Systems Using IP-addresses Within a Predefined IP Range. With the Help of Such Software, it is Possible to Attack Hundreds of Computer Systems within a few Hours.

Committing offences such as libel or online fraud needs nothing more than a computer and Internet access and can be carried out from a public Internet café. More sophisticated offences can be committed using specialist software tools. The tools needed to commit complex offences are widely available over the Internet, often without charge. More sophisticated tools cost several thousand dollars. Using these software tools, offenders can attack other computer systems at the press of a button.

Standard attacks are now less efficient, as protection software companies analyse the tools currently available and prepare for standard hacking attacks. High-profile attacks are often individually designed for specific targets.

Software tools exist to:

- Carry out DoS attacks;
- Design computer viruses;
- Decrypt encrypted communication; and
- Illegally access computer systems.

A second generation of software tools has now automated many cyber-scams and enables offenders to carry out multiple attacks within a short time. Software tools also simplify attacks, allowing less experienced computer users to commit cyber crime. Spam-toolkits are available that enable virtually anybody to send out spam e-mails. Software tools are now available that can be used to up- and download files from file-sharing systems.

With greater availability of specially-designed software tools, the number of potential offenders has risen dramatically. Different national and international legislative initiatives are being undertaken to address cyberscam software tools–for example, by criminalising their production, sale or possession.

INTELLECTUAL PROPERTY AND COMPUTER CRIME

Although existing criminal laws will continue to provide effective weapons to combat cyber crimes committed upon the traditional service industries that offer their services and products through e-commerce, Congress and the global community must move swiftly to provide an effective array of substantive laws designed specifically for Internet transactions. That array should include laws and treaties to provide law enforcement and the private sector with the tools essential for the detection and investigation of cyber crime.

Some Congressional attention has focused on peripheral issues such as privacy and encryption, and there are signs that Congress is beginning to address Internet-specific issues. Five pending Congressional bills suggest that Congress is aware that law enforcement must be equipped with adequate resources and remedies to combat cyber crime.

A High Tech Crime Bill was introduced on February 24, 2000 by senators Charles Schumer and John Kyl.

This bill proposes amendments to the computer fraud statute that would include fraudulent acts committed upon "protected computers" in the United States, by persons in foreign countries and would include damage done to computers and computer systems irrespective of property damage losses. That amendment would encompass damage caused by, for example, denial of service attacks.

The proposed bill also would amend 18 U.S.C. § 3123 (c), enabling law enforcement to employ trap and trace devices to assist in the investigation of computer attacks. The Internet Security Act of 2000, introduced in April 2000 by Senator Leahy, would expand the jurisdictional scope of the computer fraud statute to include international hacking. It would amend section 3123 to enable law enforcement to employ trap and trace devices, impose encryption standards, and authorise the prosecution of juvenile hackers. It would also appropriate $25 million for each of the next four fiscal years for law enforcement training Programmes in computer fraud investigations.

Both bills seek to react to recent attacks upon e-Commerce sites, including the denial of service attacks. The Internet Integrity and Critical Infrastructure Protection Act of 2000, introduced on April 13, 2000 by Senator Hatch, co-sponsored by Senator Schumer, would impose criminal penalties for cyber hacking committed by persons under 18 years old, create a National Cyber Crime Technical Support Center to serve as a resource center for federal, state and local law enforcement and assist them in the investigation of computer-related crimes, and provide the implementation of computer crime mutual assistance agreements in order to enable reciprocal assistance for foreign authorities.

Also on April 13, 2000, Senator Hutchinson introduced S. 2451 that would increase the criminal penalties for computer fraud committed in violation of 18 U.S.C. § 1030 and establish a National Commission on Cyber security to study incidents of computer crimes and the need for enhanced methods of combating such crimes. Finally, on May 9, 2000, Congressman Boehlert introduced the Law Enforcement Science and Technology Act of 2000, co-sponsored by Congressman Stupak. This bill would establish an Office of Science and Technology in the Office of Justice Programmes of the Department of Justice.

The mission of that office would be:

- To serve as the national focal point for work on law enforcement technology; and
- To carry out Programmes to improve the safety and effectiveness of, and access to, technology to assist Federal, State and local law enforcement agencies.

The bill would direct the appropriation of $40 million for regional National Law Enforcement and Corrections Technology Centers, $60 million for research and development of forensic technologies and methods to improve crime laboratories, and $20 million for the testing and evaluation of technologies. Additional governmental attention must be focused on extradition and mutual assistance treaties that will enable the United States to prosecute cyber crimes committed by international terrorists and hackers.

IMPACT OF TECHNOLOGY ON ECONOMIC CRIME

The growth of the information age and the globalization of Internet communication and commerce have impacted significantly upon the manner in which economic crimes are committed, the frequency with which those crimes are committed, and the difficulty in apprehending the perpetrators. A recent survey conducted by the Gartner Group of 160 retail companies selling products over the Internet reveals that the amount of credit card fraud is twelve times higher online than in the physical retail world. There is no reason to believe that this figure is unique to the credit card industry. Another recent study indicates that the number of search warrants issued by the federal government for online data has increased 800 per cent over the past few years. Technology has contributed to that increase in four major respects—anonymity, security (or insecurity), privacy (or the lack of it) and globalization. Additionally, technology has provided the medium or opportunity for the commission of traditional crimes.

Criminals continue to make false statements in credit applications submitted over the Internet, bank employees continue to embezzle funds by wire transfer or account takeover, and swindlers continue to misrepresent products at auction sites over the Internet. However, it is the widespread use of technology and the Internet for business transactions and communications, and the confluence of anonymity, security, privacy and globalization that have exposed the public and private sectors to an alarming new array of cyber attacks. In addition to their inability to prevent such attacks, both government and the private sector lack effective enforcement tools and remedies to bring the perpetrators to justice. Technology and the Internet have contributed to the growth of economic crime in each of the identified industries in similar ways.

Anonymity enables the criminal to submit fraudulent online applications for bank loans, credit card accounts, insurance coverage, brokerage accounts, and health care coverage or to construct a counterfeit web site in order to establish an inflated value for publicly traded stock in order to sell the stock at a falsely inflated price ("pump and dump" schemes). Anonymity also enables employees to pilfer corporate assets. For example, bank employees can embezzle money through electronic fund transfers and employees of credit card issuers can capture account numbers and sell them to outsiders, electronically transferring the account numbers to the coconspirators.

Further, anonymity provides enhanced opportunities for two types of perpetrators—the organised crime mobster and the teenage hacker. Security, or the lack of it, enables criminal hackers to disrupt e-commerce in several ways. They can engage in denial of service attacks, compromise payment systems in online banking, penetrate web sites and extract credit card account numbers for resale or as ransom for the extortion of cash from the card issuer, or hijack a web site for the purpose of stealing the identity of the e-commerce merchant, directing the proceeds of sales to the hijacker. Privacy protections enable thieves to take advantage of the benefits of anonymity, while hampering the efforts of law enforcement and private sector fraud investigators to track the thieves. Lastly, the Internet enables communication and commerce to occur beyond or without borders, presenting significant problems in the prevention, investigation and enforcement of those crimes.

BANKING

There is no pending legislation that specifically addresses frauds in connection with online banking. The Internet provides fertile ground for those intending to defraud financial institutions. Because the online customer is anonymous, the risk of fraud is greater. Projected increases in the volume of online transactions and repeal of the Glass-Steagall Act, which has expanded the types of institutions that may provide banking services, could increase the exposure to cyber attack. Congressional focus is currently on cyber laundering, specifically the electronic transfer of funds into U.S. banks from sources outside the country and subsequent transfers by those banks to cyber laundering havens. On the regulatory side, the Federal Trade Commission and other agencies have proposed regulations dealing with the privacy of financial data, the circumstances when disclosure may be made, and the conditions precedent to such disclosures.

Those regulations, which are scheduled to take effect on November 13, 2000, require financial institutions to provide privacy notices to consumers, limit the disclosure of Non-public personal information to Non-affiliated third parties, and allow consumers to opt-out of certain restrictions. The Electronic Signature in Global and National Commerce Act, which became law on July 1, 2000, is a major effort to facilitate the consummation of contracts, including agreements with banking and financial institutions, electronically. While the Act facilitates e-Commerce, it provides yet another opportunity for the theft of a significant aspect of one's identity—the signature. The Act contains no provision imposing criminal sanctions for the theft or piracy of one's signature. The access device statute should be amended to include electronic and digital signatures as a "means of identification. Additional legislation is essential to reduce the risks presented by anonymity and database insecurity, including prescribed authentication procedures and encryption protections.

CREDIT CARD

The use of credit cards for online retail purchases, as well as for online gambling and to gain access to pornography and child pornography sites, is expected to increase exponentially. Online transactions are not conducted face-to-face; therefore, the merchant cannot identify the customer in the traditional manner. The increased volume of online transactions and the absence of face-to-face interaction provide greater opportunity for fraud, including identity theft for the purpose of conducting an online transaction.

While substantive laws provide ample redress for the criminal use of credit cards (and debit cards) in cyberspace, the implementation of new technologies for credit purchases, such as smart cards and electronic wallets, may raise issues regarding the applicability of existing criminal statutes. Those statutes should be amended to prohibit the theft or fraudulent sale, distribution or possession of a counterfeit, stolen or fictitious account number regardless of whether that account number is used in connection with a plastic card, electronic wallet or other form of digital storage.

The amendment should also state that the crime applies to the theft by computer of account numbers or information that could be used to identify an account number. There is currently no pending legislation that would regulate the use of credit cards for online transactions. However, S. 699, the Telemarketing Fraud and Seniors Protection Act, would amend the wire fraud statute to include schemes or artifices to defraud, perpetrated via Internet communications. Because credit card fraud can be prosecuted under this statute, the proposed legislation would enhance significantly the enforcement arsenal for credit card fraud. Further, the proposed Identity Theft Protection Act of 2000 would strengthen protection against fraudulent practices committed with stolen credit cards.

That Act requires the card issuer to confirm any reported change of address and notify the cardholder of any request for additional cards. It also requires credit-reporting agencies to inform the card issuer if the address on the application for a credit card is different than the address shown in the consumer's records. Section 4 of the Act would also add a requirement that, upon the request of the consumer, a consumer reporting agency must include a fraud alert in the consumer's file and notify each person seeking credit information of the existence of that alert. That Act would provide significant protection from the technological identity theft.

HEALTH CARE

Currently, there is no pending legislation designed to address health care frauds committed in cyberspace. Future legislative attention should focus on the attributes of the Internet and e-commerce that promote fraudulent activity in the provision of health care products and services.

INSURANCE

There currently are no pending federal laws or regulations that address insurance fraud committed in cyberspace. Historically, regulation of the insurance business has been the province of the states. The 1999 Gramm-Leach-Bliley Act, which repealed the Glass-Steagall Act, enabled financial institutions to provide a variety of services, including insurance. The federal government should establish broad legislation designed to regulate and secure the online sale of insurance products.

Arguably, the only effective weapon at the disposal of federal prosecutors is the wire fraud statute. Additional legislation that requires secure connections and seeks to prevent fraudulent activity regarding online insurance applications and claims should be a priority.

Moreover, because the Internet is an instrument of interstate commerce, Congress should rethink that portion of the Gramm-Leach-Bliley Act which leaves the regulation of issues such as the use of Non-public information by insurance companies to the state regulators. Federal involvement in this area would provide uniform regulation and would not subject financial institutions that provide banking, securities and insurance products to a different regulatory scheme for the offering of insurance products.

SECURITIES

The Internet is an instrument of interstate commerce. Thus, section 10(b) of the Securities Exchange Act of 1934 and Rule 10b-5 provide criminal sanctions for fraudulent acts committed in cyberspace involving the purchase or sale of securities. Also, the mail fraud and wire fraud statutes provide an additional weapon for the prosecution of frauds and swindles involving securities.

Again, substantive criminal laws provide ample sanction for fraudulent conduct impacting upon the securities industry. The Securities Exchange Commission is, however, faced with the difficult task of detecting and investigating securities frauds committed in the online venue. It has created a new enforcement unit to deal specifically with online trading and frauds committed with respect to securities, but legislation is required to assist investigators in the detection and investigation of such frauds. The Online Investor Protection Act of 1999, S. 1015, would be a start in that direction.

TELECOMMUNICATIONS

Section 699, The Telemarketing Fraud and Senior Protection Act would amend the wire fraud statute to prohibit fraudulent telemarketing practices over the Internet. That statute should be further amended to prohibit fraudulent conduct over the Internet transacted in part through a wireless connection.

CYBER CRIME AND FUND-RAISING

Cyber crime has increased in past years, and several recent terrorist events appear to have been funded partially through online credit card fraud. Extremist hackers have reportedly used identity theft and credit card fraud to support terrorist activities by Al Qaeda cells. When terrorist groups do not have the internal technical capability, they may hire organised crime syndicates and cybercriminals through underground digital chat rooms. Reports indicate that terrorists and extremists in the Middle East and South Asia may be increasingly collaborating with cybercriminals for the international movement of money and for the smuggling of arms and illegal drugs. These links with hackers and cybercriminals may be examples of the terrorists' desire to refine their computer skills, and the relationships forged through collaborative drug trafficking efforts may also provide terrorists with access to highly skilled computer programmers.

CYBERATTACKS

Although terrorists have been adept at spreading propaganda and attack instructions on the web, it appears that their capacity for offensive computer network operations may be limited. The Federal Bureau of Investigation (FBI) reports that cyberattacks attributed to terrorists have largely been limited to unsophisticated efforts such as e-mail bombing of ideological foes, denial-ofservice attacks, or defacing of Web sites. However, it says, their increasing technical competency is resulting in an emerging capability for network-based attacks.

The FBI has predicted that terrorists will either develop or hire hackers for the purpose of complementing large conventional attacks with cyberattacks. During his testimony regarding the 2007 Annual Threat Assessment, FBI Director Robert Mueller observed that "terrorists increasingly use the Internet to communicate, conduct operational planning, proselytise, recruit, train and to obtain logistical and financial support. That is a growing and increasing concern for us." In addition, continuing publicity about Internet computer security vulnerabilities may encourage terrorists' interest in attempting a possible computer network attack, or cyberattack, against U.S. critical infrastructure.

The Internet, whether accessed by a desktop computer or by the many available handheld devices, is the medium through which a cyberattack would be delivered. However, for a targeted attack to be successful, the attackers usually require that the network itself remain more or less intact, unless the attackers assess that the perceived gains from shutting down the network entirely would offset the accompanying loss of their own communication.

A future targeted cyberattack could be effective if directed against a portion of the U.S. critical infrastructure, and if timed to amplify the effects of a simultaneous conventional physical or chemical, biological, radiological, or nuclear (CBRN) terrorist attack.

The objectives of a cyberattack may include the following four areas:

1. loss of integrity, such that information could be modified improperly;
2. loss of availability, where mission-critical information systems are rendered unavailable to authorised users;
3. loss of confidentiality, where critical information is disclosed to unauthorised users; and
4. physical destruction, where information systems create actual physical harm through commands that cause deliberate malfunctions.

Publicity would also potentially be one of the primary objectives for a terrorist cyberattack. Extensive media coverage has shown the vulnerability of the U.S. information infrastructure and the potential harm that could be caused by a cyberattack. This might lead terrorists to believe that even a marginally successful cyberattack directed at the United States would garner considerable publicity.

Some suggest that were such a cyberattack by an international terrorist organization to occur and become known to the general public, regardless of the level of success of the attack, concern by many citizens and cascading effects might lead to widespread disruption of critical infrastructures. For example, reports of an attack on the international financial system's networks could create a fiscal panic in the public that could lead to economic damage. According to security experts, terrorist groups have not yet used their own computer hackers nor hired hackers to damage, disrupt, or destroy critical infrastructure systems.

Yet reports of a recent disruptive computer worm that has spread through some government networks, including that of the National Aeronautics and Space Administration, have found a possible link to a Libyan hacker with the handle "Iraq Resistance" and his online hacker group "Brigades of Tariq ibn Ziyad," whose stated goal is "to penetrate U.S. agencies belonging to the U.S. Army." References to both the hacker and group have been found in the worm's code.

However, this does not provide conclusive evidence of involvement, as e-mail addresses can be spoofed and code can be deliberately designed to implicate a target while concealing the true identity of the perpetrator.

The recent emergence of the Stuxnet worm may have implications for what potential future cyberattacks might look like. Stuxnet is thought to be the first piece of malicious software (malware) that was specifically designed to target the computer-networked industrial control systems that control utilities, in this case nuclear power plants in Iran.

Although many experts contend that the level of sophistication, intelligence, and access required to develop Stuxnet all point to nation states, not only is the idea now in the public sphere for others to build upon, but the code has been released as well. An industrious group could potentially use this code as a foundation for developing a capability intended to degrade and destroy the software systems that control the U.S. power grid, to name one example.

CONVENTION ON CYBER CRIME

The Convention on Cyber crime includes a provision on illegal access protecting the integrity of the computer systems by criminalising the unauthorised access to a system. Noting inconsistent approaches at the national level, the Convention offers the possibility of limitations that – at least in most cases – enable countries without legislation to retain more liberal laws on illegal access.

THE PROVISION

- Article 2 – Illegal access: Each Party shall adopt such legislative and other measures as may be necessary to establish as criminal offences under its domestic law, when committed intentionally, the access to the whole or any part of a computer system without right. A Party may require that the offence be committed by infringing security measures, with the intent of obtaining computer data or other dishonest intent, or in relation to a computer system that is connected to another computer system.

THE COVERED ACTS

The term "access" does not specify a certain means of communication, but is open-ended and open to further technical developments. It shall include all means of entering another computer system, including Internet attacks, as well as illegal access to wireless networks. Even unauthorised access to computers that are not connected to any network (*e.g.,* by circumventing a password protection) are covered by the provision.

This broad approach means that illegal access not only covers future technical developments, but is also covers secret data accessed by insiders and employees. The second sentence of Article 2 offers the possibility of limiting the criminalisation of illegal access to access over a network. The illegal acts and protected systems are thus defined in a way that remains open to future developments. The Explanatory Report lists hardware, components, stored data, directories, traffic and content-related data as examples of the parts of computer systems that can be accessed.

Mental Element

Like all other offences defined by the Convention on Cyber crime Art. 2 requires that the offender is carrying out the offences intentionally. The Convention does not contain a definition of the term "internationally". In the Explanatory Report the drafters pointed out that the definition of "intentionally" should happen on a national level.

Without Right

Access to a Computer can only be prosecuted under Article 2 of the Convention, if it should happen "without right". Access to a system permitting free and open access by the public or access to a system with the authorisation of the owner or other rights-holder is not "without right".

In addition to the subject of free access, the legitimacy of security testing procedures is also addressed. Network administrators and security companies that test the protection of computer systems in order to identify potential gaps in the security measures were wary of the possibility of criminalisation under illegal access. Despite the fact that these professionals generally work with the permission of the owner and therefore act legally, the drafters of the Convention emphasised that "testing or protection of the security of a computer system authorised by the owner or operator, are with right". The fact, that the victim of the crime handed out a password or similar access code to the offender does not necessary mean that the offender then acted with right when he accessed the computer system of the victim.

If the offender persuaded the victim to disclose a password or access code due to a successful social engineering approach it is necessary to verify if the authorisation given by the victim does cover the act carried out by the offender. In general this is not the case and the offender therefore acts without right.

Restrictions and Reservations

As an alternative to the broad approach, the Convention offers the possibility of restricting criminalisation with additional elements, listed in the second sentence. The procedure of how to utilise this reservation is laid down in Article 42 of the Convention. Possible reservations relate to security measures, special intent to obtain computer data, other dishonest intent that justifies criminal culpability, or requirements that the offence be committed against a computer system through a network. A similar approach can be found in the EU Framework Decision on Attacks against Information Systems.

Commonwealth Computer and Computer Related Crimes Model Law

A similar approach can be found in Sec. 5 of the 2002 Commonwealth Model Law:

- Sec. 5.: A person who intentionally, without lawful excuse or justification, accesses the whole or any part of a computer system commits an offence punishable, on conviction, by imprisonment for a period not exceeding, or a fine not exceeding or both.

The main difference to the Convention on Cyber crime is the fact that Sec. 5 of the Commonwealth Model Law does, unlike Art. 2 Convention on Cyber crime, not contain options to make reservations.

Stanford Draft Convention

The informal 1999 Stanford Draft Convention recognises illegal access as one of those offences the signatory states should criminalise.

The Provision

- Art. 3 – Offences:
  - 1. Offenses under this Convention are committed if any person unlawfully and intentionally engages in any of the following conduct without legally recognised authority, permission, or consent:

- (c) enters into a cyber system for which access is restricted in a conspicuous and unambiguous manner;

The Covered Acts

The draft provision shows a number of similarities to Art. 2 of the Convention on Cyber crime. Both require an intentional act that is committed without right/without authority. In this context requirement of the draft provision (*"without legally recognised authority, permission, or consent"*) is more precise than the term "without right" used Convention on Cyber crime and explicitly aims to incorporate the concept of selfdefence. The main difference to the Convention is the fact that the draft provision uses the term "cyber system".

The cyber system is defined in Art. 1, paragraph 3 of the Draft Convention. It covers any computer or network of computers used to relay, transmit, coordinate, or control communications of data or Programmes.

This definition shows many similarities to the definition of the term 'computer system" provided by Art. 1 a) Convention on Cyber crime. Although the Draft Convention refers to acts related to the exchange of data and does therefore primarily focus on network based computer systems both definitions include interconnected computer as well as stand alone machines.

DATA ESPIONAGE

The Convention on Cyber crime as well as the Commonwealth Model Law and the Stanford Draft Convention provide legal solutions for illegal interception only. It is questionable whether Article 3 of the Convention on Cyber crime applies to other cases than those where offences are carried out by intercepting data transfer processes. The question of whether illegal access to information stored on a hard disk is covered by the Convention was discussed with great interest.

Since a transfer process is needed, it is likely that Art. 3 of the Convention on Cyber crime does not cover forms of data espionage other than the interception of transfer processes. One issue frequently discussed in this context is the question if the criminalisation of illegal accesses renders the criminalisation of data espionage unnecessary. In those cases where the offender has legitimate access to a computer system (*e.g.* because he is ordered to repair it) and on this occasion (in violation of the limited legitimating) copies files from the system, the act is in general not covered by the provisions criminalising illegal access.

Given that much vital data is today stored in computer systems, it is essential to evaluate whether existing mechanisms to protect data are adequate or whether other criminal law provision are necessary to protect the user from data espionage. Today, computer users can use various hardware devices and software tools in order to protect secret information.

They can install firewalls, access control systems or encrypt stored information and by this decrease the risk of data espionage. Although user-friendly devices are available, requiring only limited knowledge by users, truly effective protection of data on a computer system often requires knowledge that few users have.

Especially data stored on private computer systems is often not adequately protected against data espionage. Therefore criminal law provisions can offer an additional protection.

Examples

Some countries have decided to extend the protection that is available through technical measures by criminalising data espionage. There are two main approaches. Some countries follow a narrow approach and criminalise data espionage, only where specific secret information is obtained - an example is 18 U.S.C § 1831, that criminalises economic espionage. The provision does not only cover data espionage, but other ways of obtaining secret information as well.

Economic Espionage

(a) In General — Whoever, intending or knowing that the Offence will benefit any foreign government, foreign instrumentality, or foreign agent, knowingly—
   (1) Steals, or without authorization appropriates, takes, carries away, or conceals, or by fraud, artifice, or deception obtains a trade secret;
   (2) Without authorization copies, duplicates, sketches, draws, photographs, downloads, uploads, alters, destroys, photocopies, replicates, transmits, delivers, sends, mails, communicates, or conveys a trade secret;
   (3) Receives, buys, or possesses a trade secret, knowing the same to have been stolen or appropriated, obtained, or converted without authorization;
   (4) Attempts to commit any Offence described in any of paragraphs (1) through (3); or
   (5) Conspires with one or more other persons to commit any Offence described in any of paragraphs (1) through (3), and one or more of such persons do any act to effect the object of the conspiracy, shall, except as provided in subsection (b), be fined not more than $500,000 or imprisoned not more than 15 years, or both.

(b) Organizations — Any organization that commits any Offence described in subsection (a) shall be fined not more than $10,000,000.

Other countries have adopted a broader approach and criminalised the act of obtaining stored computer data, even if they do not contain economic secrets.

Section 202a. Data Espionage

(1) Any person who obtains without authorization, for himself or for another, data which are not meant for him and which are specially protected against unauthorised access, shall be liable to imprisonment for a term not exceeding three years or to a fine

(2) Data within the meaning of subsection 1 are only such as are stored or transmitted electronically or magnetically or in any form not directly visible.

This provision not only covers economic secrets, but stored computer data in general. In terms of its objects of protection, this approach is broader compared to § 1831 USC, but the application of the provision is limited as obtaining data is only criminalised where data are specially protected against unauthorised access. The protection of stored computer data under German criminal law is thus limited to persons or businesses that have taken measures to avoid falling victim to such offences.

Relevance of Such Provision

The implementation of such provision is especially relevant with regard to cases, where the offender was authorised to access a computer system (*e.g.* because he was ordered to fix a computer problem) and then abused the authorisation to illegally obtain information stored on the computer system. With regard to the fact that the permission covers the access to the computer system it is in general not possible to cover with provisions criminalising the illegal access.

Without Right

The application of data espionage provisions in general requires that the data was obtained without the consent of the victim. The success of phishing attacks clearly demonstrates the success of scams based on the manipulation of users. Due to the consent of the victim offenders who succeed in manipulating of users to disclose secret information cannot be prosecuted on the basis of the above mentioned provisions.

ILLEGAL INTERCEPTION

The use of ICTs is accompanied by several risks related to the security of information transfer. Unlike classic mail order operations within a country, data transfer processes over the Internet involve numerous providers and different points where the data transfer process could be intercepted. The weakest point for intercept remains the user, especially users of private home computers, who are often inadequately protected against external attacks.

As offenders generally always aim for the weakest point, the risk of attacks against private users is great, all the more so given:

- The development of vulnerable technologies; and
- The rising relevance of personal information for offenders.

New network technologies (such as "wireless LAN") offer several advantages for Internet access. Setting up a wireless network in a private home, for example, allows families to connect to the Internet from anywhere inside a given radius, without the need for cable connections. But the popularity of this technology and resulting comfort is accompanied by serious risks to network security.

If an unprotected wireless network is available perpetrators can log on to this network and use it for criminal purposes without the need to get access to a building. They simply need to get inside the radius of the wireless network to launch an attack. Field tests suggest that in some areas as many as 50 per cent of private wireless networks are not protected against unauthorised interception or access. In most cases, lack of protection arises from a lack of knowledge as to how to configure protection measures. In the past, perpetrators concentrated mainly on business networks for illegal interceptions. Interception of corporate communications was more likely to yield useful information, than data transferred within private networks. The rising number of identity thefts of private personal data suggests that the focus of the perpetrators may have changed. Private data such as credit card numbers, social security numbers, passwords and bank account information are now of great interest to offenders.

The Convention on Cyber crime

The Convention on Cyber crime includes a provision protecting the integrity of non-public transmissions by criminalising their unauthorised interception. This provision aims to equate the protection of electronic transfers with the protection of voice conversations against illegal tapping and/or recording that currently already exists in most legal systems.

The Provision

- Article 3 – Illegal interception: Each Party shall adopt such legislative and other measures as may be necessary to establish as criminal offences under its domestic law, when committed intentionally, the interception without right, made by technical means, of non-public transmissions of computer data to, from or within a computer system, including electromagnetic emissions from a computer system carrying such computer data. A Party may require that the offence be committed with dishonest intent, or in relation to a computer system that is connected to another computer system.

The Covered Acts

The applicability of Article 3 is limited to the interception of transmissions realised by technical measures. Interceptions related to electronic data can be defined as any act of acquiring data during a transfer process. The question if illegal access to information stored on a hard disk is covered by the provision is controversially discussed. In general the provision only applies to the interception of transmissions - access to stored information is not considered as an interception of a transmission.

The fact that the application of the provision is discussed even in cases where the offender physically access a standalone computer system partly arises as a result of the fact, that the Convention on Cyber crime does not contain a provision related to data espionage and the Explanatory Report to the Convention contains two slightly imprecise explanations with regard to the application of Art. 3:

- The Explanatory Report first of all points out that the provision covers communication processes taking place within a computer system. However, this still leaves open the question of whether the provision should only apply in cases where victims send data that are then intercepted by offenders or whether it should apply also when the offender himself operates the computer.
- The guide points out that interception can be committed either indirectly through the use of tapping devices or "through access and use of the computer system". If offenders gain access to a computer system and use it to make unauthorised copies of stored data on an external disc drive, where the act leads to a data transfer (sending data from the internal to the external hard disc), this process is not *intercepted*, but rather *initiated*, by offenders. The missing element of technical interception is a strong argument against the application of the provision in cases of illegal access to stored information.

The term "transmission" covers all data transfers, whether by telephone, fax, e-mail or file transfer. The offence established under Article 3 applies only to non-public transmissions.

A transmission is "non-public", if the transmission process is confidential. The vital element to differentiate between public and non-public transmissions is not the nature of the data transmitted, but the nature of the transmission process itself. Even the transfer of publicly available information can be considered criminal, if the parties involved in the transfer intend to keep the content of their communications secret. Use of public networks does not exclude "nonpublic" communications.

Mental Element

Like all other offences defined by the Convention on Cyber crime, Article 3 requires that the offender is carrying out the offences intentionally. The Convention does not contain a definition of the term "internationally". In the Explanatory Report the drafters pointed out that the definition of "intentionally" should happen on a national level.

Without Right

The interception of communication can only be prosecuted under Article 3 of the Convention, if it should happen "without right".

The drafters of the Convention provided a set of examples for interceptions that are not carried out without right:

- Action on the basis instructions or by authorisation of the participants of the transmission;
- Authorised testing or protection activities agreed to by the participants;
- Lawful interception on the basis of criminal law provisions or in the interests of national security.

Another issue raised within the negotiation of the Convention was the question if the use of cookies would lead to criminal sanctions based on Art. 3. The drafters pointed out that common commercial practices (such as cookies) are not considered to be interceptions without right.

Restrictions and Reservations

Article 3 offers the option of restricting criminalisation by requiring additional elements listed in the second sentence, including a "dishonest intent" or relation to a computer system connected to another computer system.

Commonwealth Computer and Computer Related Crimes Model Law

A similar approach can be found in Sec. 8 of the 2002 Commonwealth Model Law.

- Sec. 8.: A person who, intentionally without lawful excuse or justification, intercepts by technical means:
  (a) Any non-public transmission to, from or within a computer system; or
  (b) Electromagnetic emissions from a computer system that are carrying computer data; commits an offence punishable, on conviction, by imprisonment for a period not exceeding, or a fine not exceeding, or both.

Stanford Draft Convention

The informal 1999 Stanford Draft Convention does not explicitly criminalise the interception of computer data.

DATA INTERFERENCE

The protection of tangible, or physical, objects against intentional damage is a classic element of national penal legislation. With continuing digitalisation, more critical business information is stored as data. Attacks or obtaining of this information can result in financial losses. Besides deletion, the alteration of such information could also have major consequences. Previous legislation has in some not completely brought the protection of data in line with the protection of tangible objects. This enabled offenders to design scams that do not lead to criminal sanctions.

Convention on Cyber crime

In Article 4, the Convention on Cyber crime includes a provision that protects the integrity of data against unauthorised interference.

The aim of the provision is to fill existing gaps in some national penal laws and to provide computer data and computer programmes with protections similar to those enjoyed by tangible objects against the intentional infliction of damage.

The Provision

- Article 4 – Data interference:
  (1) Each Party shall adopt such legislative and other measures as may be necessary to establish as criminal offences under its domestic law, when committed intentionally, the damaging, deletion, deterioration, alteration or suppression of computer data without right.
  (2) A Party may reserve the right to require that the conduct described in paragraph 1 result in serious harm.
- The covered acts:
  - The terms "damaging" and "deterioration" mean any act related to the negative alteration of the integrity of information content of data and programmes;
  - "Deleting" covers acts where information is removed from storage media and is considered comparable to the destruction of a tangible object. While providing the definition the the drafters of the Convention did not differentiate between the various ways data can be deleted. Dropping a file to the virtual trash bin does not remove the file from the hard disk. Even "emptying" the trash bin does not necessary remove the file. It is therefore uncertain if the ability to recover a deleted file hinders the application of the provision.
  - "Suppression" of computer data denotes an action that affects the availability of data to the person with access to the medium, where the information is stored in a negative way. The application of the provision is especially discussed with regard to Denial-of-Service attacks. During the attack the data provided on the targeted computer system are not available anymore for potential user as well as the owner of the computer system.
  - The term "alteration" covers the modification of existing data, without necessarily lowering the serviceability of the data. This

act is especially covering the installation of malicious software like spyware, viruses or adware on the victim's computer.

Mental Element

Like all other offences defined by the Convention on Cyber crime Article 4 requires that the offender is carrying out the offences intentionally. The Convention does not contain a definition of the term "internationally". In the Explanatory Report the drafters pointed out that the definition of "intentionally" should happen on a national level.

Without Right

The acts must be committed "without right". The right to alter data was discussed, especially in the context of "remailers". Remailers are used to modify certain data for the purpose of facilitating anonymous communications. The Explanatory Reports mention that, in principle, these acts are considered a legitimate protection of privacy and can thus be considered as being undertaken with authorisation.

Restrictions and Reservations

Article 4 offers the option of restricting criminalisation by limiting it to cases where serious harm arises, a similar approach to the EU Framework Decision on Attacks against Information Systems, which enables Member States to limit the applicability of the substantive criminal law provision to "cases which are not minor".

Commonwealth Computer and Computer Related Crimes Model Law

An approach in line with Art. 4 Convention on Cyber crime can be found in Sec. 8 of the 2002 Commonwealth Model Law.

Sec. 6

(1) A person who, intentionally or recklessly, without lawful excuse or justification, does any of the following acts:
   (a) Destroys or alters data; or
   (b) Renders data meaningless, useless or ineffective; or
   (c) Obstructs, interrupts or interferes with the lawful use of data; or
   (d) Obstructs, interrupts or interferes with any person in the lawful use of data; or
   (e) Denies access to data to any person entitled to it; commits an offence punishable, on conviction, by imprisonment for a period not exceeding or a fine not exceeding [amount], or both.

(2) Subsection (1) applies whether the person's act is of temporary or permanent effect.

Stanford Draft Convention

The informal 1999 Stanford Draft Convention contains two provisions that criminalise acts related to interference with computer data.

The Provision

Art. 3:

1. Offenses under this Convention are committed if any person unlawfully and intentionally engages in any of the following conduct without legally recognised authority, permission, or consent:
   (a) Creates, stores, alters, deletes, transmits, diverts, misroutes, manipulates, or interferes with data or Programmes in a cyber system with the purpose of causing, or knowing that such activities would cause, said cyber system or another cyber system to cease functioning as intended, or to perform functions or activities not intended by its owner and considered illegal under this Convention;
   (b) Creates, stores, alters, deletes, transmits, diverts, misroutes, manipulates, or interferes with data in a cyber system for the purpose and with the effect of providing false information in order to cause substantial damage to persons or property;

The Covered Acts

The main difference between the Convention on Cyber crime and the Commonwealth Model Law and the approach of the Draft Convention is the fact, that Draft Convention does only criminalise the interference with data if this interferes with the functioning of a computer system (Art. 3, paragraph 1a) or if the act is committed with the purpose of providing false information in order to causing damage to a person or property (Art. 3, paragraph 1b). Therefore the draft law does not criminalise the deletion of a regular text document of a data storage device as this does neither influence the functioning of a computer nor does it provide false information.

The Convention on Cyber crime and the Commonwealth Model Law both follow a broader approach by protecting the integrity of computer data without the mandatory requirement of further effects.

SYSTEM INTERFERENCE

People or businesses offering services based on ICTs depend on the functioning of their computer systems. The lack of availability of webpages that are victim to Denial-of-Service (DOS) attacks demonstrates how serious the threat of attack is.

Attacks like these can cause serious financial losses and affect even powerful systems. Businesses are not the only targets. Experts around the world are currently discussing possible scenarios of "cyber terrorism" that take into account attacks against critical infrastructures such as power supplies and telecommunication services.

Convention on Cyber crime

To protect access of operators and users to ICTs, the Convention on Cyber crime includes a provision in Article 5 criminalising the intentional hindering of lawful use of computer systems.

The Provision

Article 5 – System interference:

- Each Party shall adopt such legislative and other measures as may be necessary to establish as criminal offences under its domestic law, when committed intentionally, the serious hindering without right of the functioning of a computer system by inputting, transmitting, damaging, deleting, deteriorating, altering or suppressing computer data.

The Covered Acts

The application of the provision requires that the functioning of a computer system was hindered.

- "Hindering" means any act interfering with the proper functioning of the computer system. The application of the provision is limited to cases where hindering is carried out by one of the mentioned acts.

The list of acts by which the functioning of the computer system was influences in a negative way is conclusive.

- The term "inputting" is neither defined by the Convention itself, nor by the drafters of the Convention. With regard to the fact, the transmitting is mentioned as an additional act in Art. 5 the term "inputting" could be defined as any act related to use of physical input-interfaces to transfer information to a computer system whereas the term "transmitting" is covering acts that go along with the remote input of data.
- The terms "damaging" and "deteriorating" are overlapping and defined by the drafters of the Convention in the Explanatory Report with regard to Art. 4 as negative alteration of the integrity of information content of data and programmes.
- The term "deleting" was also defined by the drafters of the Convention and the Explanatory Report with regard to Article 4 covers acts where information is removed from storage media.
- The term "alteration" covers the modification of existing data, without necessarily lowering the serviceability of the data.

- "Suppression" of computer data denotes an action that affects the availability of data to the person with access to the medium, where the information is stored in a negative way.

In addition, the provision applies limited to cases where hindering is "serious". It is the parties' responsibility to determine the criteria to be fulfilled in order for the hindering to be considered as serious. Possible restrictions under national law could include a minimum amount of damage, as well as limitation of criminalisation to attacks against important computer systems.

Application of the Provision with Regard to Spam

It was discussed whether the problem of spam e-mail could be addressed under Article 5, since spam can overload computer systems. The drafters stated clearly that spam may not necessarily lead to "serious" hindering and that "conduct should only be criminalised where the communication is intentionally and seriously hindered".

The drafters also noted that parties may have a different approach to hindrance under their own national legislation *e.g.,* by making acts of interference administrative offences or subject to sanction.

Mental Element

Like all other offences defined by the Convention on Cyber crime Art. 5 requires that the offender is carrying out the offences intentionally. This includes the intent to carry out one of listed acts as well as the intention to seriously hinder the functioning of a computer system. The Convention does not contain a definition of the term "internationally". In the Explanatory Report the drafters pointed out that the definition of "intentionally" should happen on a national level.

Without Right

The act needs to be carried out "without right". Network administrators and security companies testing the protection of computer systems were afraid of the possible criminalisation of their work. These professionals work with the permission of the owner and therefore act legally. In addition, the drafters of the Convention explicitly mentioned that testing the security of a computer system based on the authorisation of the owner is not without right.

Restrictions and Reservations

Unlike Articles 2 – 4, Article 5 does not contain an explicit possibility of restricting the application of the provision to implementation in the national law.

Nevertheless, the responsibility of the parties to define the gravity of the offence gives them the possibility to restrict its application. A similar approach can be found in the European Union Framework Decision on Attacks against Information Systems.

Commonwealth Computer and Computer Related Crimes Model Law

An approach in line with Article 5 of the Convention on Cyber crime can be found in Sec. 7 of the 2002 Commonwealth Model Law.

Sec 7:

(1) A person who intentionally or recklessly, without lawful excuse or justification:

(a) Hinders or interferes with the functioning of a computer system; or

(b) Hinders or interferes with a person who is lawfully using or operating a computer system; commits an offence punishable, on conviction, by imprisonment for a period not exceeding [period], or a fine not exceeding [amount], or both.

In subsection (1) "hinder", in relation to a computer system, includes but is not limited to:

(a) Cutting the electricity supply to a computer system; and

(b) Causing electromagnetic interference to a computer system; and

(c) Corrupting a computer system by any means; and

(d) Inputting, deleting or altering computer data.

The main differences to the Convention is the fact, that based on Sec. 7 of the Commonwealth Model Law even reckless acts are criminalised.

With this approach the Model Law even goes beyond the requirements of the Convention on Cyber crime. Another difference is the fact, that the definition of "hindering" in Sec. 7 of the Commonwealth Model Law lists more acts compared to Article 5 of the Convention on Cyber crime.

Stanford Draft Convention

The informal 1999 Stanford Draft Convention contains a provision that criminalises acts related to the interference with computer systems.

The Provision

Art. 3:

1. Offenses under this Convention are committed if any person unlawfully and intentionally engages in any of the following conduct without legally recognised authority, permission, or consent:

(a) Creates, stores, alters, deletes, transmits, diverts, misroutes, manipulates, or interferes with data or Programmes in a cyber system with the purpose of causing, or knowing that such activities would cause, said cyber system or another cyber system to cease functioning as intended, or to perform functions or activities not intended by its owner and considered illegal under this Convention.

The Covered Acts

The main difference between the Convention on Cyber crime and the Commonwealth Model Law and the approach of the Draft Convention is the fact, that Draft Convention does cover any manipulation of computer systems while the Convention on Cyber crime and the Commonwealth Model Law limit the criminalisation to the hindering of the functioning of a computer system.

FUTURE NEEDS AND CHALLENGES

LAW ENFORCEMENT TRAINING

Specialised training in the areas of economic and computer crime, and how they affect specific industries, as well as computer forensics, needs to continue to increase for law enforcement personnel. Without an understanding of how specific industries function, it is difficult to investigate or prosecute economic crimes.

New career paths within law enforcement organizations could be established before promotions and reassignments drain agencies of their limited skilled personnel in technically sophisticated areas. Often, individuals develop expertise and then are promoted or reassigned, making it necessary to train new people from ground zero. Unless the individuals who have expertise, experience, and contacts in industry are given an incentive to stay in their units, this cycle will continue and the investigation and prosecution of economic crime will not increase or improve.

LAWS, REGULATIONS AND REPORTING SYSTEMS

In the United States, government (federal, state and local), with limited exceptions, has allowed self-regulation of the Internet. Government regulation has, for the most part, focused on cyber crimes that are not economic crimes, such as child pornography and cyber stalking.

Fortunately, that attitude appears to be changing. There are numerous bills pending in Congress that address criminal frauds committed on the Internet, identity theft, and issues involving Internet security and attacks upon web sites. This legislation should use language that will be easily adaptable to future technological changes to help deter future economic crimes. However, there are other gaps in legislation. There are many regulations that require businesses to protect themselves by working to prevent fraud (*i.e.* know your customer). However, the government sends conflicting signals when it will not assist in prevention efforts by cleaning up regulations and enacting new supporting laws, as well as providing prosecutorial support. Current government regulations covering certain industries prohibit companies from sharing information with each other. This eliminates the possibility of an instrument, such as a central database of fraud, which companies could use in their procedures for preventing and detecting fraud. It is important that legislation addressing this be written and passed. Other legislation is also necessary, such as laws that keep pace with the changing nature of credit card payment and online payment systems.

PUBLIC-PRIVATE PARTNERSHIPS

No one group will be able to solve the complex problem posed by economic crime. Coalitions of private and public groups need to work together to combat economic and cyber crime. As more of these alliances develop, there will be more resources available to reverse the trend of economic crime. College and universities need to revamp their existing Programmes, *e.g.* criminal justice, accounting, computer science, or create new ones to meet the changing needs of society in this area.

At this time there are only two undergraduate Programmes and one graduate Programme addressing these issues – the Economic Crime Investigations Programmes at Utica College (Utica, NY) and Hilbert College (Hamburg, NY) and the Economic Crime Management Master's Programme at Utica College.

These Programmes are supported by advisory boards consisting of individuals at the top of their fields from the credit card, banking, insurance, and telecommunications industries, as well as representatives from government agencies, such as the U.S. Secret Service and the FBI. Further Congress, through the Identity Theft Assumption and Deterrence Act requires the FTC and industry to work together. Presidential Directive 63 required industry and government to work together in combating Internet/e-commerce fraud.

BALANCING PRIVACY INTERESTS

The growth of e-commerce and the creation of new law enforcement techniques to combat cyber crime raise critical issues concerning consumer, business and governmental privacy.

The protection of individual privacy, while considered almost sacred, in the world of economic and cyber crime can actually work to the criminal's advantage. The new FBI tool, Carnivore, is an attempt to gather intelligence information, without compromising privacy.

According to the FBI's web site,

- In recent years, the FBI has encountered an increasing number of criminal investigations in which the criminal subjects use the Internet to communicate with each other or to communicate with their victims. Because many Internet service providers (ISP) lack the ability to discriminate communications to identify a particular subject's messages to the exclusion of all others, the FBI designed a diagnostic tool, called Carnivore.
- The Carnivore device provides the FBI with a "surgical" ability to intercept and collect the communications which are subject of the

lawful order while ignoring those communications which they are not authorised to intercept.

- This is a matter of employing new technology to lawfully obtain important information, while providing enhanced privacy protection.

Carnivore provides law enforcement with the ability to keep pace with the technical advances in communication. However, this tool raises "Big Brother" concerns for the public. The controversy that Carnivore has evoked in its infancy points to the issue of trust that government, industry, and society as a whole need to resolve. BITS, Financial Services Roundtable adopted privacy principles in late 1997 that are guidelines for banking industry self-regulation concerning privacy. Industry, in general, sees self-regulation as preferable to government rule.

The BITS policy includes guidelines in each of these areas.

- Recognition of a customer's expectation of privacy
- Use, collection, and retention of customer Information
- Maintenance of accurate information
- Limiting employee access to information
- Protection of information via established security procedures
- Restrictions on the disclosure of account information
- Maintaining customer privacy in business relationships with third parties
- Disclosure of privacy principles to customers

Several other industry organizations are developing similar guidelines. Their aim is to have self-regulation rather than government intervention. By informing customers of privacy policies, industry is attempting to engender their trust. There is a delicate balance between protecting one's privacy, legitimate business use of personal data, and fraud prevention. However, the use of personal data for fraud prevention and interdiction is beneficial to society. Therefore, fraud and risk management exceptions should be built into any and all laws, regulations, and policies.

In fact, the use of personal data for identity theft prevention directly reduces the number of identity theft victims. Further, many industries (*i.e.* insurance, banking and securities) require fraud prevention through regulation to protect consumers, customers, shareholders, and employees.

Effective authentication in an e-commerce transaction is not possible without the use of independent, personal verification data. Authentication is critical to the growth and confidence of e-commerce. Fraudsters have quickly learned to defeat our technical systems.

If they are allowed to opt out of databases, they will rapidly exploit our vulnerabilities to the financial detriment of the general public. Global cooperation is also needed in this area. The United States must take a leadership role in fostering cooperation throughout the global community in the development of uniform laws, meaningful and comparable privacy policies, effective assistance to prosecutions by foreign countries, and a sharing of information. The U.S. already has surrendered a leadership role in the areas of privacy and information sharing. The European Union developed a comprehensive privacy directive applicable to all member nations in 1995, and the European Parliament recently refused to allow its member nations to share data and Non-public information with the U.S. With respect to information sharing, Interpol has announced its intention to provide private industries throughout the world with intelligence information regarding the vulnerability of those industries or specific companies to cyber attacks. At this point, the global community perceives the U.S. as a reluctant partner, not a leader.

5

Refugees, Crime and Law

REFUGEES

The 1951 Convention Relating to the Status of Refugees, the cornerstone of refugee protection, defines a refugee as "a person who, as a result of well-founded fear of being persecuted for reasons of race, religion, nationality, membership of a particular social group, or political opinion, is outside the country of his nationality, and is unable to or, owing to such fear, is unwilling to avail himself of the protection of that country." The basic principle of the Convention is that the rights of refugees in the country of refuge must be at least equal to those of other resident foreigners in that country.

Refugees are protected by the principle of non-refoulement, meaning that they cannot be forced to return to their home country if they have a reasonable fear that to do so would endanger their lives. The Convention was introduced in the wake of refugee movements in Europe after World War II. Although the Convention does not specifically address persons from armed conflict, some interpretations accept such people as refugees.

This is enshrined in, for example, the Organization of African Unity (OAU) Convention Governing the Specific Problems of Refugees in Africa drawn up in 1969, and the 1984 Cartagena Declaration on Refugees in Central America. The UN High Commissioner for Refugees (UNHCR) generally accepts those fleeing from conflict as refugees. However, a number of governments (including the US and most European governments) determine the status of asylum seekers on the basis of individual fears of persecution.

INTERNALLY DISPLACED PERSONS (IDPS)

The 1998 Guiding Principles on Internal Displacement (the Guiding Principles) describe internally displaced persons as "persons or groups of persons who have been forced or obliged to flee or to leave their homes or places of habitual residence, in particular as a result of, or in order to avoid the effects of armed conflict, situations of generalised violence, violations of human rights or natural or human-made disasters, and who have not crossed an internationally recognised State border." Armed conflict and other forms of mass violence are specifically as possible causes of flight. Both individuals and groups fall within the definition. International humanitarian and human rights law protects civilian IDPs through a number of instruments. These include the 1949 Geneva Conventions and 1977 Additional Protocol, which, among other things, prohibit parties to an armed conflict from arbitrarily displacing civilian populations.

Other relevant mechanisms include the Convention on the Elimination of All Forms of Discrimination Against Women (CEDAW), which establishes women's human rights. However, there is no single mechanism designed specifically to address IDP rights. Since the early 1990s, the international community has been increasingly concerned about IDPs because of their growing numbers and a growing awareness of their vulnerability. This concern was reflected in 1992 in the appointment of the Special Representative of the UN Secretary General on Internally Displaced Persons. The Special Representative drew up the Guiding Principles to clarify the status and rights of IDPs and to identify the responsibilities of different parties towards them. While not legally binding, they are drawn from, and are consistent with, existing laws and conventions. In 2003, the number of IDPs was estimated to be more than twice that of refugees. The increase in IDP numbers may reflect continuing reluctance by governments to accept responsibility for refugees, so that people in flight are increasingly unable to cross borders. It may also reflect the growing number of contexts in which governments are unable or unwilling to protect citizens from abuse or from the absence of adequate care in the face of disaster. IDPs are often considered to be more vulnerable than refugees. It has been estimated that half the countries with IDPs crises have failed to provide protection with reported abuses including sexual exploitation and forced labour. Moves to introduce specific protection measures for IDPs have been resisted by many countries on the grounds that to do so would infringe on national sovereignty. However, while international law upholds the concept of national sovereignty, because IDPs remain resident in their own country, their protection is the responsibility of the government concerned.

The Guiding Principles confirm that the rights of IDPs (assuming they are citizens of the country within which they have moved) are equal to those of other citizens and are therefore protected by international human rights legislation. The Guiding Principles assert the rights to protection and assistance for IDPs in all phases of displacement. If observed, the Guiding Principles can prevent displacement as a result of conflict, provide protection if it happens and help IDPs return home after hostilities have ceased.

WHAT PROBLEMS DO REFUGEES AND IDPS FACE?

People who have been displaced, whether within their own country's borders or internationally, often have to leave behind all but a few of their worldly possessions. In most cases their search for refuge takes them long distances, often on foot. Flight itself is arduous: families can lose contact with each other, sick and elderly relatives may have to be left behind and refugees in flight can be vulnerable to violent attack and exploitation. The trauma of being uprooted from one's home and of becoming separated from family members adds to the terrifying experiences that many undergo before and during their flight.

Lack of language skills and unfamiliarity with new surroundings, coupled with fear and concern about events back home, create added burdens. IDPs and refugees have usually been torn from their established environment and their economic resources. As a result they have lost their livelihoods and the means of generating an independent income. They may be obliged to settle in isolated or economically marginal areas where land is poor or where the potential for formal or informal employment is restricted. Where violence ravages rural areas, those displaced may be forced into towns and trading centres where a precarious living in the informal sector may be the only option. Legal restrictions on employment and income generation often make refugees and IDPs permanently dependent on the good will of hosts and on humanitarian assistance. This can reduce their capacity for self-reliance and their determination to survive, giving rise to what assistance providers sometimes describe as a "culture of dependency."

Host communities often see refugees and IDPs as a drain on their already meagre resources, and assistance provided to them may become the source of resentment from hosts, who may themselves be among the most marginalised segments of their own community. Refugees and IDPs can be exploited by employers, receive harsh treatment at the hands of the authorities and be at the mercy of landlords. They are vulnerable to abuse (including high levels of sexual violence and exploitation) from officials and other powerful members of their own and host communities. Especially when flight is the result of armed conflict, resolving the situation of IDPs and refugees may require political agreements that are hard to come by. Palestinian refugees have been unable to return home for four generations, pending a political resolution to their situation, and their existence has been used as justification for further aggression by all sides in other conflicts. Many long-term refugees and IDPs feel that politicians manipulate their situation.

In the Caucasus, given the still unresolved status of Abkhazia after the Georgia-Abkhazia conflict in which national boundaries were being disputed, ethnic Georgians returning to Abkhazia are viewed as internally displaced by Georgia, but as refugees by Abkhazia. In Bangladesh, the government has provided displaced Bengalis with land in areas inhabited by the ethnic minority Hilly people in the Chittagong Hill Tract, a move seen by the Hilly as part of a process of denying them their identity. Where refugees and IDPs are living in camps or organised settlements, conditions can be damaging to their physical, psychological and social health. Conditions in camps are often overcrowded, leading to public health problems and a lack of privacy. Living in such conditions for prolonged periods can prevent people from maintaining links with family members and may lead to the erosion of cultural practices that contribute to the socialisation of children and a sense of identity. In Northern Uganda, 1.4 million IDPs now live in camps, where overcrowded and impoverished living conditions have eroded the tradition of firesides after the evening family meal, when older people would tell stories and offer advice to the young. The psychological impact of camp life is particularly marked in cases where the situation of refugees or IDPs has remained unresolved for a number of years, as with the approximately 400,000 Bhutanese refugees who have lived in Nepal since the early 1990s.

Health and educational facilities are crucial to all displaced populations. Education is often ignored by assistance providers working with the displaced, as it is seen as a long-term, rather than an emergency, requirement. Yet for many displaced, education is a way out of their impoverishment and cultural isolation. Displaced populations are particularly poorly served with secondary education, without which adolescents and young people have difficulty finding employment. Health services for displaced populations are critical because of the physical and psychological stresses of displacement. Sexual and reproductive health is a major issue for refugee and IDP populations although, like education, it is often overlooked by assistance providers. Displacement, and the unaccustomed lifestyles encountered in exile or in IDP camps, can change sexual behaviour—refugee and internally displaced populations often experience increased transmission rates of HIV/AIDS and other sexually transmitted diseases. Population growth among such communities can be a politically sensitive issue, affecting access to contraceptives and to maternal and child health services. The return of displaced populations to their homes may also raise a broad range of problems. Refugees and the internally displaced have the right to a safe return. They cannot be forced to return to a country where they are likely to face persecution or torture.

Those who wish to return may not have the funds to do so, especially when intensive efforts are required to renovate homes, fields, equipment, markets and to restock animals. For communities returning to rural environments, food aid will be required until crops can be harvested. When flight has been caused by armed conflict, returnees may face unexploded landmines and other ordnance in fields, roads and even homes. Avoiding these dangers may mean not one but several relocations before security can be assured. Where displaced populations have been away a long time, the size of the community may have increased in exile, generating heightening pressure on resources upon return. Displaced populations who wish to return home may face difficulty claiming property and other entitlements.

Repossessing rights to houses or land, for example, can involve lengthy legal procedures. The problems are particularly acute for IDPs, who have no single UN agency mandated to ensure their welfare and who are primarily dependent on their own government to uphold their rights. In many cases it is these same governments whose neglect and abuse has given rise to the displacement and who have failed to put in place adequate mechanisms for IDPs to express their grievances. Refugees and IDPs also may be seen as contributors to the insecurity of others, especially where they themselves have been directly involved in political disturbances. They can perpetuate conflicts through fundraising, supporting the shipment of arms, international public relations and other activities.

In many instances the connection is more direct. Many of the Rwandan Interahamwe militias who fled to the Democratic Republic of the Congo (DRC) in 1994, were widely seen as the perpetrators of the April 1994 genocide, continued their attacks, while hiding among refugee populations. In addition, long-term camps— such as those for Burmese refugees in Bangladesh, originally set up in the 1980s—can effectively be forgotten by the international community, leaving refugees to become prey to arms and drugs smugglers. The September 11, 2001, events in the US gave rise to concerns in some quarters that refugee and IDP populations might be harbouring terrorists.

This prompted UNHCR to issue a statement, in September 2004, emphasising that the 1951 Refugee Convention excludes persons who have committed serious crimes and provides terrorists with no protection from prosecution.

The statement further urges governments to seek to improve security measures but to ensure that during the process, refugees are not exposed to racism and xenophobia, exclusion, withdrawal of refugee status, deportation and the suspension of resettlement programmes. Despite the complexity of their experiences and the challenges that many displaced populations face, it is important not to generalise about their plight. Many refugees successfully settle and thrive in their new environments.

They gain new skills and experience, often bringing home expertise and financial resources, as well as new perspectives and views. In Iran for example, despite receiving limited international assistance, Afghan refugees, including women, have had access to education, health care and jobs. Many Iraqi and Afghan refugee women who settled in Pakistan, Iran, Europe and North America have returned home in recent years and have been instrumental in advancing women's rights.

They have established NGOs to build the capacity of women and advocate for empowerment and channelled direct resources to efforts on the ground. In states of the former Yugoslavia, expatriates are a liberalising force, promoting the transition to democracy. Malian women refugees in Mauritania often resisted calls from their husbands to return home, as they had found new opportunities in exile. In many other places, refugees and IDPs who have permanently resettled are an extremely significant source of capital for the home country.

TO ENSURE REFUGEE AND IDP WOMEN'S PROTECTION

- Review basic documents such as the Guiding Principles on Internal Displacement and consider how they apply to women in the context that concerns you. Are its provisions being respected? How can you address those areas that are not being addressed adequately?
- Find out which body or bodies within your context (national government and UN) are responsible for protection and assistance to refugees and the internally displaced and how they intend to implement the Guiding Principles.
- If you are a refugee or displaced woman, find out about your rights in the country where you are located to determine the opportunities and support to which you are entitled.
- Find out the procedures for determining the status of asylum seekers, and advocate against inadequate implementation of international laws and guidelines.

TO ENSURE REFUGEE AND IDP WOMEN'S VOICES ARE HEARD

- If you wish to support refugee women and IDPs, find out about their background—what circumstances have they come from, what led them to flee, their experiences en route, the skills and expectations they bring with them, how they are living, what problems they and their families face now and what laws and other opportunities exist for them.
- Identify the gaps in understanding between the displaced and their hosts. Work to establish mutual understanding and practical links between women of the displaced and host communities, building on their common concerns.
- Ensure that assistance-providing organisations recognise the contribution that women's organisations already make, and ensure they are supported so that practical and other barriers can be overcome.

TO ENSURE EFFECTIVE ASSISTANCE FOR REFUGEE AND IDP WOMEN

- Consider the specific vulnerabilities of refugee and IDP women and make provisions to combat them. This might mean demanding increased maternal and child health or education services, advocating for survivors of human rights abuses or removing legal impediments faced by women entrepreneurs
- Enable refugees and IDPs to participate in the management and implementation of assistance programmes to help people overcome the impact of displacement and dependency and increase self-reliance. Ensure that assistance programmes are run with this in mind.

- Organise with other women and disseminate information to refugees and IDPs about the rights and opportunities available for work, access to services and social or legal support. Consider how to advocate with government and other assistance providers to address your needs.

REFUGEE PROTECTION SYSTEM

It is the responsibility of States to protect their citizens. When governments are unwilling or unable to protect their citizens, individuals may suffer such serious violations of their rights that they are forced to leave their homes, and often even their families, to seek safety in another country. Since, by definition, the governments of their home countries no longer protect the basic rights of refugees, the international community then steps in to ensure that those basic rights are respected.

In the aftermath of World War II, the United Nations General Assembly created the Office of the United Nations High Commissioner for Refugees (UNHCR). UNHCR is mandated to protect and find durable solutions for refugees.

Its activities are based on a framework of international law and standards that includes the 1948 *Universal Declaration of Human Rights* and the four *Geneva Conventions* on international humanitarian law, as well as an array of international and regional treaties and declarations, both binding and Non-binding, that specifically address the needs of refugees.

INTERNATIONAL LAWS AND STANDARDS

1951 Convention Relating to the Status of Refugees

The *Convention Relating to the Status of Refugees* is the foundation of international refugee law. The Refugee Convention defines the term "refugee" and sets minimum standards for the treatment of persons who are found to qualify for refugee status. Because the Convention was drafted in the wake of World War II, its definition of a refugee focuses on persons who are outside their country of origin and are refugees as a result of events occurring in Europe or elsewhere before 1 January 1951.

As new refugee crises emerged during the late 1950s and early 1960s, it became necessary to widen both the temporal and geographical scope of the Refugee Convention. Thus, a Protocol to the Convention was drafted and adopted.

1967 Protocol Relating to the Status of Refugees

The 1967 Refugee Protocol is independent of, though integrally related to, the 1951 Convention. The Protocol lifts the time and geographic limits found in the Convention's refugee definition.

Together, the Refugee Convention and Protocol cover three main subjects:

1. The basic refugee definition, along with terms for cessation of, and exclusion from, refugee status
2. The legal status of refugees in their country of asylum, their rights and obligations, including the right to be protected against forcible return, or *refoulement*, to a territory where their lives or freedom would be threatened
3. States' obligations, including cooperating with UNHCR in the exercise of its functions and facilitating its duty of supervising the application of the Convention

By acceding to the Protocol, States agree to apply most of the articles of the Refugee Convention to all persons covered by the Protocol's refugee definition. Yet the vast majority of States have preferred to accede to both the Convention and the Protocol. In doing so, States reaffirm that *both* treaties are central to the international refugee protection system.

REGIONAL LAWS AND STANDARDS

1969 Organization of African Unity (OAU) Convention Governing the Specific Aspects of Refugee Problems in Africa

The conflicts that accompanied the end of the colonial era in Africa led to a succession of large-scale refugee movements. These population displacements prompted the drafting and adoption of not only the 1967 Refugee Protocol but also the 1969 *OAU Convention Governing the Specific Aspects of Refugee Problems in Africa*. Asserting that the 1951 Refugee Convention is "*the basic and universal instrument relating to the status of refugees*", the OAU Convention is, to date, the only *legally binding* regional refugee treaty. Perhaps the most important portion of the OAU Convention is its definition of a refugee. The OAU Convention follows the refugee definition found in the 1951 Convention, but includes a more objectively based consideration: any person compelled to leave his/her country because of "*external aggression, occupation, foreign domination or events seriously disturbing public order in either part or the whole of his country of origin or nationality*". This means that persons fleeing civil disturbances, widespread violence and war are entitled to claim the status of refugee in States that are parties to this Convention, regardless of whether they have a well-founded fear of persecution.

The Cartagena Declaration

In 1984, a colloquium of government representatives and distinguished Latin American jurists was convened in Cartagena, Colombia to discuss the international protection of refugees in the region. This gathering adopted what became known as the Cartagena Declaration. The Declaration recommends that the definition of a refugee used throughout the Latin American region should include the 1951 Refugee Convention definition and also persons who have fled their country *"because their lives, safety or freedom have been threatened by generalised violence, foreign aggression, internal conflicts, massive violation of human rights or other circumstances which have seriously disturbed public order"*. Although the Declaration is not legally binding on States, most Latin American States apply the definition as a matter of practice; some have incorporated the definition into their own national legislation. The Declaration has been endorsed by the Organization of American States (OAS), the UN General Assembly, and UNHCR's advisory Executive Committee.

UN GENERAL ASSEMBLY RESOLUTIONS - THE 1967 DECLARATION ON TERRITORIAL ASYLUM

In 1967, the UN General Assembly adopted a Declaration on Territorial Asylum directed towards States. The Declaration reiterates that granting asylum is a peaceful and humanitarian act that cannot be regarded as unfriendly by any other State, and notes that it is the responsibility of the country of asylum to evaluate a person's claim for asylum.

UNHCR'S EXECUTIVE COMMITTEE CONCLUSIONS

UNHCR's *Executive Committee* (ExCom) advises the High Commissioner on the exercise of his/her functions. The annual Conclusions adopted by ExCom form part of the framework of the international refugee protection regime. They are based on the principles of the Refugee Convention and are drafted and adopted by consensus in response to particular protection issues. Executive Committee Conclusions represent the agreement of more than 50 countries that have great interest in and experience with refugee protection. These and other countries often refer to ExCom Conclusions when developing their own laws and policies.

NATIONAL LAWS AND STANDARDS

The adoption of national refugee legislation that is based on international standards is key to strengthening asylum, making protection more effective and providing a basis for seeking solutions to the plight of refugees. Incorporating international law into national legislation is particularly important in areas on which the Refugee Convention is silent, such as procedures for determining refugee status.

INTERNATIONAL HUMANITARIAN LAW

International humanitarian law provides that victims of armed conflict, whether displaced or not, should be respected, protected against the effects of war, and provided with impartial assistance. Because many refugees find themselves in the midst of international or internal armed conflict, refugee law is often closely linked to humanitarian law. *The Fourth Geneva Convention*

Relative to the Protection of Civilian Persons in Time of War contains an article that deals specifically with refugees and displaced persons. The Additional Protocol I provides that refugees and stateless persons are to be protected under the provisions of Parts I and III of the Fourth Geneva Convention. But humanitarian law can protect refugees only where it applies, *i.e.,* in situations of international or internal armed conflict. If a refugee flees armed conflict, but finds asylum in a country that is not involved in international or internal armed conflict, humanitarian law will not apply to that refugee.

WHAT PARLIAMENTS AND THEIR MEMBERS CAN DO

Parliaments and their members have a crucial role to play in ensuring protection to refugees both in law and in practice.

Key to that effect are the following steps:

- *Incorporate the principle of non-refoulement:* The principle of *non-refoulement* should be incorporated into national legislation. To do so, laws concerning the entry of foreigners and border-control requirements must reflect the difference between those seeking asylum and others who may want to enter a country for other reasons. Review of national legislation on immigration may be necessary. Asylum-seekers should be offered a fair and efficient procedure in which to present their claims for asylum.
- *Broaden the refugee definition*: Parliaments and their members may wish to consider incorporating an expanded refugee definition, such as that found in the OAU Convention and the Cartagena Declaration, in national legislation. Parliamentarians may also wish to review the situation of internally displaced persons in their country, if any, to facilitate their protection and to bring their plight to the attention of the international community.
- *Accede to international treaties*: The government should be encouraged to take steps with a view to accession to the Refugee Convention and Protocol, if it has not already done so. Accession to international human rights treaties relevant to refugee protection, particularly the *Convention against Torture* and the *Convention on the Rights of the Child*, and to international humanitarian law treaties should also be considered. On the regional level, parliaments in African countries that have not acceded to the OAU Convention should consider accession. Regional human rights treaties in Africa, Europe and the Americas also provide standards relevant to refugee protection. Countries in those regions should consider acceding to them.
- *Review reservations and restrictive interpretations*: The validity of reservations and restrictive interpretations ought to be reviewed periodically. In the absence of any steps to that effect by the

Executive, Members of Parliament may put questions to the Government or even present a private Member bill.

- *Implement international standards:* Inspiration can be drawn from a significant body of international standards - including the Conclusions adopted by UNHCR's Executive Committee and guidelines, produced by UNHCR, on a range of refugee-related issues - in devising national systems of refugee protection. UNHCR offices can assist parliamentarians by providing information on these standards and commenting on proposed legislation.
- *Encourage cooperation with UNHCR:* Parliamenta-rians can ensure that their government provides UNHCR with information on the number and condition of refugees on the national territory, the implementation of the Refugee Convention, and the laws, regulations and decrees in force related to refugees. Parliamentarians can also seek UNHCR's views on matters related to refugee protection, including proposed or pending legislation, court cases and policy decisions. Since UNHCR has offices in nearly 120 countries, parliamentarians in most countries will find a UNHCR office in their capital city.
- *The Role of UNHCR:* A humanitarian and non-political organization, UNHCR is mandated by the United Nations to protect refugees and help them find solutions to their plight. As the problem of displacement has grown in complexity over the past half century, UNHCR has also grown to meet the challenge. The Office, founded in 1950, has expanded from a relatively small, specialized agency with an envisioned three-year lifespan to an organization of over 4,000 staff members with offices in nearly 120 countries and an annual budget of US$1 billion. In addition to offering legal protection, UNHCR now also provides material relief in major emergencies, either directly or through partner agencies. In its first fifty years, UNHCR has protected and assisted more than 50 million people and its work has earned two Nobel Peace Prizes. At the international level, UNHCR promotes international refugee agreements and monitors government compliance with international refugee law. UNHCR staff promote refugee law among all people who are involved in refugee protection, including border guards, journalists, NGOs, lawyers, judges and senior governmental officials. At the field level, UNHCR staff work to protect refugees through a wide variety of activities, including responding to emergencies, relocating refugee camps away from border areas to improve safety; ensuring that refugee women have a say in food distribution and social services; reuniting separated families; providing information to refugees on conditions in their home country so they can make informed decisions about return; documenting a refugee's need for resettlement to a second country of asylum; visiting detention

centres; and giving advice to governments on draft refugee laws, policies and practices. UNHCR seeks long-term solutions to the plight of refugees by helping refugees repatriate to their home country, if conditions are conducive to return, integrate into their countries of asylum, or resettle in second countries of asylum.

REFUGEES ARRIVING IN LARGE NUMBERS

When large numbers of refugees cross the border at once, their arrival may overwhelm the local capacity to protect and assist them. The international community needs to share the responsibility of assisting the country of asylum. Nevertheless, the observance of fundamental protection principles such as *Non-refoulement* is an independent obligation and cannot be conditioned on burdensharing. UNHCR makes every effort to assist asylum States to keep borders open, and to mobilize international support.

The right response to a large-scale influx of refugees will save lives, promote regional stability and encourage international cooperation. When refugees are pouring across a border, it is impractical if not impossible to examine individual asylum requests, even when there may be a doubt that the people should be recognized as refugees.

When the circumstances under which large numbers of people flee indicate that members of the group could be considered individually as refugees, it makes sense for the country of asylum to use "*prima facie*" or group status determination. This allows for basic protection and assistance to be extended to those in need, pending arrangements for a durable solution, without initially addressing the question of their status under the Refugee Convention and Protocol.

- "The Executive Committee recognizes that international solidarity and burden-sharing are of direct importance to the satisfactory implementation of refugee protection principles; stresses, however, in this regard, that access to asylum and the meeting by States of their protection obligations should not be dependent on burdensharing arrangements first being in place, particularly because respect for fundamental human rights and humanitarian principles is an obligation for all members of the international community."

Temporary Protection

Temporary protection is an immediate, short-term response when large numbers of people arrive after fleeing armed conflict, massive violations of human rights or other forms of persecution.

The purpose of temporary protection, as developed by European countries for people fleeing the former Yugoslavia, is to ensure protection in the "frontline" countries of asylum as well as to provide a coherent regional response. Temporary protection is based on the principles of the international refugee protection regime, since all those displaced are refugees within UNHCR's mandate and many also fulfil the Refugee Convention definition.

- "The Conference urges governments and parliaments to condemn the use of refugees either as human shields in armed conflicts or as political pawns." — 99th Conference of the Inter-Parliamentary Union, April 1998

Countries of asylum may end temporary protection when there is a fundamental change in the circumstances that prompted people to flee. When such change occurs, experience shows that the vast majority of people can and will return home voluntarily, even when the situation is far from ideal. Countries of asylum should take care not to push for premature returns, since that can destabilize the home country. Too rapid a return of too many people can put great pressure on a fragile peace and on what is likely to be a devastated infrastructure. In addition, countries of asylum must identify and protect the small minority who cannot return to their home countries, including those who have compelling reasons arising out of past persecution. Those who do not want to return should be given access to asylum procedures. Temporary protection should not continue for too long, even if the underlying circumstances have not improved, because people should not be left under minimum conditions of protection indefinitely. States should either employ their usual asylum procedures, or regularize the beneficiaries' residence.

UNHCR can offer advice on such issues as when to institute temporary protection, what treatment should be accorded beneficiaries, and when and how such protection should be ended.

- "The Conference urges the international community to provide timely and speedy humanitarian assistance and support to countries affected by an influx of refugees and displaced persons, and to help them particularly with the care and maintenance of large populations."— 99th Conference of the Inter-Parliamentary Union, April 1998

REFUGEE EMERGENCIES

WHAT IS A REFUGEE EMERGENCY

Refugee emergencies are times of crisis for the refugees and often for the country of asylum. Lives are at stake and a speedy response is essential. The country of asylum may be under tremendous pressure, and often under media scrutiny, and may not have had experience in handling the arrival of large numbers of hungry, sick, wounded or frightened people. Refugee emergencies almost always occur in the context of armed conflict and, in that sense, can be seen as an emergency within a larger catastrophe. Parliamentarians can take steps ahead of time to help ensure that refugees are protected during such difficult times. If a national legal framework and institutional structures are in place, UNHCR can mobilize international support much more quickly and effectively.

Responsibilities in an Emergency

The aim of emergency response is to provide protection and ensure that the necessary assistance reaches people in time. The country of asylum is responsible for the safety of, assistance to, and law and order among refugees on its territory. Governments often rely on the international community to help share the financial burden; UNHCR provides assistance to refugees at the request of governments. UNHCR is usually responsible for coordinating the response of the UN system, working closely with the World Food Programme, UNICEF, the United Nations Development Programme (UNDP), and others. NGOs play a critical role in assisting refugees in emergencies. Through implementing arrangements, the country of asylum, UNHCR and the various NGOs involved in the emergency divide responsibilities. Ideally, well-designed implementing arrangements avoid duplicated efforts and close gaps in assistance.

PROTECTION IN EMERGENCIES

When People flee War: Defining a Refugee

While within Africa and some Latin American States people fleeing from armed conflict are defined as refugees (under the OAU Convention and the Cartagena Declaration, respectively), people *anywhere* fleeing from armed conflict are refugees within UNHCR's mandate. However, in countries outside of Africa and Latin America, there may be a gap between the protection provided by States under the Refugee Convention, which requires that the person have a wellfounded fear of persecution linked to one of the five Convention grounds, and the protection provided by UNHCR under its broader mandate. This legal gap can result in very practical problems for victims of armed conflict. Parliamentarians can ensure that national legislation makes full provision for protection under the wider refugee definition, including for victims of armed conflict.

Relationship Between Conflict and Persecution

Conflict and persecution can exist side by side; indeed, conflict may be the very method chosen by the persecutor to repress or eliminate certain groups. In most cases, people who are fleeing from armed conflict will fit within the definition of a refugee found in the Refugee Convention. That is, *in addition* to being caught up in war, they will have a well-founded fear of persecution because of their race, religion, nationality, membership of a particular social group, or political opinion. People fleeing from "ethnic cleansing" in the former Yugoslavia or from genocide in Rwanda, for example, were escaping persecution based on a Convention ground, in which the means of persecution was the war itself. These are examples of large-scale persecution that were conducted along with, or as part of, military campaigns. Individuals may also be targeted for persecution during armed conflict for reasons reflected in the Refugee Convention definition.

Protection for People who do not Fit the Refugee Convention Definition

Those who flee from armed conflict are not always recognized as refugees in asylum countries that do not use the wider definition of refugee found in the OAU Convention and the Cartagena Declaration. Nevertheless, in practice it is recognized that people escaping from war cannot be returned to their home countries. Most States grant these individuals some type of permission to remain under domestic legislation or administrative discretion. Parliamentarians in countries that do not adopt the expanded refugee definition may want to consider making provision in national law for persons who do not meet the Refugee Convention definition but who are, nevertheless, in need of protection.

Group Determination

In a refugee emergency, securing protection is the first priority. When it is obvious that large numbers of people are fleeing armed conflict or other mass violations of human rights, it is neither practical nor necessary to examine individual claims for refugee status.

UNHCR and States usually resort to refugee status determination for the entire group based on their knowledge of objective conditions in the country of origin. Every member of the group is considered a refugee *prima facie*, *i.e.*, in the absence of evidence to the contrary.

Relationship Between Mass Influx and Asylum

In countries that haven't used *prima facie* recognition on a group basis, temporary protection has usually been offered, allowing people immediate access to safety and protecting their basic human rights. Temporary protection is a device used to respond to an emergency when there are clear protection needs but little or no possibility to determine such needs quickly on an individual basis.

Temporary protection needs to last only until there is a fundamental change in the circumstances that prompted people to flee. When this fundamental change occurs, the country of asylum may presume that the need for protection no longer exists and that the vast majority of beneficiaries can return in safety. Nevertheless, countries of asylum must be aware that some people will continue to be in need of protection, including for reasons related to past persecution. States will have to have a mechanism, normally the refugee status determination system, for identifying such people.

Exclusion

Some people do not deserve international protection. Individuals can be excluded from refugee status even if a group determination has been made.

Identifying and returning excludable individuals may be very difficult for the country of asylum. It is advisable that States seek UNHCR's advice and assistance at the outset of an emergency to assess the profile of the refugee population and the resources available for separating those excluded from protection from the rest of the refugees.

PROTECTING REFUGEE WOMEN

Specific Conditions Affecting Women as Refugees

Women comprise at least half of any refugee population. Refugee women have many of the same needs as refugee men: protection against forced return, respect for their human rights while in exile and help in finding durable solutions to their plight. However, they also have different and additional needs throughout their experience as refugees. In the often-chaotic conditions of a large-scale refugee emergency, women are extremely vulnerable to sexual and other forms of violence. In addition, they frequently bear responsibility for other, more vulnerable, family members such as children and the elderly. Women are often separated from male family members who may be taking part in the conflict or staying behind to guard the family's property.

In camp situations, the disruption of traditional patterns of decision-making may leave women without a voice in matters that affect their daily lives and their security. For example, if men, or a certain faction of men, control the distribution of aid, women may be forced to exchange sexual favours for food. Women may also be at risk of sexual violence from other refugees, the local population, nearby combatants and the police or security forces in the country of asylum. In countries with individual status determination procedures, women travelling with male family members may not be given an opportunity to present their own claim, even if the man's claim is denied. Women may find it more difficult to speak frankly to a male interviewer or through a male interpreter, particularly if some aspect of their refugee claim involves sexual violence or questions of family honour. In addition to procedural obstacles in status determination systems, there may be legal impediments to the accurate assessment of gender-related claims.

Gender-related Persecution

Gender-related persecution is a term used in international refugee law to describe a variety of claims, including some presented by men. While gender is not specifically mentioned in the Refugee Convention (the fear of persecution must be on account of race, religion, nationality, membership of a particular social group, or political opinion), it is accepted that gender can influence or dictate the type of persecution suffered and/or the reasons for such treatment. Gender-related claims have typically encompassed acts of sexual violence, family violence, coerced family planning, female genital mutilation, punishment for transgression of social mores and homosexuality. These claims may be quite different from each other in that they mix *forms* of persecution with *reasons* for persecution. What they have in common, however, is gender as a relevant factor in determining the claim.

In this light, persecution is not necessarily or only caused by the victim's gender, but by the perpetrator's ideology: that people deviating from their proscribed gender role shall be persecuted. For example, women who fear persecution because they transgress social mores are not usually persecuted because they are women, but because they refuse to be "proper" women.

The Refugee Convention definition must be interpreted in a gender-sensitive way. Just as information about an asylum applicant's home country is crucial for determining a "typical" refugee claim, so is understanding the socially-defined roles in the home country essential to correctly interpreting the refugee definition. This approach has been endorsed by a number of international bodies, including UNHCR's Executive Committee.

Examining Women's Asylum Requests

UNHCR and a few States have issued guidelines on how to examine women's asylum requests, including gender-related claims. There is a growing body of jurisprudence on such cases and many States have expressed an interest in incorporating this thinking into their protection framework.

In addition to the general body of international human rights law applicable to all people, there are a number of human rights standards that directly address the situation of women refugees and asylum-seekers. The pre-eminent international legal instrument is the *Convention on the Elimination of All Forms of Discrimination against Women* and its *Optional Protocol*.

This Convention establishes standards for States in a number of areas that are important to refugee women, including:

- Suppression of all forms of traffic in women and exploitation of prostitution
- Nationality
- Education
- Employment
- Health care
- Particular problems of rural women
- Equality before the law
- All matters pertaining to marriage and family relations

Other relevant international standards include the UN General Assembly Declaration on the Elimination of Violence against Women, which recognizes refugee women as one of the groups especially vulnerable to violence and calls upon States to adopt measures directed towards the elimination of violence against women.

CRIME AGAINST REFUGEES: AVOIDING VICTIMIZATION

Although official crime statistics do not account separately for victimization among refugees, it is valid to assume that newcomers have certain vulnerabilities that make them targets of criminals. Refugees who are uncertain about the workings of the American criminal justice system, who speak or understand little English, and who may be reluctant to talk freely with police authorities due to experiences in their native land, open themselves to a wide array of crimes, many of which are never reported.

Crime victimizes a community in many ways:

- Residents fear and distrust people around them. Neighbourhood anxiety and tension increase.
- Criminals take over public spaces, such as parks, forcing residents back into their houses.
- The prices of goods and services may increase to cover losses incurred due to crimes.
- Local businesses may close or move to a safer neighbourhood, thus decreasing opportunities for employment and services available to local communities.
- Abandoned buildings attract further criminal activity ¾ drug sales, arson, and vandalism.
- The sense of community cohesion and pride may deteriorate as individual isolation increases.
- Crime also interferes with civic activity, such as welcoming and supporting refugees. It interferes with a community's ability to deal with constructive change.

Groups or individuals associated with refugee resettlement - and refugees themselves can take steps to decrease their chances of refugee victimization:

- Encourage community familiarity and solidarity. Plan picnics, festivals, or other social events to draw neighbours out of their houses. Plan a wide range of opportunities sports events, concerts, summer day camps, art shows ¾ for neighbours to get to know each other. Neighbours who know each other watch out for each other.
- Get in touch with law enforcement and experienced community crime prevention organizations. Ask them to come into the community to make presentations, such as how to report crimes and participate in court processes.
- Organize a youth patrol ¾ teens who help clean up the neighbourhood, provide baby-sitting services, or assist elderly residents with routine chores.
- Contact government agencies, such as housing and transportation, to address physical problems in the neighbourhood, such as abandoned cars, deteriorating housing, and poor street lighting.

- Organize a citizens' committee to design neighbour-hood strategies for increased personal and neighbourhood safety.

Victimization rates decrease when community members learn both how to work together to prevent crime as well as how to work with the police when crimes occur.

HOW REFUGEES CAN HELP LAW ENFORCEMENT PROTECT THEM

Refugees can contribute to the safety and security of their neighbourhoods by learning to work in an effective partnership with law enforcement officials. They can learn how to use crime prevention skills and how to report suspicious activities to the police department. Documents that explain the following steps can be translated into the native language o the refugees in the community.

- *Anyone witnessing or experiencing a crime should do the following*:
  - Call the police (in most communities, 9-1-1) immediately.
  - Try to stay calm, even though the experience may be upsetting.
  - Tell the police what happened, where it happened, and the caller's name.
  - If anyone is hurt, ask for medical assistance.
  - Write down everything about the crime to tell the police.
  - Try to remember as possible, such as the scene of the crime, number and description of suspects (age, sex, colour of hair, height, weight, distinguishing features) or description of criminal's vehicle (make, model, colour, license number) and which direction it traveled when it left the scene.
  - If asked to make a complaint or testify in court, do so. Cooperation might keep the criminal from victimizing someone else.
  - If asked to identify a suspect in a lineup, do the best possible job, and remember that the suspect can not see the people looking at him.

JOINING GROUPS: BECOMING AN INVOLVED COMMUNITY MEMBER

When refugees first arrive in their new community, they are faced with the immediate challenges of learning a new language, adjusting to a new social atmosphere, seeking employment, and establishing a daily routine that fits into the standards and traditions of a new culture. This period of adjustment may take many months ¾ or longer ¾ but at some point, the initial shock of resettlement will be replaced by a feeling of familiarity and accommodation. While going through this period of adjustment, refugees will find that there are people and organized groups who share common interests with them in neighbourhood improvement, community safety, recreational activities, political issues environmental concerns, and economic progress, among other things.

These groups are able to bring support and power to an issue that individuals alone could not. They work for the betterment of the community in many ways. Many have funds that enable the group to reach its goals more easily. By becoming active in efforts to improve their community, refugees find their concerns get greater attention from the community. Involvement in local groups such as neighbourhood associations, school organizations, service clubs, and church-related groups bring their refugee interests and concerns to a wider audience, resulting in partnerships for positive action.

For example, if members of a Polish refugee group in Chicago find that there are insufficient business networks that include Polish merchants, they can join a neighbourhood merchants' association that works closely with the Chamber of Commerce. Through this link, the Polish merchants can bring their concerns to the attention of the Chamber, requesting inclusion in Chamber-sponsored events, such as neighbourhood business breakfasts and seminars. As a result, Polish refugees become acquainted with other business owners and are exposed to a wider range of economic opportunities.

USING EXISTING SYSTEMS TO EDUCATE OTHERS

Part of the challenge for refugees is to learn about life in the United States. The other part is to teach Americans about the refugees' native cultures. This two-way educational process is critical for mutual understanding and trust. Many avenues for cultural education already exist. There are ready-made audiences in schools, special interest groups, law enforcement-sponsored events, religious institutions, neighbourhood organizations, civic groups, businesses, and youth clubs. Newcomers can share information about national history, religious traditions, holidays, cooking styles, literature, music, or art.

Approaching a group to offer cultural education can be as simple as making a phone call or writing a letter. Find out the name of the person in charge of scheduling special events. Ask if there are people in the group interested in learning about another culture.

Tell the scheduling chairman:

- The subject of the talk is (probably something that would be of specific interest to them, such as a presentation on schooling in the refugee's home country to an assembly at the local elementary school);
- When the talk can be given (ask when it would be convenient for them);
- How long the presentation will take (this will depend on the age of the audience; younger groups tend to become restless during long presentations);
- Whether special equipment, such as a microphone, slide projector, blackboard, or record player will be needed; and whether materials will be handed out.
- Whether materials will be handed out.

A brief, one-time presentation may expand to become a yearly ¾ or more frequent ¾ event for all the students at the high school, or for a local art museum association, or for a group of music historians. Find out how many and who the audience will be. Tailor the presentation to the audience's interest, bring artifacts or examples, and leave time to answer questions.

CRIME PREVENTION: PERSONAL SAFETY, NEIGHBOURHOOD AND BUSINESS WATCH

Teaching personal safety and organizing crime prevention programmes in multi-cultural communities pose unique challenges. Refugees may take a long time to adjust to their new surroundings, not immediately welcoming what they may perceive as intrusions into their lifestyle. Once trust has been established, interest in and acceptance of local programmes will come, even if the process is slow. The language barrier is the first problem. It can be overcome at least in part with competent interpreters and welltranslated materials. When approaching new people in a refugee community, law enforcement will be received with greater hospitality and less reluctance if accompanied by someone the refugees trust, such as a representative from the volunteer agency that helped with the initial resettlement process. It is important when teaching crime prevention techniques to avoid increasing a newcomer's fear of crime, which could result in isolation from the rest of the community.

Accurate information can also emphasize the positive skills of self-protection. Assure newcomers that neighbours, police officers, and community groups are there to help them live safely in their new community. Developing or expanding a crime prevention programme that addresses the concerns of refugees is more successful when it couples efforts to teach personal safety techniques with those that bring the neighbourhood together. Personal safety should emphasize such basic rules as locking doors and window, even when someone is home; leaving lights on outside the home after dark; keeping a list of emergency phone numbers posted by the phone, storing large sums of money or valuables in a safety deposit box rather than at home and keeping money safely concealed, except when paying for something. Neighbourhood programmes, such as Neighbourhood Watch and Business Watch, encourages residents to watch for suspicious activity in the community and summon appropriate help. When educating neighbours to be more alert in recognizing suspicious activities, also teach them the appropriate action to take. Newcomers to the neighbourhood may be willing to join a watch programme when they feel comfortable being around their American neighbours.

Watch organizers should make special attempts to make refugees feel welcome and carefully explain the details of the programme. When organizing a Neighbourhood or Business Watch group, ask for help from local government agencies, private advocacy and service organizations, religious institutions, mediation services, and other groups experienced in working with refugees or immigrants. An interpreter will be helpful during meetings. Print materials in appropriate languages, if reliable translators are available.

EVALUATING BRIDGE-BUILDING AND CROSSING EFFORTS

It is vitally important to be able to evaluate efforts to build and cross cultural bridges with the refugee population in the community. Programme evaluation is a practical tool.

It shows whether the programme should keep doing what it's doing, do more of it, do it differently, or stop doing it.

- Evaluation tells if goals have been reached, such as:
- Reducing crime in refugee communities;
- Reducing the fear of crime;
- Developing long-term programmes that help refugees become participating members of the community;
- Helping refugees become self-sufficient;
- Keeping young refugees out of gangs or other trouble;
- Increasing reports of crimes against refugees; and
- Raising the quality of life for refugees moving into the Community.

Programme evaluation has other useful benefits. Valid records of successes (or failures) ¾ barriers faced, lessons learned ¾ will affect the amount of public, volunteer, and other support the programme might attract as well as the amount of future funding it receives. When setting up a programme, think in terms of the goals (desired outcome) of the programme, what elements must go into programme to reach the goals, and the expected results.

For example, if a youth programme was established to deal with high school graffiti that makes ethnic slurs against Jewish teens from the former Soviet Union, the program's success might be assessed this way:

- *The desired outcome*: Greater cultural sensitivity among teens and reduction or elimination of ethnic-bias hate crimes at school and after school.
- *Programme elements*: A multicultural youth club that sponsors an athletic programme, social opportunities for young people from differing ethnic backgrounds, a graffiti paintout squad, and a twiceyearly assembly programme featuring skits and ethnic songs and dances for all students.
- *Programme results*: The athletic programme developed into one of the sports highlights of the year, resulting in a yearly tennis tournament with other school teams. After two assembly programmes, the American students expressed an interest in sponsoring a multicultural food fair as a fund-raiser. Incidents and perpetrators of anti-refugee graffiti were reported to school security and the police department. Six months after the youth club was organized, the graffiti

> problem was under control. Only one incident and that was non-ethnic - had been reported in the six months compared with six or seven at the program's start, all of which were anti-semitic.

In this example, the measurements of success are twofold: simply put, the problem ¾ anti-ethnic graffiti ¾ was resolved. Additionally, attitudes towards refugee students changed, as measured by increased interest, involvement, and acceptance by the American students. These changes can be gauged by student surveys, crime reports, clippings from the student newspaper or the local media, or interviews with teachers, coaches, and other school personnel. Crime data are valuable as pre- and post-programme measurements.

They measure the situation before the programme began and compare it with the situation after the programme has been in effect for a reasonable amount of time, which varies with the type of programme. Mid-programme evaluations are also valuable for recording problems that may have developed. If the programme is not eliciting the desired outcome, it may be wise to conduct a midcourse correction by changing some of the programme elements. A midterm evaluation may also reveal that the programme is not working at all and that the best choice is to discontinue that effort and develop a substitute or alternate programme.

In these times of limited resources, it is also useful to determine whether the programme is cost-effective. Measure both direct and indirect costs that have gone into the programme, such as costs for printing translated educational pamphlets, purchasing athletic equipment, and providing refreshments. Indirect costs can include time at the school, talking with parents about the programme, and any travel costs incurred. If graffiti at the high school is costing $3,000 a year to clean up and the programme that eliminates graffiti costs $1,750 a year, the programme is certainly cost effective. After the programme has achieved measurable success, with evidence that it is making a difference not only at the school but also in the reduced amount of graffiti on buildings in the community, business owners may be willing to become partners by donating funds to support a programme expansion ¾ or at least a continuation. They may prefer to donate sports equipment, food for social events, or other inkind items. Always remember to publicly acknowledge donations from benefactors. Public recognition will elicit continued support from current partners and encourage new partners to get on the bandwagon.

SUCCESSFUL BRIDGE-CROSSING: A SUMMARY OF ACTIONS LAW ENFORCEMENT CAN TAKE

- When refugees have resettled in the community, take the lead - assign officers to patrol their neighbourhood on foot to get to know them, one-on-one. This process may take time, but the time and effort are worth it.

- Ask a qualified bi-lingual member of the refugee community to volunteer or work as a liaison between the refugee and law enforcement communities.
- Set up a storefront in a refugee neighbourhood to provide decentralized police and interpreter services. Encourage other government agencies social services, medical, family assistance - to offer services and information through the storefront.
- Start a community outreach programme that strengthens trust between law enforcement and refugees through counseling, athletic programmes, housing assistance, and other services.
- Make a special effort to befriend young refugees who often find barriers easier to overcome than do their parents. Teaching children to roller skate may help them win acceptance from American children in the neighbourhood. Coaching a young boy or girl on a softball team may keep him or her from joining a gang.
- Educate the community about bias- or hatemotivated crimes. Community intolerance of hateful prejudice is the keystone of hate-crime prevention.
- Develop personal safety and Neighbourhood or Business Watch programmes that include refugees. Take a little extra time for people who are just learning to speak and understand English.

REFUGEES FOR THE LAW ENFORCEMENT COMMUNITY

This stage will help members of the criminal justice community develop methods for serving refugee communities more effectively. It offers suggestions for getting to know newly resettled refugees and helping them learn how to live safely. It also discusses the problems of youth gangs and bias-motivated crimes. Finally, it describes successful crosscultural law enforcement programmes and the challenges they encountered - in communities around the country.

Though many Americans have lived and worked beside people who grew up in a different culture, a large number have not. For those who have never shared experiences with people from other cultures, the "American way of doing things" might seem to be the "right" way, or the "only" way.

They are not sensitive to the fact that there are other valid cultural values around the world. This cultural insensitivity may not be intentional, but it becomes a serious barrier to helping refugees through the difficult process of settling in a new community. Differences between cultures affect basic standards of behaviour, religious or holiday traditions, verbal and non-verbal communication patterns, styles of dressing, social attitudes, work ethics, and family relations.

But "different" doesn't mean "wrong." Different cultures can exist even within a region. The statement that a community of Southeast Asian refugees has settled in a city or town is not very specific. Similar to the regional differences found between residents of New Orleans, Louisiana, and Bronx, New York, substantial differences exist between refugees from Cambodia, Vietnam, and Laos. "Southeast Asian" is a term covering a broad expanse of cultures, all of them in the same section of the world but all having distinctive histories, religions, and social heritages. Regional differences occur between natives of different towns in those Southeast Asian countries. The languages, which may sound similar, have substantive differences in connotation and phrasing. A comparable example from the English language is the British use of "bonnet" for the hood of a car or "lift" for an elevator. Other refugees also come to the U.S. with adjustment problems - some similar and some quite dissimilar to those faced by Southeast Asians and with a variety of background experiences. One early study of Afghan refugees found that many of them viewed their stay as temporary and did not put much effort into assimilating into their new community. In 1986, Ethiopians who resettled into the U.S. had high education levels ¾ in fact, many of them had been college students - but their work experience was relatively limited. Knowledge of English varied greatly. The study found that Ethiopians had serious difficulty adjusting to the U.S. Polish refugees, many of whom were highly educated, were able to find employment more easily than some other refugee groups, the same study showed. Romanians were generally well-educated, highly motivated to find jobs, and hard-working. However, as a group they did not socialize with existing residents; their churches were their main focus of community interaction.

WHY LEARN ABOUT THE CAMBODIANS, THE ROMANIANS, THE HAITIANS, OR THE LAOTIANS

The answer is simple. They are members of the community that law enforcement protects and serves. Certainly, members of the community share the responsibility for keeping themselves safe, but they can do so only if they understand how, when, and why. That is why they need to understand the police, and the police need to understand them. Minority ethnic residents may currently represent only a small portion of a jurisdiction's total population, but consider some projections for the future. A study published in 1992 estimates a remarkable shift in American cultural diversity over the next 50 years. By the year 2040, it is projected that the nation's population will grow to 355.5 million and experience a profound change in its racial and ethnic makeup.

That total is expected to include:

- 210.5 million (non-Hispanic) European Americans, an increase of less than 13%;
- 44.1 million African Americans, an increase of almost 50%;
- 34.5 million Asian and Pacific Islander Americans, an increase of nearly 400%; and
- 64.2 million Hispanics, an increase of nearly 200%.

If refugees (or other cultural minorities) live in a community, its law enforcement personnel need to be culturally competent to be able to do their job well. The Community Relations Service of the U.S. Department of Justice says that 'becoming culturally competent is a developmental process for the individual and for the system. It is not something that happens because one reads a book or attends a workshop or happens to be a member of a minority group. It is a process born of commitment to provide quality services to all. " Becoming culturally competent requires understanding how values, beliefs, attitudes, and traditions influence behaviour.

COMING TO AMERICA: A REFUGEE'S EXPERIENCE IN A NEW LAND

The formal process of refugee resettlement begins with an official approval from the U.S. Department of State for the refugee, and possibly his or her family, to come to the United States. After arriving in a U.S. refugee camp, the refugee is processed through a Volunteer Assistance Agency (VOLAG) that contracts with the State Department to attend to the refugee's immediate needs for language training, medical credentials, job development and training, living arrangements, and skills leading to selfsufficiency. The refugee may meet with a representative from the state Office of Refugee Resettlement, a sponsor, or a member of a Mutual Assistance Association, who may help him or her with cultural adjustment.

This process ¾ and the assistance provided - is highly variable, and in some cases, the resettled refugee may have received little practical assistance before reaching a community. Try to imagine being suddenly removed from familiar surroundings in Houston, Topeka, Jersey City, or Jacksonville. Imagine being suddenly transported with limited possessions to a community in Poland or Russia where few people speak English. There is some assistance from a local group with housing and immediate needs, but that is all. Imagine being responsible for assimilating yourself and your family into a new community. Imagine being in this young Vietnamese woman's shoes: Six months after she arrived in the Portland area, she became a victim of sexual assault. She spoke very little English, felt overwhelmed by the strange surroundings, and was terrified after the incident. Even though women in her culture traditionally don't speak of such personal things, she was encouraged to talk to the police about her assault and was assisted with the reporting procedure. She was also referred to the Women's Strength Programme of the Portland Police Bureau that teaches women self-defence tactics. Unfortunately, she could not attend the programme because she spoke so little English.

However, Portland reports that the programme is currently developing a course for non- English-speaking newcomers. In Lincoln, Nebraska, a Vietnamese family was threatened in their home by a young male who set fire to their trash can after midnight. The suspect then knocked on the door and demanded a hundred dollars to extinguish the fire. The family called the police but were unable to explain in English what had happened. The next day, the family went to the Lincoln Police Department and, with the help of a community service liaison as interpreter. The police officer and the interpreter suggested that the family have a home security survey and join Operation I.D. With the family's consent, the community service liaison accompanied the home security officer as he conducted the survey. In New Jersey, a Vietnamese woman was injured and robbed by a group of teenagers. She was scared and didn't report the crime to anyone because, based on her experiences in her home country, she thought no one would pay attention. The teens returned to her apartment to harass and threaten her, saying they would kill her if she told anyone.

They phoned her, sent her threatening letters, and rang her doorbell. She and her mother, who lived with her, felt frightened and helpless. The woman gathered her courage and reported her experiences to the International Institute of New Jersey. The Institute's Crime Victimization Coordinator, the woman sought help from the Crime Victimization Programme, which acted as a bridge to services from the local police department. 'She now freely reports crimes to the police with the aid of a translator and sees the police as supportive public servants," reports Nguyen. The complicated realities of laws, rights, and regulations can overwhelm a new resident. The confusion of their new experiences is compounded by strange driving regulations, unfamiliar symbols on street signs, grocery stores with unusual foods, unaccustomed school enrollment procedures, congested traffic, and the many differences in dayto-day commerce. And everything is labeled in a strange new language. For some refugees, it means starting life completely anew. When they feel comfortable in asking for help, newcomers look to people who can explain the social regulations and institutions that now shape their lives. If law enforcement reaches out with a patient and friendly hand, it can erase old stereotypes and build strong, safe bridges of understanding.

TAKING THE LEAD

Although a partnership is a two-way street, the host community often has the resources and the community base to take the lead in reaching out to new residents. Additionally, police officers and other members of the criminal justice system are role models for the community at large. If law enforcement takes the first step in working with families from another culture, others will follow that lead. This sets the stage for community-wide action to work more closely with refugees. To become culturally competent, take the first step to get to know the new members of the community. Take time out to talk with Cambodian shopkeepers. Spend an hour each afternoon at the playground in the area where Russian families have settled. Ask to talk about home security to a women's group, with help from an interpreter. Actively reach out to all the ethnic groups in the community. Check with local refugee resettlement groups for guidance.

GAINING ACCESS TO REFUGEE COMMUNITIES INFORMALLY AND FORMALLY

Research conducted by the Ford Foundation, positive personal interaction is key to gaining access to refugee communities.' Law enforcement often has excellent opportunities to do this through day-to-day application of community policing techniques.

Walking through housing complexes, talking with merchants, attending social or holiday gatherings, getting to know children playing on the street - these techniques are building blocks of inter-cultural trust.

- In Willows, California, ethnic tensions among youth have decreased since a Community Service Officer began meeting with the parents of Asian gang members.
- In Portland, Oregon, police meet regularly with H'mong community leaders and clan heads to discuss problems in their community. As a result of a better understanding between refugees and law enforcement, refugees are more comfortable in reporting crime, and community members are experiencing both a decrease in fear and a sense of increased protection.
- In Abbeville, Louisiana, the Office of Migration and Refugee Services and the Vietnamese-American Voters Association invited the mayor, a district court judge, and the chief of police to a town meeting focusing on crime reduction. A translator served as liaison in the dialogue.

One of the more effective methods of gaining access to the refugee population is through a local Mutual Assistance Association (MAA) or voluntary agency that has assisted or sponsored a local refugee resettlement. Although MAAs don't yet exist in all communities where refugees have settled, they are part of a growing movement to enable foreign-born residents to settle in the United States with a greater sense of cultural accommodation. Some MAAs are loosely structured; others are sophisticated, incorporated organizations. The groups provide a range of services to newcomers, varying from emergency assistance to formal employment and social service programmes to long-term community development.

They can be categorized into six major types, primary service or programme focus:

1. Cultural preservation and social activities: generally operating on a voluntary basis and picking up where the domestic resettlement system left off by helping newcomers find a home in American society.
2. Religious services: providing traditional religious and cultural services and/or informal counseling; usually headed by a monk, priest, or other religious leader.
3. Special constituency groups: including women's groups, senior citizen societies, specific fraternal groups (such as veterans), students, and

professional societies. These groups are usually able to mobilize volunteers and carry out well-organized programmes of activities that address the interests of their membership.

4. Resettlement/social services: providing a range of services with access to limited public funding. These groups usually have more demands on their services than they can meet.
5. Business and economic development: providing programmes with the potential to enhance refugee economic power. These groups lay the groundwork for local refugee business associations, chambers of commerce, and community development corporations.
6. Advocacy and political action: focusing on political action and advocacy, including election year politicking, voter registration drives, and working for selected candidates.

MAAs are an excellent source of help for law enforcement officers seeking to reach out to the refugee community. Many MAAs rely on a network of volunteers to offer interpreter/translation services or to serve as liaison between refugees and elements of the criminal justice system. They also help ease tensions if there is a lack of understanding between newcomers and law enforcement and work directly with law enforcement to establish personal safety, crime prevention, or other education programmes. Lists of local MAAs and of Volunteer Assistance Agencies (VOLAGS) are usually available from state offices of the Office of Refugee Resettlement or from the contact for volunteer organizations in the governor's office.

HUMAN RIGHTS LAW

In an attempt partially to overcome many of the structural and conceptual problems in engaging with human rights law, Lynn Freedman has proposed an alternative approach to expand the reach and relevance of human rights "on the ground." Her strategy is innovative in that it seeks to supplement the dominant approach to human rights work that takes place within international institutions as academic and legal discussions, and instead focuses on holding governments accountable for upholding human rights. We suggest Freedman's approach as our Path 2. Freedman advocates a strategy that extracts various values and principles from existing human rights law and applies them to local contexts — the on-the-ground analysis of the causal chain of ill health and mortality. While Freedman focuses on addressing maternal mortality, and her approach fits nicely with our example of the right to sutures, this strategy could be applied to addressing any health issue.

Motivated by the understanding that human dignity is the core value of human rights law and is meant to inspire profound and fundamental change in everyday interactions, Freedman proposes communities identify a set of values and principles in human rights law and then articulate how they can help guide community-level programmes to address maternal mortality. Using the case of the right to sutures, following Freedman's path would mean that we do not look for a right to sutures in the law but that the values and principles of human rights law can help communities identify, analyze, and address maternal mortality. In fact, Freedman interprets the legal discourse on the human right to health as encompassing the right not to die an avoidable death in pregnancy and childbirth. This right then translates into a societal obligation to provide emergency obstetric care, which would entail the provision of sutures when needed. But even when dealing with Non-governmental actors and a concern not just about sutures but maternal mortality more broadly, Freedman argues that the two values of human dignity and non-discrimination (among others), which are central to human rights law, can and should guide the manner in which emergency obstetric care is provided to patients and families as well as how it impacts hospital staff. This strategy may be seen as expanding human rights work, perhaps even liberating human rights from the existing legal language and mechanisms of international law. Importantly, rather than making rights into causal components of health and well-being, Freedman suggests that human rights values and principles, when combined with other health-related disciplines such as epidemiology, medicine, and operations research, can provide a plan of action for communities and states — in other words, human rights discourse can become a community health planning tool.

Although it is an important and worthwhile strategy to apply human rights law to the reality of how individuals are living their daily lives, this path also suffers from insufficient power as a tool for motivation. It is unclear as to why the values and principles that Freedman uses to guide maternal mortality programmes should be convincing to others simply on the basis of their presence in human rights legislation. Indeed, is it not ethical reasoning that first produced the values that then became enshrined as various rights in human rights law? That is, why would individuals and communities change their views and behaviors from the status quo to be in line with these values because these values are derived from human rights law? Granted, there is an international consensus embodied in such laws, but how convincing is it that individuals need to work and interact or programmes are designed and operated in accordance with certain values and principles because they were derived from human rights law? Perhaps more persuasive would be an ethical or moral argument. Why not present these values and principles as being important in the analysis of health issues and require allegiance because it is the right thing to do, or is what is demanded by social justice? Dignity, non-discrimination, equality, and participation are all values than can be highlighted within the ethical reasoning concerning what to do about maternal mortality in communities throughout the world. Synthesizing scientific and empirical insights from fields such as epidemiology, medicine, operations research, and public health with ethical reasoning about social justice by communities should be just as motivating — if not more so — for taking action than arguing that certain value-motivated actions are required simply because the values can be found in human rights law. The first path, in its best form, seeks to link the causal and distributional analysis of health issues with international human rights law. The second path seeks to craft and guide a social response by integrating various values with necessary and helpful insights from different fields while remaining grounded in human rights law.

The third path can be seen as being a step farther away from either of the first two, as it seeks to derive values from ethical reasoning that takes place at community-level, national, regional, and global spheres. The initial conclusion of that ethical reasoning, which took place within the Commission and is now ongoing and open to all, was to classify ill health and health inequalities that are avoidable through reasonable means as inequities. Furthermore, the Commission determined that such manifest inequities must be addressed as a matter of social justice. In addition to this ethical argument — that if one can reasonably prevent ill health and death, one should do so — is the argument that one must act to address social determinants of ill health and health inequalities on the basis of the duties to protect, promote, and fulfil relevant human rights.

There is broad convergence between research and action on rights-based approaches and social determinants of health when existing international agreements about human rights encompass actions to address the relevant social determinants. Indeed, perhaps it can be argued that enunciated rights and values implicit in human rights law cover the entire gamut of the social determinants of ill health and mortality.

However, social epidemiology has more explanatory potential than human rights approaches because the objects of research are not themselves ethical assertions, nor is the scope of social epidemiology limited by what is written in the law. Yet human rights law has the power to bridge social epidemiology with social action. The power of human rights lies in its prescriptive power to guide prospective social action through identifying legal obligations as well as underlying moral obligations of societies to act in particular ways. However, local and global discussions that link social epidemiological analysis with ethical reasoning about social justice would involve more actors and allow for a broader scope of social action, more expansive rights and responsibilities, and easier social acceptance. It is necessary to find a way to integrate these two approaches.

Perhaps one method that avoids the conflation of causal factors and human rights is to incorporate rights as distal factors in the chain of causation. A social environment that does not protect, promote, or fulfil the rights to food, clothing, shelter, or civil and political liberties can be understood to have a role in the chain of causation and distribution of ill health without being a direct causal factor. It would also make understandable the assertion that if individuals have a right to health, then they should also have a right to the determinants of health. In this way, integrating epidemiology and human rights — or constitutional rights for that matter — would illuminate the role of the lack of rights in the causal chain of ill health and mortality, while also avoiding having to show that every violation of a human right is bad for health. Such an integrated framework could move forward the agenda to improve health and health equity by harnessing the power of both human rights and epidemiology.

HEALTH EQUITY AND SOCIAL CONDITIONS

The human rights agreements referred to here include the Universal Declaration of Human Rights (UDHR), the International Covenant on Civil and Political Rights (ICCPR), the International Covenant on Economic, Social and Cultural Rights (ICESCR), and the officially recognized documents interpreting the ICESCR — the General Comments by the UN Committee on Economic, Social and Cultural Rights (CESCR), Limburg Principles on the Implementation of the ICESCR and the Maastricht Guidelines on Violations of Economic Social and Cultural Rights.

Together the UDHR, ICCPR, and ICESCR are referred to as the International Bill of Human Rights. The International Convention on the Elimination of All Forms of Racial Discrimination (ICERD) is also cited in this chapter.

The Right to Education

In countries of all levels of economic development, education — meaning general schooling, rather than health education — appears to be one of the most powerful social determinants of health. Education has appeared to be a stronger predictor of some health outcomes in some contexts than income or other measures of material resources; income or other material measures have, however, seemed more powerful predictors of other health outcomes, or in other contexts. It is difficult to disentangle education from material resources, given the importance of each in determining access to the latter.

The ICESCR expresses "the right of everyone to education . . . directed to the full development of the human personality." It notes that "education shall enable all persons to participate effectively in a free society." Sen's concept of basic capabilities has been influential in thinking about both human rights and health equity. In line with that concept, education, along with health, can be seen as a fundamental capability essential for fully achieving one's health potential as well as one's ability to function in society, including the capacity to earn a living and participate in the political process, concretely illustrating the interconnectedness of rights.

While the right to a standard of living adequate for health might not appear, in itself, necessarily to call for more than a minimum standard, consideration of the indivisibility of all human rights also would invoke the "right to the highest attainable standard of health." By extension, the human rights obligation would be to ensure to all citizens a standard of living required to achieve the highest attainable standard of health.

The "right to health" — or to the "highest attainable standard of health," as expressed in Article 12 of the ICESCR and other human rights agreements — has been criticized at times, however, for being vague or unrealistic, and therefore of limited use to guide policies. Despite the criticisms, there is evidence of its practical utility in the policy arena. Nevertheless, it is worth examining some of the shortcomings that have been articulated.

Some have pointed out that governments cannot be responsible for guaranteeing that everyone enjoys good health, let alone enjoys the highest possible levels of health. It is also reasonable to ask how one would monitor compliance with the right to health and how one would determine the highest attainable state of health for individuals or groups. Furthermore, without more rigorous definition, at least in theory, the right to the highest attainable standard of health could be used by some, in individual-level litigation, to justify unlimited expenditures on expensive medical technology for a few articulate, empowered individuals, to the detriment of investments in more equitable interventions with greater effectiveness in improving population health and reducing disparities. The CESCR's General Comment No. 14 on the right to the highest attainable standard of health as expressed in the ICESCR, however, explicitly emphasizes that, "[t]he right to health is not to be understood as a right to be *healthy*," because too many factors beyond a state's control influence health. Rather, it is "the right to a system of health protection which provides equality of opportunity to enjoy the highest attainable level of health."

Despite the fact that the indivisibility of rights implicitly links the right to health with the right to a standard of living adequate for health, the right to health has often been interpreted as applying only to medical care, and not as frequently used to argue for the need for greater equity in social conditions. CESCR General Comment No. 14, however, makes it clear that the right to health is not limited to medical care or traditional public health domains, stating, "On the contrary, the drafting history and the express wording [of the language of the right to health] acknowledge that the right to health embraces a wide range of socioeconomic factors that promote conditions in which people can lead a healthy life, and extends to the underlying determinants of health, such as food and nutrition, housing, access to safe and potable water and adequate sanitation, safe and healthy working conditions, and a healthy environment." A subsequent statement also notes, "The Committee interprets the right to health . . . as an inclusive right extending not only to timely and appropriate health care but also to the underlying determinants of health." Furthermore, UDHR Article 25.1, on the right to a standard of living adequate for health, is explicit about the connection between social conditions and health. Alicia Ely Yamin has noted that "rights must be realized inherently within the social sphere," and that this "formulation immediately suggests that determinants of health and ill health are not purely biological or 'natural' but are also factors of societal relations."

The Indivisibility of all Human Rights

The principle of the *indivisibility, interdependence, and inter-relatedness of all human rights,* as expressed in the International Bill of Rights (UDHR, ICCPR, and the ICESCR), has great relevance to both health equity and the link between social conditions and health. According to this principle, all human rights — civil, political, economic, social, and cultural — are interdependent and indivisible from one another. For example, according to this principle, the inability to realize one's economic and social rights (for example, the right to a standard of living adequate for health; the right to education; and the right to the highest attainable standard of health) is recognized as an impediment to realizing one's civil and political rights (for example, freedom of speech and assembly; and the right to participate in the political process in one's society). Similarly, denial of civil and political rights can constitute a serious threat to health, as illustrated not only by examples of genocide and torture, but also by the health consequences of apartheid and other regimes in which particular population groups have been systematically disenfranchised.

The knowledge gained over the past decade or two on the social determinants of health and health equity can contribute to human rights discussions by providing an empiric illustration supporting the principle of the indivisibility of all human rights.

The indivisibility of all human rights contributes to the concept of health equity in part by underscoring, for example, that failure to realize one's full health potential can have negative consequences for the ability to exercise one's civil and political rights, thereby strengthening arguments regarding a societal obligation to create conditions permitting everyone to achieve her or his health potential. It also can strengthen the arguments for the need to pursue equity in all the determinants of health, including living standards, education, and the ability to participate fully in society and the political process.

Article 25.1 of the UDHR explicitly acknowledges the link between living conditions and health: "Everyone has the right to a standard of living adequate for the health and well-being of himself and of his family" The right to a standard of living adequate for health is of clear, direct, and substantial relevance to health equity, in that health equity requires an equitable distribution not only of medical care, but also of the social and economic conditions necessary for health.

The right to "a standard of living adequate for health" does not entail an obligation to ensure equal standards of living, so long as a standard adequate for health is achieved.

It seems reasonable that increases in living standards above a certain high level might not necessarily translate into increases in health; however, a US study including an unusually wide range of income levels showed incremental improvements in health (as reflected by functional limitations among the elderly) with income levels up to seven times the federal poverty level. In addition, income gradients in multiple child and adult health indicators in the US have been demonstrated in studies where the most affluent group had incomes at least four times the federal poverty level.

Non-discrimination

Another human rights principle with strong and pervasive links to core concepts of health equity and relevance to the role of social conditions in health is the cross-cutting principle of non-discrimination. Non-discrimination applies to all rights; the International Bill of Human Rights and multiple General Comments specify that everyone is entitled to all human rights without distinction based on "race, colour, sex, language, religion, political or other opinion, national or social origin, property, birth or other status." In ICESCR General Comment 20, the CESCR added "ethnic origin" to this list ("'race and colour,' which includes an individual's ethnic origin"), referring to all these categories as the "express grounds" for which discrimination is prohibited. It is worth noting that the language explicitly includes both socioeconomic resources and social position as prohibited bases for discrimination; the terms "social origin," "property," and "birth" refer unambiguously and explicitly to wealth and to the relative social and economic standing of the family into which an individual is born.

General Comment 20 also addresses the "other status" category of prohibited grounds for discrimination, stating that the "nature of discrimination varies according to context and evolves over time," therefore requiring a "flexible approach to interpreting 'other status.'" Referring to ICESCR Article 2, paragraph 2, the following paragraph subheadings within General Comment 20 (as a non-exhaustive list, given the fluid nature of discrimination) identified additional "implied grounds" for which discrimination is prohibited under the "other status" category: disability (paragraph 28), age (paragraph 29), nationality (paragraph 30), marital and family status (paragraph 31), sexual orientation and gender identity (paragraph 32), health status (paragraph 33), place of residence (paragraph 34), and economic and social situation (paragraph 35).

While the ICESCR itself does not state that priority attention should be given to disadvantaged groups, the UN Committee on Social, Economic and Cultural Rights, has made it unambiguously clear, both in their General Comments on the ICESCR, and in their comments on the reports that state parties are required to submit at regular intervals, that giving priority attention to vulnerable and marginalized groups is one of the Covenant's main intents, and a core obligation of states.

Other official interpretations of the ICESCR supporting the obligation to prioritize vulnerable groups are stated in the Limburg Principles on the Implementation of the International Covenant on Economic, Social and Cultural Rights (1986), and The Maastricht Guidelines on Violations of Economic, Social and Cultural Rights (1997). Affirmative action to preferentially promote the achievement of rights by groups who are vulnerable because they have historically experienced discrimination is justified, so long as the preference is not permanent, and is removed once a group is no longer vulnerable.

The ICERD states: Special measures taken for the sole purpose of securing adequate advancement of certain racial or ethnic groups or individuals requiring such protection as may be necessary in order to ensure such groups or individuals equal enjoyment or exercise of human rights and fundamental freedoms shall not be deemed racial discrimination, provided, however, that such measures do not, as a consequence, lead to the maintenance of separate rights for different racial groups and that they shall not be continued after the objectives for which they were taken have been achieved.

Similarly, the CESCR stated the following in General Comment 16 (under "Temporary Special Measures"): The principles of equality and non-discrimination, by themselves, are not always sufficient to guarantee true equality. Temporary special measures may sometimes be needed in order to bring disadvantaged or marginalized persons or groups of persons to the same substantive level as others.

Temporary special measures aim at realizing not only de jure or formal equality, but also de facto or substantive equality for men and women. However, the application of the principle of equality will sometimes require that States parties take measures in favour of women in order to attenuate or suppress conditions that perpetuate discrimination.

As long as these measures are necessary to redress de facto discrimination, and are terminated when de facto equality is achieved, such differentiation is legitimate. States have the responsibility not only to strive to end intentionally discriminatory actions and structures, but also to strive to end de facto discrimination, that is, structural or institutional patterns resulting in, exacerbating, or perpetuating inequality in obstacles to realizing rights, regardless of intent.

The ICERD states: "Each State Party shall take effective measures to review governmental, national and local policies, and to amend, rescind or nullify any laws and regulations which have *the effect* of creating or perpetuating racial discrimination wherever it exists."

Similarly, the CESCR's General Comment 20 defined discrimination as "any distinction, exclusion, restriction or preference or other differential treatment that is directly or indirectly based on the prohibited grounds of discrimination and which has the *intention or effect* of nullifying or impairing the recognition, enjoyment or exercise on an equal footing of [ICESCR] rights." Gillian MacNaughton has noted examples of reports from the International Committee for Civil and Political Rights in which the issues singled out as manifesting discriminatory patterns involve underlying social inequality between groups; for example, the disproportionate representation of African Americans among homeless people in the US.

Equality

The equality of all persons "in dignity and rights" can be seen as the basis for non-discrimination as well as for all human rights; this is paralleled by the basis for the concept of equity, which rests on valuing all persons equally. The operational definition of equality in the field of human rights — apart from equality before the law — has been much debated.

The concept of equality has been no less contentious in the field of health equity. Equity and equality are seen by many as distinct, with equity potentially requiring inequality, that is, allocating more resources (including resources addressing social determinants as well as medical care) to those who need more.

Two dimensions are often distinguished: horizontal equity, or equal resources for equal need, and vertical equity, or more resources for greater need; defining need can be challenging, however. Furthermore, in situations where a particular group of persons — for example, women, or people of a lower caste — is especially disenfranchised, a clear call for equality rather than equity may be essential, because some definitions of equity may leave too much room for interpretation. For example, more enfranchised groups may argue that the treatment of a disenfranchised group is "equitable," given the latter's best interests and proper role in society. In any case, equity cannot be assessed without measuring equality and inequality: progress towards greater equity is measured by reductions in health inequalities.

Other Human Rights Principles

Human rights instruments acknowledge that governments, particularly in developing countries, often will be unable to immediately remove all obstacles to their populations' realization of all rights, particularly the economic and social rights, and therefore require states to show good faith efforts at progressively moving Towards that goal. Governments are obligated to ensure the immediate fulfilment of some rights (generally those prohibiting active infringements on rights), and, at least, to progressively take steps Towards ensuring that all persons can realize all of their rights. Governmental obligation lies not only in not violating (that is, respecting) the rights of their populations, but also in protecting these rights against violations by other parties, and actively promoting the realization of rights by all persons.

6

Society and Cultural Sociology

INTRODUCTION

Society refers to a group of people who share a defined territory and a culture. Society is often understood as the basic structure and interactions of a group of people or the network of relationships between entities. A distinction is made between society and culture in sociology. Culture refers to the meanings given to symbols or the process of meaning-making that takes place in a society. Culture is distinct from society in that it adds meanings to relationships. All human societies have a culture and culture can only exist where there is a society. Distinguishing between these two components of human social life is primarily for analytical purposes—for example, so sociologists can study the transmission of cultural elements or artifacts within a society. This chapter will present a brief overview of some of the types of human societies that have existed and continue to exist. It will then present some classic approaches to understanding society and what changing social structure can mean for individuals.

SOCIETAL DEVELOPMENT

The sociological understanding of societal development relies heavily upon the work of Gerhard Lenski. Lenski outlined some of the more commonly seen organizational structures in human societies.

Classifications of human societies can be based on two factors:

1. The primary means of subsistence and
2. The political structure.

This chapter focuses on the subsistence systems of societies rather than their political structures. While it is a bit far-reaching to argue that all societies will develop through the stages outlined below, it does appear that most societies follow such a route. Human groups begin as huntergatherers, move towards pastoralism and/or horticulturalism, develop towards an agrarian society, and ultimately end up undergoing a period of industrialization. The reason this is presented as a model is because not all societies pass through every stage.

Some societies have stopped at the pastoral or horticultural stage, though these may be temporary pauses due to economic niches that will likely disappear in time. Some societies may also jump stages as a result of the introduction of technology from alien societies and culture. Another reason for hesitancy in presenting these categories as distinct groups is that there is often overlap in the subsistence systems used in a society. Some pastoralist societies also engage in some measure of horticultural food production. Industrial societies have agrarian components.

HUNTER-GATHERER

The hunter-gatherer way of life is based on the exploitation of wild plants and animals. Consequently, hunter-gatherers are relatively mobile, and groups of hunter-gatherers have fluid boundaries and composition. Typically in hunter-gatherer societies men hunt larger wild animals and women gather and hunt smaller animals. Hunter-gatherers use materials available in the wild to construct shelters or rely on naturally occurring shelters like overhangs. Their shelters give them protection from predators and the elements.

The majority of hunter-gatherer societies are nomadic. It is difficult to be settled under such a subsistence system as the resources of one region can quickly become exhausted. Huntergatherer societies also tend to have very low population densities as a result of their subsistence system. Agricultural subsistence systems can support population densities 60 to 100 times greater than land left uncultivated, resulting in denser populations. Hunter-gatherer societies also tend to have non-hierarchical social structures, though this is not always the case. Because hunter-gatherers tend to be nomadic, they generally do not have the possibility to store surplus food.

As a result, full-time leaders, bureaucrats, or artisans are rarely supported by hunter-gatherer societies. The hierarchical egalitarianism in hunter-gatherer societies tends to extend to gender-based egalitarianism as well. Although disputed, many anthropologists believe gender egalitarianism in hunter-gatherer societies stems from the lack of control over food production, lack of food surplus—which can be used for control, and an equal gender contribution to kin and cultural survival.

Archeological evidence to date suggests that prior to twelve thousand years ago, all human beings were hunter-gatherers. While declining in number, there are still some hunter-gatherer groups in existence today. Such groups are found in the Arctic, tropical rainforests, and deserts where other forms of subsistence production are impossible or too costly.

In most cases these groups do not have a continuous history of hunting and gathering; in many cases their ancestors were agriculturalists who were pushed into marginal areas as a result of migrations and wars.

Examples of huntergatherer groups still in existence include:

- The Haida of British Columbia

- Bushmen of South Africa

The line between agricultural and hunter–gatherer societies is not clear cut. Many huntergatherers consciously manipulate the landscape through cutting or burning unuseful plants to encourage the growth and success of those they consume. Most agricultural people also tend to do some hunting and gathering. Some agricultural groups farm during the temperate months and then hunt during the winter.

PASTORALIST

A pastoralist society is a society in which the primary means of subsistence is domesticated livestock. It is often the case that, like hunter-gatherers, pastoralists are nomadic, moving seasonally in search of fresh pastures and water for their animals. Employment of a pastoralist subsistence system often results in greater population densities and the development of both social hierarchies and divisions in labour as it is more likely there will be a surplus of food. Pastoralist societies still exist.

For instance, in Australia, the vast semi-arid areas in the interior of the country contain pastoral runs called sheep stations. These areas may be thousands of square kilometers in size. The number of livestock allowed in these areas is regulated in order to reliably sustain them, providing enough feed and water for the stock.

Other examples of pastoralists societies still in existence include:

- The Maasai of Kenya
- The Boran
- The Turkana of Kenya
- The Bedouin of Northern Africa

HORTICULTURALIST

Horticulturalist societies are societies in which the primary means of subsistence is the cultivation of crops using hand tools. Like pastoral societies, the cultivation of crops increases population densities and, as a result of food surpluses, allows for a division of labour in society. Horticulture differs from agriculture in that agriculture employs animals, machinery, or some other non-human means to facilitate the cultivation of crops while horticulture relies solely on humans for crop cultivation.

SOCIETY AND GENDER ROLES

Psychologists such as Sandra Bem, one cognitive process that seems nearly inevitable in humans is to divide people into groups. We can partition these groups on the basis of race, age, religion, and so forth. However, most of the times we split humanity on the basis of gender. The first thing we instantly determine, when meeting someone new, is their gender. This process of categorizing others in terms of gender is both habitual and automatic. It's nearly impossible to suppress the tendency to split the world in half, using gender as the great divider. When we divide the world into two groups, males and females, we tend to consider all males similar, all females similar, and the two categories of "males" and "females" very different from each other. In real life, the characteristics of women and men tend to overlap. Unfortunately, however, gender polarization often creates an artificial gap between women and men and gender roles that are very difficult to change in time.

GENDER STEREOTYPES FOR MALES AND FEMALES

Stereotypes are representative of a society's collective knowledge of customs, myths, ideas, religions, and sciences. It is within this knowledge that an individual develops a stereotype or a belief about a certain group. Social psychologists feel that the stereotype is one part of an individual's social knowledge. As a result of their knowledge, or lack of knowledge, the stereotype has an effect on their social behaviour. Stereotypic behaviour can be linked to the way that the stereotype is learned, transmitted, and changed and this is part of the socialization process as well.

The culture of an individual influences stereotypes through information that is received from indirect sources such as parents, peers, teachers, political and religious leaders, and the mass media. In order to understand stereotyping, an individual must first be made knowledgeable about the definition of a stereotype. Stereotyping is how we perceive each other, especially individuals outside our group. What we believe to be "normal" is associated with who we are hanging out with.

Which are usually our friends and social networks. Gender stereotypes are related to cognitive processes because we have different expectations for female and male behaviour and the traditional gender roles help to sustain gender stereotypes, such as that males are supposed to be adventurous, assertive aggressive, independent and task-oriented, whereas females are seen as more sensitive, gentle, dependent, emotional and people-oriented. Here as suggested, deal with the opposite male dominance and feeling superior to women.

Of course, not all men have power and arrogantly dominate women; indeed, according to Miller, many men are dominated by "the system" and considered disposable. Also, women are given certain advantages and "protected" in many ways that men do not enjoy. Clearly, each sex has and utilizes power in certain ways and we are getting more equal, but, clearly, the sexes aren't equal yet. The most recent suggestion to solve this problem is to completely disassociate gender from all personality traits. Within the two career families of today, the women-are-inferior attitude is muted and concealed, but the archaic sex role expectations are still subtly there.

The old rules still serve to "put down women and keep them in their place." By nature, men and women have some biological differences, but it is life experience that reinforces or contradicts those differences. The truth lies in differential socialization, which claims that males and females are taught different appropriate behaviours for their gender.

GENDER SOCIALISATION

Socialisation is the process, through which the child becomes an individual respecting his or her environment laws, norms and customs. Gender socialisation is a more focused form of socialisation, it is how children of different sexes are socialised into their gender roles and taught what it means to be male or female. Gender socialisation begins the moment we are born, from the simple question "is it a boy or a girl?".

We learn our gender roles by agencies of socialisation, which are the "teachers" of society. The main agencies in Western society are the family, peer groups, schools and the media. In respect with gender socialisation, each of the agencies could reinforce the gender stereotypes. Gender differences result from the socialization process, especially during our childhood and adolescence.

The classical example of gender socialisation is the experiment done with babies that were introduced as males to half of the study subjects and as females to the other half. The results are interesting and quite disturbing at the same time. The participants behave differently according to the sex they had been told. These findings show that other people contribute a lot to how we see ourselves only on the basis of gender.

THE FAMILY AS GENDERED RELATIONSHIPS: INFLUENCES ON GENDER SOCIALIZATION PROCESS

It is said before that parents are the primary influence on gender role development in the early years of one's life. With regard to gender difference, the family in fact, unlike other groups, is characterized by a specific way of living and constructing gender differences through a process that is surely biological, but also relational and social. The family is " the social and symbolic place in which difference, in particular sexual difference, is believed to be fundamental and at the same time constructed ". In particular, in the family the gender characterization reflects the individualities of the parents. The family is therefore a "gender relation".

In the family, the relation with the father and the mother assumes therefore one fundamental importance in the definition of the gender belonging, because it 's the first experience of relation with males and females. Gender identities and the expectations towardss male and female roles are socialized within the parents-children relationship; such expectations are today various and new compared with the past.

The models from which fathers and mothers take inspiration need to be verified because "the crisis of the paternal authority has given more space to the father in shaping the educational relation with the child. They think that the important thing is to converse and to build convincing representations of the world". The gender socialization inside the familiar relations evidences therefore also the temporal dimension of the transmission of styles and expectations between parents and children.

The parents ' generation, in comparison with the child 's one, can highlight marked differences too. Parents today probably have different expectations from those their parents had, and their children have even more different expectations. We must go deeper into the matter on how transmission of gender differences happens today and how the gender belonging is constructed..

If such differences seem to diminish on the one side, on the other instead they move on different areas in comparison with the past. Between children in fact the sexual difference "produces various models of belongings and continuity", and they are today completely different from those of the previous generations. In the past, families had different educational demands for their sons and daughters after puberty , they then tended to differentiate them in the sense to promote the autonomy of the males and the dependency of the females.

It was implicit that the boy should realise himself, even if against familiar ties, while the girl had, in some ways, to accept and to conserve them. This difference has always favoured the fact that young women lived their desire of autonomy with a sense of guilt and of independency with intolerance.

A child's parents are the first socialization agents he or she will come into contact with. Parents teach stereotypes through different ways and behaviour : "the way they dress their children, they way they decorate their children's rooms, the toys they give their children to play with, their own attitudes and behaviour".

A RELATIONAL APPROACH TO GENDER ROLES SOCIALIZATION

The most important aspect of the sociological reflection is the ability to use the concepts elaborated in the theoretical debate at an empirical level, realizing "a hermeneutic" connection between the interpretative framework and social life. Gender socialization can be read like a "relational process". It is unavoidable that in the transformation a simplification is put into effect, a reduction of the complexity of the terms in game, because you need to lead back to the factors that explain a social phenomenon to one more rigid pattern of reality: in order not to fall into the trap of the merely casual interpretation it is necessary to always place, to the centre of attention, the relation between different factors that concur to see the phenomena from more points of view, in a multidimensional perspective. The relational model is assumed like the point of observation to verify the hypotheses in order to characterize those that are the gender socializing outcomes in the contemporary society. Within a risky society the relational model considers every phenomenon as the outcome of a process in which the challenges and the resources are put implicitly or explicitly in comparison.The risk therefore is given from the relation of adequacy/inadequacy between challenges and resources. That appears clear if it is believed that every choice is linked to multidimensional situations, which are relational contexts, in which the phenomena are networks of phenomena and every node represents interlaces of challenges, ties and resources.

Speaking about challenges and resources in gender socialization simplifies reality and circumscribes a point of view from which to observe a phenomenon, but it always takes into account that is a relational phenomenon, in which more dimensions are intersected. Consequently the gender socialization process is divided into two orders of factors, one leads the challenges and the other the resources, in the hypothesis that behind every phenomenon there are however the intentions of the actors who arrange in a more or less balanced way, with reference to the context of options that delimits the action, objects to reach and strategies of participation.

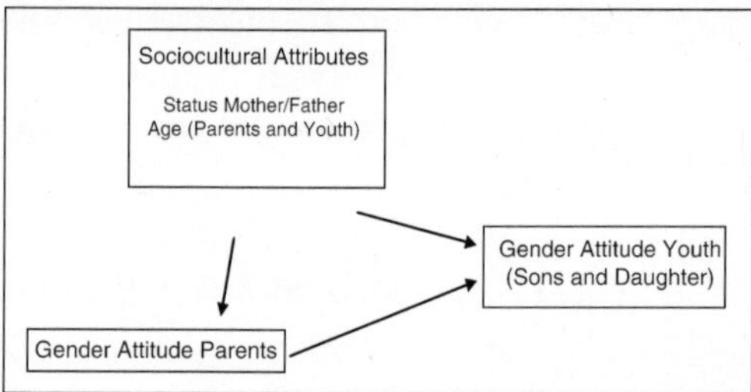

Fig. Analytical Framework for the Relationships between Soci-Demographic Attributes, Gender Attitude Parents and Gender Attitudes Youth.

RELIGION IN TRIBAL SOCIETIES

CHIEF FEATURE OF TRIBAL SOCIETIES: EASY FORM OF RELIGION

Every religious system consists of a set of three essential elements:

- Belief in the subsistence of a superhuman world;
- Human's connection to it; and
- Practice of ritual as an instrument of establishing connection.

Here:

- Refers to the belief system,
- To the value system, and
- To the action system.

The form and meaning of these elements, *i.e.*, religious belief, religious value and religious action, may differ from one order to another. Religion of a tribe is easy insofar as it is expressed in everyday language and experienced in everyday life. It is descriptive, demonstrative and readily discernible. In the middle of the tribe's religious myth, belief, religious value and religious action are not treated as something separately from other types of belief and behaviour, as followed in social, economic and political contexts. Yet, the meaning of beliefs and behaviour of the tribal's appears mysterious to the outsiders. This is precisely because theirs is a religion without explanation. Though, tribal religion is no less complete than the highly urbanised form of intricate religion to the extent that its implicit philosophy recognises the similar universal truth.

Let us now explain to you all these characteristics of tribal religion, its implicit philosophy and the worldview. This we will do through discussing tribal lifestyle, tribal ritual intricate and tribal worldview.

Tribal Lifestyle

Religion pervades all characteristics of tribal life that is why for understanding the tribal lifestyle we need to first understand the tribe's religious notions. To explain this, we will take an instance of the rustic Toda of the Nilgiri in South India. Through their own explanation, the Toda and their extensive horned buffaloes were created on the high massif of the Nilgiri Hills through the great goddess Teikirzi. Their resolution is marked through the unique barrel-vaulted homes and dairy structures. The dairy structures are temples.

The Toda are socially organised into two endogamous sections, named *Tarthoral* and *Teivaliol*. The division is based on ritual specialisation. The *Tarthar* people alone can own the mainly sacred dairy temples with their associated herds; the *Teivaliol* men, described 'the servants of the gods' fulfil the highest priestly tasks associated with them. Their economic and social lives are centred on the buffaloes. The greater part of their religious observance is also focused on this animal. The buffaloes are ritually guarded. Every task of the dairyman, every substance and lay associated with the herds has received the impress of ritual. The Toda observe a number of special ceremonies related to the dairies, the buffaloes and the pastures. There are rites through which they honour the dairy, purify it when it has been defiled, and create offerings to it. There are rites associated with rebuilding and rethatching. After that are the rites for naming a buffalo, milking a temple buffalo for the first time, giving salt to the herds and moving them to the new pastures. There is also the rite of lighting the gods' fire to ensure the fertility of the pastures.

Life's major events are highly ritualised in the middle of the Toda. The first pregnancy of a Toda woman is seen as ritually contaminating and hence in almost fifth month she spends a complete lunar month in a temporary 'pollution hut' outside her hamlet. In her seventh month of pregnancy, the husband ritually provides her a bow-and-arrow to set up the social paternity of the unborn child. If a child were born to a woman who had not been given a bow, it would be a bastard with no patrician affiliation. In former days when polyandry was the norm, the many husbands of a woman took turns to assume the paternity of her children. Childbirth is a polluting event. It is not only the mother and her child who are ritually defiled, but also all other people and things which approach in secure get in touch with them. Purificatory rite is performed on or presently before the day of the new moon after birth. The 'face-uncovering' ceremony is performed some time flanked by one and three months after the birth of a child. It is only then the Toda child is recognised as a social being.

The name-giving ceremony follows it. Marriage is initiated in childhood and completed at maturity. Meanwhile the ear-piercing ceremony is performed for all boys. For a girl there are two separate rites supposed to precede her entry into womanhood. The two rites essentially are symbolic and an actual defloration is performed before a girl's first menstruation. When the partners in a marriage alliance reach maturity, arrangements are made for their cohabitation and for the subsequent payment of dowry. On this occasion the girl's father performs 'the girl-sending' ceremony. The passage of a Toda man or woman into middle or old age is not marked through ritual. As death approaches, the elders can look forward to an afterlife not radically dissimilar from their present one. As the goddess Teikirzi rules in excess of the livelihood Toda and their buffaloes, so does her brother, On, who reigns in excess of the dead. Death generates the greatest profusion of ritual. The corpse of the deceased is cremated at the end of the first funeral ceremony throughout which buffaloes are sacrificed so that they may accompany the spirit to the afterworld. A second ceremony is held, usually months after the first, in which a relic of the deceased is cremated.

What comes through this account of the Toda passage through life cycle, as also the organisation of their territory, society and economy, is the great importance of religion. You have seen how the intricate web of ritual is woven approximately the comparatively easy tasks of the husbandry man. One might, so, conclude that tribal life and society cannot be fully understood without understanding their religion. Though, as Winter has pointed out, in some societies religion plays a much more significant role in group structure than it does in others. This has been illustrated with reference to African tribes. The social structure of the Iroquois cannot be described without taking religion into explanation; that of the Amaba can be described in such a manner.

Tribal Ritual Intricate

For a religious human, the superhuman world is the real world, which is ritually replicated in legroom and time. The believer communicates with this world through a symbolic code which Saraswati calls the ritual language, consisting of:

- Esoteric word, *mantra,*
- Gesture, *mudra*,
- Sound, *dhvani,*
- Everyday language of interaction, *vyavahariki*.

The tribal ritual intricate may be described beside this row. Here we will first speak of ritual legroom and then of ritual time. After that, we will talk about ritual language in conditions of *mantra, mudra, dhvani,* and *vyavahariki*.

Ritual Legroom

In the tribal perception the legroom is filled with spiritual beings. There are two classes of legroom: cosmic legroom and physical, or substance legroom. The Santal consider that the creator *Thakur Jiu* dwells up in the sky; the *Sin Bonga* or the Sun God also occupies the cosmic legroom. There is also the *Hanapuri*, or the land of the dead. The spirits inhabit concrete objects in and approximately their resolution. Such spaces are named after the spirits associated with them. For instance, the spirit of the region, the spirit of the village boundary, the home spirit, the spring spirit, the mountain spirit, the forest spirit, the spirit of the rice field, the spirit of the threshing floor, cremation ground, etc.

The ritual legroom is dissimilar from the ordinary legroom inasmuch as it is sacred effective. But any ordinary legroom can become a ritual legroom, depending on its association with the spirit. Usually, it is allowed to retain its natural form. For instance, the Jaher, or the sacred grove of the Santal consists of a clump of sal tree with one *mahua* standing close to. Three trees in a row are dedicated to Mama Buru, the spirit who dwelt with the first Santal, Jaher Era, the spirit of the sacred grove, and to More ko Turuc ko, the spirit described Five-Six. Another *sal* tree is dedicated to Pargana Bonga, the spirit of the region, while *Mahua* tree is reserved for Gosae Era, the spirit of the sacred home. At the base of each of these trees, a stone is embedded and all five are recognised as *Bonga* trees. An easy construction may also spot the sacred legroom. The Santal Manjhithan consists of smoothly cemented plinth of mud with two stories to symbolise the founder of the village, Manjhi and his wife, a centre pillar of *sal* wood, a second and smaller pillar supporting a pot of water and finally a roof of thatch or tiles.

Tribes, through and big, entertain no notion of hierarchy of the sacred spaces. But, as Walker has reported, the Toda dairy temples are graded into an intricate hierarchy just as to relative sanctity. The higher they are, the more elaborate is the ritual associated with the daily tasks of the dairyman, and the higher necessity is the purity in which the dairy, its appurtenances, and the dairyman himself are maintained.

Ritual Time

The tribes order their ritual time on the Nature's signal, *i.e.*, on the blossoming plants and trees, on the location of stars and moon, the biological time, and, if the circumstances so demand, through direct divination. The principal festival of the Oraon is described *Sarhul*, the Feast of the *Sal* Blossoms, also recognised as the Marriage of the Earth. Another festival recognised as *Kadlota*, is celebrated when rice granules have shaped in the rice plants. The Toda perform their rituals just as to the location of stars and new moon. The star described ket, the 18th *naksatra* or lunar mansion, is measured to have a malignant power. Mainly rituals are performed on or in relation to the new moon. The moon-time is followed rather strictly. The Toda regard childbirth pollution particularly dangerous to the ritual condition of the sacred dairies of the hamlet. Therefore they insist that a new mother and her child should be taken, as soon as the woman could move, out of her hamlet to the pollution hut. The length of the time mother and child were compelled to remain in this hut depended upon whether or not the child was her first. In the case of the second or subsequent child, the era of seclusion would last until the new moon following the birth, perhaps presently a few days.

Therefore, if a woman had given birth to her first child presently after a new moon, she would have to endure approximately two months of seclusion. On the third day of the new moon the newly delivered mother receives butter and buttermilk from the dairy, which event marks the end of the restriction on her drinking milk and consuming milk products from the dairy. The 'social paternity rite' or 'bow-and-arrow ceremony' is performed on the day of the new moon. The first funeral rite is also held on the day of the new moon. Mainly tribes consider biological time as an occasion to perform ritual, such as the first menstruation, childbirth, and death.

Impact of other Religious Belief Systems

Several tribal religions have blended with other faiths of non-tribal groups. Of these Hinduism and Christianity are the major religious systems which have affected the tribal societies. Let us first consider the impact of Hinduism on tribal religious beliefs and practices.

Hinduism and Tribal Religions

Ethnographic studies of dissimilar tribal groups illustrate that the get in touch with of the tribal's with their neighbours varied from part-separation to complete assimilation. The Tharu and the Khasa, the two central Himalayan tribes in North India are a good instance of totally assimilated or Hinduised tribes. Through adopting Hindu caste names, wearing the sacred thread, establishing social links with the local Rajput and Brahmin groups, these tribal's have incorporated their identity with high caste Hindus.

Likewise, the Kshatriya model of Hinduism has been adopted in middle India through the Chero, Kharwar, Pahariya of Bihar and the Bhumij of Madhya Pradesh. The Bhumij Kshatriya Association, founded in 1935, showed wider implications of Hinduisation of the tribal's. The concept of tribal Rajput continuum was evolved in the course of historical studies of the Bhumij Raj of Birbhum. In Eastern India the Bauri of West Bengal accepted to observe the prescribed number of days of pollution for mourning, wear the sacred thread, go to pilgrimage and follow Vaishnavism. They now claim to belong to the Brahmin caste. Adhering to beliefs in the Hindu concepts of Karma, pollution, merit *(punya)* and observing Hindu life cycle rituals, the Mahali of West Bengal have adopted and assimilated the elements of local belief and practices of the Hindus. Likewise, in several of the Oraon villages of Chotanagpur, Hindu gods and goddesses are worshipped; Hindu priests are employed to carry out ritual performances throughout life-cycle ceremonies. In Western India also, we discover that several of the Hindu deities are worshipped through the tribal's. For instance, Mahadev is the main deity of the Bhil tribe. Shah has shown that in Gujarat the Dubla, Naika, Gamit and Dhanaka are quite Hinduised and employ a Brahmin to perform the rituals.

Looking at the situation in South India, we discover that beliefs and practices of the neighbouring Hindu castes have been adopted through the Chenchu, Kadar and Muthuvan. Hindu gods and goddesses like Aiyappan, Maruti and Kali are worshipped through the Kadar. Presiding deities of Madurai temple, Palaniandi and Kadavallu are treated as their chief deities through the Muthuvan.

Here we would like to also mention that contacts flanked by the tribals and their Hindu neighbours have not only resulted in the impact of Hinduism on tribal beliefs and practices, "We discover also the impact of tribal religions on the practices of sure Hindu group's livelihood in tribal villages. For instance, the procedure of triplication in the Bastar region of Madhya Pradesh reflected in acceptance through high caste Hindus of tribal morals, rituals and belief. Majumdar mentions the concept of trans-culturation in the middle of the Ho of Singhbhum, signifying reciprocal impact of tribal culture on local Hindu castes. Hutton observed that Hinduism and tribal religions share a general base, while Bose is of the opinion that the tribal population of India has contributed to the creation of Hinduism.

It is not out of lay here to mention that the tribal groups have also been affected through their neighbours. In upper Lahaul and the Ladakh region, the Bhot tribals are mainly Buddhists. Likewise, the Gujjar of the North-Western Himalayan region and the Bhil of Rajasthan have secure contacts with Muslim groups and are affected through their beliefs and practices. We have basically mentioned in relation to the neighbouring groups' impact on the tribal groups. We have not discussed the procedure of these changes. This point will be examined in the after that unit on *Tribes and Modernisation in India.* Let us now look at Christianity, which has affected several of the tribal groups in India.

Christianity and Tribal Religions

Beginning with the conversion of the Khasi of Assam in 1813, of the Oraon of Chotanagpur in 1850 and of the Bhil of Madhya Pradesh in 1880 through Christian missionaries, Christianity has brought in relation to the several changes in the cultural life of the tribals in India.

The missionaries attempted to convert numerically major tribes. As a result, minor tribes remained untouched through the new religion while mass conversion of major tribes gave the impression of the hold of Christianity on tribal India. Of the total population of Christians in India at least one sixth belong to tribal groups. Mainly of the tribal Christians are establish in the North-East Himalayan zone. Elwin estimated that ranging from half to approximately the whole population of the Mizo, Garo and Naga tribes professed Christianity. In middle India, two-thirds of the Khasi, one-fourth of the Munda and one fourth of the Oraon follow Christianity. In the tribal regions of Madhya Pradesh and Orissa, we discover little pockets of Christian tribals. The tribes like the Chero, Kharwar, Pahariya, Birhor, Baiga, Balhudi, Bedia, Karmali, do not have a single Christian convert.

In South India, Hill Pulaya, Malayarayan and Palliar tribals of Kerala have been proselytised and almost two-third of their population has accepted Christianity. Conversion to Christianity gave the tribals a model of westernisation. Here it will suffice to say that the Church organisation, western education, values and morals reached the tribals through Christianity. Their introduction implied a demand to provide up tribal belief and practices. In some cases, traditional festivals were reinterpreted in conditions Christianised myths. For instance, origin of the festival Sarhul of the Munda was, after conversion, associated through them to the fight flanked by Alexander and King Porus in 400 B.C. Sahay has concluded that the Oraon of Chainpur in Ranchi district of Jharkhand gave up their faith in traditional Sarna religion and adopted Christian faith. This resulted in considerable changes in celebration of festivals, village organisation, economic life and other characteristics of their culture. Therefore, some scholars have viewed Christianity as a source of disintegration of tribal religion.

We can also mention the element of fusion with Christianity introduced in the middle of the tribal groups. Under the rubric of one denomination of Christianity some of the previously separated tribal groups came jointly and even accepted marital dealings crossways tribal boundaries. Under the Church organisational network, several tribal groups scattered in excess of a wider region came jointly and built contacts not only with the provincial and national but also international Church bodies. Sahay has studied the procedure of Christianisation of the Oraon tribals and recognised a set of five procedures, signifying dissimilar shapes of interaction flanked by the tribal Christian norms and values. Under the patronage of British rule, conversion to Christianity had establish a favourable environment while in self-governing India, several revivalist movements in the middle of the tribal groups have led the tribals to go back to their traditional religious beliefs and practices.

Socio-Religious Movements

All in excess of the world, socio-religious movements have evolved in approximately all religions. These range from cargo cults to millenarian movements. The word millenarian means, literally, a thousands years and refers to the belief that the world order is soon going to end, giving method to a new and perfect society. Ethnographic material is well researched and documented to explain the emergence of such movements. Here we will look at the emergence of some of the socio-religious movements in the middle of the tribal groups as products of change within the group, of get in touch with the out-group, and of reinterpretation of the sacred realm. Through focusing on these movements in the middle of the tribal groups, we do not mean to say that such movements do not happen in the middle of other groups.

In information, several such movements have been recorded in the middle of the untouchable and middle castes in India. Examples of such movements in the middle of the tribals are the Munda Rebellion, Jatra Bhagat Movement and Kharwar Movement. All these examples illustrate that the tribals (in the middle of whom the movements appeared) were never totally in accessibled from the main currents of Indian society. Secondly, the exploitative forces (against whom the movements were addressed) were not only colonisers, but also the non-tribal upper castes. Thirdly, the influencing get in touch with the out-group did not approach only from Christian missionaries but also from Hindus and Muslims.

We may have to enquire ourselves the question as to why it is that no socio-religious movement had appeared in the North-Eastern Boundary Agency while several did in the middle of the tribals of Chotanagpur. If we go through the theory of deprivation as one of the causes of emergence of such movements, it may appear that perhaps the tribals of Chotanagpur were deprived to the worst extent and hence in the middle of them a multiplicity of such movements arose. We may also look at the question of duration of contacts flanked by dissimilar cultures. We may enquire, at what stage of get in touch with, does a socio-religious movement arises?

Due to varying intensity of crises, several durations may be necessary in scrupulous groups for the movements to crystallise. Also, a movement may emerge, become active and then lie dormant. Again, a socio-religious movement may approach at the initial stage of get in touch with or it may approach after the completion of acculturation.

When one culture meets the other, one social order is affected through the other. Here, while re-emphasizing the similar, it can be said that mainly of the time meeting of cultures has been prompted through colonisation. The colonisers (be they foreigners or other cultural groups within the country) integrate their colonies into wider markets through introducing dissimilar shapes of economy, through exporting the local products and raw materials. As a result rapid changes take lay and the existing social order breaks down. In the case of tribal India, big level changes were introduced through the missionaries.

These changes, in turn, produced disturbance in the method society was previously organised in the middle of the tribals. The disturbances caused several a dilemmas for the people, leading to both psychological social deprivations. These are the situations, which triggered the path to socio-religious movements.

With this background of their emergence, let us now take two examples of socio-religious movements, namely, the Tana Bhagat Movement in the middle of the Oraon of Bihar (Jharkhand) and the Birsa Munda movement of the Munda in and approximately the districts of Ranchi and Singhbhum in Chotanagpur Division of present day Jharkhand. Both these movements are essentially religious in nature. Here, Jatra Bhagat and Birsa Munda, the tribal leaders of the respective movements were essentially fighting the foreign exploiters, like the landlords and contractors. The tribals, feeling deprived and in accessibled, establish through these movements a sense of unity and a general identity. Yet, the two movements also differed from each other. Let us consider each of them separately.

Tana Bhagat Movement

In Tana Bhagat Movement, as in other Bhagat movements, an effort is made to emulate the method of life of the Hindu higher castes. Tana Bhagat movement is one type of the Bhagat movement that appeared in the middle of the Oraon of Chotanagpur, Jharkhand. There were other Bhagat movements like Nemha Bhagat and Bachidan Bhagat. The term Bhagat has been employed in several parts of Bihar and Jharkhand to refer to sorcerers and magicians. In the middle of the Oraon it is though applied to a separate section of the tribe which subscribes to the cult of Bhakti. The whole Bhagat movement, attempting as it did to raise the status of its members in the eyes of the nearby Hindu society, is characterised big level incorporation of Hindu belief-practices into its ideology. The leader of Tana Bhagat movement was described Jatra Oraon who existed in village Beparinwatoli in Bishanpur Thana of Gumla sub-division of Ranchi district. In 1914, this person announced in the month of April that Dharmesh, the high god of the Oraon, had revealed to him that the people would have to provide up the worship of ghosts and spirits and the practice of exorcism. He told his people that they would have to refrain from animal sacrifice, meat eating, liquor drinking etc. Even farming through plough with the use of animal power was rejected. It was whispered that god had given to Jatra sure songs or spells through which fever, sties, and other ailments could be cured.

The leaders of this movement whispered that the tribal spirits and deities whom they had been worshipping were of no use to them since it did not help them alleviate the socioeconomic ills of their society. They also tried to prove that in information it was these deities who were responsible for their present state of misery and degradation. Through asserting that these tribal deities were of Munda origin, the founders of Tana Bhagat movement embarked on a programme of proselytisation and agitation for the exorcism of the foreign spirits and deities. The cult emphasized a return to the original Oraon religion. Its earliest manifestation was in the expulsion of evil spirits imported from the Munda and in the active rebellion against unfair landlords who exploited them. Even when their leader Jatra Bhagat was imprisoned, some of the cult members refused to pay rents to their landlords and ceased to cultivate their lands. Such and other rebellious behaviours like ghost-hunting drive and holding meetings through the followers of the Tana Bhagat movement were regarded with suspicion and branded as 'disloyal and illegal' gatherings.

This movement broke up into many smaller cults after sometime. Some of these cults are extremist and orthodox like Sibu Bhagat. The rest are mixtures of tribal and Hindu religious beliefs and practices.

Birsa Munda Movement

Throughout the second half of the nineteenth century the whole of Chotanagpur underwent a tremendous change. The old Munda system of *khuntkatti* tenure gave method to a new and alien system of use through the landlords recognised as *Jagirdar* and *Thikadar*. Under their greed and cruelty the tribal population was squeezed out of their land and other possessions. Suffering economically and politically, the Munda were assigned low social status. Later the Christian missionaries tried to provide the Munda back their rights on their land. But this too had a price, which was conversion to Christianity. A big number of the Munda did convert to Christianity. But in due course they realised that this was not the solution. The missionaries had failed to redeem them from abject poverty and oppression.

At this time when the Munda society was seething with discontent, in 1895, Birsa Munda of Chalked started a movement. In him the Munda establish the embodiment of their aspirations. He gave them leadership, a religion and a code of life. He held before them the prospect of Munda Raj in lay of a foreign rule. Under the power of a learned Satnami Pandit, Birsa Munda became a vegetarian and the religion that he preached had elements of both Hinduism and Christianity. His religion promised to end the misery of his society and so it was a means to an end. His religion had the element of charisma. Birsa came to be regarded as an embodiment of god *'Birsa Bhagwan'*; his people whispered that Birsa could bring the dead back to life. Whenever there was epidemic he visited his people and cured them. He had the magic touch and proclaimed himself to be the prophet of Sing-Bonga, the one and only God. So distant Birsa was seen as a provider of new and better life for his people, But later his movement assumed quasi-political and militaristic form. As he organised a force to fight oppressive landlords, Christian missionaries and British officials, he was imprisoned. Since his people whispered in Birsa's magical power, they did not enquire for his release, rather they wanted to go to jail with him. They whispered that within three days he will himself approach out of jail. He was released only after two years.

Out of jail, Birsa asked his people to ready their arms to fight injustice. He trained his army and became the politician leading his people to their goal of self-rule. He was though arrested again and died in jail. Yet the seeds of unrest were sown in the middle of his people and they sustained to fight against injustice. The erstwhile, 'Jharkhanda Movement', which ultimately culminated in the formation of the Jharkhand State has its roots in this movement. Our account of both the Tana Bhagat movement and Birsa Munda movement underlines the importance of a 'prophet-like' figure, who is the guiding spirit of the movement. He draws his legitimacy from the divine revelation. His prophecy appeals to the crisis situation. He becomes the epicentre of the communal expectations of his people.

He suggests rejection of sure behaviours, rituals and customs. He incorporates new elements and adapts sure components of out-group culture to suit the needs of communal expectations. He reinterprets the myth, reformulates the ritual and prepares his people for communal action. We say that cult myths are dynamic characteristics of tribal religion as they express the hopes of the people. We can conclude here that through discussing some of the socio-religious movements in the middle of the tribals we have gained an added understanding of tribal religions.

ELEMENTS OF SOCIALIZATION

As socialization is a fundamental sociological concept, there are a number of components to this concept that are important to understand. While not every sociologist will agree which elements are the most important, or even how to define some of the elements of socialization, the elements outlined below should help clarify what is meant by socialization.

GOALS OF SOCIALIZATION

Arnett, in presenting a new theoretical understanding of socialization outlined what he believes to be the three goals of socialization:

1. Impulse control and the development of a conscience
2. Role preparation and performance, including occupational roles, gender roles, and roles in institutions such as marriage and parenthood
3. The cultivation of sources of meaning, or what is important, valued, and to be lived for

In short, socialization is the process that prepares humans to function in social life. It should be re-iterated here that socialization is culturally relative—people in different cultures are socialized differently. This distinction does not and should not inherently force an evaluative Judgement. Socialization, because it is the adoption of culture, is going to be different in every culture. Socialization, as both process or an outcome, is not better or worse in any particular culture.

PRIMARY AND SECONDARY SOCIALIZATION

Socialization is a life process, but is generally divided into two parts. Primary socialization takes place early in life, as a child and adolescent. Secondary socialization refers to the socialization that takes place throughout one's life, both as a child and as one encounters new groups that require additional socialization.

While there are scholars who argue that only one or the other of these occurs, most social scientists tend to combine the two, arguing that the basic or core identity of the individual develops during primary socialization, with more specific changes occurring later secondary socialization in response to the acquisition of new group memberships and roles and differently structured social situations. The need for later life socialization may stem from the increasing complexity of society with its corresponding increase in varied roles and responsibilities.

Mortimer and Simmons outline three specific ways these two parts of socialization differ:

1. *Content:* Socialization in childhood is thought to be concerned with the regulation of biological drives. In adolescence, socialization is concerned with the development of overarching values and the self-image. In adulthood, socialization involves more overt and specific norms and behaviours, such as those related to the work role as well as more superficial personality features.
2. *Context:* In earlier periods, the socializee more clearly assumes the status of learner within the context of the family of orientation, the school, or the peer group. Also, relationships in the earlier period are more likely to be affectively charged, *i.e.,* highly emotional. In adulthood, though the socializee takes the role of student at times, much socialization occurs after the socializee has assumed full incumbency of the adult role. There is also a greater likelihood of more formal relationships due to situational contexts, which moderates down the affective component.
3. *Response*: The child and adolescent may be more easily malleable than the adult. Also, much adult socialization is self-initiated and voluntary; adults can leave or terminate the process at any time.

Socialization is, of course, a social process. As such, it involves interactions between people. Socialization, as noted in the distinction between primary and secondary, can take place in multiple contexts and as a result of contact with numerous groups. Some of the more significant contributors to the socialization process are: parents, friends, schools, siblings, and co-workers. Each of these groups include a culture that must be learned and to some degree appropriated by the socializee in order to gain admittance to the group.

TOTAL INSTITUTIONS

Not all socialization is voluntary nor is all socialization successful. There are components of society designed specifically to resocialize individuals who were not successfully socialized to begin with. For instance, prisons and mental health institutions are designed to resocialize the people who are deemed to have not been successfully socialized. Depending on the degree of isolation and resocialization that takes place in a given institution, some of these institutions are labeled total institutions.

In his classic study of total institutions, Erving Goffman gives the following characteristics of total institutions:

- All aspects of life are conducted in the same place under the same authority
- The individual is a member of a large cohort, all treated alike
- All daily activities are tightly scheduled
- There is a sharp split between supervisors and lower participants
- Information about the member's fate is withheld

The most common examples of total institutions include mental hospitals, prisons, and military boot camps, though there are numerous other institutions that could be considered total institutions as well. The goal of total institutions is to facilitate a complete break with one's old life in order for the institution to resocialize the individual into a new life. Mortimer and Simmons note a difference in socialization methodologies in different types of institutions. When the goal of an institution is socialization, the institution tends to use normative pressures. When the goal of an institution is resocialization of deviants, coercion is frequently involved

BROAD AND NARROW SOCIALIZATION

An interesting though seldom used distinction in types of socialization was proposed by Arnett.

Arnett distinguishes between broad and narrow socialization:

- Broad socialization is intended to promote independence, individualism, and self-expression; it is dubbed broad because this type of socialization has the potential of resulting in a broad range of outcomes
- Narrow socialization is intended to promote obedience and conformity; it is dubbed narrow because there is a narrow range of outcomes

These distinctions correspond to Arnett's definition of socialization, which is: the whole process by which an individual born with behavioural potentialities of enormously wide range, is led to develop actual behaviour which is confined with a much narrower range; the range of what is customary and acceptable for him just as to the standards of his group Arnett explains that his understanding of socialization should not be understood as having just two options, broad or narrow.

Instead, the author argues that socialization can be broad or narrow within each of the seven socializing forces he outlines. Because each force can be either broad or narrow, there is a wide variety of possible broad/narrow socialization combinations. Finally, Arnett notes two examples where his distinction is relevant.

First, Arnett argues that there are often differences in socialization by gender. Where these differences exist, argues Arnett, socialization tends to be narrower for women than for men. Arnett also argues that Japanese socialization is narrow as there is more pressure towards conformity in that culture. Arnett argues that this may account for the lower crime rates in Japan.

THE IMPORTANCE OF SOCIALIZATION

One of the most common methods used to illustrate the importance of socialization is to draw upon the few unfortunate cases of children who were, through neglect, misfortune, or willful abuse, not socialized by adults while they were growing up.

RESEARCH IN SOCIOLOGY OF CULTURE

THEORETICAL CONSTRUCTS IN BOURDIEU' S SOCIOLOGY OF CULTURE

French sociologist Pierre Bourdieu's influential model of society and social dealings has its roots in Marxist theories of class and disagreement. Bourdieu characterises social dealings in the context of what he calls the field, defined as a competitive system of social dealings functioning just as to its own specific logic or rules. The field is the location of thrash about for power flanked by the dominant and subordinate classes. It is within the field that legitimacy—a key aspect defining the dominant class—is conferred or withdrawn.

Bourdieu's theory of practice is practical rather than discursive, embodied as well as cognitive and durable though adaptive. A valid concern that sets the agenda in Bourdieu's theory of practice is how action follows regular statistical patterns without the product of accordance to rules, norms, and/or conscious intention. To explain this concern, Bourdieu explains habitus and field. Habitus explains the mutually penetrating realities of individual subjectivity and societal objectivity after the function of social construction. It is employed to transcend the subjective and objective dichotomy.

CULTURAL CHANGE

The belief that culture is symbolically coded and can therefore is taught from one person to another means that cultures, although bounded, can change. Cultures are both predisposed to change and resistant to it. Resistance can approach from habit, religion, and the integration and interdependence of cultural traits. Cultural change can have several causes, including: the environment, inventions, and get in touch with other cultures.

Many understandings of how cultures change approach from anthropology. For instance, in diffusion theory, the form of something moves from one culture to another, but not its meaning. For instance, the ankh symbol originated in Egyptian culture but has diffused to numerous cultures. Its original meaning may have been lost, but it is now used through several practitioners of New Age Religion as an arcane symbol of power or life forces. A variant of the diffusion theory, incentive diffusion, refers to an element of one culture leading to an invention in another.

Get in touch with flanked by cultures can also result in acculturation. Acculturation has dissimilar meanings, but in this context refers to replacement of the traits of one culture with those of another, such as what happened with several Native American Indians. Related procedures on an individual stage are assimilation and trans-acculturation, both of which refer to adoption of a dissimilar culture through an individual.

Griswold outlined another sociological approach to cultural change. Griswold points out that it may appear as though culture comes from individuals – which, for sure elements of cultural change, is true – but there is also the superior, communal, and extensive-lasting culture that cannot have been the creation of single individuals as it predates and post-dates individual humans and contributors to culture. The author presents a sociological perspective to address this disagreement,

Sociology suggests an alternative to both the view that it has always been an unsatisfying method at one extreme and the sociological individual genius view at the other. This alternative posits that culture and cultural works are communal, not individual, creations. We can best understand specific cultural objects... through seeing them not as unique to their creators but as the fruits of communal manufacture, fundamentally social in their genesis.

In short, Griswold argues that culture changes through the contextually dependent and socially situated actions of individuals; macro-stage culture powers the individual who, in turn, can power that similar culture. The logic is a bit circular, but illustrates how culture can change in excess of time yet remain somewhat constant.

It is, of course, significant to recognise here that Griswold is talking in relation to the cultural change and not the actual origins of culture. Because Griswold does not explicitly distinguish flanked by the origins of cultural change and the origins of culture, it may appear as though Griswold is arguing here for the origins of culture and situating these origins in society. This is neither accurate nor a clear representation of sociological thought on this issue.

Culture, presently like society, has lived since the beginning of humanity. Society and culture co-exist because humans have social dealings and meanings tied to those dealings. Culture as a super-phenomenon has no real beginning except in the sense that humans have a beginning.

This, then, creates the question of the origins of culture moot – it has lived as extensive as we have, and will likely exist as extensive as we do. Cultural change, on the other hand, is a matter that can be questioned and researched, as Griswold does.

Culture Theory

The cultureless theory, was urbanised in the 1980s and 1990s. One strand of research focuses on the audiences and how they interact with media; the other strand of research focuses on those who produce the media, particularly the news.

CURRENT RESEARCH

Computer-mediated Communication as Culture

Computer-mediated communication (CMC) is the procedure of sending messages—primarily, but not limited to text messages—through the direct use through participants of computers and communication networks. Through restricting the definition to the direct use of computers in the communication procedure, you have to get rid of the communication technologies that rely upon computers for switching technology but do not require the users to interact directly with the computer system via a keyboard or same computer interface.

To be mediated through computers in the sense of this project, the communication necessity is done through participants fully aware of their interaction with the computer technology in the procedure of creating and delivering messages. Given the current state of computer communications and networks, this limits CMC to primarily text-based messaging, while leaving the possibility of incorporating sound, graphics, and video images as the technology becomes more sophisticated.

Cultural Institutions Studies

Cultural behaviours are institutionalised; the focus on institutional settings leads to the investigation "of behaviours in the cultural sector, conceived as historically evolved societal shapes of organising the conception, manufacture, sharing, propagation, interpretation, reception, conservation, and maintenance of specific cultural goods". Cultural Institutions Studies is so a specific approach within the sociology of culture.

SOCIALIZATION AND SOCIAL CLASS

Ellis, Lee, and Peterson developing a research agenda begun by Melvin L. Kohn explored differences in how parents raise their children relative to their social class. Kohn found that lower class parents were more likely to emphasize conformity in their children whereas middle-class parents were more likely to emphasize creativity and selfreliance.

Ellis et. al. proposed and found that parents value conformity over self-reliance in children to the extent that conformity superseded self-reliance as a criterion for success in their own endeavors.

In other words, Ellis et. al. verified that the reason lower-class parents emphasize conformity in their children is because they experience conformity in their day-today activities. For example, factory work is far more about conforming than innovation. Another study in this same area explored a slightly different component of this relationship. Erlanger was interested in a correlation between social class and physical violence. While he did not find a strong correlation indicating lower class individuals were more likely to employ physical violence in punishing their children, he did present evidence concerning several outdated propositions.

Erlanger's findings include:

- Physical punishment does not lead to working class authoritarianism
- Childhood punishment experiences do not explain the greater probability that working class adults, as opposed to middle class adults, will commit homicide
- General use of corporal punishment is not a precursor to child abuse
- Use of corporal punishment is not part of a subcultural positive evaluation of violence

It should be noted that this is an older study and that more recent findings may have shed more light on these issues. It should also be noted that Erlanger readily points out when his findings are strongly supported or weakly supported by his data.

SOCIALIZATION AND DEATH PREPARATION

Marshall interviewed a number of retirement home residents to explore how their environment influenced their thinking about death. In essence, Marshall was examining secondary socialization concerning mortality. Marshall found that a combination of relationships, behavioural changes, and retirement home culture contributed to a conception of death that was both accepting and courageous. Residents of this particular retirement home found themselves with more time on their hands—to think about death because they no longer had to care for their own homes. Additionally, they found themselves surrounded by people in a situation similar to their own: they were basically moving into the retirement home to prepare for death. The prevalence of elderly people facilitated discussions of death, which also helped socialize the residents into their acceptance of mortality.

Finally, the retirement home community encouraged a culture of life and fulfillment in part to counter-act the frequency of death. Some residents calculated there was one death per week in the retirement home. In light of such numbers, it was important to the success of the community to maintain a positive culture that embraced life yet accepted death. In summary, Marshall found that numerous factors contributed to the socialization of residents into a positive lifestyle that was also accepting of and preparatory for their impending deaths.

DO COLLEGE PREPARATION CLASSES MAKE A DIFFERENCE?

Rosenbaum was interested in the effects of high school tracks on IQ. High school tracks are the different levels or types of courses students can take; for instance, many high schools now include college preparation tracks and general education tracks. Rosenbaum's theory was that students who followed the lower tracks would score lower on IQ tests over time than would students who followed the higher tracks. Considering that school is one of the primary contributors to socialization, it makes sense that participation in a given track can also result in the adoption of the norms, values, beliefs, skills, and behaviours that correspond to that track.

In other words, tracks can turn into a type of selffulfilling prophecy: you may start out at the same level as someone in a higher track, but by the time you have completed the lower track you will have become like the other students in your track. To reduce confounding variables and ensure notable test effects, Rosenbaum selected a homogeneous, white, working class public school with five different, highly stratified classes. Rosenbaum then compared IQ scores for individuals in the different tracks at two time points.

As it turns out, tracking does have a significant effect on IQ. People in lower tracks can actually see a decline in IQ compared to a possible increase among those in the upper track. In other words, tracks socialize their students into their corresponding roles.

THE CHANGING CONCEPT OF CULTURE

Today most social scientists reject the cultured vs. uncultured concept of culture and the opposition of culture to human nature. They recognize that non-elites are as cultured as elites; they are just cultured in a different way.

During the Romantic Era, scholars in Germany, especially those concerned with nationalism, developed a more inclusive notion of culture as worldview. That is, each ethnic group is characterized by a distinct and incommensurable world view. Although more inclusive, this approach to culture still allowed for distinctions between civilized and primitive or tribal cultures. By the late 19th century, anthropologists had changed the concept of culture to include a wider variety of societies, ultimately resulting in the concept of culture-objects and symbols, the meaning given to those objects and symbols, and the norms, values, and beliefs that pervade social life.

This new perspective has also removed the evaluative element of the concept of culture and instead proposes distinctions rather than rankings between different cultures. For instance, the high culture of elites is now contrasted with popular or pop culture. In this sense, high culture no longer refers to the idea of being cultured, as all people are cultured. High culture simply refers to the objects, symbols, norms, values, and beliefs of a particular group of people; popular culture does the same.

THE ORIGINS OF CULTURE

Attentive to the theory of evolution, anthropologists assumed that all human beings are equally evolved, and the fact that all humans have cultures must in some way be a result of human evolution. They were also wary of using biological evolution to explain differences between specific cultures—an approach that either was a form of, or legitimized forms of, racism.

Anthropologists believed biological evolution produced an inclusive notion of culture, a concept that anthropologists could apply equally to non-literate and literate societies, or to nomadic and to sedentary societies.

They argued that through the course of their evolution, human beings evolved a universal human capacity to classify experiences, and encode and communicate them symbolically. Since these symbolic systems were learned and taught, they began to develop independently of biological evolution. That this capacity for symbolic thinking and social learning is a product of human evolution confounds older arguments about nature versus nurture.

Thus, Clifford Geertz has argued that human physiology and neurology developed in conjunction with the first cultural activities, and Middleton concluded that human "instincts were culturally formed." This view of culture argues that people living apart from one another develop unique cultures. However, elements of different cultures can easily spread from one group of people to another. Culture is dynamic and can be taught and learned, making it a potentially rapid form of adaptation to change in physical conditions.

Anthropologists view culture as not only a product of biological evolution but as a supplement to it; it can be seen as the main means of human adaptation to the natural world. This view of culture as a symbolic system with adaptive functions, which varies from place to place, led anthropologists to conceive of different cultures as defined by distinct patterns of enduring, although arbitrary, conventional sets of meaning, which took concrete form in a variety of artifacts such as myths and rituals, tools, the design of housing, and the planning of villages.

Anthropologists thus distinguish between material culture and symbolic culture, not only because each reflects different kinds of human activity, but also because they constitute different kinds of data that require different methodologies to study. This view of culture, which came to dominate between World War I and World War II, implied that each culture was bounded and had to be understood as a whole, on its own terms. The result is a belief in cultural relativism.

LEVEL OF ABSTRACTION

Another element of culture that is important for a clear understanding of the concept is level of abstraction. Culture ranges from the concrete, cultural object to micro-level interpersonal interactions to a macro-level influence on entire societies. It is important when trying to understand the concept of culture to keep in mind that the concept can have multiple levels of meaning.

MEANING AND NATURE OF SOCIAL CHANGE

Change is a very broad concept. Though change is all approximately us, we do not refer to all of it as social change. Therefore, physical growth from year to year, or change of seasons does not fall under the concept of social change. In sociology, we look at social change as alterations that happen in the social structure and social connection. The International Encyclopaedia of the Social Science looks at change as the significant alterations that happen in the social structure, or in the pattern of action and interaction in societies. Alterations may happen in norms, values, cultural products and symbols in a society.

Other definitions of change also point out that change implies alteration in the structure and function of a social system. Institutions, patterns of interaction, work, leisure behaviours, roles, norms and other characteristics of society can be altered in excess of time as a result of the procedure of social change.

THREE CHARACTERISTICS OF SOCIAL CHANGE

From these and other definitions of social change, we can see that:

- Social change is essentially a procedure of alteration with no reference to the excellence of change.
- Changes is society are related/connected to changes in culture, so that it would be sometimes useful to talk in relation to the 'socio-cultural change. Some sociologists, though, differentiate flanked by social change and cultural change. Social change is defined as alterations in the social structure, (including the changes in the mass of society) or in scrupulous social institutions, or in the connection flanked by institutions. They feel that social change refers mainly to actual human behaviour. Cultural change, on the other hand, refers to difference in cultural phenomena such as knowledge and ideas, art, religion moral doctrines, values, beliefs, symbol systems and so on. This distinction is abstract, because in several situations it is hard, or almost impossible to decide which kind of change is occurring. For instance, growth of contemporary technology as part of the culture, has been closely associated with alterations in the economic structures, on significant part of the society.
- Social change can vary in its scope and in speed. We can talk of little level or big level changes. Changes can take a cyclical pattern, *e.g.* when there is the recurrence of centralisation and decentralisation in administrative organisations. It can also be revolutionary. Revolutionary change can be seen when there is an overthrow of government in a scrupulous nation. Change can also contain short term changes (*e.g.* in migration rates) as well as extensive term changes in economic structures. We can contain in social change, both growth and decline in membership and mass of social institutions. Change may contain continuous procedures like specialisation, and also contain discontinuous procedures such as a scrupulous technological or social invention which appears at some point of time.

Change also varies in scope, in that it may power several characteristics of a society and disrupt the whole social system. In contrast, the substitution of matches for rubbing sticks to start a fire had a relatively limited scope. Some changes happen rapidly but others take a extensive time. Several of the Western nations took several decades to become industrialised, but developing nations are trying to do it more quickly.

They do this through borrowing or adapting from those nations which have already achieved it. Today mainly sociologists assume that change is a natural, inevitable, ever present part of life in every society. When we are looking at social change, we are focusing not on changes in the experiences of an individual, but on variations in social structures, institutions and social connection.

Some Allied Concepts

Social change is seen to be a neutral concept. The two other conditions that have often been allied with this concept are 'development' and 'progresses.

- Development expresses stability and direction of change. It means more than growth. 'Growth' implies a direction of change but essentially in mass or excellence. Development involves something more intrinsic, a change not only in mass but also of structure.
- Progress implies change in direction towards some final desired goal. It involves a values judgement.

All changes are not evolutionary and all changes are not progressive. Discussion of the direction of change need not involve any value judgements. The diminishing mass of the family, and the rising mass of economic units, are matters of historical information. 'Social change' is a value-neutral term, in the sense that the sociologists do not revise social change in conditions of "good or bad", desirable or undesirable. One necessity admit, though, that it is a hard task indeed to create a value-free critical analysis of changes, taking lay in the structure of a society.

THEORIES ON SOCIAL CHANGE

The major sociological theories of change can be classified in several methods. One can, for instance create a distinction flanked by evolutionary, (linear) and cyclical theories of social change. In the middle of the former, the mainly important are those of Comte, Spencer, Hobhouse and Marx.

In the middle of the latter, the mainly prominent ones are those of Spengler, Pareto, and Sorokin. In this unit, we shall briefly look at the following perspectives on change:

- The evolutionary perspective,
- The cyclical perspective,
- The structural-functional perspective, and
- The disagreement perspective.

The Evolutionary Perspective

The notion of social development was taken from the theories of biological development. Spencer propounded an analogy flanked by social and organic growth and flanked by society and an organisation. The theories of social development are composed of one or more of the following principles change, order, direction, progress and perfectibility. The principle of change states that the present system is the outcome, of more or less continuous modification from its original state. Some evolutionists add to the principles of change the notion that change necessity have an order.

Other evolutionists combine the principles of change and order with the principle of direction, thereby suggesting that there is a natural linear order of change in a social system. The evolutionary procedure of change implies, that every society goes through distinctive and successive states of subsistence and orientation. Comte, for instance, proposed a directional theory of society. He suggested that a society evolves from a theological orientation, to a metaphysical orientation to a positivistic orientation. Durkheim classified societies into easy societies united through parallel of their members, (what he described mechanical solidarity) and intricate societies based on specialisation and functional interdependence of members (what he described organic solidarity). This also suggests a directional evolutionary pattern.

It has been pointed out that it is sometimes hard in evolutionary theory, to differentiate easy direction from progress. The general theme in much of the evolutionary literature is that society's progress in excess of time, to a point where they industrialise and develop in the path and manner of western nations. Extreme expressions of this location are contained in the notion of perfectibility. Societies continue to move towards some ideal advanced state of industrialisation. Though, the neo-evolutionary theories that have appeared in recent years, are more tentative than the evolutionary theories of the 19th century and early 20th century. These neo-evolutionary theorists do not assert that change proceeds beside the similar path. They suggest that there is a common trend towards a more elaborate division of labour. They take on a relativistic view, in that they recognise that dissimilar cultures have dissimilar ideas of what constitutes progress. One of the greatest troubles of older theories of development was that they too often contained untreatable, sometimes ethnocentric propositions.

Cyclical Theories

The vital premise of the cyclical theories is: cultures and civilizations pass through stages of change, starting and often ending with the similar stage. This passing through stages is described a cycle. The cycle when completed, repeats itself in excess of and in excess of again. The ancient civilizations in Greece, China and India for instance, can be explained through the principle of cycles.

Some cyclical theorists are pessimistic in that they think that decay is inevitable. Oswald Spengler whispered that every society is born, matures, decays and eventually dies. The Roman Empire rose to power and then slowly collapsed. The British empire grew strong, and then deteriorated. Spengler whispered that social change may take the form of progress or of decay, but that no society lives for ever. Pareto presented in his theory of the circulation of elites, an interpretation of history just as to which social change is brought in relation to the, through the thrash about flanked by groups for political power. His theory was inadequate in that it was based on a limited instance of the circulation of elites in ancient Rome. His conception of political change ignored the growth of democratic government in contemporary times.

More recently Sorokin has presented theories which have some characteristics of the cyclical perspective. Sorokin's theory is based on the principle of immanent socio-cultural change. This implies that any socio-cultural system alters through virtue of its own forces and properties. This principle is interlinked to another principle, namely, the principle of limited possibilities of change. There is a limit to the number of alterations that can develop in a system. For instance, there is a limit to the new shapes of change, and to new patterns of behaviour, that can emerge in a society.

The system basically runs out of combinations in due time. If it does not die, it eventually starts running through the changes again. Therefore, there is "recurrence" or "rhythm" in the histories of socio-cultural systems.] Sorokin also creates a distinction flanked by three broad kinds of culture-ideational, idealist and sensate-which he conceives as succeeding each other in cycles, in the history of societies.

Ideational culture is spiritualistic, mystical and indeterminate. Sensate culture is the realm of science and of direct sensory experiences. Idealistic culture has sure feature of both the ideational and sensate cultures. These three kinds of cultures are looked upon as three views of reality that change just as to the two principles.

Sorokin's work is especially noteworthy not only because it contains a mass of historical analogies and comments on scrupulous social transformations, but also because it saw societies as 'changing' rather than necessarily progressing or decaying.

Structural Functionalist Perspective

In the middle of modern scholars it is mainly closely associated with the work of Parsons and Merton. Structural functionalists consider that society, like the human body, is a balanced system. Each institution serves a function in maintaining society.

When events outside or inside the society, disrupt the social order, social institutions create adjustments to restore stability. They also argue that change usually occurs in a gradual, adjective fashion and not in a sudden violent, radical fashion. Even changes which appear to be drastic, have not been able to create a great or lasting impact on the core elements, of the social and cultural systems. Change just as to them comes from basically three sources:

- Adjustment of the system to exogenous change,
- Growth through structural and functional differentiation,
- Innovations through members of groups within society.

The mainly significant and vital factor creation for social integration and stability, just as to this school of thought, is value consensus. The term 'cultural lag' is often used to describe the state of disequilibrium flanked by material and non-material characteristics of a culture. Ogburn who coined this word, explained that 'cultural lag' occurs when parts of a culture that were once in adjustment with each other change at dissimilar rates, and become incompatible with each other. Ogburn pointed out how the non-material culture (values, beliefs, norms, family, and religion) often lags behind material culture (technology, means of manufacture output of the economic system). For instance, family scheduling technologies (*i.e.* material culture) have advanced, but people take their time to accept them. Some sections of the population may reject the very thought of 'family scheduling' and consider in having a big family. Again, when an event such as augment in population or a depletion in natural possessions cause a strain in society, it takes some time for the society to understand and absorb the strain and alter its values and institutions to adapt to the change. But in order to function smoothly, societies adjust to uphold and restore themselves.

Critics have pointed out that the amount and type of changes that can be explained, with the help of the structural functionalist perspective is limited. This view neglects revolutionary changes which are profound and sudden. It also overlooks the possibility of a society going through extensive periods of malintegration, as throughout times of economic recession.

Disagreement Perspective

The disagreement theory takes the principle of dialectic (opposites) as central to social life. Disagreement theory also has its origins in early sociology, especially in the works of Marx. Disagreement theorists do not assume that societies smoothly evolve to higher or intricate stages. Just as to this school every pattern of action, belief and interaction tends to generate an opposing reaction. Contemporary life is full of examples. The legalisation of abortion has provoked the anti-abortion movement. The feminist movement has stimulated a reaction from men and women. The liberalization of sexual mores has led to open denunciation. The vital premise is that one of the outcomes of disagreement in the middle of groups is social change. The greatest limitation of this approach is that it lays too much emphasiz on disagreement, as the mainly significant factor of change. In more recent sociological writing, there is yet another perspective of social change described the 'development perspective'.

The development perspective grew from three main sources:

- From the revise of economic growth. Economists and to a great extent other social scientists, view quantitative growth in the economic sphere of life, as an significant indicator of a country's progress. For instance, they point out that a country's prosperity can be measured in conditions of GNP (Gross National Product) or per capita income.
- From the categorisation of all societies into technologically advanced, and less technologically advanced. Sometimes, the emphasiz is on industrialisation and consequently societies that are highly industrialised, are seen to be more urbanised than societies which are basically agricultural.
- From the comparison of the capitalist countries with the socialist or communist countries.

Several social scientists have compared the socialist economy and social organisation with Western capitalist economy and organisation. At this juncture we will not elaborate on this perspective, as you are going to look at it in the after that unit. The development approach to social change, brought into sharp focus, the need for formulating a broad relative perspective, which would take into explanation the intricate and diverse relationships flanked by developing countries, flanked by technologically advanced countries, and flanked by technologically advanced countries and developing nations. It can be said from the above discussion of the several perspective, that no single theory cans explanation for the complexity of social change.

FACTORS IN SOCIAL CHANGE

The troubles of why change occurs and why it has been made possible, and what affects the rate of change, is closely connected with the common problem of the factors in social change. It is more general to speak of the factors that affect social change, rather than the causes of change. Why? A cause implies that a phenomenon or event, is both necessary and enough to produce a predictable effect. The word 'necessary' suggests that we can never have the effect without the preceding cause. The word 'enough' implies that the cause alone produces the effect. It is very hard to set up 'necessity and sufficiency' in the social sciences. We prefer to speak of "factors of change" rather than "causes" of social change.

Three Vital Sources of Social Change

Some sociologists propose that social change takes lay basically in one or more of the following three methods:

- *Detection:* A shared human perception of an aspect of reality which already exists *e.g.* detection of blood circulation in biology. It is an addition to the world's store of verified knowledge. Though, it becomes a factor in social change only when it is put to use, not when it is merely recognised.

- *Inventions:* A new combination or a new use of existing knowledge *e.g.* the assembling of the automobile from an already existing thought. The thought of combining them was new. Inventions can be material (technology) and social (alphabet, deal union). Each invention may be new in form (*i.e.* in form or action) in function (what it does) or in meaning (its extensive range consequences) or in principle (the theory or law on which it is based).
- *Diffusion:* Diffusion refers to the spread of cultural traits from one group to another. It operates both within and flanked by societies. It takes lay whenever societies approach into get in touch with each other. Diffusion is a two method procedure. The British gave us their language and made tea an significant ritual for us Indians; but they adopted many conditions in English from us, for instance, Pacca Sahib, Chchota haziri, Jaggernaut, etc. Diffusion is also a selective procedure. Majority of the Indians may adopt the English language, but not their beef-eating habits. Diffusion usually involves some modification of the borrowed elements of culture either in form, function or meaning

Exogenous and Endogenous Origin of Change

It is very hard to determine where and how change originates. Some sociologists have offered a distinction flanked by endogenous change (change originating from within) and exogenous change (change entering from outside). In practice, the origin of change, can only rarely be assigned wholly to one or the other category. It can be argued that wars and conquest (exogenous origin) have played an active part in bringing in relation to the major social changes in societies crossways the world. Again it could be said that in the contemporary world, the changes taking lay in the developing countries have been stimulated to a big extent, through Western technology which was introduced in mainly cases following colonial rule. But in all societies, including those in which the initial impetus has approach from outside, social change has depended to a great extent upon the behaviours of several social groups within the society. A major part of sociological analysis consists in identifying the spheres and groups, that are principally affected, and the methods in which innovations are diffused from one sphere to another

Acceptance of and Resistance to Social Change

This leads us on to another in social change, namely acceptance of and resistance to social change. Innovations (inventions and detection are jointly termed as innovations) are rarely accepted totally. The specific attitudes and values of the society in question, the manifest usefulness of the innovations, the compatibility of the innovations with the existing culture, vested interests, and the role of change mediators are some of the significant factors that affect the degree of acceptance of and resistance to social change.

Some Factors that Affect Direction and Rate of Change

Social change has two significant characteristics: direction and rate. Here, we shall talk about the factors that affect the direction and rate of changes in society.

Geography, Population and Ecology

These factors are seen to bring in relation to the sudden changes or set a limit on social change. Climatic circumstances, natural possessions, physical site of a country, natural disasters can be significant sources of change. A natural disaster like floods may destroy whole population, force people to migrate to another lay, or create them rebuild their society all in excess of again. Likewise, augment and decrease in the mass of human population through birth, death or migration can pose a serious challenge to economic, and political institutions. Today, several geographic alterations and natural disasters are induced through the behaviours of the inhabitants or a region. Soil erosion, water and air pollution may become severe enough to trigger off new norms and laws concerning how to use possessions and dispose waste products.

Technology

Technology is recognised as one of the mainly crucial factors in social change. You may read Ogburn's concept of 'culture lag' in detail, to understand how technology has been an significant factor in social change. The contemporary factory, means of transportation, medicine, surgery, mass media of communications, legroom and computers technology etc. have affected the attitudes, values and behaviour of people crossways societies. To take a easy instance, automobiles and other means of contemporary transportation have spread culture, through rising interaction in the middle of people who live distant absent from each other. The technological feats in the region of transport and communication have altered leisure behaviours, helped in maintaining social networks, and stimulated the formation of new social relationships.

Values and Beliefs

The role of values in social change has been clearly brought out in Max Weber's book, The Protestant Ethic and the Spirit of Capitalism. Weber proposed that some historical situations, doctrines or ideas may independently affect the direction of social change. He tried to illustrate that the rise of contemporary capitalism was mainly rooted in religious values as contained in ascetic Protestantism. Disagreement in excess of incompatible values and beliefs can be an significant source of change. For instance values concerning racial or caste superiority, may conflict with the values of equality of opportunity and status. New laws have appeared to ensure that people do not face discrimination on the foundation of caste or race. Conflicts flanked by group within a society, have been and are a major source of innovation and change. For instance, the establishment of political democracy in Western Europe can be said to be mainly the outcome of class struggles.

The Great Men and Women: The Role of Individuals in Social Change

It has been pointed out that the contribution through men of genius and leaders to social change is significant. The "great men" (which comprises many women leaders as well) faced a set of circumstance, and their power arose in part from their skill to drawout persuasively the latent aspirations, anxieties and fears of big numbers of people. They were also charismatic leaders. These leaders owed their positions to personal qualities, and left upon events the spot of their own convictions. There are several more factors that can be discussed while dealing with the questions why, how and at what rate change occurs.

RELEVANCE OF ANALYSING SOCIAL CHANGE

No single theory or factor can explain the origin, direction, manner or consequences of social change. Change is such a intricate procedure, that it is hard to explain its causes, limits and consequences in a definitive specific manner. Sociological research studies in recent years have concentrated on specific procedure of social change, and its effects on society. Though, sociologists say that they are trying to look at change in an objective manner, the thought of progress is still very much present in contemporary social thought. Just as to Bottomore, it is apparent in the serious commitment to economic growth in the industrial countries, and subsequently in the countries of the Third World.

More recently, he feels, it has provided the impetus for critical evaluation of unlimited and uncontrolled economic growth. The effects of technology on the environment have animated powerful ecology movements, in mainly of the industrial and industrialising countries. There are debates in relation to the nature of a "good society" in relation to the rapid advance of science and technology and to unrestrained consumerism. Just as to Bottomore, it is not the business of the sociologist as such to describe, a "good" society "or a desirable excellence of life" but it is his/her responsibility indeed to:

- Be aware of those issues relating to human welfare.
- Outline as precisely as possible the alternative courses of change and their implications, and
- Indicate what social forces are at work in producing one outcome rather than another.

CULTURAL CHANGE

The belief that culture is symbolically coded and can thus be taught from one person to another means that cultures, although bounded, can change. Cultures are both predisposed to change and resistant to it. Resistance can come from habit, religion, and the integration and interdependence of cultural traits. For example, men and women have complementary roles in many cultures. One sex might desire changes that affect the other, as happened in the second half of the 20th century in western cultures while the other sex may be resistant to that change.

Cultural change can have many causes, including: the environment, inventions, and contact with other cultures. For example, the end of the last ice age helped lead to the invention of agriculture. Some inventions that affected Western culture in the 20th century were the birth control pill, television, and the Internet. Several understandings of how cultures change come from Anthropology.

For instance, in diffusion theory, the form of something moves from one culture to another, but not its meaning. For example, the ankh symbol originated in Egyptian culture but has diffused to numerous cultures. It's original meaning may have been lost, but it is now used by many practitioners of New Age Religion as an arcane symbol of power or life forces.

A variant of the diffusion theory, stimulus diffusion, refers to an element of one culture leading to an invention in another. Contact between cultures can also result in acculturation. Acculturation has different meanings, but in this context refers to replacement of the traits of one culture with those of another, such as what happened with many Native American Indians. Related processes on an individual level are assimilation and transculturation, both of which refer to adoption of a different culture by an individual. One sociological approach to cultural change has been outlined by Griswold. Griswold points out that it may seem as though culture comes from individuals which, for certain elements of cultural change, is true but there is also the larger, collective, and long-lasting culture that cannot have been the creation of single individuals as it predates and post-dates individual humans and contributors to culture. The author presents a sociological perspective to address this conflict.

Sociology suggests an alternative to both the unsatisfying it has always been that way view at one extreme and the unsociological individual genius view at the other. This alternative posits that culture and cultural works are collective, not individual, creations. We can best understand specific cultural objects... by seeing them not as unique to their creators but as the fruits of collective production, fundamentally social in their genesis.

In short, Griswold argues that culture changes through the contextually dependent and socially situated actions of individuals; macro-level culture influences the individual who, in turn, can influence that same culture. The logic is a bit circular, but illustrates how culture can change over time yet remain somewhat constant. It is, of course, important to recognize here that Griswold is talking about cultural change and not the actual origins of culture. Because Griswold does not explicitly distinguish between the origins of cultural change and the origins of culture, it may appear as though Griswold is arguing here for the origins of culture and situating these origins in society. This is neither accurate nor a clear representation of sociological thought on this issue. Culture, just like society, has existed since the beginning of humanity. Society and culture co-exist because humans have social relations and meanings tied to those relations. Culture as a super-phenomenon has no real beginning except in the sense that humans have a beginning. This, then, makes the question of the origins of culture moot it has existed as long as we have, and will likely exist as long as we do. Cultural change, on the other hand, is a matter that can be questioned and researched, as Griswold does.

CULTURAL CHANGE IN SECULARIZATION

Secularization is the transformation of a society from close identification with religious values and institutions towards non-religious values and secular institutions. *Secularization thesis* refers to the belief that as societies "progress", particularly through modernization and rationalization, religion loses its authority in all aspects of social life and governance. The term secularization is also used in the context of the lifting of the monastic restrictions from a member of the clergy.

Secularization has many levels of meaning, both as a theory and a historical process. Social theorists such as Karl Marx, Sigmund Freud, Max Weber, and Émile Durkheim, postulated that the modernization of society would include a decline in levels of religiosity. Study of this process seeks to determine the manner in which, or extent to which religious creeds, practices and institutions are losing social significance. Some theorists argue that the secularization of modern civilization partly results from our inability to adapt broad ethical and spiritual needs of mankind to the increasingly fast advance of the physical sciences.

The term also has additional meanings, primarily historical and religious. Applied to church property, historically it refers to the seizure of monastic lands and buildings by anti-clerical European governments during the 18th and 19th centuries, which resulted in the expulsion and suppression of the religious communities which occupied them. Otherwise, secularization involves the abandonment of goods by the Church where it is sold to purchasers after the government seizes the property, which most commonly happens after reasonable negotiations and arrangements are made. In Catholic canon law, the term can also denote the permission or authorization given for a member of a religious Order to live outside his or her religious community or monastery, either for a fixed or permanent period.

BACKGROUND

Secularization is sometimes credited both to the cultural shifts in society following the emergence of rationality and the development of science as a substitute for superstition — Max Weber called this process, "the disenchantment of the world" — and to the changes made by religious institutions to compensate. At the most basic stages, this begins with a slow transition from oral traditions to a writing culture that diffuses knowledge. This first reduces the authority of clerics as the custodians of revealed knowledge.

As the responsibility for education has moved from the family and community to the state, two consequences have arisen:

1. The *collective conscience* as defined by Durkheim is diminished; and
2. Through the fragmentation of communal activities, religion becomes more a matter of individual choice rather than an observed social obligation.

A major issue in the study of secularization is the extent to which certain trends such as decreased attendance at places of worship indicate a decrease in religiosity or simply a privatization of religious belief, where religious beliefs no longer play a dominant role in public life or in other aspects of decision-making.

The issue of secularization is discussed in various religious traditions. The government of Turkey is an often cited example, following the abolition of the Ottoman Caliphate and foundation of the Turkish republic in 1923. This established popular sovereignty in a secular republican framework, in opposition to a system whose authority is based on religion. As one of many examples of state modernization, this shows secularization and democratization as mutually re-enforcing processes, relying on a separation of religion and state. In expressly secular states like India, it has been argued that the need was to legislate for toleration and respect between quite different religions, and likewise, the secularization of the West was a response to drastically violent intra-Christian feuds between Catholicism and Protestantism. Some have therefore argued that Western and Indian secularization is radically different in that it deals with autonomy from religious regulation and control. Considerations of both tolerance and autonomy are relevant to any secular state.

DEFINITIONS

John Sommerville outlined six uses of the term secularization in the scientific literature.

The first five are more along the lines of 'definitions' while the sixth is more of a 'clarification of use':

1. When discussing macro social structures, secularization can refer to *differentiation*: a process in which the various aspects of society, economic, political, legal, and moral, become increasingly specialized and distinct from one another.
2. When discussing individual institutions, secularization can denote the transformation of a religious into a secular institution. Examples would be the evolution of institutions such as Harvard University from a predominantly religious institution into a secular institution.

3. When discussing activities, secularization refers to the transfer of activities from religious to secular institutions, such as a shift in provision of social services from churches to the government.
4. When discussing mentalities, secularization refers to the transition from *ultimate* concerns to *proximate* concerns. *E.g.*, individuals in the West are now more likely to moderate their behaviour in response to more immediately applicable consequences rather than out of concern for *post-mortem* consequences. This is a personal religious decline or movement towards a secular lifestyle.
5. When discussing populations, secularization refers to broad patterns of societal decline in levels of religiosity as opposed to the individual-level secularization of (4) above. This understanding of secularization is also distinct from (1) above in that it refers specifically to religious decline rather than societal differentiation.
6. When discussing religion, secularization can only be used unambiguously to refer to religion in a generic sense. For example, a reference to Christianity is not clear unless one specifies exactly which denominations of Christianity are being discussed.

OPPOSITION

Abdel Wahab Elmessiri outlined two meanings of the secularization term:

1. Partial Secularization: which is the common meaning of the word, and expresses "The separation between religion and state".
2. Complete Secularization: this definition is not limited to the partial definition, but exceeds it to "The separation between all values, and but also to, so that the holiness is removed from the world, and this world is transformed into a usable matter that can be employed for the sake of the strong".

7

Social Problems in Society

PROBLEM OF CASTEISM

Caste is closely connected with the Hindu philosophy and religion, custom and tradition. It is believed to have had a divine origin and sanction. It is deeply rooted social institution in India. There are more than 2800 castes and sub-castes with all their peculiarities. The term caste is derived from the Spanish word caste meaning breed or lineage. The word caste also signifies race or kind. The Sanskrit word for caste is varna which means colour. The caste stratification of the Indian society had its origin in the chaturvarna system. This doctrine the Hindu society was divided into four main varnas—Brahmins, Kashtriyas, Vaishyas and Shudras. The Varna system prevalent during the Vedic period was mainly based on division of labour and occupation. The caste system owns its origin to the Varna system. Ghurye says any attempt to define caste is bound to fail because of the complexity of the phenomenon. Risely caste is a collection of families bearing a common name claiming a common descent from a mythical ancestor professing to follow the same hereditary calling and regarded by those who are competent to give an opinion as forming a single homogeneous community.

MacIver and Page when status is wholly predetermined so that men are born to their lot without any hope of changing it, then the class takes the extreme form of caste. Cooley says that when a class is somewhat strictly hereditary we may call it caste. M.N Srinivas sees caste as a segmentary system.Every caste for him divided into sub castes which are the units of endogamy whose members follow a common occupation, social and ritual life and common culture and whose members are governed by the same authoritative body, *viz.* the panchayat. Bailey caste groups are united into a system through two principles of segregation and hierarchy. For Dumont caste is not a form of stratification but as a special form of inequality. The major attributes of caste are the hierarchy, the separation and the division of labour. Weber sees caste as the enhancement and transformation of social distance into religious or strictly a magical principle. For Adrian Mayer caste hierarchy is not just determined by economic and political factors although these are important.

MAIN FEATURES OF CASTE SYSTEM

Caste system hierarchically divides the society. A sense of highness and lowness or superiority and inferiority is associated with this gradation or ranking. The Brahmins are placed at the top of the hierarchy and are regarded as pure or supreme. The degraded caste or the untouchables have occupied the other end of the hierarchy. The status of an individual is determined by his birth and not by selection nor by accomplishments. Each caste has its own customs, traditions practices and rituals. It has its own informal rules, regulations and procedures. The caste panchayats or the caste councils regulate the conduct of members. The caste system has imposed certain restrictions on the food habitats of the members these differ from caste to caste.

In North India Brahmin would accept pakka food only from some castes lower than his own. But he would not accept kachcha food prepared with the use of water at the hands of no other caste except his own. As a matter of rule and practice no individual would accept kachcha food prepared by an inferior casteman.The caste system put restriction on the range of social relations also. The idea of pollution means a touch of lower caste man would pollute or defile a man of higher caste. Even his shadow is considered enough to pollute a higher caste man.

The lower caste people suffered from certain socio-religious disabilities. The impure castes are made to live on the outskirts of the city and they are not allowed to draw water from the public wells. In earlier times entrance to temples and other places of religious importance were forbidden to them. Educational facilities, legal rights and political representation were denied to them for a very long time. If the lower castes suffer from certain disabilities some higher caste like the Brahmins enjoy certain privileges like conducting prayers in the temples etc. There is gradation of occupations also. Some occupations are considered superior and sacred while certain others degrading and inferior. For a long time occupations were very much associated with the caste system.

Each caste had its own specific occupations which were almost hereditary. There was no scope for individual talent, aptitude, enterprise or abilities. The caste system imposes restrictions on marriage also. Caste is an endogamous group. Each caste is subdivided into certain sub-castes which are again endogamous. Intercaste marriages are still looked down upon in the traditional Indian society.

FUNCTIONS OF THE CASTE SYSTEM

The caste system is credited to ensure the continuity of the traditional social organisation of India. It has accommodated multiple communities including invading tribes in the Indian society. The knowledge and skills of the occupations have passed down from one generation to the next. Through subsystems like Jajmani system the caste system promoted interdependent interaction between various castes and communities with in a village. The rituals and traditions promoted cooperation and unity between members of the different castes.

The Dysfunctions

Caste system promoted untouchability and discrimination against certain members of the society. It hindered both horizontal and vertical social mobility forcing an individual to carry on the traditional occupation against his or her will and capacity. The status of women was affected and they were relegated to the background. The caste system divided the society into mutually hostile and conflicting groups and subgroups.

DOMINANT CASTE

This concept given by M.N. Srinivas holds that a caste is dominant when it is numerically higher than the other castes. In the Mysore village he described the peasant Okkalinga composed of nearly half of the population made up of nineteenth jati group. The Okkalinga were the biggest land owner.

The chief criteria of domination of a caste are:

- Economic strength
- Political power
- Ritual purity
- Numerical strength

The dominant caste also wields economic and political power over the other caste groups. It also enjoys a high ritual status in the local caste hierarchy. The dominant caste may not be ritually high but enjoy high status because of wealth, political power and numerical strength. The presence of educated persons and high occupation rate also play an important role in deciding its dominance over other caste groupings. Sometimes a single clan of dominant caste controls a number of villages in areas. The dominant caste settle dispute between persons belonging to their own and other jati.The power of the dominant caste is supported by a norm discouraging village from seeking justice from area,govt official, court or police located outside the village. The members of the dominant caste particularly those from the wealthy and powerful families are representative of this village in dealing with the officials.

PURITY AND POLLUTION

The notions of purity and pollution are critical for defining and understanding caste hierarchy. These concepts, Brahmins hold the highest rank and Shudras the lowest in the caste hierarchy. The Varna System represents a social stratification which includes four varnas namely—Brahmans, Kshatriyas, Vaisyas and Shudras. The Shudras were allocated the lowest rank of social ladder and their responsibilities included service of the three Varnas. The superior castes tried to maintain their ceremonial purity. Dumont holds the notion of purity and pollution interlinked with the caste system and untouchability.

The hierarchy of caste is decided just as to the degree of purity and pollution. It plays a very crucial role in maintaining the required distance between different castes. But the pollution distance varies from caste to caste and from place to place.

Dipankar Gupta observes that the notion of purity and pollution as Dumont observed is integrally linked with the institution of untouchability. But unlike untouchability the notion of purity and pollution is also a historical accretion. Over time this notion freed itself from its specific and original task of separating untouchables from the others and began to be operative at different planes of the caste system. The concept of purity and pollution plays a very crucial role in maintaining the required distance between different castes. But the pollution distance varies from caste to caste and from place to place.

HISTORY

There is no universally accepted theory about the origin of the Indian caste system. The Indian classes are similar to the ancient Iranian classes wherein the priests are Brahmins, the warriors are Kshatriya, the merchants are Vastriya, and the artisans are Huiti.

Varna and Jati

The ancient Hindu scriptures, there are four "varnas". The Bhagavad Gita says varnas are decided based on Guna and Karma. Manusmriti and some other shastras name four varnas: the Brahmins, the Kshatriyas, the Vaishyas, and Shudras. This theoretical system postulated Varna categories as ideals and explained away the reality of thousands of endogamous Jâtis actually prevailing in the country as being the result of historical mixing among the "pure" Varnas --Varna Sankara. All those who did not subscribe to the norms of the Hindu society, including foreigners, tribals, nomads and certain criminals, were considered contagious and untouchables. Another group excluded from the main society was called Parjanya or Antyaja.

This group of people formerly called "untouchables", now self-described as the Dalits, was considered either the lowest among the Shudras or outside the Varna system altogether. Passages from scriptures such as Manusmriti indicate that the varna system was originally non-hereditary. Several critics of Hinduism state that the caste system is rooted in the varna system declared in the ancient Hindu scriptures. However, many groups, such as ISKCON, consider the modern Indian caste system and the varna system two distinct concepts. Many European administrators from the colonial era incorrectly regarded the Manusmriti as the "law book" of the Hindus, and thus concluded that the caste system is a part of Hinduism, an assertion that is now rejected by most scholars, who state that it is a social practice, not a religious belief. Manusmriti was a work of reference for some Brahmins of north India, especially in Bengal, and was largely unknown in southern India. Although many Hindu scriptures contain passages that can be interpreted to sanction the caste system, they also contain indications that the caste system is not an essential part of Hinduism. The Vedas placed no importance on the caste system, mentioning caste only once, almost in passing, out of tens of thousands of verses.

Most Vedic scholars believe even this to be a subsequent and artificial insertion; B. R. Ambedkar concluded after a thorough study that this is a much later interpolation, and gave strong evidence to support his conclusion. In the Vedic period, there was no prohibition against anyone, including the Shudras, listening to the Vedas or participating in any religious rite. In Early Evidence for Caste in South India, George L. Hart stated that "the earliest Tamil texts show the existence of what seems definitely to be caste, but which antedates the Brahmins and the Hindu orthodoxy."

He believes that the origins of the caste system can be seen in the "belief system that developed with the agricultural civilization", and was later profoundly influenced by "the Brahmins and the Brahmanical religion". These early Tamil texts also outline the concept of equality. Saint Valluvar has stated "pirapokkum ella uyirkkum", which means "all are equal at birth". Likewise, Saint Auvaiyaar has stated that there are only two castes in the world: those who contribute negatively and those who contribute positively. From these statements, it can be inferred that the caste system is a socio-economic class system.

Caste and Social Status

Traditionally, although the political power lay with the Kshatriyas, historians portrayed the Brahmins as custodians and interpreters of Dharma, who enjoyed much prestige and many advantages. Fa-Hien, a Buddhist pilgrim from China, visited India around 400 A.D. "Only the lot of the Chandals he found unenviable; outcastes by reason of their degrading work as disposers of dead, they were universally shunned... But no other part of the population were notably disadvantaged, no other caste distinctions attracted comment from the Chinese pilgrim, and no oppressive caste 'system' drew forth his surprised censure." In this period kings of Sudra and Brahmin origin were as common as those of Kshatriya varna and caste system was not wholly prohibitive and repressive.

The castes did not constitute a rigid description of the occupation or the social status of a group. Since British society was divided by class, the British attempted to equate the Indian caste system to their own social class system. They saw caste as an indicator of occupation, social standing, and intellectual ability. Intentionally or unintentionally, the caste system became more rigid during the British Raj, when the British started to enumerate castes during the ten year census and codified the system under their rule. The Harijans, or the people outside the caste system, had the lowest social status. The Harijans, earlier referred to as untouchables by some, worked in what were seen as unhealthy, unpleasant or polluting jobs.

In the past, the Harijans suffered from social segregation and restrictions, in addition to extreme poverty. They were not allowed temple worship with others, nor water from the same sources. Persons of higher castes would not interact with them. If somehow a member of a higher caste came into physical or social contact with an untouchable, the member of the higher caste was defiled, and had to bathe thoroughly to purge him or herself of the impurity. Social discrimination developed even among the Harijans; sub-castes among Harijans, such as the dhobi and nai, would not interact with lower-order Bhangis, who were described as "outcastes even among outcastes". Sociologists have commented on the historical advantages offered by a rigid social structure as well as its drawbacks. While caste is now seen as anachronistic, in its original form the caste system served as an instrument of order in a society where mutual consent rather than compulsion ruled; where the ritual rights and the economic obligations of members of one caste or sub-caste were strictly circumscribed in relation to those of any other caste or sub-caste; where one was born into one's caste and retained one's station in society for life; where merit was inherited, where equality existed within the caste, but inter-caste relations were unequal and hierarchical.

A well-defined system of mutual interdependence through a division of labour created security within a community. In addition, the division of labour on the basis of ethnicity allowed immigrants and foreigners to quickly integrate into their own caste niches. The caste system played an influential role in shaping economic activities, where it functioned much like medieval European guilds, ensuring the division of labour, providing for the training of apprentices and, in some cases, allowing manufacturers to achieve narrow specialisation. For instance, in certain regions, producing each variety of cloth was the speciality of a particular sub-caste. Additionally, some philosophers have argued that the majority of people would be comfortable in stratified endogamous groups, as they were in ancient times.

Caste Mobility

Some scholars believe that the relative ranking of other castes was fluid or differed from one place to another prior to the arrival of the British. Sociologists such as Bernard Buber and Marriott McKim describe how the perception of the caste system as a static and textual stratification has given way to the perception of the caste system as a more processual, empirical and contextual stratification. Other sociologists such as Y.B. Damle have applied theoretical models to explain mobility and flexibility in the caste system in India. These scholars, groups of lower-caste individuals could seek to elevate the status of their caste by attempting to emulate the practices of higher castes. Flexibility in caste laws permitted very low-caste religious clerics such as Valmiki to compose the Ramayana, which became a central work of Hindu scripture. There is also precedent of certain Shudra families within the temples of the Sri Vaishnava sect in South India elevating their caste.

The following is a list of changes in varna cited in Hindu texts:

- Manu eldest son [Priyavrata] became king, a Kshatriya. Out of his ten sons seven became kings while three became Brahman. Their names were Mahavira, Kavi and Savana.
- Kavashailush was born to a Sudra and attained varn of a Rishi. He became mantra-drashta to numerous Vedic mantras in Rig-Veda 10th Mandal.
- Jabala's son [Satyakama] born from unknown father became Rishi by his qualities.
- [Matanga] became a Rishi after his birth in low Varna.

Some psychologists, mobility across broad caste lines may have been "minimal", though sub-castes may have changed their social status over the generations by fission, re-location, and adoption of new rituals. Sociologist M. N. Srinivas has also debated the question of rigidity in Caste. In an ethnographic study of the Coorgs of Karnataka, he observed considerable flexibility and mobility in their caste hierarchies. He asserts that the caste system is far from a rigid system in which the position of each component caste is fixed for all time; instead, movement has always been possible, especially in the middle regions of the hierarchy.

It was always possible for groups born into a lower caste to "rise to a higher position by adopting vegetarianism and teetotalism" *i.e.* adopt the customs of the higher castes. While theoretically "forbidden", the process was not uncommon in practice. The concept of sanskritization, or the adoption of upper-caste norms by the lower castes, addressed the complexity and fluidity of caste relations. The fact that many of the dynasties were of obscure origin suggests some social mobility: a person of any caste, having once acquired political power, could also acquire a genealogy connecting him with the traditional lineages and conferring Kshatriya status. A number of new castes, such as the Kayasthas and Khatris, are declared in the sources of this period. The Brahmanic sources, they originated from intercaste marriages, but this is clearly an attempt at rationalizing their rank in the hierarchy. Khatri appears to be unquestionably a Prakritised form of the Sanskrit Kshatriya. Many of these new castes played a major role in society. The hierarchy of castes did not have a uniform distribution throughout the country.

Reforms

There have been challenges to the caste system from the time of Buddha, Mahavira and Makkhali Gosala. Opposition to the system of varna is regularly asserted in the Yoga Upanic-ad-s and is a constant feature of Cina-acara tantrism, a Chinese-derived movement in Asom; both date to the medieval era. The Natha system, which was founded by Matsya-indra Natha and Go-rakc-a Natha in the same era and spread throughout India, has likewise been consistently opposed to the system of varna. Many Bhakti period saints rejected the caste discriminations and accepted all castes, including untouchables, into their fold. During the British Raj, this sentiment gathered steam, and many Hindu reform movements such as Brahmo Samaj and Arya Samaj renounced caste-based discrimination.

The inclusion of so-called untouchables into the mainstream was argued for by many social reformers. Mahatma Gandhi called them "Harijans" although that term is now considered patronizing and the term Dalit is the more commonly used. Gandhi's contribution towards the emancipation of the untouchables is still debated, especially in the commentary of his contemporary. Dr. B. R. Ambedkar, an untouchable who frequently saw Gandhi's activities as detrimental to the cause of upliftment of his people. The practice of untouchability was formally outlawed by the Constitution of India in 1950, and has declined significantly since then, to the point of a society allowing former untouchables to take high political office, like former President K. R. Narayanan, who took office in 1997, and former Chief Justice K. G. Balakrishnan.

British Rule

The fluidity of the caste system was affected by the arrival of the British. Prior to that, the relative ranking of castes differed from one place to another. The castes did not constitute a rigid description of the occupation or the social status of a group. The British attempted to equate the Indian caste system to their own class system, viewing caste as an indicator of occupation, social standing, and intellectual ability.

During the initial days of the British East India Company's rule, caste privileges and customs were encouraged, but the British law courts disagreed with the discrimination against the lower castes. However, British policies of divide and rule as well as enumeration of the population into rigid categories during the 10 year census contributed towards the hardening of caste identities. During the period of British rule, India saw the rebellions of several lower castes, mainly tribals that revolted against British rule.

These were:

- Halba rebellion
- Bhopalpatnam Struggle
- Bhil rebellion
- Paralkot rebellion
- Tarapur rebellion
- Maria rebellion
- First Freedom Struggle

- Bhil rebellion, begun by Tantya Tope in Banswara
- Koi revolt
- Gond rebellion, begun by Ramji Gond in Adilabad
- Muria rebellion
- Rani rebellion
- Bhumkal

MODERN STATUS OF THE CASTE SYSTEM

In some rural areas and small towns, the caste system is still very rigid. Caste is also a factor in the politics of India. The Government of India has officially documented castes and sub-castes, primarily to determine those deserving reservation through the census. The Indian reservation system, though limited in scope, relies entirely on quotas.

The Government lists consist of Scheduled Castes, Scheduled Tribes and Other Backward Classes:

- *Scheduled castes*: Scheduled castes generally consist of "Dalit". The present population is 16% of the total population of India. For example, the Delhi state has 49 castes listed as SC.
- *Scheduled tribes*: Scheduled tribes generally consist of tribal groups. The present population is 7% of the total population of India *i.e.* around 70 million.
- *Other Backward Classes*: The Mandal Commission covered more than 3000 castes under OBC Category and stated that OBCs form around 52% of the Indian population. However, the National Sample Survey puts the figure at 32%. There is substantial debate over the exact number of OBCs in India; it is generally estimated to be sizable, but many believe that it is lower than the figures quoted by either the Mandal Commission or the National Sample Survey.

The caste-based reservations in India have led to widespread protests, such as the 2006 Indian anti-reservation protests, with many complaining of reverse discrimination against the forward castes. Many view negative treatment of forward castes as socially divisive and equally wrong.

CASTE-RELATED VIOLENCE

Independent India has witnessed a considerable amount of violence and hate crimes motivated by caste. Various incidents of violence against Dalits, usually by other backward castes such as Kherlanji Massacre and the killings in 2010 at Mirchpur, have been reported from many parts of India. Many violent protests by Dalits, such as the 2006 Dalit protests in Maharashtra, have also been reported.

An exception to the norm is the Ranvir Sena, a caste-supremacist fringe paramilitary group based in Bihar, which committed violent acts against Dalits. Phoolan Devi, who belonged to the Mallah lower caste, was mistreated and raped by upper-caste Thakurs at a young age. She became a bandit and carried out violent robberies against upper-caste people. In 1981, her gang massacred twenty-two Thakurs, most of whom were not involved in her kidnapping or rape. Later, she became a politician and Member of Parliament.

CASTE POLITICS

B. R. Ambedkar and Jawaharlal Nehru had radically different approaches to caste, especially concerning constitutional politics and the status of untouchables. Since the 1980s, caste has become a major issue in the politics of India. The Mandal Commission was established in 1979 to "identify the socially or educationally backward" and to consider the question of seat reservations and quotas for people to redress caste discrimination. In 1980, the commission's report affirmed the affirmative action practice under Indian law, whereby additional members of lower castes—the other backward classes—were given exclusive access to another 27 per cent of government jobs and slots in public universities, in addition to the 23 per cent already reserved for the Dalits and Tribals.

When V. P. Singh's administration tried to implement the recommendations of the Mandal Commission in 1989, massive protests were held in the country. Many alleged that the politicians were trying to cash in on caste-based reservations for purely pragmatic electoral purposes. Many political parties in India have openly indulged in caste-based votebank politics. Parties such as Bahujan Samaj Party, the Samajwadi Party and the Janata Dal claim that they are representing the backward castes, and rely on OBC support, often in alliance with Dalit and Muslim support, to win elections. Remarkably, in what is called a landmark election in the history of India's biggest state of Uttar Pradesh, the Bahujan Samaj Party was able to garner a majority in the state assembly elections with the support of the high caste Brahmin community.

CRITICISM

There has been criticism of the caste system from both within and outside of India. Criticism of the Caste system in Hindu society came both from the Hindu fold and Dalit.

Historical Criticism

Many bhakti period saints, including Nanak, Kabir, Caitanya, Dnyaneshwar, Eknath, Ramanuja and Tukaram, rejected all caste-based discrimination and accepted disciples from all the castes. Many Hindu reformers such as Swami Vivekananda believe that there is no place for the caste system in Hinduism. The 15th century saint Ramananda accepted all castes, including untouchables, into his fold. Most of these saints subscribed to the Bhakti movements in Hinduism during the medieval period that rejected casteism. Nandanar, a low-caste Hindu cleric, also rejected casteism and accepted Dalits. Some other movements in Hinduism have also welcomed lower-castes into their fold, the earliest being the Bhakti movements of the medieval period. Early Dalit politics involved many reform movements; these arose primarily as a reaction to the advent of Christian missionaries in India and their attempts to convert Dalits, who were attracted to the prospect of escaping the caste system. In the 19th Century, the Brahmo Samaj under Raja Ram Mohan Roy actively campaigned against untouchability and casteism. The Arya Samaj founded by Swami Dayanand also renounced discrimination against Dalits. Sri Ramakrishna Paramahamsa and his disciple Swami Vivekananda founded the Ramakrishna Mission that participated in the emancipation of Dalits.

Upper-caste Hindus such as Mannathu Padmanabhan participated in movements to abolish untouchability against Dalits; Padmanabhan opened his family temple to Dalits for worship. Narayana Guru, a pious Hindu and an authority on the Vedas, also criticized casteism and campaigned for the rights of lower-caste Hindus within the context of Hinduism. The first upper-caste temple to openly welcome Dalits into their fold was the Laxminarayan Temple in Wardha in the year 1928; the move was spearheaded by reformer Jamnalal Bajaj. The caste system has also been criticized by many Indian social reformers. Some reformers, such as Jyotirao Phule and Iyothee Thass, argued that the lower caste people were the original inhabitants of India, who had been conquered in the ancient past by "Brahmin invaders." Mahatma Gandhi coined the term Harijan, a euphemistic word for untouchable, literally meaning Sons of God. B. R. Ambedkar, born in Hindu Dalit community, was a heavy critic of the caste system.

He pioneered the Dalit Buddhist movement in India, and asked his followers to leave Hinduism, and convert to Buddhism. India's first Prime Minister, Jawaharlal Nehru, based on his own relationship with Dalit reformer Ambedkar, supported the eradication of untouchability for the benefit of the Dalit community. In 1936, the Maharaja proclaimed that "outcastes should not be denied the consolations and the solace of the Hindu faith". Even today, the Sri Padmanabhaswamy temple that first welcomed Dalits in the state of Kerala is revered by the Dalit Hindu community.

Contemporary Criticism

Organisations such as the Rashtriya Swayamsevak Sangh have actively criticized the caste system. Some activists consider the caste system a form of racial discrimination. At the United Nations Conference Against Racism in Durban, South Africa in March 2001, participants condemned discrimination based on the caste system and tried to pass a resolution declaring caste as a basis for segregation and oppression a form of apartheid. However, no formal resolution was passed. The alleged maltreatment of Dalits in India has been described by some authors as "India's hidden apartheid". Critics of the accusations point to substantial improvements in the position of Dalits in post-independence India, consequent to the strict implementation of the rights and privileges enshrined in the Constitution of India, as implemented by the Protection of Civil rights Act, 1955.They also note that India has had a Dalit president, K. R. Narayanan, and argue that the practise had disappeared in urban public life. William A. Haviland, however:

- Although India's national constitution of 1950 sought to abolish cast discrimination and the practice of untouchability, the caste system remains deeply entrenched in Hindu culture and is still widespread throughout southern Asia, especially in rural India. In what has been called India's "hidden apartheid", entire villages in many Indian states remain completely segregated by caste. Representing about 15 per cent of India's population—or some 160 million people—the widely scattered Dalits endure near complete social isolation, humiliation, and discrimination based exclusively on their birth status. Even a Dalit's shadow is believed to pollute the upper classes. They may not cross the line dividing their part of the village from that occupied by higher castes, drink water from public wells, or visit the same temples as the higher castes. Dalit children are still often made to sit in the back of classrooms.

Sociologists Kevin Reilly, Stephen Kaufman and Angela Bodino, while critical of casteism, conclude that modern India does not practice any apartheid since there is no state-sanctioned discrimination. They write that casteism in India is presently "not apartheid. In fact, untouchables, as well as tribal people and members of the lowest castes in India benefit from broad affirmative action programmes and are enjoying greater political power." The Constitution of India places special emphasis on outlawing caste discrimination, especially the practice of untouchability.

Caste and Race

Allegations that caste amounts to race were addressed and rejected by B.R. Ambedkar, an advocate for Dalit rights and critic of untouchability. He wrote that "The Brahmin of Punjab is racially of the same stock as the Chamar of Punjab. The Caste system does not demarcate racial division. The Caste system is a social division of people of the same race", Such allegations have also been rejected by sociologists such as Andre Béteille, who writes that treating caste as a form of racism is "politically mischievous" and worse, "scientifically nonsensical" since there is no discernible difference in the racial characteristics between Brahmins and Scheduled Castes. He states, "Every social group cannot be regarded as a race simply because we want to protect it against prejudice and discrimination". The Indian government also rejects the claims of equivalency between caste and racial discrimination, pointing out that the caste issues are essentially intra-racial and intra-cultural. Indian Attorney General Soli Sorabjee insisted that "[t]he only reason India wants caste discrimination kept off the agenda is that it will distract participants from the main topic: racism. Caste discrimination in India is undeniable but caste and race are entirely distinct." Many scholars dispute the claim that casteism is akin to racism. Sociologist M. N. Srinivas has debated the question of rigidity in caste. Others have applied theoretical models to explain mobility and flexibility in the caste system in India. These scholars, groups of lower-caste individuals could seek to elevate the status of their caste by attempting to emulate the practices of higher castes.

Democracy and Authoritarianism in South Asia, Pakistani-American sociologist Ayesha Jalal writes, "As for Hinduism, the hierarchical principles of the Brahmanical social order have always been contested from within Hindu society, suggesting that equality has been and continues to be both valued and practiced." In India, some observers felt that the caste system must be viewed as a system of exploitation of poor low-ranking groups by more prosperous high-ranking groups.

In many parts of India, land is largely held by high-ranking property owners of the dominant castes, who economically exploit low-ranking landless labourers and poor artisans. Matt Cherry claims that karma underpins the caste system, which traditionally determines the position and role of every member of Hindu society. Caste determines an individual's place in society, the work he or she may carry out, and who he or she may marry and meet. Hindus believe that the karma of earlier life will determine the caste an individual will be (re)born into. On 29 March 2007, the Supreme Court of India, as an interim measure, stayed the law providing for 27% reservation for Other Backward Classes in educational institutions. This was done in response to a public interest litigation—Ashoka Kumar Thakur *vs.* Union of India. The Court held that the 1931 census could not be a determinative factor for identifying the OBCs for the purpose of providing reservation. The court also observed, "Reservation cannot be permanent and appear to perpetuate backwardness." However, the Supreme Court later upheld the reservation.

GENETIC ANALYSIS

There have been several studies examining caste members as discrete populations, examining the hypothesis that their ancestors have different origins. A 2002–03 study by T. Kivisild *et al.* concluded that the "Indian tribal and caste populations derive largely from the same genetic heritage of Pleistocene southern and western Asians and have received limited gene flow from external regions since the Holocene." Studies point to the various Indian caste groups having similar genetic origins and having negligible genetic input from outside south Asia. Because the Indian samples for this study were taken from a single geographical area, it remains to be investigated whether its findings can be safely generalized.

An earlier 1995 study by Joanna L. Mountain et al. of Stanford University had concluded that there was "no clear separation into three genetically distinct groups along caste lines", although "an inferred tree revealed some clustering just as to caste affiliation". A 2006 study by Ismail Thanseem et al. of Centre for Cellular and Molecular Biology concluded that the "lower caste groups might have originated with the hierarchical divisions that arose within the tribal groups with the spread of Neo-lithic agriculturalists, much earlier than the arrival of Aryan speakers", and "the Indo-Europeans established themselves as upper castes among this already developed caste-like class structure within the tribes."

The study indicated that the Indian caste system may have its roots long before the arrival of the Indo-Aryans; a rudimentary version of the caste system may have emerged with the shift towards cultivation and settlements, and the divisions may have become more well-defined and intensified with the arrival of Indo-Aryans. A 2006 genetic study by the National Institute of Biologicals in India, testing a sample of men from 32 tribal and 45 caste groups, concluded that the Indians have acquired very few genes from Indo-European speakers. More recent studies have also debunked the British claims that so-called Aryans and Dravidians have a racial divide.

A study conducted by the Centre for Cellular and Molecular Biology in 2009 analysed half a million genetic markers across the genomes of 132 individuals from 25 ethnic groups from 13 states in India across multiple caste groups. The study establishes, based on the impossibility of identifying any genetic indicators across caste lines, that castes in South Asia grew out of traditional tribal organisations during the formation of Indian society, and was not the product of any Aryan invasion and subjugation of Dravidian people.

DOWRY PROVLEM

The basic definition of dowry have remained unclear. As discussed by Menski, there are definitely several concepts of dowry which interlink with each other. Some writers have defined dowry as wealth given to a daughter at her marriage for contributing to the practical life of the newly married couple. They are transfers given from parents to the daughter to take with her into marriage. Technically, the property belongs to the wife and ought to stay within her control, though the husband usually has rights of management. Corresponding to the spirit of the dowry institution, dowry given to a wife ought to form part of the conjugal estate, to be enjoyed by husband and wife and to be transmitted in time to their children.

Another definition to dowry is the property a woman brings to the marriage partnership. In this meaning, dowry can be the dowry a bride receives from her parents, property she previously inherited and brings to the marriage, or property she owns as a widow and brings when she remarries. Dowry has also been referred to as a gift or transfer by a bride's family to the groom or his family at the time of marriage. Dowry as bequest have given way to groomprice, a direct transfer to the groom, in numerious historical instances. This form of transfer has been termed by M. N. Srinivas, leading Indian Sociologist, as "new dowry" and Anderson as "real dowry payments". Studies have shown that the crux of the dowry problem appears to lie with this particular concept of dowry. Definitions apart, there are many variations, across time and space, to the practice of dowry payments—the size, form and function of payments.

RELATED CONCEPTS

Payments between families on the occasion of marriage existed during the history of most developed countries and are currently widespread in many areas of the developing world. With regard to dowry, two related forms of marriage payments—brideprice/bridewealth and dower.

Bridewealth/Brideprice

The custom of brideprice dates back to 3000 B.C.E. Usually considered to be the payment a groom owes the bride's parents for the right to her labour and reproductive capabilities, a transaction involving bridewealth occurs when the bridegroom and his family transfer property to the bride's kin. Brideprice tends to exist more often in societies that tend to be homogenous, primitive, and nomadic. Boserup emphasized that brideprice societies are characterized by high female reproductive and economic autonomy, high female contribution to agricultural work, and a high incidence of polygynous marriage. This connection appears to be supported by the occurrence of brideprice in sub-Saharan Africa, where women's participation in agriculture is relatively high and more than 95 per cent of societies are traditionally polygynous.

Tambiah also contended that "bridewealth can neatly tie with polygyny, with concubinage and with men of high status or great wealth 'acquiring' women of low status or in poor circumstances. When such propensities are carried to extremes there is a distinct flavour of 'purchasing' women, of maintaining 'harems' and the like." Bridewealth is not to be seen as the mirror opposite of dowry, which involves the transmission of property not to the bride's kin, but to herself. Instead of being used in the course of wedding celebrations, bridewealth goes to the bride's male kin in order that they can themselves secure a wife. Hence, unlike dowry, bridewealth is not normally given to the couple as capital for setting up the household.

Dower

Dower refers to payments from the groom's family to the bride. Unlike brideprice, in which the transfer is made to the bride's family, dower is given directly to the bride. Dower, which remains with the conjugal couple and is the formal property of the wife throughout the marriage, serves as a form of provision for her support in case of divorce or her husband's death. Anderson, dower is most typical of traditional Islamic marriages and is prevalent in the Islamic countries of the Middle East.

THEORIES OF DOWRY

Attempts to explain dowry have centred on the very understanding of what dowry represents—a price or bequest. In what follows, I summarize the relevant literature on the theories of dowry as bequest and dowry as price, and put forward some critiques.

DOWRY AS BEQUEST

The bequest theory views dowry as an intergenerational transfer of inheritance to the bride from her kin, under her control, upon marriage.

Pre-mortem Inheritance

In general, regardless of gender, parents tend to provide transfers to children who marry off and leave the paternal household. In patrilocal/virilocal societies, where married daughters leave their parental home and married sons do not, married sons have a comparative advantage in working with the family assets in comparison to their married sisters as they live with their parents. But married sons will not obtain the full benefits of extending the family wealth and may supply too little effort if their married sisters are to fully share in their parent's bequests.

Hence, in patrilocal/virilocal societies with individual property rights, altruistic parents provide dowries for daughters and bequests for sons to alleviate a potential free-riding problem among their married sons and daughters. Dowry can be seen as a pre-mortem inheritance to the bride at the time of her marriage. The bequest theory, while sons obtain their inheritance upon the death of the parents, daughters receive their share of the family wealth at marriage. In line with this notion of inheritance is Goody's suggestion that dowry can be a form of "diverging devolution", a situation in which the parents' property "diverged" by passing into the possession of children of both sexes - dowry is part and parcel of the transfer of familial property.

Dowry as Price

First formalized by Becker, the price model sees dowries as transfers between families. Brides do not directly benefit from such transfers. Instead, dowries are transferred from the bride's families to the groom's families to equilibriate the marriage market. Hence, price models of dowry "yields a dowry function that maps characteristics of the bride, groom, and their respective families, as well as underlying features of the marriage market, to a dowry amount".

Theory of Equalizing Differentials

An influential view that can be subsumed under the price model is that dowry is given to compensate the groom's family for supporting a women after her marriage, as women are often prohibited by social customs from entering the productive economy and earning an income that would contribute economically to the family. In line with this view is Dalmia and Lawrence's theory that marital arrangements between households are "manifestations of implicit contracts serving to 'equalize' the imbalance in the value of marriage". It was proposed that a combination of traits of the groom, bride and their respective households determines the "price" of that marriage.

Kodoth's analysis of the matrilineal castes of northern Kerala suggested that dowry was demeaning and transacted as compensations only in"exceptional" circumstances, by women"marked by a combination of poor economic, social and normative feminine attributes".

Dowry is transacted in the local discourse when women are considered"old", where over-age is considered a deficit of a normative conception of femininity. It was the price socially vulnerable and poor families were called upon to pay to avoid the possibility of sexual liaisons that were condemned or enforced spinsterhood. Hence, in Kerala, gender, caste and the emphasis on conjugality work together to provide a basis for dowry.

Female Competition Model

From a neo-Darwinian perspective, dowry is the product of competition among women to attract resourceful men so as to maximise genetic representation in future generations. Females prefer males who provide the best supply of resources, as females who do so would have the highest reproductive success.

Dowries are investments of resources and reproductive tactics used by prospective brides and their kinsmen to attract the wealthiest bridegroom. The price model views dowry as an instrument whereby parents of daughters secure alliances with high-quality in-laws.

Dowries are considered as opportunities for daughters to attract resourceful men and means to ensure a better future for one's daughter and to enhance one's own prestige in the community. In this way, dowry is a gift for alliance and not a marriage payment.

Although dowry does not involve a transfer that is provided in exchange for a transfer of rights between families, there is the necessary connotation that something is expected to be obtained in return for the dowry.

The female competition model seems particularly relevant to understanding the Indian marriage market as "Hindu social organisation is essentially hierarchical, and dowry there has been traditionally linked to hypergamy."

DOWRY PAYMENTS

There are many variations, across time and space, to the practice of dowry payments—the size, form and function of payments. The following entries consider some of the functions of dowry, and various sizes and forms of dowry.

FUNCTIONS OF DOWRY

The example of Kerala reveals that while the transaction may only seem symbolic, there are probably social meanings or functions to dowry.

Economic Dimension

Other aspects of social organisation, particularly the economy, plays an integral aspect in the dowry system. Dowry has economic functions and is a way of redistributing property. Involving the transmission of property, dowry as price is essentially an economic exchange between the bride-giver and bride-taker.

In certain societies, dowry is transformed into a commercial transaction in which monetary considerations receive precedence over the personal merits of a bride; it has led to the commodification of women. As daughters are increasingly seen as expensive and costing the family too much, they grow to be less powerful in the economic exchange within the joint family system. But dowry may also improve the welfare of brides by serving as a form of pre-mortem inheritance. As a wife's dowry can constitute to what is necessary for the couple to start their conjugal unit, it can help to improve the wife's bargaining power in the marital household.

Political Dimension

Dowry often has a marked political dimension. Noble but not well-to-do families may aspire to marry their sons to women from wealthy families whose dowries would thus enhance their own financial situations. Likewise, newly wealthy families may improve their social standings through the use of rich dowries to form marriage alliances with those of a higher status.

Size and Form of Dowry

Size of Dowry Payments

Dowry is essentially variable. A number of factors may determine the size of the dowry. Various characteristics of the bride and groom affect the size of dowry. For instance, wealthier families and families of older brides tend to pay greater amounts; grooms of good jobs or prospects and good family background may demand a higher dowry. Dowry payments are also influenced by broader social changes and the prevalence of dowry payments within a context.

Form of Dowry Payments

Dowry may consist of any property whatsoever—physical objects in the form of household goods, land, cash, jewellery, etc. But anthropological work has indicated that the form of dowry payment changes with the transition in the function of dowry. For instance, as the prevalence of dowry as bequest declines, dowry increasingly began to be paid in cash, wherein the brides rarely exercised control in their new conjugal household.

DOWRY-PAYING SOCIETIES

Underlying Patterns

Dowry is generally found in societies with more complex societal structures. These societies appear to exhibit substantial socioeconomic differentiation and class stratification. As put forth by Yalman, it seems expected that the "development of social hierarchies is associated with the emerging variations in marriage and inheritance behaviour." It was observed that as many ancient civilizations flourished and grew, the practice of brideprice began to diminish and a transformation to the custom of dowry occurred. A predominance of dowry over brideprice in China during the Sung dynasty corresponded to the development of a more complex social order; there was an increased emphasis on the attainment of education in comparison with the prior Tang period, in which the possibility of upward mobility was precluded for other classes by a small number of ruling aristocrat families.

The theory that dowry is mainly found in societies exhibiting substantial class stratification and socioeconomic differentiation is substantiated by Goody's sample of 857 preindustrial societies and Murdock's sample of 1167 societies. Dowry-paying societies' marriage practices are typically monogamous/Non-polygynous, virilocal, patrilineal and endogamous. But dowry has also been traditionally linked to hypergamy. Gaulin and Boster claim a high rate of accurate prediction in a cross-cultural sample—dowry was 50 times more common in stratified, monogamous societies. Dowry-paying societies have also been associated to heavy plow agriculture where the role for women is limited.

Boserup in her study of the position of women in rural communities, distinguished two major types of societies: "... the first type is found in regions where shifting cultivation predominates and the major part of agricultural work is done by women.

In such communities, we can expect to find a high incidence of polygamy, and bridewealth being paid by the future husband or his family. The women are hardworking... The second group is found where plough cultivation predominates and where women do less agricultural work than men. In such communities, we may expect to find only a tiny minority of marriages, if any, are polygamous; that a dowry is usually paid by the girl's family; that a wife is entirely dependent upon her husband for economic support; and that the husband has an obligation to support his wife and children, at least as long as the marriage is in force."

Hence, dowry societies feature low female contribution to agriculture, low incidence of polygyny and high levels of dependence of women and children on husband's economic support.

Brideprice societies are in contrast characterized by a high female contribution to agriculture, high female reproductive and economic autonomy and high incidences of polygyny. Anderson contended that this connection appears to be supported by the reemergence of dowry in medieval Europe, which corresponded to a period of economic expansion coinciding with the introduction of heavier plough agriculture technology. In turn, this technology led to greater productivity, more surplus for trade, growth in commerce, and a rise of towns, all of which have been argued to increase the amount of household-bound activity for women.

THE DOWRY SYSTEM IN INDIA

The dowry system is so deeply rooted in Indian culture, that sometimes one feels that there's going to be no way out— at least not for another century. Even modern, well-educated families start saving up money for their daughter's dowry as soon as she is born, so what can one expect from the uneducated masses, whose only form of education is tradition?

When demands for dowry are not met, the bride is subject to torture, and often even killed. The reason many parents don't want to have daughters is because of the dowry they will have to shell out at her marriage, and the stress they go through due to never ending demands from her in-laws.

Dowry is an evil, evil system and all of us, at some level, condone it and even contribute to it. Often the boys parents don't demand dowry, but our culture is such that we feel we must give something to the in-laws. In such cases, give as much as you receive.

When you go out of your way because you are the parents of the girl, you are contributing to this evil. Come festivals like Diwali or Holi, and the parents of the daughter flood her in-laws with gifts. If gifts are expected - your daughter is married into the wrong family. If such giving is self-inflicted, you're making a mistake.

Give a token present to your daughter. If you want to give her something more, do so, but don't feel pressured to give anything more than you receive to her in-laws. You don't need to if your daughter is happily married and has a supportive husband - so DON'T.

Educate Your Daughters

An astounding number of parents still don't lay enough emphasis on educating their daughters. They believe their daughters will get married eventually, and husbands will support them, so why push them so hard? Poorer parts of society would rather send their daughters out to work and earn some money, to help them save up for her dowry. Those from regular middle and upper class backgrounds do send their daughters to school, but don't emphasise career options. They view education as a rite of passage.

If their daughters do well, it's something to brag about at kitty parties. Similarly, very wealthy parents will happily support their daughters until they get married. Because of the family status and their ability to fork out a high dowry, they know they will get good matches for their daughter, and don't take their daughters education very seriously. Get serious about your daughter's education. Encourage her to have a career of her own, no matter what your financial standing.

One of the reasons parents of the boy ask for dowry, is that they often expect that their son will be earning and supporting the wife, and it is only fair that she contribute somewhat towards the household by way of dowry. If your daughter is educated and has as good a career as her husband to be, you've got a strong step in your favour.

Instead of giving her dowry so everyone is nice to her at her new home, give her a great career, so they can't help but respect her. So if they treat her badly, she can walk out, as she is not dependent on them. So they need her monthly contribution to the household expenses and dare not mess with her. Providing your daughter with a solid education, and encouraging her to pursue a career of her choice is the best dowry any parent can ever give their daughter.

DOWRY DEATHS

Paying and accepting dowry has been illegal in India for more than forty years, but the practice is still rampant. The BBC's Lucy Ash reported on dowry in India in 2003; she spoke to Ranjana Kumari, who runs seven domestic violence shelters in Delhi, and who estimates that fights over dowry result in up to seventy deaths and serious injuries a month. "Sometimes women are tortured to squeeze more money out of their families and in extreme cases they're killed," she told Ash. "Then the husband is free to remarry and get another dowry."

If the groom or husband and his family are not satisfied with the wife's dowry, they may humiliate, harass, and physically abuse her. Wives have been confined to their houses, beaten, poisoned, and subjected to unimaginable brutality. A Bangalore-based women's group called Vimochana estimates in Ash's BBC piece that three to five women per day arrive at the city hospital's burns unit suffering from massive burns. "Bride burnings" of women by a husband's family are often reported as kitchen accidents, since many households use kerosene stoves. Many victimized wives see no alternative but to stay in their husbands' households. This is the only option they believe they have in a society that does not accept divorce and where husbands can retaliate with impunity. Attitudes that stigmatize unmarried or divorced women convince many families to give in to dowry demands, even if it leads to financial ruin.

They don't expect legal redress because offenders are usually acquitted when families do take their cases to court. One study reported that out of 799 cases of dowry death taken to court, there was only one conviction. India's National Crime Record Bureau statistics show that husbands and in-laws killed 7,026 women in 2005 over "inadequate" dowry payments. One dowry death is reported every seventy-seven minutes. This problem cuts across all social and class lines, affecting rich and poor, educated and illiterate, urban and rural. Anti-Dowry Acts were passed in the early 1960s in India and Bangladesh, but they are rarely enforced. The practice of dowry in India and Bangladesh goes back thousands of years in Hindu marriage traditions. There are two traditional aspects of dowry. *Stridhan* was given directly to the bride by her family and was meant to be an asset to her in times of adversity. Under Hindu law, it was her own property, with full right to dispose of as she wished, and it was passed on to her daughters.

Its original intent was to equip a woman for her new life with gifts of bedding, clothing, furniture, or utensils, and to be a consolation for daughters not being included in the inheritance process. The second aspect, *dakshina,* was a gift given out of affection from the family of the bride to the groom; it included any gifts made after the marriage. This usually consisted of gold or cash, in accordance with the family's financial ability.In earlier times dowry was voluntary, and the amount or lack of the gift did not interfere with the completion of a marriage. The dowry system was originally intended to provide security to, and celebrate, a newly married couple in their new life together. Dowry gradually changed, and the custom came to represent an obligatory gift to the groom's family, required to finalize a marriage for wealthy families, rather than a gift to the couple.

It was not until the mid-nineteenth century that ordinary families became socially obligated to provide elaborate dowries, especially families trying to improve their social status. It became so important a custom that the cost might ruin a family—or an insufficient dowry might stop a marriage. As intercaste mixing in schools and jobs has increased, families of lower-status girls have tried to improve their status by marrying their daughters to higher-status husbands and the practice of dowry has become commercialized as grooms and their families try to improve their wealth by demanding excessive dowries from families that are desperate to enter the superior class. Meanwhile, *stridhan* has disappeared and is no longer practiced. Since India opened up to foreign investment in 1990, the country has seen a rise in dowry-related violence alongside its economic boom. The numbers of reported dowry deaths surged from four hundred a year in the mid-1980s to fifty-eight hundred a year in the mid-1990s, just as to a 2001 report in *Time* magazine, and the number may be even greater because government statistics account for only a fraction of the total number of dowry killings.

The fact that more people are coming forward to report the crimes accounts for only a part of this increase. "A new acquisitiveness permeates society," reports *Los Angeles Times* staff writer Henry Chu in September 2007, "with more consumer and luxury goods showing up on store shelves and in television commercials." In 2006, Delhi Commission for Women member Varsha Jah told the *International Herald Tribune,* "Everyone is becoming more and more Westernized; they want expensive clothes, they want the consumer objects which are constantly advertised on television.

A dowry is seen as an easy way to get them." In many cases, the bride is pressured for more cash, jewelry, and expensive consumer items well past the wedding day. Dowries have become such a burden that many families avoid having girls. In all castes, because girls are not expected to work—and even if they actually do work—they represent costs to the family without the return a son is expected to bring when he is old enough to support his parents.

Women are viewed as a financial drain. Infant mortality for female babies is 40 per cent higher than that of male babies. Poverty is the main reason, but dowry is the second. Pregnant women can determine the sex of the baby with ultrasound technology and abort the female fetuses.

The 2001 census showed that there are just 933 women for every thousand men in India. Legislation against sex determination tests was passed ten years ago, but the practice is still widespread. A 2006 UN report estimated that female infanticide and sex-selective abortions account for ten million "missing" Indian girls over the past twenty years.

Domestic violence was criminalized in the country in 1983, but generally, abused women who are economically dependent on their husbands have been afraid of the repercussions of turning their abusers in. Activists hope that this will soon change. The Protection of Women Against Domestic Violence Act went into effect in India on October 29, 2006.

A coalition of women's rights organizations came together in agreement to successfully campaign for this law; it defines domestic violence broadly to include marital rape, emotional abuse, and economic harassment. It specifically targets dowry harassment. It is revolutionary because of its broader definition of domestic violence but also because of the recourse it offers to victims. The new act entitles a wife to a portion of the marital estate, and it guarantees financial assets to women who leave abusive husbands.

PROBLEM OF CHILD MARRIAGE

Child marriage is a violation of human rights whether it happens to a girl or a boy, but it represents perhaps the most prevalent form of sexual abuse and exploitation of girls. The harmful consequences include separation from family and friends, lack of freedom to interact with peers and participate in community activities, and decreased opportunities for education. Child marriage can also result in bonded labour or enslavement, commercial sexual exploitation and violence against the victims. Because they cannot abstain from sex or insist on condom use, child brides are often exposed to such serious health risks as premature pregnancy, sexually transmitted infections and, increasingly, HIV/AIDS. Parents may consent to child marriages out of economic necessity. Marriage may be seen as a way to provide male guardianship for their daughters, protect them from sexual assault, avoid pregnancy outside marriage, extend their childbearing years or ensure obedience to the husband's household.

FACTS AND FIGURES

- Globally, 36 per cent of women aged 20-24 were married or in union before they reached 18 years of age.
- An estimated 14 million adolescents between 15 and 19 give birth each year. Girls in this age group are twice as likely to die during pregnancy or childbirth as women in their twenties.
- Marriage of young girls is most common in sub- Saharan Africa and South Asia. In Niger, 77 per cent of 20- to 24-year-old women were married before the age of 18. In Bangladesh, this rate was 65 per cent.

BUILDING A PROTECTIVE ENVIRONMENT FOR CHILDREN

Government Commitment and Capacity

The role of government and civil-society institutions is to develop and implement systems to prevent or discourage this practice. Government action is required to review customary and civil law. Because child marriage is closely associated with poverty, government commitment to poverty reduction is likely to lead to a decrease in child marriages.

Legislation and Enforcement

Governments need to establish 18 as the legal age of marriage for girls, as well as boys, and ensure its implementation. Promoting birth and marriage registration will help enforce these laws.

Attitudes, Customs and Practices

Ending child marriage is challenging because even parents who understand its negative impact may find it hard to resist economic and societal pressures and traditions. Addressing attitudes and customs that promote or condone the practice is vital to changing the acceptable age for marriage.

Open Discussion

Marriage is regarded as a private subject in many cultures. Communication campaigns can help create circumstances in which it can be discussed and traditional beliefs about marriage can be examined. To foster behavioural change from within communities, human rights should be emphasized, particularly those of women–including equality, access to education and freedom from exploitation and discrimination.

Children's Life Skills, Knowledge and Participation

Expanding children's knowledge and empowerment is crucial, particularly for girls. Educated girls are less likely to agree to marry at a young age. Attempts to close gender gaps in education can include the establishment of child-friendly schools, cash incentives for parents and the expansion of non-formal education.

Capacity of Families and Communities

Community-level women's organisations need support to act as effective advocates and educators. Human rights-based development and education programmes can create dynamics leading to a change in customs, hierarchies and prejudices linked to the tradition of child marriage.

Essential Services, Including Prevention, Recovery and Reintegration

Counselling services on abuse, reproductive health and protection from HIV infection are imperative for young girls. Girls who run away from marriages need emergency support, as do those running away from parents forcing them into an unwanted marriage.

Monitoring, Reporting and Oversight

Demographic Health Surveys and Multiple Indicator Cluster Surveys collect valuable data on prevalence and reasons for child marriage. Community level monitoring systems can also help record frequency of child marriage. Marriage registration should be promoted.

CHILD SEXUAL ABUSE

Sexual abuse is defined as "all sexually oriented conduct, commentary or gestures, intentional and repeated, not desired or accepted freely by their object, for whom it is an imposition, a humiliation or attack on their dignity". The term *abuse* includes physical as well as non-physical acts. There is enough evidence to suggest that it often receives wider familial sanction. It is institutionalised in various forms, ranging from long hours of labour, often within and outside the home, denial of food, neglect of ailments and verbal abuse to physical violence by the husband and sometimes other family members. Far more difficult to acknowledge are problems caused by the narrow definition of sexuality as a means of perpetuating control over their minds and bodies in a conjugal relationship. Legally child sexual abuse is interpreted as 'rape' of a child who is below 16 years of age and rape as defined in Indian Penal Code is penetration without her consent.

However, in Indian law has interpreted and defined rape as penile-vaginal penetration. This definition is inadequate as in most of the child sexual abuse cases, Sakshi has worked with, there has been no sexual penetration. Child sexual abuse is the physical or mental violation of a child with sexual intent.

Thus Narang, 1998 defines child sexual abuse as follows:

- An adult exposing his/her genitals to a child or persuading the child to do the same.
- Adult touching a child's genitals or making the child touch the adult's genitalia
- An adult involving a child in pornography which includes exposing a child to pornographic material.
- An adult having oral, vaginal or anal intercourse with a child
- Any verbal or other sexual suggestion made to a child by an adult
- An adult persuading children to engage in sexual activity

Kemps sexual abuse is defined as "the involvement of dependent, developmentally immature children and adolescents in sexual activities they do not really comprehend, to which they are unable to give informed consent, or that violate the social taboos of family roles. Sexual abuse is defined as any sexual misuse of the child by a care-taking adult.

Sexual abuse includes incest, oral-genital contact; sodomy, molestation, digital manipulation and so on. RAHI includes exploitative sexual activity, whether or not they involve physical contact, between a child and another person, who by virtue of his power over the child due to age, strength, position, or relationship uses the child to meet his or her own sexual and emotional needs to the definition of child sexual abuse. The act though sexual in nature is also about the abuse of power and the betrayal of trust.

A child's dependency needs for nurturance, touch, caring, caressing, and the like are not the same as adult sexual desires. The adult or older person completely disregards the child's own developmental immaturity and inability to understand sexual behaviours. The act, therefore, is not only a gross violation of the child's body but also of the trust implicit in a care giving relationship. Child sexual abuse, just as to the report is any sexual contact between a child and an adult.

The contact covers a wide range of behaviours. It may or may not involve physical contact, force or violence, but always involves coercion. It can also include fondling of the breast or genitals, rape, oral sex, and/or sodomy.It can also include an adult demanding that a child touch his/her genitals either directly or through clothing. Non-physical sexual contact also includes exhibitionism, obscene talk or pornography. Child sexual abuse takes place in all cultures, races and in every strata of the society. Both males and females are sexually abused. Girls however, are abused more frequently and over a longer period of time. Findings based on research done at Sakshi as well as international statistics on child sexual abuse indicate that at least 2 out of 4 girls and 1 out of 6 boys are victims of sexual abuse. A study carried out by a Bangalore based NGO, Samvada, in 1994 of 348 girls from Karnataka, revealed that 83% of the respondents had experienced some form of child sexual abuse.

The preliminary report of an ongoing survey of Sakshi with about 650 girl students indicates that about 60% of the girls had experienced some form of abuse till the age of 15 years. Out of these 60%, about 20% had suffered abuse by close relatives. DCP S.B.K.Singh reported in a daily newspaper, 'The Pioneer', that 85% of the rape cases registered in the District during 1997, involved persons known to the victims.

The World Health Organisation, one in every ten child is sexually abused. In a 1980 study of 1000 victims of child abuse, A.B.Dave, et al found that 81 per cent could be classified as victims of physical abuse, 7 per cent of what the authors call neglect, 9.3 per cent of sexual abuse and 2.7 per cent of emotional abuse. None of these categories can be treated as exclusive and it is important to note that studies of this kind are extremely difficult to undertake. This particularly so in the area of sexual relations where the overall attitude of secrecy and suppression which governs any discussion or reference to sex making it difficult to come to any definite conclusion on the extent of sexual abuse of children.

Yet of available figures, of almost 10,000 reported rapes in 1990, an alarming 25 per cent are of girl children below the age of 16 and about a fifth are those under ten. A recent analysis done by the Crimes Against Women Cell, Delhi Police, points out that of the 143 rape cases registered between January and June 1992, 107 or almost 75 per cent were in the age range 7 - 18 years. Forty of the rapists were immediate neighbours and seven were relatives.

Conversations with those in charge of the cell indicate that such cases are on the increase. Sixty per cent of 650 school girls questioned in a survey said they had suffered abuse, close relatives having abused twenty per cent of them. The word perpetrator is used in relation to the person or people who are directly abusing a child or children. Although this can be applied to the person responsible for any other form of mistreatment, it tends to relate to those committing child sexual abuse.

It is not used to refer to other adults who may have played a role but were not directly involved, such as a non-abusing parent who might have been aware of the abuse but unable to intervene. In most cases, the abuser is known to the child family friend, sibling, relative, servant, teacher and so on. There have also been cases where the abusers have been very close relatives—father, grandfather, brother and uncle. The abuser is usually an older person who is in some position of trust and/or power vis-avis the child. Even though both men and women can sexually abuse a child, most abusers are male. The abuser violates a relationship of trust with the child. They may use tricks or threats to persuade the child to take part in a sexual activity. The abuse generally takes place in the child's home or the abuser's home. Given that the abuser is often known to the child and usually has both access to as well as authority over the child, the abuse does not commonly involve physical violence and generally continues over a long period of time. The abuser uses threats or blackmail to warn the child against telling any one about the abuse. This may be the primary cause for the child's silence.

Child sexual abuse is on the increase because of the responses to it and towards the victims. One of the response being denial of its existence and disbelief: Many people with whom Sakshi has interacted, deny any existence of child sexual abuse especially within a family. The concept of Indian families is perhaps the most sensitive and revered.

Therefore, it is difficult to believe that sexual abuse in the families really happens. For them, if at all the concept of child sexual abuse exists, it is limited to a particular class. The popular belief is that it is very rare and happens only in low class families. Even if some people believe that child sexual abuse exists, there is denial publicly as it is difficult for them to deal with the fact that it is prevalent in our traditional Indian families.

Due to ignorance, denial of its existence, and inability of adults to deal with the subject, the child is met with disbelief when he/she finally summons up the courage to confide in someone about the experience and trauma of being sexually abused. Thus the child is forced to suffer in silence giving the abuser greater power over the child. Sexual abuse is shrouded in shame and secrecy. Sexual organs or any reference to sex is considered to be shameful. Children are not given proper answers when they ask questions about sexual organs.

They get the messages that certain body parts are dirty and they should never be talked about. So, when a child is abused, there is total silence. The child knows that there is something wrong going on, yet the child does not have the language or the words to express it. There is loneliness because the child cannot talk about it to anybody and does not know whom to approach. This hampers disclosure and thus the abuse continues. In families where parents/relatives accept and realise that a child has suffered sexual abuse, the child is forced into silence given the culture of privacy, family prestige and family unity.

The child generally does not receive much support from the family as they do not want the matter to be disclosed and the family name exposed. Thus the abuser is not confronted and the child is encouraged to 'forget' the traumatic experience. The child and her future are sacrificed for the image of the family. A healthy environment is a family situation where family communication is clear, direct and specific and rules are flexible.

Children can freely approach elders or adults with questions or concerns about sexual experiences in the full knowledge that the adults concerned will address these issues with the child's welfare in mind. In this situation no trusted older individual violates the child's person and the child feels the freedom to say no to potential abusers and report the incident with full confidence that he or she will be protected. Families in which incest occurs often appear to be like any other family. However, they are riddled with secrets and psychological stress. Incestuous families tend to be closed, inward families lacking in any real emotional connection to people outside the family.

These families often have a history of problems for several generations, which increase the potential for incest. Frequently the mothers of abused children were themselves molested as children. Many victims assume that being dominated and treated poorly by the offender is just a fact of life and not something to be challenged. However it is vital to note that, while family influences may contribute to incest, the dysfunction itself cannot cause an individual to become sexually abusive. However, the situation makes it easier for the symptoms to play themselves out.

The offender is the sole person responsible for the abuse. In some cases, the mothers do not want to take action against the abused as they are constrained by the status of the abuser within the family, for example; a father. Economic dependence, low self esteem, lack of power within the family, incapacity to accept the responsibility of single parent and moral shame of the act keep the mother quite Members of voluntary organisations says that a mother would often suppress and wish away the event, not only because of a sense of shame and outrage, but also out of fear of reprisals from her husband, son, or other relatives.

In 1992–93, there were eight cases of rape and molestation reported by mothers to Crime Against Women Cell in Delhi. Officials at the cell pointed out that this was a significant development as hardly any such instances were reported earlier. At the same time, wives expected the police to merely caution their husbands; filing a case against them would be unheard of.

Society constantly judges women including young girls and children. They are made to feel responsible, guilty or persecuted. Girls are very scared of this judgement, and of being exposed, which forces them into silence. Abusers are aware of this societal attitude towards women and this becomes their power. Society's attitude enables them to go scott-free. Child sexual abuse is usually dismissed because in most cases it is not 'rape' as defined by law. It is met with disbelief and girls are accused of being destructive when the complaint is against a family member.

In cases where there is no penile penetration or when rape cannot be proved due to inadequate evidence, the accused is charged for 'outraging the modesty of a woman' where they may be sentenced only for a period of six months of two years. In most cases, the accused are acquitted in absence of adequate laws on child sexual abuse and inadequate interpretation of existing laws. The court room environment is hostile and girls are humiliated over and over again. This poses to be a major obstacle for girls who want to file a complaint against their abuser.

The effects of child abuse are long lasting and are carried into adulthood leaving deep scars on the personality of the abused. Healing is an important process and must begin as early as possible. Singh has pointed out that child sexual abuse triggers a host of complexities in the child's psyche. Periodic bouts of low self esteem, sexual dysfunctioning, guilt are some of the problems that arise out of child sexual abuse and which continue to haunt the individual well into adulthood.

Sexual abuse is not the only childhood experience that causes difficulty for people as they mature. Long term effects are often identical to those of other early developmental setbacks. The difference however is that most of them can be talked about freely and without involving embarrassment. The person who is sexually abused in childhood is faced with the taboo of talking about it.

Most former victims keep their experiences a secret for many years. Consequently their emotions are likely to run very deep and when they eventually surface the effects can be devastating. The abuser conveys the message that the abuser's needs come first and so it destroys the basis for child-adult trust. Victims of sexual abuse grow up without a sense of protection and security, something that is essential for them to build inner strength and venture into new experiences.

As a result, they also have difficulty in trusting others and forming relationships. Survivor's sexual activity as children were dominated by perpetrators emotional needs and selfish orientation towards sexuality. Tension, fear, betrayal, pain and mistrust coloured the victim's sexual awakening. Consequently, as adults, the sexual behaviour of survivors is severely impacted. They face issues such as sexual maladjustment, abstaining from sex or compulsively seeking it out.

Adult women victimised as children are also more likely to manifest depression, self destructive behaviour, anxiety, feelings of isolation, low self esteem, a tendency towards substance abuse, over-eating and various other addictions. The most disturbing effect of child sexual abuse is that the worst scars are on the emotional and mental health, which may show up as unidentifiable symptoms. Children are prone to a variety of psychological and behavioural disturbances caused by the trauma of abuse. These include bed wetting, nightmares, sleep disorders, depression, anxiety, running away from home, multiple personality disorders, low self esteem caused by guilt and shame.

Many children also develop a negative attitude towards their body as they blame themselves for the abuse. Renu, victim of sexual abuse began hating herself and her body. She started eating constantly, as she wanted to look ugly and so that she would not fall prey to abuse again. Thus it can lead to disturbing the child's relationship with her sexual identity/sexuality and she can fall anywhere in the spectrum, which extends from promiscuity to frigid.

It effects her self worth and the future interactions that she will have, especially with men. Shobha Srinath NIMHANS, points out to a fact that a young child below ten may not always be aware that her sexual violation is in fact qualitatively different from thrashing and abuse; it is only with the onset of puberty that she becomes aware of her sexuality.

In fact in an environment where physical contact, both affectionate and abusive, by relatives of both sexes is not uncommon, child rape needs to be viewed a little differently from the rape of a post-pubertal girl. Not unexpectedly, the families rarely talk about the rape of their young daughter: when the rapist is a father or brother, the chances of reporting is even lower. A victim of incest may attempt suicide, may have bouts of panic attack and depression.

The child may not even confide in the parents. He adds that, the wide prevalence of the crime can be gauged by the fact that just as to a study, 16 per cent of the patients being treated for genito-urinary symptoms in the dermatology and sexually transmitted diseases department of a public hospital in New Delhi, were below 14 years of age.

The child feels three Ds—dirty, damaged and different. There is a lot of anger, shame and guilt involved. There are suicidal tendencies, drug addiction and alcoholism. They also exhibit self-mutilating behaviour and have panic attacks and depression. At times the impact plays itself out in certain compulsive behaviour like over-eating, bulimia, anorexia nervosa generally seen in abused girls. There would be a slump in academic performance, increased temper tantrums, "different" conduct with some members, exhibition of sexual awareness in crude manner which are indicators of abuse. Most often children do not have the language to describe sexual activity.

It is difficult for a child to articulate his or her experience. Moreover, they are extremely traumatised as they try to make sense of what has happened to them. Hurt and fear of disclosure or punishment are the initial responses that prevent a child from speaking out.

Hence it is very important to cultivate openness within the immediate family where the children can confide in their parents without the fear of ridicule or reproach. Parents can look for certain telltale signs and reactions to find out how safe their children are, says Singh,

- The child tries to stay away from friends and people he was close to earlier. This could be due to guilt that has flooded his little conscience.
- He or she may seem depressed. Depression itself may not be easy to gauge in children but it is translated into more expressible emotions such as being irritable, withdrawn and listless
- The child may resume bed-wetting if he or she has stopped it. Sometimes he or she can get incontinent while awake.

- He or she may avoid a particular individual and show fear when forcibly made to come face to face with this person. This person could be abuser or someone who looks like him.
- Difficulty in concentrating or failing tests at school
- Sudden use of sexual language and swear words.
- Sexual exploitation or exploration of other children.
- Irritation in throat and bladder infections.
- Sexually transmitted infections.

DIVORCE PROBLEM IN SOCIETY

Divorce is the final termination of a marital union, cancelling the legal duties and responsibilities of marriage and dissolving the bonds of matrimony between the parties. In most countries divorce requires the sanction of a court or other authority in a legal process. The legal process for divorce may also involve issues of spousal support, child custody, child support, distribution of property and division of debt. In most Western countries, a divorce does not declare a marriage null and void, as in an annulment, but it does cancel the married status of the parties. Where monogamy is law, this allows each former partner to marry another. Where polygyny is legal, divorce allows the woman to marry another. Divorce laws vary considerably around the world. Divorce is not permitted in some countries, such as in Malta and in the Philippines, though an annulment is permitted. From 1971 to 1996, four European countries legalised divorce: Spain, Italy, Portugal and the Republic of Ireland.

WESTERN LAW

In some Western jurisdictions, divorce does not require a party to claim fault of their partner that leads to the breakdown of marriage. But even in jurisdictions which have adopted the "no fault" principle in divorce proceedings, a court may still take into account the behaviour of the parties when dividing property, debts, evaluating custody, and support; facts which almost always have considerable weight in fault proceedings. In most jurisdictions, a divorce must be certified by a court of law to become effective. The terms of the divorce are usually determined by the court, though they may take into account prenuptial agreements or postnuptial agreements, or simply ratify terms that the spouses may have agreed to privately.

In the absence of agreement, a contested divorce may be stressful to the spouses and lead to expensive litigation. Less adversarial approaches to divorce settlements have recently emerged, such as mediation and collaborative divorce, which negotiate mutually acceptable resolution to conflicts. In some other countries, when the spouses agree to divorce and to the terms of the divorce, it can be certified by a non-judiciary administrative entity. The effect of a divorce is that both parties are free to marry again. The subject of divorce as a social phenomenon is an important research topic in sociology. In many developed countries, divorce rates increased markedly during the twentieth century. Among the nations in which divorce has become commonplace are the United States, the United Kingdom, Canada, Germany, Australia and Scandinavia. Japan and Italy retain a lower divorce rate, and it has decreased recently. The only western country where divorce is still illegal is the British Crown Dependency of Sark.

TYPES OF DIVORCE

Though divorce laws vary between jurisdiction, there are two basic approaches to divorce: fault based and no-fault based. However, even in some jurisdictions that do not require a party to claim fault of their partner, a court may still take into account the behaviour of the parties when dividing property, debts, evaluating custody, and support. Laws vary as to the waiting period before a divorce is effective. Also, residency requirements vary. However, issues of division of property are typically determined by the law of the jurisdiction in which the property is located.

No-fault Divorce

Under a no-fault divorce system, the dissolution of a marriage does not require an allegation or proof of fault of either party. The application can be made by either party or by both parties jointly.

At-fault Divorce

Prior to 1975, countries which permitted divorces also required proof by one party that the other party had committed an act incompatible to the marriage. This was termed "grounds" for divorce and was the only way to terminate a marriage. Most jurisdictions around the world still require such proof of fault. In the United States, no-fault divorce is now available in all 50 states and the District of Columbia—New York, the last state to still require fault-based divorce, passed a bill in 2010 permitting no-fault divorce. Fault-based divorces can be contested; evaluation of offenses may involve allegations of collusion of the parties, or condonation, connivance, or provocation by the other party. Contested fault divorces can be expensive, and not usually practical as eventually most divorces are granted. Comparative rectitude is a doctrine used to determine which spouse is more at fault when both spouses are guilty of breaches.

Summary Divorce

A summary divorce, available in some jurisdictions, is used when spouses meet certain eligibility requirements, or can agree on key issues beforehand.

Key factors:

- Short marriage
- No children

- Minimal or no real property
- Marital property is under a threshold
- Each spouse's personal property is under a threshold

Uncontested Divorce

It is estimated that upwards of 95% of divorces in the U.S. are "uncontested," because the two parties are able to come to an agreement about the property, children and support issues. When the parties can agree and present the court with a fair and equitable agreement, approval of the divorce is almost guaranteed. If the two parties cannot come to an agreement, they may ask the court to decide how to split property and deal with the custody of their children. Though this may be necessary, the courts would prefer parties come to an agreement prior to entering court. Where the issues are not complex and the parties are cooperative, a settlement often can be directly negotiated between them. In the majority of cases, forms are acquired from their respective state Web sites and a filing fee is paid to the state. Most US states charge between $175 and $350 for a simple divorce filing.

Collaborative divorce and mediated divorce are considered uncontested divorces. In the United States, many state court systems are experiencing an increasing proportion of self-representation without of a lawyer in divorce cases. In San Diego, for example, the number of divorce filings involving at least one self-representing litigant rose from 46% in 1992 to 77% in 2000, in Florida from 66% in 1999 to 73% in 2001. Urban courts in California report that approximately 80% of the new divorce filings are filed *per se*.

Collaborative Divorce

Collaborative divorce is a method for divorcing couples to come to agreement on divorce issues. In a collaborative divorce, the parties negotiate an agreed resolution with the assistance of attorneys who are trained in the collaborative divorce process and in mediation, and often with the assistance of a neutral financial specialist and/or divorce coach(es). The parties are empowered to make their own decisions based on their own needs and interests, but with complete information and full professional support.

Once the collaborative divorce starts, the lawyers are disqualified from representing the parties in a contested legal proceeding, should the collaborative law process end prematurely. Most attorneys who practice collaborative divorce claim that it can be more cost effective than other divorce methods, *e.g.* going to court.

Expense, they say, has to be looked at under the headings of financial and emotional. Also, the experience of working collaboratively tends to improve communication between the parties, particularly when collaborative coaches are involved and the possibility of going back to court post separation or divorce is minimized. In the course of the collaboration should the parties not reach any agreements, any documents or information exchanged during the collaborative process cannot be used in court except by agreement between the parties. Neither can any of the professional team retained in the course of the collaboration be brought to court. Essentially they have the same protections as in mediation.

There are two exceptions:

1. Any affidavit sworn in the course of the collaboration and vouching documentation attaching to same.
2. Any interim agreement made and signed off on in the course of the collaboration or correspondence relating thereto.

The parties are in control of the time they are prepared to give their collaboration. Some people need a lot of time to complete and others will reach solutions in a few meetings.

Collaborative practitioners offer a tightly orchestrated model with meetings scheduled in advance every two weeks and the range of items to be discussed apportioned in advance of signing up as well as the more open ended process, the clients decide.

Electronic Divorce

Electronic divorce is a means that allows two persons married under certain jurisdictions, such as Portugal, to file an electronic request for no-fault collaborative divorce in a Non- judiciary administrative entity. Specific cases, with no children, real property, alimony, or common address, can be decreed as summary within one hour.

Mediated Divorce

Divorce mediation is an alternative to traditional divorce litigation. In a divorce mediation session, a mediator facilitates the discussion between the two parties by assisting with communication and providing information and suggestions to help resolve differences. At the end of the mediation process, the separating parties have typically developed a tailored divorce agreement that can be submitted to the court.

Mediation sessions can include either party's attorneys or a neutral attorney or an attorney-mediator who can inform both parties of their legal rights, but does not provide advice to either, or can be conducted with the assistance of a facilitative or transformative mediator without attorneys present at all. Divorce mediators may be attorneys who have experience in divorce cases or they may be professional mediators who are not attorneys, but who have training specifically in the area of family court matters

. Divorce mediation can be significantly less costly, both financially and emotionally, than litigation. The adherence rate to mediated agreements is much higher than that of adherence to court orders.

CAUSES OF DIVORCE

An annual study in the UK by management consultants Grant Thornton, estimates the main proximal causes of divorce based on surveys of matrimonial lawyers.

The main causes in 2004 were:

- Extra-marital affairs - 27%
- Emotional/physical abuse - 17%
- Mid-life crisis - 13%
- Addictions, *e.g.* alcoholism and gambling - 6%
- Workaholism - 6%

This survey, men engaged in extra-marital affairs in 75% of cases; women in 25%. In cases of family strain, women's families were the primary source of strain in 78%, compared to 22% of men's families. Emotional and physical abuse were more evenly split, with women affected in 60% and men in 40% of cases. In 70% of workaholism-related divorces it was men who were the cause, and 30% women. The 2004 survey found that 93% of divorce cases were petitioned by women, very few of which were contested. 53% of divorces were of marriages that had lasted 10 to 15 years, with 40% ending after 5 to 10 years. The first 5 years are relatively divorce-free, and if a marriage survives more than 20 years it is unlikely to end in divorce. The age at which a person gets married is also believed to influence the likelihood of divorce; delaying marriage may provide more opportunity or experience in choosing a compatible partner.

RELIGION AND DIVORCE

In some countries, the government defines and administers marriages and divorces. While ceremonies may be performed by religious officials on behalf of the state, a civil marriage and thus civil divorce is also possible. Due to differing standards and procedures, a couple can be legally unmarried, married, or divorced by the state's definition, but have a different status as defined by a religious order. Other countries use religious law to administrate marriages and divorces, eliminating this distinction. In these cases, religious officials are generally responsible for interpretation and implementation.

Islam allows divorce, and it can be initiated by either the husband or the wife. However, the initiations are subject to certain conditions and waiting periods, which are meant to force the initiating party to reconsider. Dharmic religions do not allow divorce. Christian views of divorce vary, with Catholic teaching allowing only annulment, but most other denominations discouraging but allowing divorce. Jewish views of divorce differ, with Reform Judaism considering civil divorces adequate. Conservative and Orthodox Judiasm require that the husband grant his wife a divorce in the form of a get. Several countries use sharia to administrate marriages and divorces. Marriage in Israel is administered separately by each religious community and there is no provision for interfaith marriages other than marrying in another country. For Jews, marriage and divorce are administered by Orthodox rabbis. Partners can file for divorce either in rabbinical court or Israeli civil court to have the household divided.

GENDER AND DIVORCE

A study published in the American Law and Economics Review, women currently file slightly more than two-thirds of divorce cases in the United States. There is some variation among states, and the numbers have also varied over time, with about 60% of filings by women in most of the 19th century, and over 70% by women in some states just after no-fault divorce was introduced, just as to the document. Evidence is given that among college-educated couples, the percentages of divorces initiated by women is approximately 90%.Regarding divorce settlements, just as to the 2004 Grant

Thornton survey in the UK, women obtained a better or considerably better settlement than men in 60% of cases. In 30% of cases the assets were split 50-50, and in only 10% of cases did men achieve better settlements.

The report concluded that the percentage of shared residence orders would need to increase in order for more equitable financial divisions to become the norm. Some jurisdictions give unequal rights to men and women when filing for divorce. For couples to Conservative or Orthodox Jewish law, the husband must grant his wife a divorce through a document called a get.

If the man refuses, the woman can appeal to a court or the community to pressure the husband. A woman whose husband refuses to grant the get or who is missing is called an agunah, is still married, and therefore cannot remarry. Under Orthodox law, children of an extramarital affair involving a married Jewish woman are considered mamzerim and cannot marry non-mamzerim.

DIVORCE PROBLEM IN INDIA

THE LAW

All major religions have their own laws which govern divorces within their own community, and separate regulations exist regarding divorce in interfaith marriages.

Hindus, including Buddhists, Sikhs and Jains, are governed by the Hindu Marriage Act, 1955; Christians by the Indian Divorce Act, 1869; Parsis by the Parsi Marriage and Divorce Act, 1936; and Muslims by the Dissolution of Muslim Marriages Act, 1939, which provides the grounds on which women can obtain a divorce, and the uncodified civil law.

Civil marriages and inter-community marriages and divorces are governed by the Special Marriage Act, 1956.Other community specific legislation includes the Native Converts' Marriage Dissolution Act, 1866 that allows a Hindu to appeal for a divorce if a spouse converts to Christianity.

Grounds for Divorce

In most Western nations, there are approximately 16 distinct reasons for which divorces are granted. In India, however, only five main reasons are generally accepted as sufficient grounds for divorce.

- *Adultery*: While no formal definition of adultery exists, it does have "a fairly established meaning in matrimonial law", namely "the voluntary sexual intercourse of a married man or woman with a person other than the offender's wife or husband". While the law considers it valid grounds for either sex, adulterous women are "judged more harshly" than men. The various religious regulations are not unanimous on this issue. The law regarding Hindus allows divorce to be granted on the grounds of infidelity of either husband or wife. The Christian law, however, would traditionally not have granted a divorce to a woman solely on the grounds of adultery. She would have had to prove another violation, such as cruelty. A recent Bombay High Court decision "recognised cruelty and desertion as independent grounds for the dissolution of a Christian marriage," striking down a part of the law that allowed for an unconstitutional distinction between the sexes.
- *Desertion*: The three main components of desertion are the "disruption of cohabitation, absence of just or reasonable cause and their combination throughout three years" before the abandoned spouse may petition for a divorce. There also must be an obvious intent on the part of the offending spouse to remain permanently apart from the other. This statute also applies to cases in which a spouse has been heard from for at least seven years.
- *Cruelty*: As with adultery, "the definition of the type of behaviour that constitutes cruelty varies just as to the gender of the petitioner" of the divorce. "Despite the fact that cruelty is often equally available to husbands and wives, the way in which the law is interpreted and applied suggests that women and men are evaluated by rather different standards." This category includes both physical and mental abuse and neglect. A court decision made in early May 1997 made cruelty sufficient grounds for a Christian woman to obtain a; previously, the law required both adultery and cruelty to be proven. The national Indian Christian community seems to have embraced this Judgement.
- *Impotency*: This refers to the physical inability of the couple to consummate the marriage or the refusal by one spouse to do so. Some cases have established that sterility can be construed to mean non-consummation if the other partner is not aware of the condition before the marriage.

- *Chronic Disease*: Both mental and physical illnesses are included in this category, as well as sexually transmitted diseases. Not all religions recognize identical diseases as grounds for divorce. Christians and Parsis do not allow divorce for a sexually transmitted disease or leprosy while the other communities do.

Divorce under Muslim Law

Muslims are governed by their personal laws under which "Nikah" is a contract and may be permanent or temporary and permits a man 4 wives if he treats all of them equally. To have a valid "Nikah" under the Muslim Law, presence of a Qazi is not necessary. Merely a proposal in the presence and hearing of two sane males or one sane male and two sane female adults, all Muslims and acceptance of the said proposals at the same time constitute a valid Nikah under the Muslim Personal Law. A husband can divorce his wife without any reasons merely by pronouncing thrice the word "Talak". However for a Muslim woman to obtain divorce certain conditions are necessary.

MEASURES TO SOLVE GENDER INEQUALITY

Every problem has its own solution elsewhere or what ever the problem is? Like this phenomenon this problems has many measures out of which some of the simple one are stated below.

- *Changes at District level mechanism*: A clear cut administrative should be made available at the district level for monitoring and reviewing the incidence of inequality against women. This district level machinery headed by District Magistrate should consist of representatives of police, prosecution machinery, judiciary and the representatives of prominent individuals of women's organisations in the Districts. This committee should review progress of investigation and prosecution. At least one special cell should be created at the district level for ensuring better registration and progress of investigation and monitoring of crimes against gender equality. This special cell should network with community groups and women's organisations and help to create an atmosphere in which people would feel encouraged to freely report the cases of gender injustice. At present, most, non-reporting of the cases is due to lack of confidence in enforcement machinery. The reporting of violence against women from the Thana to the district level and from district level to the state level gets obscured in the overall mass and complexities of the currently prescribed reporting system. Specific format should be created and implemented for reporting on gender-related crimes.
- *Changes at State level mechanism*: Similarly, like District level mechanism there should be State level machinery at the State level in which there should be special entry for those cases which needs

prompt actions. This institution will make a full control over the district level machinery. So that there should nit be any corruption or fraud with innocent persons.

- *Law of Torts*: An area of civil wrong is tort law. Tort law is probably one of the most underutilised areas of the law with respect to the problem of gender injustice.
  The torts that are directly applicable are:
  - Assault
  - Battery
  - Unlawful imprisonment
  - Nuisance
  - Tort of harassment
  - Tort of Medical prenatal test
  - It means that there can be punishment under tort law also.
- *Sensitization of Criminal Justice System*: The police officers, prosecutors, and judges at all levels of hierarchy need to be exposed to the gender equality education which would enlighten them on existing assumptions, myths and stereotypes of women and how these can interfere with fair and equitable administration of justice. Judicial system should comprise of all types of officers *i.e.* from judiciary *i.e.* judges, police officers and which should take immediate action in serious cases.
- *Family Law*: Another of wrong is family law also. In this accused can be punished under Domestic Violence Act, 2005 and Dowry Prohibition Act, 1987 other laws relating to family disputes. The suit/ case can be filed for domestic violence or any other household wrong.

The most significant factor in continued use of law to enforce patriarchal privilege is that men still control not only the legal process and the interpretation of laws, but also the subject matter and vantage point of law. If the subject matter of law is male concerns and if the perspective employed within the legal process are those of men, then women should actually have no reason to expect that mere reform of existing law will materially improve the condition of women. This is particularly true when attempts to improve the statutes of women are made through incremental reforms that are not grounded in an understanding of how women's oppressions are constructed. Reforms of rape law will not materially improve the status of women when the point of rape laws is their no enforcement. It has been shown that law is strictly restricted in it capacity to deliver gender justice, which in itself is contingent on the nature of law and its functioning.

In this connection it is worthwhile to recall that the law itself is not a monolithic entity, which simply progresses or regresses. Historically, the development of law has been an uneven one. That is to say, more than not, what law promises on document cannot carry through in reality. That is why law-as-legislation and law-in-practice are most of the time in contradiction with each other. To cite an example, the Indian constitution explicitly enshrines formal equality for women. However, the lives and experiences of India women relentlessly continue to be characterized by substantive inequality, inequity and discrimination.

Gender justice may not be then that much of a caste in the sky. Finally, one must at least clearly suggest what ought to be done. The present feminist analysis is such a modest endeavour which not only attempts to understand the reality but also tries to explain how to change it.

8

Health and Society

AN INTRODUCTION

Public health is "the science and art of preventing disease, prolonging life and promoting health through the organized efforts and informed choices of society, organizations, public and private, communities and individuals". It is concerned with threats to health based on population health analysis. The population in question can be as small as a handful of people or as large as all the inhabitants of several continents. The dimensions of health can encompass "a state of complete physical, mental and social well-being and not merely the absence of disease or infirmity", as defined by the United Nations' World Health Organization. Public health incorporates the interdisciplinary approaches of epidemiology, biostatistics and health services. Environmental health, community health, behavioural health, health economics, public policy and occupational health are other important subfields.

The focus of public health intervention is to improve health and quality of life through the prevention and treatment of disease and other physical and mental health conditions, through surveillance of cases and the promotion of healthy behaviours. Promotion of hand washing and breastfeeding, delivery of vaccinations, and distribution of condoms to control the spread of sexually transmitted diseases are examples of common public health measures.

Modern public health practice requires multidisciplinary teams of professionals including physicians specializing in public health/community medicine/infectious disease, epidemiologists, biostatisticians, public health nurses, medical microbiologists, environmental health officers, dental hygienists, dietitians and nutritionists, health inspectors, veterinarians, public health engineers, public health lawyers, sociologists, community development workers, communications officers, and others.

OBJECTIVES

The focus of a public health intervention is to prevent and manage diseases, injuries and other health conditions through surveillance of cases and the promotion of healthy behaviours, communities and environments. Many diseases are preventable through simple, non-medical methods. For example, research has shown that the simple act of hand washing with soap can prevent many contagious diseases. In other cases, treating a disease or controlling a pathogen can be vital to preventing its spread to others, such as during an outbreak of infectious disease, or contamination of food or water supplies. Public health communications programmes, vaccination programmes, and distribution of condoms are examples of common public health measures.

Public health plays an important role in disease prevention efforts in both the developing world and in developed countries, through local health systems and non-governmental organizations. The World Health Organization (WHO) is the international agency that coordinates and acts on global public health issues. Most countries have their own government public health agencies, sometimes known as ministries of health, to respond to domestic health issues. For example in the United States, the front line of public health initiatives are state and local health departments.

The United States Public Health Service (PHS), led by the Surgeon General of the United States, and the Centers for Disease Control and Prevention, headquartered in Atlanta, are involved with several international health activities, in addition to their national duties. In Canada, the Public Health Agency of Canada is the national agency responsible for public health, emergency preparedness and response, and infectious and chronic disease control and prevention. In India, the Public Health Foundation of India was launched in 2006 as a response to growing concern over the emerging public health challenges in that country.

There is a vast discrepancy in access to health care and public health initiatives between developed nations and developing nations. In the developing world, public health infrastructures are still forming. There may not be enough trained health workers or monetary resources to provide even a basic level of medical care and disease prevention. As a result, a large majority of disease and mortality in the developing world results from and contributes to extreme poverty. For example, many African governments spend less than US$10 per person per year on health care, while, in the United States, the federal government spent approximately US$4,500 per capita in 2000.

HISTORY

In some ways, public health is a modern concept of human development in science, although it has roots in antiquity. From the beginnings of human civilization, it was recognized that polluted water and lack of proper waste disposal spread communicable diseases (theory of miasma). Early religions attempted to regulate behaviour that specifically related to health, from types of food eaten, to regulating certain indulgent behaviours, such as drinking alcohol or sexual relations. The establishment of governments placed responsibility on leaders to develop public health policies and programmes in order to gain some understanding of the causes of disease and thus ensure social stability prosperity, and maintain order.

The term "healthy city" used by today's public health advocates reflects this ongoing challenge to collective physical well-being that results from crowded conditions and urbanization.

EARLY PUBLIC HEALTH INTERVENTIONS

By Roman times, it was well understood that proper diversion of human waste was a necessary tenet of public health in urban areas. The Chinese developed the practice of variolation following a smallpox epidemic around 1000 BC. An individual without the disease could gain some measure of immunity against it by inhaling the dried crusts that formed around lesions of infected individuals.

Also, children were protected by inoculating a scratch on their forearms with the pus from a lesion. This practice was not documented in the West until the early-18th century, and was used on a very limited basis. The practice of vaccination did not become prevalent until the 1820s, following the work of Edward Jenner to treat smallpox.

During the 14th century Black Death in Europe, it was believed that removing bodies of the dead would further prevent the spread of the bacterial infection. This did little to stem the plague, however, which was most likely spread by rodent-borne fleas. Burning parts of cities resulted in much greater benefit, since it destroyed the rodent infestations. The development of quarantine in the medieval period helped mitigate the effects of other infectious diseases. However, the plague model of governmentality was later controverted by the cholera model.

A Cholera pandemic devastated Europe between 1829 and 1851, and was first fought by the use of what Foucault called "social medicine", which focused on flux, circulation of air, location of cemeteries, etc. All those concerns, born of the miasma theory of disease, were mixed with urbanistic concerns for the management of populations, which Foucault designated as the concept of "biopower". The German conceptualized this in the *Polizeiwissenschaft* ("Police science").

The science of epidemiology was founded by John Snow's identification of a polluted public water well as the source of an 1854 cholera outbreak in London. Dr. Snow believed in the germ theory of disease as opposed to the prevailing miasma theory. Although miasma theory correctly teaches that disease is a result of poor sanitation, it was based upon the prevailing theory of spontaneous generation. Germ theory developed slowly: despite Anton van Leeuwenhoek's observations of Microorganisms, (which are now known to cause many of the most common infectious diseases) in the year 1680, the modern era of public health did not begin until the 1880s, with Louis Pasteur's germ theory and production of artificial vaccines. Other public health interventions include latrinization, the building of sewers, the regular collection of garbage followed by incineration or disposal in a landfill, providing clean water and draining standing water to prevent the breeding of mosquitoes. This contribution was made by Edwin Chadwick in 1843 who published a report on the sanitation of the working class population in Great Britain at the time. So began the inception of the modern public health.

The industrial revolution had initially caused the spread of disease through large conurbations around workhouses and factories. These settlements were cramped and primitive and there was no organised sanitation. Disease was inevitable and its incubation in these areas was encouraged by the poor lifestyle of the inhabitants.

MODERN PUBLIC HEALTH

With the onset of the epidemiological transition and as the prevalence of infectious diseases decreased through the 20th century, public health began to put more focus on chronic diseases such as cancer and heart disease. Previous efforts in many developed countries had already led to dramatic reductions in the infant mortality rate using preventative methods. For instance in the United States, public health worker Dr. Sara Josephine Baker established many programmes to help the poor in New York City keep their infants healthy, leading teams of nurses into the crowded neighbourhoods of Hell's Kitchen and teaching mothers how to dress, feed, and bathe their babies.

During the 20th century and early in the next, the dramatic increase in average life span is widely credited to public health achievements, such as vaccination programmes and control of many infectious diseases including polio, diphtheria, yellow fever and smallpox; effective health and safety policies such as road traffic safety and occupational safety; improved family planning; tobacco control measures; and programmes designed to decrease non-communicable diseases by acting on known risk factors such as a person's background, lifestyle and environment. One of the major sources of the increase in average life span in the early 20th century was the decline in the "urban penalty" brought on by improvements in sanitation. These improvements included chlorination of drinking water, filtration and sewage treatment which led to the decline in deaths caused by infectious waterborne diseases such as cholera and intestinal diseases. In Cutler and Miller's, "The Role of Public Health Improvements in Health Advances", they display evidence of the decline in typhoid fever deaths in Chicago, Baltimore, Cincinnati, and Cleveland after these American cities adopted chlorination, filtration, or a sewage improvement.

Meanwhile, large parts of the developing world remained plagued by largely preventable/treatable infectious diseases and poor maternal and child health outcomes, exacerbated by malnutrition and poverty. The WHO reports that a lack of exclusive breastfeeding during the first six months of life contributes to over a million avoidable child deaths each year. Intermittent preventive therapy aimed at treating and preventing malaria episodes among pregnant women and young children is one public health measure in endemic countries.

Front-page headlines continue to present society with public health issues on a daily basis: emerging infectious diseases such as SARS, rapidly making its way from China to Canada, the United States and other geographically distant countries; reducing inequities in health care access through publicly funded health insurance programmes; the HIV/AIDS pandemic and its spread from certain high-risk groups to the general population in many countries, such as in South Africa; the increase of childhood obesity and the concomitant increase in type II diabetes among children; the social, economic and health impacts of adolescent pregnancy; and the ongoing public health challenges related to natural disasters such as the 2004 Indian Ocean tsunami, 2005's Hurricane Katrina in the United States and the 2010 Haiti earthquake.

Since the 1980s, the growing field of population health has broadened the focus of public health from individual behaviours and risk factors to population-level issues such as inequality, poverty, and education. Modern public health is often concerned with addressing determinants of health across a population.

There is a recognition that our health is affected by many factors including where we live, genetics, our income, our educational status and our social relationships - these are known as "social determinants of health." A social gradient in health runs through society, with those that are poorest generally suffering the worst health. However even those in the *middle classes* will generally have worse health outcomes than those of a higher social stratum. The *new* public health seeks to address these health inequalities by advocating for population-based policies that improve health in an equitable manner.

Public Health 2.0

Public Health 2.0 is the term given to a movement within public health that aims to make the field more accessible to the general public and more user-driven. There are three senses in which the term "Public Health 2.0" is used. In the first sense, "Public Health 2.0" is similar to the term "Health 2.0" and is used to describe the ways in which traditional public health practitioners and institutions are reaching out (or could reach out) to the public through social media.

In the second sense, "Public Health 2.0" is used to describe public health research that uses data gathered from social networking sites, search engine queries, cell phones, or other technologies. In the third sense, "Public Health 2.0" is used to describe public health activities that are completely user-driven. An example this type of Public Health 2.0 is the collection and sharing of information about environmental radiation levels following the March 2011 tsunami in Japan. In all cases, Public Health 2.0 draws on ideas from Web 2.0, such as crowdsourcing, information sharing, and user-centred design.

EDUCATION AND TRAINING

Education and training of public health professionals is available throughout the world in Medical Schools, Veterinary Schools, Schools of Nursing, Schools of Public Health, and Schools of Public Affairs. The training typically requires a university degree with a focus on core disciplines of biostatistics, epidemiology, health services administration, health policy, health education, behavioural science and environmental health.

DEFINITIONS OF HEALTH

There are many definitions of health. Health can be defined by its presence or its absence and it can have individual or societal parameters. In 1946 the World Health Organisation (WHO) defined health as 'a state of complete physical, mental and social well-being and not merely the absence of disease or infirmity'. In this definition, health is defined as a positive experience rather than the absence of sickness and as a social rather than a solely individual phenomenon. Critics argue that it defines health as 'perfect health', a concept which is unable to be measured or obtained and is always future-oriented.

Definitions of health and what health planners do, however, vary according to the frames of reference used. Doctors, administrators and consumers may view health differently and therefore have different views on how health needs should be met, what health services are needed and how they should be delivered. Major health frames of references include biological/biomedical, clinical health sciences, population health, ecological public health, social health and everyday life. Planners typically focus on population issues, morbidity and demography.

DETERMINANTS OF HEALTH

The causes of illness are complex and the social, cultural and environmental impacts on health are now well documented. The determinants of health interact in complex ways, with diseases sharing common risk factors and risk factors clustered in socioeconomic groups.

Broad determinants of health may include socioeconomic structures, physical, human-made and ecological environments, health service access or quality, individual biology, cultural beliefs, personal behaviour and lifestyle choices. Specific determinants may include nutrition, infectious agents, trauma, congenital or inherited problems, the physical environment (sun, radiation, altitude), tobacco and alcohol consumption, age, gender, occupation, stress and social isolation. Epidemiological evidence increasingly points to the importance of social factors in explaining health status differences across populations.

Epidemiology is at the core of contemporary understanding of the distribution and causation of health and disease at the population level. Over the past 150 years, epidemiological concepts have undergone a number of shifts, from infectious disease epidemiology (based on germ theory) to the 'classic triad' (physical, genetic and environment causes), to the current interest in chronic diseases and multiple risk factors.

Contemporary public health approaches critique both the biomedical model and an 'illness-centred' focus on the physical risk factors of individuals and groups. The more comprehensive 'web of causation' takes biological and social factors and interventions into account and may span the genetic to the societal. The central concept in the web of causation is that many variables may be related to a single effect through direct and indirect causes. The main evidence for determinants of health comes from the prevalence of disease differences between different population sub-groups. The available data about the distribution of determinants are often poor, however and this makes planning for health (with any sophistication) difficult.

If the ultimate goal of health planning activities is to impact positively on health status, then decisions have to be taken about which of the myriad of factors/determinants are priorities for action and what can be done about them. Certainly, it is not necessary (even were it possible) to understand causal mechanisms fully in order to undertake prevention. The knowledge of small components in the web of causation can significantly contribute to prevention or improved treatment/therapy.

The Ottawa Charter suggests five core strategies for health improvement: building healthy public policy; creating supportive environments; strengthening community action; developing personal skills; and reorienting health services. The challenge in health planning is to act successfully on the social determinants of health.

HEALTH SERVICES AND THEIR IMPACT ON HEALTH STATUS

The importance of public health measures in improving health has long been recognised. The dramatic decline in mortality in the last 100 years has been widely attributed to the first public health revolution resulting in environmental improvements, including sanitation, nutrition, water supply, housing and education. These improvements led to significant overall declines in infectious diseases such as tuberculosis, typhus-typhoid, cholera, dysentery and diarrhoea, smallpox and scarlet fever.

Medical and scientific advances such as the development of antibiotics, the development of the Salk and Sabin vaccines for poliomyelitis and developments in surgery contributed to reduced death rates in the 1950s; however, these only marginally improved mortality rates. The decline in population mortality in the last century has coincided with, rather than been caused by, the rise of modern medicine.

The impact of medical access on overall health status is likely to be less than the impact of improving working and living conditions. Current studies estimate that 60–80 per cent of current disease is preventable through social change. The Centre for Disease Control in the United States attributed only 10 per cent of premature mortality to inadequate health care. Despite the contention that medical interventions have a relatively marginal impact on the overall mortality levels of a community, medicine generally enjoys great community credence. Science and the scientific method is most frequently credited with having the explanations for illness and health and the 'curative' health system continues to consume the bulk of the health budget.

Nevertheless, whilst national mortality rates tend not to respond to increases in hospital and medical resources, medical care does contribute to the reduction of non-fatal diseases, disability, discomfort and distress. Health services extend life through interventions such as immunisation, accident and trauma services and cancer treatments. Quality of life may also be improved through relief of pain, improved mobility (joint replacements) and effective treatment of many non-life-threatening conditions. The challenge for health planning is to ensure equitable access to costeffective health care while harnessing complementary strategies for health improvement.

ECOLOGY AND HEALTH

In a witty review of popular attitudes toward food, David Cort remarks that he has encountered absurdly conflicting dietary recommendations in books and articles on nutrition. One authority advises his readers to avoid fat; another advises that it should be eaten, on the theory that fat is the least fattening of all foods. Potatoes have been alternately damned and praised; mixed meals have been both frowned upon and approved; the consumption of alcohol, criticized and recommended. "The cruelty and irresponsibility of offering one single, standard dietary solution for everybody is obvious," Cort adds. "What a person eats is, in many important respects, his life. But every individual is different from every other individual. No doctrinaire solution will work for them all. Each individual has conditioned habits of eating, of taste, of appetite, of expenditure of energy, of nervous rhythms and, most important of all, of metabolism. Few modern doctors have the interest, time or genius to find out all about any one individual; and many are themselves overweight. But the individual has the time and interest and, at least about himself, perhaps the genius. After all, it's his life."

Although Cort's remarks are confined to nutrition, they are quite relevant to a number of problems in human ecology. It would be an error to form rigid concepts of a normal man, a normal diet, or a normal way of life. Any such image would be woefully lacking in biochemical and physiological support. The biologist and physician must still admit, as Carrel did nearly a quarter of a century ago, that "most of the questions put to themselves by those who study human beings remain without answer. Immense regions of our inner world are still unknown." Impressive advances, to be sure, have been made during the past two decades in solving major problems of cellular biochemistry, endocrinology and physiology. Knowledge of the transformation of energy in the cell is very far advanced, for example and great strides have been made in understanding the chemistry of the genetic material in the cell's nucleus. Despite this newly acquired knowledge, however, nutritionists have an extremely limited understanding of the function of many trace elements in the body and of the way in which vitamins prevent deficiency diseases. The nutritional requirements of the various tissues, essential details of the blood-forming system, the mechanisms of resistance to disease and many key relationships within the body await clearer understanding.

The human organism is extremely sensitive to very small quantities of hormones and nutrients. A variation by only a few drops in the daily output of insulin, a pancreatic hormone, will determine whether an individual will handle sugar properly or succumb to diabetes. A difference of a few thousandths of a gram (milligrams) in the intake of certain vitamins and trace elements makes for either well-being or nutritional disorders. According to the National Research Council, a man twentyfive years of age requires a daily intake of 1.6 milligrams of thiamine and riboflavin, 7.5 milligrams of vitamin C and 12 milligrams of iron to preserve good health.

His minimum daily requirements of iodine and copper are believed to be as little as 0.1 and 0.2 milligrams, respectively. If the daily intake of these nutrients is reduced by a few thousandths of a gram or less for a long period of time, the result will be a marked impairment of health. Despite the minute quantities involved, deficiencies of vitamins and minerals occur on a fairly large scale in the United States. If A. F. Morgan and L. M. Odland are correct in their claim that a dry, roughened skin and lesions of the eyes and mouth "may be considered a useful pointer to possible dietary faults," about 50 per cent of the adolescents examined in the affluent northeastern states and 20 per cent in the western states may have nutritional disorders.

We tend to look upon diseases as though they were localized disturbances, confined to definite parts of the body. Although it is customary to acknowledge the body's unity in sickness and in health, the whole is often overlooked in Favour of the parts and vital interrelationships are ignored in Favour of isolated events. Actually, every major deficiency and physical impairment has far-reaching effects. "Disease consists of a functional and structural disorder," Carrel notes. "Its aspects are as numerous as our organic activities.

There are diseases of the stomach, of the heart, of the nervous system, etc. But in illness the body preserves the same unity as in health. It is sick as a whole. No disturbance remains strictly confined to a single organ. Physicians have been led to consider each disease as a specialty by the old anatomical conception of the human being. Only those who know man both in his parts and in his entirety, simultaneously under his anatomical, physiological and mental aspects, are capable of understanding him when he is sick."

A clear understanding of illness and health requires a greater appreciation not only of man but of men. Physical needs and responses vary enormously from one individual to another. Roger J. Williams, one of America's most eminent biochemists, emphasizes that within the same racial groups, even in the same families, men differ from one another in the shape and weight of their vital organs, the composition of body fluids, the output of endocrine glands, the rate of metabolism, temperature control and many other respects. Individual differences in the amount of nutrients required for health and in the amount of nutrients absorbed by the body are of major practical importance. Individual requirements of calcium, trace elements, amino acids and vitamins are highly variable. For example, two normal five-year-old children who ate the same food and were exposed to the same environmental conditions showed a great variation in the amount of calcium they retained from their diets.

One child retained 264 milligrams of calcium per day for 45 days, whereas the other retained 469 milligrams, a difference of nearly 80 per cent. A high degree of variability is also found in individual responses to common environmental toxicants. Williams cites an account of 78 men who were exposed to vapors of carbon tetrachloride, of whom 15 suffered acute poisoning. Six became sufficiently ill to require hospitalization. "All were white men within 5 to 8 years of the same age and in general good health," observes Fredrich H. Harris, the source for Williams's account. "All 15 of the men poisoned were exposed from 3 to 8 hours; however, many of those who developed no symptoms were exposed for a similar length of time or longer."

The fact that man's knowledge of important bodily processes is incomplete and that many individuals exhibit marked deviations from "normal" responses and needs does not imply that the role of medicine is inconsequential in promoting health or that scientific generalizations are useless. The healthiest of men will undoubtedly require medical attention at some time in their lives and every physician must use physiological and anatomical generalizations as points of departure for the diagnosis of a disorder. Basic research in biochemistry and physiology promises to increase vastly our understanding of the preconditions for human health and well-being. But a phenomenon does not cease to exist because it cannot be readily explained by current methods and theories.

On the contrary, we are often profoundly affected by phenomena that are too complex to lend themselves to precise analysis at the present stage of scientific development. The way in which stress produces illness and the role that nutrition plays in the occurrence and prevention of chronic diseases constitute fields of research that have scarcely been penetrated. It would be a major setback if the roles of these factors were minimized simply because they present formidable problems to research. Man must try to conserve many practices that, on the basis of long experience, are known to promote good health, even if the reasons why they are beneficial cannot be stated in precise biochemical terms.

What are some of these practices? As it is clear that our bodily functions are interdependent, we should not permit any part of our biological equipment to atrophy. This means that we must use all the parts of our bodies. Our musculature must be as fully employed as our minds. Many activities and experiences that have been restricted by our sheltered civilization seem to play important roles in preserving health. There is a suspicion that modern man indirectly harms his body by failing to use certain physiological resources that once supported his ancestors during periods of hunger and cold. "There exists in the body of man, as of all animals, biological mechanisms for the storage of food developed for meeting the irregularities and cyclical changes in nature," Rene Dubos writes. "It may still turn out that a nutritional way of living permitting continuous growth at a maximum rate may have unfortunate distant results. Fasting fads may have some justification after all by providing an opportunity for the operation of certain emergency mechanisms built by nature into the human body."

Although it remains to be seen whether this conclusion will be accepted by nutritionists and physicians, it is reasonably clear that a one-sided manner of life is biologically undesirable. An existence anchored in either muscular exertion or inactivity, surfeit or poverty, stress or an overly sheltered manner of life, tends to produce physiological disequilibrium. A prolonged period of muscular exertion causes marked damage, whereas protracted physical inactivity appears to increase both the effect and the incidence of heart and circulatory disorders. When the coronary arteries of dogs are surgically narrowed to simulate atherosclerosis, a lack of exercise makes it difficult for new blood vessels to form and provide more blood to nourish the diseased area of the heart muscle.

There also seems to be more coronary illness among men whose occupations are sedentary than among those who engage in physical work. In contrast to the well-exercised individual, the "physically inactive individual shows signs of aging earlier in life," emphasizes Hans Kraus, of New York University. "He exists physiologically at a lower potential and is less well-equipped to maintain homeostasis [stable bodily conditions] and to meet daily stresses. This low level of function, combined with enforced suppression of the 'fight and flight' response, enhances the incidence of disease."

Not only does health require all the elements of a full life; it also requires that they exist in balance. A moderate amount of exertion, a balanced intake of nutriment and a reasonable amount of exposure to stress are necessary for the maintenance of well-being. Almost any kind of excess is harmful. This has become apparent in respect to nutrition. "In laboratory experiments rats fed an unlimited diet were found to die sooner than animals prevented from gaining weight by a diet severely restricted in quantity but well balanced in composition," Dubos observes. "Likewise insurance statisticians have repeatedly emphasized that in man the obese have a short expectancy of life. Indeed, obesity is now publicized as the most common nutritional disease of Western society. This was apparently true also in Imperial Rome, as during all periods of great material prosperity.

'In the old days,' wrote Lucretius in the fifth book of *De Rerum Natura, 'lack of food gave languishing limbs to Lethe; contrariwise today surfeit of things stifles us.' Thus, history repeats itself. Like the prosperous Romans of two thousand years ago, countless men of the Western world today are digging their own graves through over-eating."*

Finally, if man is to maintain good health, he requires diversity. It is hardly necessary to emphasize that a healthy psyche and a rounded response to stress are nourished by a variety of experiences and by diversified surroundings. However, it does need to be emphasized that variety is also necessary for the satisfaction of man's nutritional needs. By limiting his selection of foods, he may fail to acquire nutrients known to exist in natural foods but not yet identified by chemists or nutritionists. "Because we know that unidentified factors exist in foods of plant and animal origin," observes George M. Briggs, of the National Institutes of Health, "it is wisest to eat a wide variety of foods from the many excellent food groups." If this is done regularly, Briggs emphasizes, it is unnecessary to supplement the diet with vitamins and so-called health foods. It might be added that if food such as grain were not overly processed, it would be unnecessary to "enrich" bread with synthetic vitamins, which replace only part of the valuable nutrients lost in the milling process. In general, the more a food is processed, the greater the likelihood that identified nutrients as well as unidentified ones will be removed.

Completeness, balance and diversity should be regarded as practical ecological concepts—as important in producing healthy human communities as they are in producing stable plant-animal communities. Indeed, it is not farfetched to say that when these concepts are correctly applied, they promote human health because they produce a stable ecosystem of men, animals and plants. In the last analysis, the ecology of health is grounded in natural ecology. A complete way of life for man presupposes unrestricted access to the countryside as well as the town, to soil as well as to pavement, to flora and fauna as well as to libraries and theaters. A balanced way of life presupposes a lasting equilibrium between land and city; animals, men and plants; air, water and industry.

Diversity presupposes an awareness that nearly every species perpetuates the stability of the biosphere, either directly or indirectly. As the city encroaches on the land, however, human life becomes increasingly restricted to a polluted, nerve-racking urban environment. As the city begins to dominate the land, physical activity yields to sedentary forms of work. Finally, as the aggregations of population swell to massive proportions, foods become laden with chemicals and human activities are standardized. By oversimplifying the natural environment, we have created an incomplete man who lives an unbalanced life in a standardized world. Such a man is ill—not only morally and psychologically, but physically.

HUMAN ECOLOGY AND HEALTH

DECENTRALIZATION

Without having read any books or articles on human ecology, millions of Americans have sensed the over-all deterioration of modern urban life. They have turned to the suburbs and "exurbs" as a refuge from the burdens of the metropolitan milieu. From all accounts of suburban life, many of these burdens have followed them into the countryside. Suburbanites have not adapted to the land; they have merely adapted a metropolitan manner of life to semi-rural surroundings. The metropolis remains the axis around which their lives turn. It is the source of their livelihood, their food staples and, in large part, their tensions. The suburbs have branched away from the city, but they still belong to the metropolitan tree.

It would be wise, however, to stop ridiculing the exodus to the suburbs and to try to understand what lies behind this phenomenon. The modern city has reached its limits. Megalopolitan life is breaking down—psychically, economically and biologically. Millions of people have acknowledged this breakdown by "voting with their feet"; they have picked up their belongings and left. If they have not been able to sever their connections with the metropolis, at least they have tried. As a social symptom, the effort is significant. The reconciliation of man with the natural world is no longer merely desirable; it has become a necessity. It is a compelling need that is sending millions of people into the countryside.

The need has created a new interest in camping, handicrafts and horticulture. In ever-increasing numbers, Americans are acquiring a passionate interest in their national parks and forests, in their rural landscape and in their small-town agrarian heritage. Despite its many shortcomings, this trend reflects a basically sound orientation. The average American is making an attempt, however confusedly, to reduce his environment to a human scale. He is trying to re-create a world that he can cope with as an individual, a world that he correctly identifies with the freedom, gentler rhythms and quietude of rural surroundings. His attempts at gardening, landscaping, carpentry, home maintenance and other so-called suburban "vices" reflect a need to function within an intelligible, manipulatable and individually creative sphere of human activity.

The suburbanite, like the camper, senses that he is working with basic, abiding things that have slipped from his control in the metropolitan world—shelter, the handiwork that enters into daily life, vegetation and the land. He is fortunate, to be sure, if these activities do not descend to the level of caricature.

Nevertheless, they are important, not only because they reflect basic needs of man but because they also reflect basic needs of the things with which he is working. The human scale is also the natural scale. The soil, the land, the living things on which man depends for his nutriment and recreation are direly in need of individual care.

For one thing, proper maintenance of the soil not only depends upon advances in our knowledge of soil chemistry and soil fertility; it also requires a more personalized approach to agriculture. Thus far, the trend has been the other way; agriculture has become depersonalized and over-industrialized. Modern farming is suffering from gigantism. The average agricultural unit is getting so big that the finer aspects of soil performance and soil needs are being overlooked. If differences in the quality and performance of various kinds of soil are to receive more attention, American farming must be reduced to a more human scale. It will become necessary to bring agriculture within the scope of the individual, so that the farmer and the soil can develop together, each responding as fully as possible to the needs of the other.

The same is true for the management of livestock. Today our food animals are being manipulated like a lifeless industrial resource. Normally, large numbers of animals are collected in the smallest possible area and are allowed only as much movement as is necessary for mere survival. Our meat animals have been placed on a diet composed for the most part of medicated feed high in carbohydrates. Before they are slaughtered, these obese, rapidly matured creatures seldom spend more than six months on the range and six months on farms, where they are kept on concentrated rations and gain about two pounds daily. Our dairy herds are handled like machines; our poultry flocks, like hothouse tomatoes. The need to restore the time-honored intimacy between man and his livestock is just as pronounced as the need to bring agriculture within the horizon of the individual farmer.

Although modern technology has enlarged the elements that enter into the agricultural situation, giving each man a wider area of sovereignty and control, machines have not lessened the importance of personal familiarity with the land, its vegetation and the living things it supports. Unless principles of good land use permit otherwise, a farm should not become smaller or larger than the individual farmer can command. If it is smaller, agriculture will become inefficient; if larger, it will become depersonalized.

With the decline in the quality of urban life, on the one hand and the growing imbalance in agriculture, on the other, our times are beginning to witness a remarkable confluence of human interests with the needs of the natural world. Men of the nineteenth century assumed a posture of defiance Towards the forests, plains and mountains. Their applause was reserved for the engineer, the technician, the inventor, at times even the robber baron and the railroader, who seemed to offer the promise of a more abundant material life. Today we are filled with a vague nostalgia for the past. To a large degree this nostalgia reflects the insecurity and uncertainty of our times, in contrast with the echoes of a more optimistic and perhaps more tranquil era. But it also reflects a deep sense of loss, a longing for the free, unblemished land that lay before the eyes of the frontiersman and early settler. We are seeking out the mountains they tried to avoid and we are trying to recover fragments of the forests they removed. Our nostalgia springs neither from a greater sensitivity nor from the wilder depths of human instinct. It springs from a growing need to restore the normal, balanced and manageable rhythms of human life—that is, an environment that meets our requirements as individuals and biological beings.

Modern man can never return to the primitive life he so often idealizes, but the point is that he doesn't have to. The use of farm machinery as such does not conflict with sound agricultural practices; nor are industry and an urbanized community incompatible with a more agrarian, more natural environment. Ironically, advances in technology itself have largely overcome the industrial problems that once justified the huge concentrations of people and facilities in a few urban areas. Automobiles, aircraft, electric power and electronic devices have eliminated nearly all the problems of transportation, communication and social isolation that burdened man in past eras. We can now communicate with one another over a distance of thousands of miles in a matter of seconds and we can travel to the most remote areas of the world in a few hours.

The obstacles created by space and time are essentially gone. Similarly, size need no longer be a problem. Technologists have developed remarkable small-scale alternatives to many of the giant facilities that still dominate modern industry. The smoky steel town, for example, is an anachronism. Excellent steel can be made and rolled with installations that occupy about two or three city blocks. Many of the latest machines are highly versatile and compact. They lend themselves to a large variety of manufacturing and finishing operations. Today the more modern plant, with its clean, quiet, versatile and largely automated facilities, contrasts sharply with the huge, ugly, congested factories inherited from an earlier industrial era.

Thus, almost without realizing it, we have been preparing the material conditions for a new type of human community—one which constitutes neither a complete return to the past nor a suburban accommodation to the present. It is no longer fanciful to think of man's future environment in terms of a decentralized, moderate-sized city that combines industry with agriculture, not only in the same civic entity but in the occupational activities of the same individual. The "urbanized farmer" or the "agrarianized townsman" need not be a contradiction in terms. This way of life was achieved for a time by the Greek polis, by early republican Rome and by the Renaissance commune. The urban centers that became the wellsprings of Western civilization were not strictly cities, in the modern sense of the term. Rather, they brought agriculture together with urban life, synthesizing both into a rounded human, cultural and social development.

Whether modern man manages to reach this point or travels only part of the way, some kind of decentralization will be necessary to achieve a lasting equilibrium between society and nature. Urban decentralization underlies any hope of achieving ecological control of pest infestations in agriculture. Only a community well integrated with the resources of the surrounding region can promote agricultural and biological diversity. With careful planning, man could use plants and animals not only as a source of food but also, by pitting one species of life against another, as a means of controlling pests, thus eliminating much of his need for chemical methods. What is equally important, a decentralized community holds the greatest promise for conserving natural resources, particularly as it would promote the use of local sources of energy. Instead of relying primarily on concentrated sources of fuel in distant regions of the continent, the community could make maximum use of its own energy resources, such as wind power, solar energy and hydroelectric power.

These sources of energy, so often overlooked because of an almost exclusive reliance on a national division of Labour, would help greatly to conserve the remaining supply of high-grade petroleum and coal. They would almost certainly postpone, if not eliminate, the need for turning to radioactive substances and nuclear reactors as major sources of industrial energy. With more time at his disposal for intensive research, man might learn either to employ solar energy and wind power as the principal sources of energy or to eliminate the hazard of radioactive contamination from nuclear reactors.

It is true, of course, that our life lines would become more complex and, from a technological point of view, less "efficient." There would be many duplications of effort. Instead of being concentrated in two or three areas of the country, steel plants would be spread out, with many communities employing small-scale facilities to meet regional or local needs. But the word "efficiency," like the word, "pest," is a relative term. Although a duplication of facilities would be somewhat costly, many local mineral sources that are not used today because they are too widely scattered or too small for the purposes of large-scale production, would become economical for the purposes of a smaller community. Thus, in the long run, a more localized or regional form of industrial activity is likely to promote a more efficient use of resources than our prevailing methods of production.

It is true that we will never entirely eliminate the need for a national and international division of Labour in agriculture and industry. The Midwest will always remain the best source of our grains; the East and Far West, the best sources of lumber and certain field crops. Our petroleum, high-grade coal and certain minerals will still have to be supplied, in large part, by a few regions of the country. But there is no reason why we cannot reduce the burden that our national division of Labour currently places on these areas by spreading the agricultural and industrial loads over wider areas of the country. This seems to be the only approach to the task of creating a long-range balance between man and the natural world and of remaking man's synthetic environment in a form that will promote human health and fitness. An emphasis on agriculture and urban regionalism is somewhat disconcerting to the average city dweller. It conjures up an image of cultural isolation and social stagnation, of a journey backward in history to the agrarian societies of the medieval and ancient worlds. Actually, the urban dweller today is more isolated in the big city than his ancestors were in the countryside. The city man in the modern metropolis has reached a degree of anonymity, social atomization and spiritual isolation that is virtually unprecedented in human history.

Today man's alienation from man is almost absolute. His standards of co-operation, mutual aid, simple human hospitality and decency have suffered an appalling amount of erosion in the urban milieu. Man's civic institutions have become cold, impersonal agencies for the manipulation of his destiny and his culture has increasingly accommodated itself to the least common denominator of intelligence and taste. He has nothing to lose even by a backward glance; indeed, in this way he is likely to place his present-day world and its limitations in a clearer perspective.

But why should an emphasis on agriculture and urban regionalism be regarded as an attempt to return to the past? Can we not develop our environment more selectively, more subtly and more rationally than we have thus far, combining the best of the past and present and bringing forth a new synthesis of man and nature, nation and region, town and country? Life would indeed cease to be an adventure if we merely elaborated the present by extending urban sprawl and by expanding civic life until it completely escapes from the control of its individual human elements. To continue along these lines would serve not to promote social evolution but rather to "fatten" the social organism to a point where it could no longer move. Our purpose should be to make individual life a more rounded experience and this we can hope to accomplish at the present stage of our development only by restoring the complexity of man's environment and by reducing the community to a human scale.

Is there any evidence that reason will prevail in the management of our affairs? It is difficult to give a direct answer. Certainly we are beginning to look for qualitative improvements in many aspects of life; we are getting weary and resentful of the shoddiness in our goods and services. We are gaining a new appreciation of the land and its problems and a greater realization of the social promise offered by a more manageable human community. More and more is being written about our synthetic environment and the criticism is more pointed than it has been in almost half a century. Perhaps we can still hope, as Mumford did more than two decades ago in the closing lines of *The Culture of Cities:*

"We have much to unbuild and much more to build: but the foundations are ready: the machines are set in place and the tools are bright and keen: the architects, the engineers and the workmen are assembled. None of us may live to see the complete building and perhaps in the nature of things the building can never be completed: but some of us will see the flag or the fir tree that the workers will plant aloft in ancient ritual when they cap the topmost story."

PRINCIPLES FOR PROMOTING HEALTHY EATING

The following issues need to be considered before embarking on any interventions.

In the present context, an intervention is usually a deliberate change that is made to the child's environment with the purpose of altering the child's feeding behaviours to improve the child's health and nutrition status. This 'deliberate change' can be general or highly specific. A key aim of children's healthy eating promotion is to bring about sustainable long term dietary improvements. This usually involves altering the ways in which families, child care organisations or schools operate, thus the importance of food policies.

Behavioural change takes time and persistence, and needs to involve the help of many people and agencies. Working out exactly which changes are required and setting a schedule of goals for the child, parents, teachers, schools and other organisations are important steps. Many parents and community health and education workers are willing to help implement healthy eating programmes for children. In any locality or setting, it is important to consult with these stakeholders to decide on the desired outcomes of any healthy eating programme and to work out ways in which to evaluate progress towards project goals.

A school community, for example, might decide to develop a food policy that will aim to transform the canteen sales to include more fruit and vegetable products. If a policy with goals and responsibilities is written, then the success of the policy can be reviewed from time to time and actions can be taken to either modify the goals or strengthen actions to better meet the goals.

THE PRACTITIONERS' ROLE IN HEALTHY EATING PROMOTION

The role of practitioners in healthy eating promotion varies just as to their occupation and the settings in which they work. Setting good examples is an essential role of all practitioners, so it is important for practitioners to set their own healthy eating goals and act to achieve them. An equally important general role is listening to parents' and children's views, needs and wants. Healthy eating should be a natural part of everyone's lives; practitioners have to find ways in which to fit healthy eating into people's lives. The Review of Children's Healthy Eating Interventions found little evidence that the design and implementation of many published interventions had accounted for children's and parents' opinions and life experiences. Yet, children and parents are the *key people* in any healthy eating programme, and they should be heavily involved in the design, implementation and evaluation of any interventions, in keeping with the principles of sound community health promotion. For many people, food and eating are moral issues—that is, some ways of eating are perceived as 'wrong' and others as 'right'. Practitioners need to avoid becoming labelled as the 'diet police', which can happen if their activities are too prescriptive. There are many ways to eat healthily; the essence of good practice is to enable people to choose their own ways of doing so. In summary, the practitioner's role is to facilitate children's, parents' and professionals' access to information and food resources to enable children and families to eat in healthy ways; practitioners should not try to 'own' the project.

AIMING FOR SMALL, MEASURABLE, SUSTAINABLE, SYSTEMIC CHANGES

A key finding of the Review of Children's Healthy Eating Interventions was that large scale externally funded interventions were often no more effective than small scale interventions, and that very few interventions were sustainable in the long term. Often, when external funding ceased, the programmes ceased. Several practitioners interviewed for that review noted that small, systemic but significant changes in daily practice are preferable to one-off 'gee whiz' campaigns because they are more likely to be feasible in the long term. Again, this approach is consistent with the local community focus of effective health promotion. It suggests healthy eating promotion should be a normal part of a teacher's, nurse's, carer's or parent's 'job'.

THE IMPORTANCE OF SOUND INFORMATION

Although parents and carers do not need to be mini-nutritionists to help children eat healthy, enjoyable foods, there is little doubt that they require sound knowledge of key nutritional and behavioural principles. However, many adults have less than optimal knowledge of nutritional principles and the distribution of this knowledge appears to be differentiated among social economic groups, with lower socioeconomic status groups having less knowledge. Several stakeholders interviewed for the Review of Children's Healthy Eating Interventions noted substantial demand for clear information about the feeding of children. Without an understanding of the basic principles of nutrition and child development, parents, teachers and other carers may find it difficult to alter children's food consumption habits. Good examples of suitable information materials include *What's there to eat? The practical guide to feeding families*, the 'Filling the Gap' tip sheets, *The Australian Dietary Guidelines for Children and Adolescents*, publications by Nutrition Australia, the National Heart Foundation's manual for out-of-school hours carers, and *The Australian Guide to Healthy Eating*.

A FOCUS ON EATING, NOT JUST NUTRITION

Healthy eating should be enjoyable. Unfortunately, there is a widespread perception among children that healthy food *must* be distasteful. This perception may be related to some parents' and community members' overly constrictive views of food. In contrast, healthy eating involves consuming a wide variety of foods and a more relaxed approach to nutritional principles. Children can enjoy most foods so long as the foods are well prepared and eaten in a supportive social environment.

Usually, children and parents need to be involved in handling, choosing, preparing and tasting food. Good examples are school gardening and kitchen projects, the Tooty Fruity programme and the classroom-based fruit and vegetable campaigns run annually by the Western Australian Department of Health in conjunction with the horticultural industry. These projects emphasise the experiential aspects of food—learning about how food feels, smells and tastes. Useful guides to healthy, enjoyable eating can also be found in cookery books, the 'slow food' movement's publications and manuals such as the National Heart Foundation's *Eat smart, play smart* school manual, *FoodPower* and *What's there to eat?*

The practical guide to feeding families. Nutritional outcomes such as prevention of obesity and adequate nutrition status are desirable consequences of healthy eating; however, if people do not make healthy food choices in the first place, their nutrition status will be poor. The Review of Children's Healthy Eating Interventions showed that interventions during the 1980s placed little emphasis on eating behaviours and focused too much on biomedical outcomes. These goals have now been shown to be overly narrow and limited predictors of health status. An emphasis on ways of enjoying a wide variety of foods from the standard food groups avoids the risk of changes in nutritional fashions and does not confuse people.

GOAL SETTING

To change their behaviours, people need to have a clear picture of what they should change; they need clear goals and strategies to achieve those goals. This simple principle applies just as much to practitioners' work programmes as it does to parents' and children's eating behaviours. Several interventions have employed self-monitoring schemes in which children set their own eating goals, then try to meet them; if children meet their goals, they are rewarded with praise or something tangible, such as a gold star.

In moderation, such schemes are useful behavioural strategies because they focus everyone's minds on a task and they build in feedback and positive reinforcement. Again, there are useful guides to this approach. For this approach, the collection of baseline information about eating is important so any changes can be evaluated and fed back to the participants to motivate them. Reinforcement or reward of desired behaviours is a key principle of behaviour change. It does not have to be given on every occasion; often, mere recognition that the person has achieved the goal can be highly effective in maintaining the behaviour change. Several researchers, however, have warned about the dangers of using food 'treats' to reward children for 'good' behaviour. This type of reward usually makes the treat more desirable in the child's eyes.

A FOCUS ON CHILDREN'S AND CARERS' NEEDS AND WANTS

Practitioners can easily concentrate only on healthy eating goals. However, parents and children may not perceive healthy eating as a highly valuable goal. They may want to do other things instead, such as quit smoking, work longer hours to earn essential household income or, in the case of children, retain the approval of their friends, who may regard healthy eating as 'sissy'. This recognition of other goals does not prevent practitioners from adopting other strategies to reach healthy eating goals.

FoodCent$ is an excellent example of the flexible thinking required. This Western Australian programme operates for low income households. The designers of FoodCent$ were aware that many of their clients suffered from major financial hardships that tended to make nutritional considerations relatively less relevant to them. The practitioners thus used the dietary pyramid as a way of saving money, rather than as a way of talking about the healthiness of foods. As a result, most participants adopted healthier food patterns after only a few group sessions and maintained them for up to four years. In other words, the practitioners focused on the clients' expressed wants rather than solely on their professional orientation. It is important to focus on the clients' needs, wants and views of health and nutrition. Many primary and secondary school students, for example, associate the concept of 'health' with 'boredom' and other negative connotations, so some may perceive foods labelled 'healthy' as being unattractive. Some canteen managers identify the foods that children perceive as attractive and market their foods accordingly. At Loreto College in Adelaide, many students thought that Italian trends were attractive, so the canteen manager gave the healthier products Italian names to make them more attractive to the children.

As a result, salad rolls outsold meat pies and pasties four to one! Marketers do this routinely, associating their products with images that are attractive to their potential customers. Mineral water, for example, is often advertised using images showing 'sophisticated' models sipping the product poolside. While practitioners have to be concerned about health, many children are less concerned. For this reason, practitioners may need to motivate children to eat more healthily by linking healthy foods to the children's social and personal needs, especially their need for social acceptance.

THE BEST SETTINGS FOR INTERVENTIONS

The Review of Children's Healthy Eating Interventions showed that most interventions have been conducted in ante-natal and postnatal centres and in primary schools. These settings are important influences on children's eating, but other settings—for example, preschools, secondary schools and local communities—may be just as important yet have been less studied by researchers. Interestingly, the greatest percentage of effective interventions was found in secondary schools. This suggests some settings may be more amenable for researchers to study, while others may be better places to conduct effective interventions. It is important to select settings for interventions just as to their potential to facilitate healthy eating, rather than because they are convenient settings in which practitioners can work.

THE IMPORTANCE OF PARENTS

One key problem is access to parents. Parents remain major influences on many children until adulthood but it can be difficult to involve them in healthy eating programmes. Settings such as preschools, family day care and out-of-school care centres tend to involve more contact with parents, which may provide opportunities for the promotion of healthy eating. However, other approaches that may be required include: the use of mass media advertising; interventions in work sites, health centres and leisure and sporting settings; school newsletters; mail-outs of booklets and videos to children's homes; and communication via retail outlets.

Parents probably benefit as much as their children from healthy eating interventions, particularly given that over half of them are likely to be overweight or obese. Families are thus more likely to adopt programmes that target parents' eating habits as well as children's. Most parents decide which foods enter the household, so when they change their purchasing and eating habits, there is a good chance that their children will change accordingly.

LOCAL COMMUNITY PARTNERSHIPS

While most interventions have been conducted in single settings such as primary schools, most children and parents purchase or consume foods in several settings, such as the home, the supermarket, bakeries, fast food outlets, milk bars, canteens, specialty food shops, cafés, restaurants and so on. Each setting has its own influences on food consumption, so it is important to intervene in those settings in which children purchase or consume food. The formal control of these settings varies, ranging from parental control in the home, to the control of the owner of the local supermarket, corner deli or local café, to local government regulation of the sale of food. This diversity of control suggests the need for local community partnerships between the healthy eating practitioner and a variety of community and commercial groups. The wider and more integrated the partnerships, the more likely children and parents will be enabled to choose healthier foods. A novel example of a community partnership is the current obesity prevention study in a small regional town in Victoria. Facilitated through the activities of one community development officer, the project aims to build the capacity of the local community to undertake obesity prevention activities—for example, to acquire funding from VicHealth for a walking school bus initiative, to promote the drinking of water at schools, in preschool centres and in public places, to develop lunchbox guidelines for parents and to promote school canteen policies.

The development officer does not undertake any interventions, but instead communicates about healthy eating with members of the local community so they can conduct interventions of their own design in their own settings. This approach is quite different from that of the randomised control trial intervention, but it is similar to the type of work done in economic development and in community health promotion. The aim is to facilitate change by people who work in and control a wide range of settings.

It is a much more naturalistic approach than the randomised control trial intervention, relying on social cohesion and the social diffusion of innovations through the community. Other examples of the use of community partnerships to change eating behaviours include the Penrith Food Project, Eat Well SA and California's Leaders Encouraging Activity and Nutrition programme, which has succeeded in having soft-drinks banned from sale in Los Angeles schools from 2004.

LEAN is a community advocacy programme of the California Department of Human Services and the Public Health Institute. The success of this legislative change is likely to depend on the availability of adequate funding for those school activities previously funded through soft-drink sales.

SELECTING THE BEST METHOD

Many of the most effective healthy eating interventions have employed combinations of methods to change children's eating behaviours. However, other effective interventions have used only one approach. It is difficult to tell from published reports how intensively various approaches have been pursued, so a comparison of the effectiveness of various change methods is problematic. Nevertheless, multiple methods are likely to be more effective than single methods, because different methods are likely to have different effectiveness among different types of people. Some of the change approaches used have been based on specific psychological or educational theories, while others have not.

The various methods include:

- *Sessions about food and nutrition:* This category includes classroom teaching in schools, as well as lectures to members of the community and counselling sessions in hospitals and clinics. Unfortunately, most published reports do not indicate the type of teaching involved—whether it was didactic or group discovery learning, for example. There is evidence that the latter is very effective in promoting the nutrition learning of primary school children. Some sessions have been theoretical; others have involved practical cooking skills and taste appreciation.
- *Parental involvement:* This category covers many types of activity. It

may simply require parents to monitor children's homework, but more usually requires them to work with children at home on eating-related tasks. Alternatively, programmes may be directed mainly towards parents—for example, the use of videotaped sessions to teach parents how to include more fruit and vegetables in their children's diets in appealing ways. The 'Food Dudes' programme in the United Kingdom more than doubled children's fruit and vegetable intake as a result of this type of approach. Generally, few programmes have involved parents at all. This is unfortunate because parents are probably the main influence on many children's eating habits.

- *Changes to the food supply:* Several school studies have shown that the types of food served in the school canteen influence children's eating. French showed that changes in the content of vending machine foods in Minnesota schools had marked effects on students' purchasing of those foods. Students preferred low fat snacks, especially if the snacks were sold at reduced prices. It is common knowledge among catering companies that the positioning and price of foods in school canteens affects their sales. Children tend to choose foods that are close to the edge of the counter and that are lower in price than similar products.
- *Self-monitoring approaches:* These approaches are based on cybernetic and social cognitive theories of behaviour. They are personal change strategies, not unlike food policies that schools and other organisations may adopt to guide their food and nutrition activities. Participants are encouraged to become aware of aspects of their current diet, such as their daily intake of fruit. Then, they are asked to try to change this aspect in a specific way. They record their attempts and, if they succeed they are rewarded in some way. This approach is quite effective, so long as it is not carried to extremes. It teaches the learners about the virtues of goal setting, makes them think about the future and can employ powerful reinforcers. An early example of self-monitoring is the STAR system used in the South Australian Body Owner's Programme in 1980. More recently, Luepker used a form of self-monitoring in the CATCH programme.
- *Award and accreditation schemes:* At an organisational level, accreditation and award schemes are good examples of this category. Child care centres, for example, may examine the state of their staff's food and nutrition skills, enter a training scheme, and, when successful, be given a healthy eating award for a period of time, as in Western Australia's Start Right, Eat Right award system.

FAMILY AFFAIR OF HEALTHY LIFESTYLE

Give your children building blocks for a healthy lifestyle by teaching them the importance of good nutrition and regular physical activity. Eating well and being physically active every day are keys to your child's health and well-being. Eating too many high calorie foods and getting too little physical activity can lead to excessive weight gain and physical health problems, such as type 2 diabetes and high blood pressure, now being diagnosed in children. Obesity also is associated with an increased risk of other health problems such as depression. You play an important role in helping your child, and the entire family, learn about healthy eating and regular physical activity. Parents have the power to set examples. Make healthy eating and daily physical activity fun, to help children learn good habits to last a lifetime. This brochure provides some tips on how you can promote healthy eating habits and encourage active lifestyles in your family.

HEALTHY CHOICES START WITH YOU

- Help your children develop healthy eating habits at an early age. Nutritious food is something to enjoy. It helps children grow strong and gives them energy.
- Set an example for active living by moving with your kids. Your kids pay attention to you, they really do!
- Teach your children that good health depends on the right balance between what they eat and how much they move.

KEYS TO A HEALTHY DIET

The keys to healthy eating are variety, balance and moderation. Be sure your family eats a variety of foods, including plenty of vegetables, fruits and whole grain products. Also include low-fat and Non-fat dairy products, lean meats, poultry, fish and legumes. Drink water to quench your thirst, and go easy on the salt, sugar and saturated fat. Good nutrition should be part of an overall healthy lifestyle that also includes regular physical activity. To maintain weight, both kids and adults must balance the calories they eat with the calories they burn through physical activity. If you eat more calories than you use up in physical activity, you gain weight. If you eat fewer calories than you use up, you lose weight. Make a commitment to helping your family eat sensibly and move more often.

Here are some tips for healthy eating to help you get started:

- Try to keep track of your children's meal/snack and physical activity patterns so you can help them balance the amount and types of food they eat with the amount of physical activity they perform.
- Encourage your family to eat at least 5 servings of brightly coloured vegetables and fruits a day. You can start the day with 100% fruit or vegetable juice. Slice fruit on top of cereal. Serve salad with lunch and an apple as an afternoon snack. Include vegetables with dinner.
- Leave the candy, soft drinks, chips and cookies at the store. Substitute

them with fruits, vegetables, nuts, and low-fat or Non-fat milk products. Your child will soon learn to make smart food choices outside your home as well.

- Serve children child-sized portions, and let your child ask for more if still hungry. Don't force children to clean their plates. Try measuring food items to learn to estimate the amount of food on a plate.
- Choose a variety of foods. No single food or food group supplies all the nutrients in the amounts that you need for good health. If you plan for pizza one night, balance your meal with salad, low-fat or Non-fat milk and fruit.

EAT SMART

Sharing meals is an ideal way for the family to spend time together.

Whether you're eating at home or eating out on the go, it's important to eat smart:

- *Be Consistent*: Establish a family meal routine, and set times for breakfast, lunch, dinner and snacks. Eat together whenever possible.
- T*ake Charge of the Foods your Children Eat*: When you serve a meal, your child can choose to eat it or not; but don't offer to substitute an unhealthy alternative when your child refuses to eat what you've served.
- Restrict children's access to the refrigerator and snack cupboards.
- Turn off the tv during meals, and limit kids' snacking when watching tv.
- Serve a vegetable or fruit with every meal and at snack time.
- Reward your kids with praise and fun activities rather than with food.
- Involve your children in meal planning and food preparation. They are more likely to eat what they help to make.
- While shopping and cooking, teach your children about the food groups and the importance of a balanced diet. Throughout the day, choose the types and amounts of foods you need from the five food groups.
- Teach your children how to read food labels and use the 5%-20% guide to Daily Values to make better food choices.
- Limit foods that are high in saturated fat, cholesterol, sodium, and added sugars, and make sure to get enough fibre and calcium.
- Use low-fat cooking methods such as baking, roasting and grilling, and choose healthy fats when you use them, such as olive or canola oils.
- Serve water, low-fat or Non-fat milk with and between meals. Only children under two years always need to drink whole milk.
- Teach your children how to make wise food choices away from home– at school cafeterias, restaurants, and vending machines. Teach them

to pay attention to both the quality and quantity of their food choices. More food is not always better for them; appropriate portion sizes need to be understood.

MONEY-SAVING IDEAS FOR BETTER HEALTH

Good nutrition doesn't have to mean expensive grocery bills:

- *Plan Ahead*: Make a list of meal ideas for the coming week. Keep in mind the days you'll have time to cook from scratch and the days you'll be pressed for time. Then make a grocery list and stick to it.
- *Buy in-season Fruits and Vegetables*: Use local farmers' markets when possible–the foods are fresher and tend to cost less.
- Purchase canned and frozen fruits and vegetables when fresh ones are not available or affordable. They're healthy, too, and will last longer.
- Never shop for food when you're hungry.
- Review store ads and clip coupons before shopping.
- Sign up for your grocer's bonus/discount card for additional savings.
- Stock up on sale items you can use in a timely manner. Buy in bulk for quality and value, but serve healthy portions.
- Look for items on the top and bottom shelves at the grocery store. The most costly brands are often placed at eye-level. Store brands that may be cheaper and just as good are often placed higher or lower.
- Assemble snacks at home in small baggies and use foods such as nuts and seeds, low-fat cheese and fresh veggies and fruits, rather than buying less healthy and more expensive prepackaged and processed snacks.
- *Use your Food Budget Wisely*: For the price of a large bag of chips and a box of cookies, you can buy a lot of apples, bananas, carrots, potatoes, peppers and other healthy foods.

A HEALTHY WEEK-AT-A-GLANCE

An easy and fun way to keep your family active and eating right is to create a weekly calendar of healthy lifestyle activities.

Use some of the ideas below to get yourself started on building a healthy life that works for your family and your schedule:

- *Monday:* Start a daily log of what your family eats and how they keep active; review it with them at the end of each week.
- *Tuesday:* Go to your local community center and find out what physical activity or sports programmes are available.
- *Wednesday:* Make frozen juice pops instead of buying popsicles. They're healthier and cheaper!
- *Thursday:* Encourage your family to use safe and accessible stairs as an active alternative to elevators and escalators.

- *Friday:* Involve your kids in cooking and take a walk after dinner.
- *Saturday:* Take your children food shopping and let them pick out a new fruit or vegetable to try.
- *Sunday:* Review the coming week's school lunch menu with your kids, and talk about making healthy meal choices.

GET MOVING

Physical activity is good for children and adults. It strengthens muscles, bones and joints, and it gives children the opportunity to gain confidence while having fun.

Children need at least 60 minutes of physical activity every day. Playing hopscotch, tossing a ball back and forth, and dancing are some good ways for your child to be active.

Some children are good athletes, but all need many opportunities to be active, including but not limited to sports:

- Be a physically active role model and have fun with your kids. Adults need at least 30 minutes of daily physical activity.
- Walk with your child at every available opportunity–if possible to school or to the store on errands. Take a family walk after dinner instead of watching tv or playing computer games.
- Plan active weekends. Include biking, hiking, skating, walking or playing ball. Take a trip to the park, skating rink, zoo, or swimming pool.
- Offer to join your child in his/her favourite physical activity, or enroll your child in a group exercise programme.
- Include children in active chores such as dog walking, house cleaning, car washing, and yard work.
- Limit inactive brhaviour such as television watching and computer time. Do physical activity with your kids during commercials, such as marching in place or stretching. This helps reinforce the importance of movement in your child's life.
- Avoid using tv as a child sitter or pacifier. Offer active alternatives to screen time–jumping rope, playing hide-and-seek or running an errand.
- Children love when you are active with them and involve them in what you do.
- Keep tv's out of children's rooms.
- Give your children gifts that encourage physical activity–active games, sporting equipment, or a Frisbee.
- Take the President's Challenge as a family.
- Talk with your schools about ways to incorporate Non-competitive physical activity during the day.

Bibliography

Aadesh K Devgan: *Crime Against Women and Child : An Emerging Social Problem*, Cyber Tech Publication, Delhi, 2008.

Alok Kumar Kashyap: *Social Problems in Contemporary India*, Mohit Publication, Delhi, 2012.

Anjana Singh: *Crime and Criminology*, ABD Publishers, Delhi, 2011.

Anjela Kumari: *Social Problems and Welfare*, Alfa Publication, Delhi, 2008.

Bhupendra Singh: *Crime Against Women*, Mohit Publication, Delhi, 2012.

Bindeshwari Pd. Mandal: *Cultural Sociology*, Centrum Press, Delhi, 2011.

Harish Goel: *Cyber Crime*, Rajat Publication, Delhi, 2007.

Jairam Kansal and Vani Prabhakar: *Social Problems and Social Change*, Wisdom Press, Delhi, 2012.

Jayant Malik: *Cyber Crime and Terrorism*, Swastik Publication, Delhi, 2011.

Masood Ali Khan: *Cultural Sociology of India*, Arise Publication, Delhi, 2006.

Mohan Sen Gupta: *Cyber Crimes*, Centrum Press, Delhi, 2012.

Nishant Singh: *Crime Against Women*, Ancient Publishing House, Delhi, 2011.

P.K. Giri: *Crime Against Women*, Sublime Publication, Delhi, 2009.

Paul T Augastine: *Combating Cyber Crime*, Crescent Publication, Delhi, 2007.

Paul T Augustine: *Cyber Crime and Legal Issues*, Crescent Publication, Delhi, 2007.

Pradip Kumar Bose: *Health and Society in Bengal : A Selection from Late 19 Century Bengali Periodicals*, Sage Publication, Delhi, 2006.

R K Suri and T N Chhabra: *Cyber Crime*, Pentagon Press, Delhi, 2002.

R. Thilagaraj, Jianhong Liu and S. Latha: *Crime and Criminal Justice in Asia*, Mittal Publications, Delhi, 2011.

R.A.P. Singh: *Crime Against Women*, Aavishkar Publication, Delhi, 2010.

R.K. Dutta: *Crime Against Women*, Reference Press, Delhi, 2003.

R.K. Pradhan: *Cyber Crime and Cyber Terrorism*, Manglam Publication, Delhi, 2010.

Raj Kumar Sen; Asis Dasgupta and Mrinal Kumar Dasgupta: *Crime and Corruption in Indian Economy*, Deep and Deep Publication, Delhi, 2007.

Ram Ahuja: *Social Problems in India*, Rawat Publication, Delhi, 2014.

S.K. Bansal: *Cyber Crime*, A P H Publication, Delhi, 2011.

Sarita Vashistha: *Crime Against Women*, K.K. Publications, Delhi, 2012.

Seema Chandra: *Social Problems and Social Works*, ALP Books, Delhi, 2013.

Shekhar Kumar: *Crime Against Women : A Social Perspective*, Globus Press, Delhi, 2012.

Udai Veer: *Crime Against Women*, Anmol Publication, Delhi, 2004.

Vikram Singh Jaswal and Shweta Thakur Jaswal: *Cyber Crime and Information Technology Act, 2000*, Regal Publications, Delhi, 2014.

Y.K. Singh: *Cyber Crime and Law*, Shree Publication, Delhi, 2005.

Index

H

I

J

L

M

N

O

P

R

S

T

U

V

W